BEFORE THE PYRAMIDS

Baked clay, squat, round-bottomed, ledge rim jar. 12.3 x 14.9 cm. Naqada IIC. OIM E26239 (photo by Anna Ressman)

BEFORE THE PYRAMIDS

THE ORIGINS OF EGYPTIAN CIVILIZATION

edited by

EMILY TEETER

ORIENTAL INSTITUTE MUSEUM PUBLICATIONS 33

THE ORIENTAL INSTITUTE OF THE UNIVERSITY OF CHICAGO

Library of Congress Control Number: 2011922920
ISBN-10: 1-885923-82-1
ISBN-13: 978-1-885923-82-0

The Oriental Institute, Chicago

This volume has been published in conjunction with the exhibition
Before the Pyramids: The Origins of Egyptian Civilization
March 28–December 31, 2011

Oriental Institute Museum Publications 33

Series Editors

Leslie Schramer

and

Thomas G. Urban

Rebecca Cain and Michael Lavoie assisted in the production of this volume.

Published by The Oriental Institute of the University of Chicago
1155 East 58th Street
Chicago, Illinois 60637 USA
oi.uchicago.edu

For Tom and Linda

Illustration Credits
Front cover illustration: Painted vessel (Catalog No. 2). Cover design by Brian Zimerle
Catalog Nos. 1–79, 82–129: Photos by Anna Ressman
Catalog Nos. 80–81: Courtesy of the Ashmolean Museum, Oxford

Printed by M&G Graphics, Chicago, Illinois.

TABLE OF CONTENTS

FOREWORD

GIL J. STEIN

DIRECTOR, ORIENTAL INSTITUTE

The phrase "ancient Egypt" almost automatically evokes the Sphinx, the pyramids, and the golden sarcophagus of Tutankhamun. However, these iconic images represent Egypt when it was already a fully formed, powerful, and highly centralized state in the third and second millennia BC — the Old, Middle, and New Kingdoms. We need to remind ourselves that Egyptian civilization was not a static, timeless culture, and it did not spring into being *ex nihilo*. For Egyptologists and archaeologists, much of the fascinating complexity of Egypt derives from precisely the fact that it was a rich, vibrant, living culture that was constantly evolving, while at the same time grounding itself in a set of deeply rooted core elements and symbols that make it unique among the civilizations of the ancient world. How did the Egyptian state begin? This is the fundamental question addressed by the Oriental Institute's special exhibit Before the Pyramids: The Origins of Egyptian Civilization.

It is especially challenging for us to understand and reconstruct the Predynastic origins of Egypt because so many of the key developments took place before the invention of writing, about 3300 BC. Without texts, researchers are forced to rely heavily on purely archaeological evidence and the interpretation of the relatively small number of artistic depictions of key events and processes. Our exhibit presents some of the objects that are uniquely important pieces in this wordless puzzle.

Drawing on both the most current research and on excavations done more than a century ago, Before the Pyramids allows us to examine the Egyptian state at the historical moment of its birth. As volume editor and exhibit curator Emily Teeter notes, Egypt existed as a unified kingdom under pharaonic rule for more than 500 years before the construction of the pyramids in the Old Kingdom. The 120 objects in our exhibit eloquently tell the story of the emergence of Egyptian civilization from its earliest beginnings about 4000 BC down to 2600 BC. Most derive from the pioneering excavations in the late nineteenth- and early twentieth-century excavations at Hierakonpolis, Abydos, and Naqada — the most important sites for understanding the late Predynastic period.

Before the Pyramids highlights the many threads that combined to form the tapestry of an ancient state society or civilization — kingship or centralized political power, social stratification, elite groups, economic specialization, warfare, writing, and trade, to name just a few. The beautifully crafted stone and ceramic vessels show the extraordinary skill and aesthetics of the master artisans in the late Predynastic and Early Dynastic periods. The presence of imported objects shows us the far-flung trading connections of the earliest Egyptian state. We are especially fortunate to have as centerpieces of our exhibit two priceless loan objects from the Ashmolean Museum of Oxford University — the Battlefield Palette and a unique limestone statue of King Khasekhem. These extraordinary objects have never before been on display in the United States.

This catalog is a remarkable volume that pulls together the most recent research by the world's leading scholars on Predynastic Egypt. It outlines the fascinating story of Sir Flinders Petrie's initial discovery of the Predynastic period and explains the ways that art, political organization, craft production, burial practices, international trade, and the invention of writing served as key elements that defined the emerging Egyptian state in the fourth and early third millennia BC. By bringing together the actual artifacts and the theoretical frameworks used to interpret them, the chapters presented here will have lasting value for both the museum visitor and the professional researcher.

Before the Pyramids does a wonderful job highlighting the ways that earliest Egypt differed from, and gave rise to, the later, better known magnificence of the Old Kingdom. At the same time we can see unmistakable continuities in the symbolism of kingship and in the core values that flourished for millennia at the heart of Egyptian civilization. By showing us the origins of the Egyptian state, this exhibit only enhances our sense of wonder at the later achievements of this civilization when it reached its zenith. In both the exhibit and this catalog, Emily Teeter and her colleagues have done a wonderful job in bringing this little-known but crucial period of history to life.

THE CHRONOLOGY OF EARLY EGYPT

Absolute date in years BC	General culture-historical phase	Relative chronology	Major developments
2100 2685	OLD KINGDOM (Dynasties 3–8)		Administrative integration of the provinces
2890–2685 3100–2890	EARLY DYNASTIC PERIOD (Dynasties 1–2) **Dynasty 2 (selected kings)** Khasekhem(wy) Peribsen **Dynasty 1** Qa'a Semerkhet Anedjib Den Queen Merneith Djet Djer Aha Narmer	Naqada IIIC–D	Territorial unification, primary center in Memphis
3200	PROTODYNASTIC	Naqada IIIA–B	Regional proto-states, hieroglyphic writing
3600	LATE CHALCOLITHIC	Naqada IIC/D–IIIA	Commercial centers, increasing social complexity, long-distance trade
3900	EARLY CHALCOLITHIC	Naqada IB/C–IIB	Craft specialization, social ranking, interregional trade
4500	LATE NEOLITHIC	Naqada IA/B Badarian	Growth of villages
5000	EARLY NEOLITHIC	el-Omari Merimda Beni Salama Fayum A	Sedentism, agriculture, animal domestication
7000	EPI-PALEOLITHIC		Gradual human occupation of the Nile Valley
10,000 500,000	PALEOLITHIC		

Adapted from "The Rise of the Egyptian State" in this volume

Note on the Chronology of the Naqada Period

The chronology of the Naqada period is divided into three sub-periods (I, II, III), which in turn are further subdivided. Kaiser's subdivisions are expressed by lowercase letters (Naqada IIIa–c), while Hendrickx's revised chronology uses uppercase letters (Naqada IIIA–D). Köhler proposes further divisions to both the Naqada IIIC and IIID periods. For more information on Hendrickx's and Köhler's re-evaluation of Kaiser's phasing, see "Sequence Dating and Predynastic Chronology" and figure 1.1 in this volume.

INTRODUCTION

EMILY TEETER
EXHIBIT CURATOR

"Until [the excavations at Abydos in 1895–1896], the history
of prehistoric Egypt only began with the Great Pyramid."

— W. F. Petrie, *The Making of Egypt*, p. 160*

This volume and its companion exhibit are the result of several related objectives. One was the desire to exhibit objects from the spectacular Predynastic collection of the Oriental Institute Museum. The collection consists of some 2,500 objects, most of it with provenance, and much of it received from the Egypt Exploration Fund and its related offshoots in the 1890s and early 1900s. Only a handful of pieces of the collection are on permanent view in the Joseph and Mary Grimshaw Egyptian Gallery, and so when I was asked to develop an exhibition, this underutilized material seemed like an ideal focus. An added incentive was that preparing an exhibit necessitated bringing our records, especially the date and description fields, up to current standards, a pressing need with the Oriental Institute's imminent adoption of a new integrated database.

Another, perhaps more exciting, incentive to undertake the project was to bring this fascinating era, which is so seminal to the later glories of Egyptian civilization, to a wider audience. Predynastic studies have increasingly become an insular sub-specialty of Egyptology with its own journals and conferences. Much of the important research is not apparent to scholars outside an inner group, and it is generally entirely out of the grasp of the general reader. The few good overall histories, as good as they are, cannot keep pace with the new discoveries.

The inaccessibility of information on earliest Egypt is particularity unfortunate because the study of the Predynastic and Early Dynastic periods is such a rapidly evolving discipline. It is full of excitement with new discoveries and new interpretations that are upending long-held conclusions. What we know about the Predynastic period and the formation of the state of Egypt is undergoing dramatic change. A hundred and twenty years ago, nothing was known about the era. As Predynastic sites and their artifacts were recovered, they were thought not to be of Egyptian origin at all, so different were they from later Egyptian art. Only sixty years ago, scholars debated whether Predynastic cultures emerged first in northern Egypt rather than in the south. The pendulum gradually swung toward the idea that the state rose in the south as a result of a military conquest of the north by King Narmer. Now, the view is more nuanced, largely as a result of intensive excavations in the Delta, Abydos, and Hierakonpolis that have entirely changed our perception of early Egypt. The dynamic nature of this field is apparent in the essays in this volume. You will encounter differences of opinion and varying interpretations, and in many cases, questions that cannot yet be answered and iconographic features that cannot be decisively deciphered.

This volume is intended to be an overview of what is currently known about Predynastic and Early Dynastic Egypt. The volume includes copious illustrations that are not usually encouraged or allowed in scholarly publications, but which do much to make the often unfamiliar and complex conceptions more understandable.

Because the study of Predynastic Egypt is such a rapidly evolving and specialized field, it was essential to involve those who are on the forefront of the discipline. I cannot thank my colleagues enough. They showed an incredible generosity of spirit, sharing their expertise and their precious time, many of them cheerfully offering or agreeing to write catalog entries and to clarify issues. I appreciate their enthusiasm for the project,

---

* I thank Elise MacArthur for bringing this quote to my attention.

which I take as a reflection of the passion that each and every one of them has for their work and their desire to share their research with others.

In addition to the catalog authors, I would like to thank Jane Smythe, who consulted with me early on in the project, for her valuable insight on the dating of some of the objects and for her enthusiasm for ceramics. Here at the Oriental Institute, I thank faculty members Janet H. Johnson, Robert K. Ritner, and Nadine Moeller for their advice and suggestions on both the publication and the exhibit. I also thank Gil Stein, Director of the Oriental Institute, and Geoff Emberling, former Chief Curator of the Oriental Institute Museum, for their early support of the project. Aleksandra Hallman, Rozenn Bailleul-LeSuer, and Robert Wagner prepared translations of papers. I thank Margaret Moline, Lise Truex, and Elizabeth Major for help organizing bibliographies, the object documentation, and initial proofreading.

Here at the Oriental Institute Museum, our registrars, Helen MacDonald and Susan Allison, tracked the whereabouts of the constantly moving objects and Alison Whyte, Assistant Conservator, treated dozens of them. I also thank Thomas James, Assistant Curator of Digital Images, for his help, and Anna Ressman for the wonderful photography. It is such a luxury to be able to commission new photography of these objects that are so seldom seen in studio-quality color images. The simplest of stone vessels shimmer with beauty in Anna's photos. Erik Lindahl and Brian Zimerle designed the show, and I also thank Brian for the design of the book cover. Our publications department, Thomas Urban and Leslie Schramer, cannot be praised enough for their ability to create exhibit catalogs on the tightest of deadlines, yet stay cheerful.

I also acknowledge our Community Advisory Group, who was instrumental in shaping the show: Angela Adams, Randy Adamsak, Christine Carrino, Wendy Ennes, Dianne Hanau-Strain, Carole Krucoff, Nathan Mason, Patty McNamara, Beverly Serrell, and Molly Woulfe. I am not sure that the show would have worked without their input.

This project received a grant from the Antiquities Endowment Fund of the American Research Center in Egypt to fund conservation of the objects. The AEF is an inspired program whose support for conservation projects is doing so much to preserve monuments and artifacts from all periods of Egypt's history. A further grant was received from the Excelon Corporation

A last, but clearly not least, thank-you goes to Tom and Linda Heagy, who supported the publication and the exhibit. Tom's enthusiasm for King Narmer is well known to anyone in the field, and it is a pleasure to be able to bring this material to a wider audience on his behalf.

CONTRIBUTORS

About the Contributors:

Branislav Anđelković is Assistant Professor of Near Eastern Archaeology in the Department of Archaeology of the Faculty of Philosophy, University of Belgrade. His research focuses on Naqada culture, the process of state formation, and international relations in the fourth millennium BC. Since 1987, he has participated in fieldwork in Serbia and the Near East. He edited the *Journal of the Serbian Archaeological Society* from 2005 to 2008. Along with his main areas of research, he has published extensively on the Belgrade Mummy (Nesmin), and corpus of Egyptian antiquities in Serbia.

Laurel Bestock is an Assistant Professor of Egyptology and Archaeology at Brown University. She has been excavating at Abydos for ten years. She now serves as Director of the Brown University Abydos Project, which operates under the aegis of the University of Pennsylvania-Yale University-Institute of Fine Arts Expedition to Abydos. Her research thus far has centered on royal cult in the early First Dynasty, though she has lately begun to explore a series of Ptolemaic monuments as well.

Eliot Braun is an Associate Researcher in the Centre de Recherche Français de Jérusalem and a Senior Fellow of the W. F. Albright Institute of Archaeological Research, Jerusalem. He is a member of ARCANE Project (Synchronizing Cultures and Civilizations of the Ancient Near East and the Eastern Mediterranean in the Third Millennium BC) in conjunction with Tübingen University. He is widely published on salvage and rescue projects and on the Early Bronze Age. His newest publication (in press) is *Early Megiddo on the East Slope (The "Megiddo Stages"): A Report on the Early Occupation of the East Slope of Megiddo; Results of the Oriental Institute's Excavations, 1925-1933.*

Krzysztof M. Ciałowicz is the Director of the Institute of Archeology at Jagiellonian University in Kracow, Poland. He has excavated at Qasr el-Sagha (Egypt), Kadero (Sudan), Sonyat (Sudan), and Tell el-Farkha (Egypt). He is author of many articles about Tell el-Farkha as well the monographs *Les palettes égyptiennes aux motifs zoomorphes et sans décoration: Études de l'art prédynastique* (Krakow, 1991), and *La naissance d'un royaume: L'Egypte dès la période prédynastique à la fin de la Ière dynastie* (Krakow, 2001).

Günter Dreyer is presently the Director of Excavations for the German Archaeological Institute at Abydos and Saqqara. From 1997 to 2007 he was director of the Institute's excavations at Elephantine, and he served as Director of the German Archaeological Institute in Cairo from 1998 to 2008. His work at Tomb U-j at Abydos was published in the important volume *Umm el-Qaab* I: *Das prädynastische Königsgrab U-j und seine frühen Schriftzeugnisse* (Mainz, 1998).

GE **Geoff Emberling** is Visiting Scholar at the Kelsey Museum of Archaeology, University of Michigan. He was previously Museum Director and Chief Curator at the Oriental Institute and Assistant Curator of Ancient Near Eastern Art at the Metropolitan Museum of Art. He has directed excavations in Syria and Sudan. His research interests focus on cities and identities in the ancient Middle East.

Renée F. Friedman is the Heagy Research Curator of Early Egypt in the Department of Ancient Egypt and Sudan at the British Museum. She is also director of the expedition to Hierakonpolis, a site she has worked at since 1983.

SH **Stan Hendrickx** is lecturer in History of Art at the Media, Arts and Design Faculty (Hasselt, Belgium). He studied Archaeology at the Katholieke Universiteit Leuven (PhD 1989). Since 1977, he has participated in excavations and surveys at Elkab, Adaïma, Mahgar Dendera, Dayr al-Barsha, Hierakonpolis, Abu Ballas Trail/Chufu region, Kom Ombo, and Aswan. Besides ceramology, his research focuses on the Predynastic period up to the end of the Old Kingdom. He edits the "Analytical Bibliography of the Prehistory and the Early Dynastic Period of Egypt and Northern Sudan," updated yearly in the journal *Archéo-Nil*.

TH **Thomas Hikade** is Assistant Professor of Egyptology at the University of British Columbia in Vancouver. He also taught at Brown University, the University of Sydney, and the University of Trier. His main fields of research are stone tool industries from ancient Egypt and royal expeditions and the economy of the New Kingdom. He has worked at major sites in Egypt such as Buto, Maadi, Helwan, Abydos, Hierakonpolis, and Elephantine.

E. Christiana Köhler is Professor of Egyptology at the University of Vienna. She has been working on excavations in Europe, the Middle East, and Egypt for almost thirty years. Her main areas of research are Prehistoric and Early Dynastic Egypt as well as Egyptian archaeology and society. Currently, she is directing excavations in the large Early Dynastic necropolis at Helwan in order to investigate the chronology, material culture, and social development pertinent to Egypt's first capital city, Memphis.

LM **Liam McNamara** is Assistant Keeper (Curator) for Ancient Egypt and Sudan at the Ashmolean Museum of Art and Archaeology, University of Oxford. Prior to joining the Ashmolean, he was a Project Curator at the British Museum. McNamara specializes in the material culture of the late Predynastic and Early Dynastic periods. His current research focuses on the ivories from the Hierakonpolis Main Deposit in the Ashmolean Museum.

EVM **Elise V. MacArthur** is a PhD student in Egyptian Archaeology at the Department of Near Eastern Languages and Civilizations at the University of Chicago. She has worked at Giza and Tell Edfu. She is a curatorial assistant for the exhibit Before the Pyramids as well as for other recent exhibits at the Oriental Institute Museum. Her academic interests include Predynastic and Early Dynastic Egypt, early writing, GIS technology, and photography.

David O'Connor is the Lila Acheson Wallace Professor of Ancient Egyptian Art at the Institute of Fine Arts of New York University. He has directed excavations at Abydos in southern Egypt for many years, most recently focused on enigmatic but very large cult enclosures built for First Dynasty kings, one of whom was allotted no less than fourteen full-scale ships for his afterlife needs. His publications include *Abydos: Egypt's First Pharaohs and the Cult of Osiris* (2009) and co-edited (with Eric Cline) volumes on Amenhotep III (1998), Thutmose III (2006), and Ramesses III (in press).

Béatrix Midant-Reynes is the Director of the French Institute of Oriental Archeology in Cairo. She has served as head of excavations at the Predynastic site of Adaïma (1989-2005), the Predynastic necropolis of Kom el-Khilgan (2001-2006), and Tell Iswid (2006). She is the author of the highly regarded books *The Prehistory of Egypt From the First Egyptians to the First Pharaohs* and *Aux origines de l'Égypte. Du néolithique à l'émergence de l'État.*

RKR **Robert K. Ritner** is Professor of Egyptology in the Oriental Institute, Department of Near Eastern Languages and Civilizations, Program on the Ancient Mediterranean World, and the College, University of Chicago. His research interests include Egyptian religion and magic, language, and social history. His most recent monograph is *The Libyan Anarchy: Inscriptions from Egypt's Third Intermediate Period.*

Patricia Spencer is Director of the Egypt Exploration Society and Editor of its color magazine *Egyptian Archaeology.* She edited and contributed to *The Egypt Exploration Society: The Early Years* and has written several articles on the Society's history. Dr Spencer has been involved in excavations in Egypt since 1981 and has worked for the British Museum at el-Ashmunein, Tell Belim, and Tell el-Balamun, and most recently, for the Egypt Exploration Society at Tell Yetwal wa Yuksur.

AS **Alice Stevenson** is a Researcher of World Archaeology at the Pitt Rivers Museum, University of Oxford and Junior Research Fellow of St. Cross College, Oxford. She was awarded her PhD at the University of Cambridge for her thesis on the Predynastic cemetery of el-Gerzeh. She has worked for the Egypt Exploration Society and the Institute of Archaeology, University College London. She is currently researching the Egyptian collections of the Pitt Rivers Museum and contributing to the University of Oxford/UCL radiocarbon dating project "A New Chronology for the Formation of the Egyptian State."

ET **Emily Teeter** is an Egyptologist, Research Associate, and Coordinator of Special Exhibits at the Oriental Institute of the University of Chicago. She curated the exhibit Before the Pyramids. Her most recent monographs are *Baked Clay Figurines and Votive Beds from Medinet Habu* and *Religion and Ritual in Ancient Egypt*.

Yann Tristant's research interest lies in the Predynastic and Early Dynastic period with special emphasis on settlement excavation and geoarchaeology. He has worked on a number of sites in various parts of Upper and Lower Egypt as well as in the oases. Currently he is in charge of excavations at Abu Rawash and Wadi Araba (Eastern Desert), where he is undertaking an archaeological survey, as well as at Tell el-Iswid in the Delta. Dr Tristant was scientific member of the French Institute of Archaeology in Cairo (IFAO) from 2006 to 2010. He is presently teaching Egyptology in Australia at Macquarie University and he is also editor of the journal *Archéo-Nil*.

AW **Alison Whyte** holds a Master of Art Conservation degree from Queen's University, Kingston, Ontario, and is an objects conservator at the Oriental Institute Museum. She specializes in the preservation of archaeological material from the Near East.

David Wengrow is Reader in Comparative Archaeology at the Institute of Archaeology, University College London. He has conducted fieldwork in various parts of Africa and the Middle East. He has also been Junior Research Fellow at Christ Church, Oxford, and Henri Frankfort Fellow in Near Eastern Art and Archaeology at the Warburg Institute. His research explores early cultural transformations across the boundaries of Africa, Asia, and Europe, including the emergence of the first farming societies, states, and systems of writing. He is the author of two books, *The Archaeology of Early Egypt: Social Transformations in North-East Africa, 10,000 to 2650 BC* and *What Makes Civilization? The Ancient Near East and the Future of the West*.

BBW **Bruce B. Williams** has published volumes three through ten in the series Oriental Institute Nubian Expedition and other works on early Egypt and Nubia. One of these was *Decorated Pottery and the Art of Naqada III*. He has conducted fieldwork in Turkey, Egypt, and Sudan.

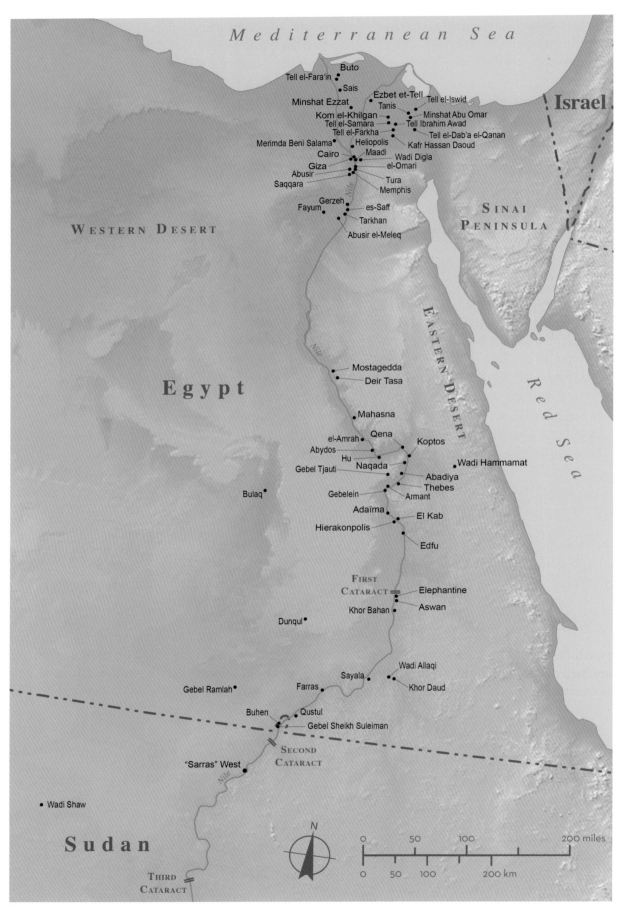

Map of principal areas and sites

14

1. SEQUENCE DATING AND PREDYNASTIC CHRONOLOGY

STAN HENDRICKX

In the winter of 1895/1896, W. Flinders Petrie excavated a huge cemetery at Naqada for which he had no parallels at that time. Although he first considered the cemetery to date from the First Intermediate Period, it soon became clear that it was in reality prehistoric and consequently named it "Predynastic" (Petrie 1896). During the following decades, Petrie excavated several more Predynastic cemeteries and worked out a relative chronology which he called "sequence dating." It was the first attempt ever in archaeology for seriation. As a first step, the pottery was arranged in a corpus of "Predynastic" pottery, consisting of nine classes of pottery and over seven hundred types (Petrie 1921). Next, all objects from each grave were noted on a slip of card with the idea of arranging them in relative chronological order after the resemblance of types. First, an earlier and a later phase were distinguished through the observation that White Cross-Lined pottery did not occur with Decorated and Wavy-Handled pottery. Second, a shape evolution from globular to cylindrical shapes was accepted for the Wavy-Handled types, in combination with the handles loosing their functionality. When all grave cards had been arranged in order, Petrie divided the cards into fifty equal groups, numbering them as "sequence dates" (SD) from 30 to 80 (Petrie 1901b, pp. 4–12). By choosing to start at SD 30, he left space for earlier cultures, which might still be discovered. Finally the fifty sequence dates were divided into three groups, which he considered to be archaeologically, culturally, and chronologically different. The "cultures" were named Amratian (SD 30–37), Gerzean (SD 38–60), and Semainean (SD 60–75), after important Predynastic cemetery sites.

Although the development of the sequence dates certainly represents one of the major intellectual performances in the study of Predynastic Egypt, a number of methodological shortcuts, such as the heterogeneous criteria used for defining pottery classes and types, inevitably resulted in errors. An essential problem is that Petrie made no clear distinction between typology and chronology (Hendrickx 1996). Also, Petrie aimed at a very detailed chronological framework, but integrating new data made it gradually less precise. However, the most striking omission in Petrie's way of working was the omission to take the horizontal distribution of the graves into consideration.

Werner Kaiser (1957) revised the Predynastic relative chronology by investigating the horizontal distribution of pottery classes within the cemetery of Armant. He distinguished three spacial zones by the relative percentages of Petrie's Black-Topped, Rough, and late wares. These zones are considered to represent chronological stages and within each of them subdivisions, called "Stufen," were recognized according to the clustering of pottery types. In this manner Kaiser distinguished three main periods of the Naqada culture, with all in all eleven Stufen. But although Kaiser included data from a number of other cemeteries, his study is essentially based on a single cemetery, which furthermore did not cover the entire Predynastic period. An update and partial revision of the "Kaiser chronology" was therefore necessary and was carried out toward the end of the 1980s, integrating all the cemeteries published at that time (Hendrickx 1989). Methodologically, there is not much difference to the method already developed by Kaiser. The identification of related groups of graves is not only based on their contents but also on their spatial distribution within the cemetery. As a result, a conflict arose between the search for closer chronological proximity of all examples of one pottery type, on the one hand, and the definition of spatially well-defined groups of graves, on the other hand, between which an equilibrium is to be reached. The system developed by Kaiser was not fundamentally contradicted and the chronological phases distinguished were maintained, although, in some cases, important differences occur in the archaeological description (Hendrickx 2006a). This is especially so for the Naqada III period, for which the number of tombs at Armant is very limited. The most recent group distinguished within Kaiser's Stufe IIIa2 was readjusted to Naqada IIIA1, while most of the original Stufe IIIa1 types, together with a large number of the Stufe IId2 types, are considered characteristic for Naqada IID2 (see fig. 1.1). Meanwhile, work on the cemeteries of Adaïma has shown that distinguishing two subphases within Naqada IID period is an artificial construction (Buchez in press).

Over the last decades, research on Predynastic sites has increased dramatically, making a large amount of new data available. Local chronological sequences have been elaborated at Abydos (Hartmann in press), Adaïma (Buchez in press), Gerzeh (Stevenson 2009b), and Tell el-Farkha (Jucha

2005, pp. 63–78; Jucha in press). Starting from the cemetery of Helwan, Köhler (2004) proposed a revision of the Naqada IIIC chronology and added phases 1–3 to Naqada IIID, the last of which dates to the end of the Second Dynasty (see "The Early Chronology of Egypt" in this volume). However, all this research has yet to be integrated into an overall chronological framework that allows for regional differentiation.

FURTHER READING

Buchez in press; Hartmann in press; Hendrickx 1989, 1996a, and 2006a; Jucha 2005 and in press; Kaiser 1957; Köhler 2004; Petrie 1896, 1901b, and 1921; Stevenson 2009b

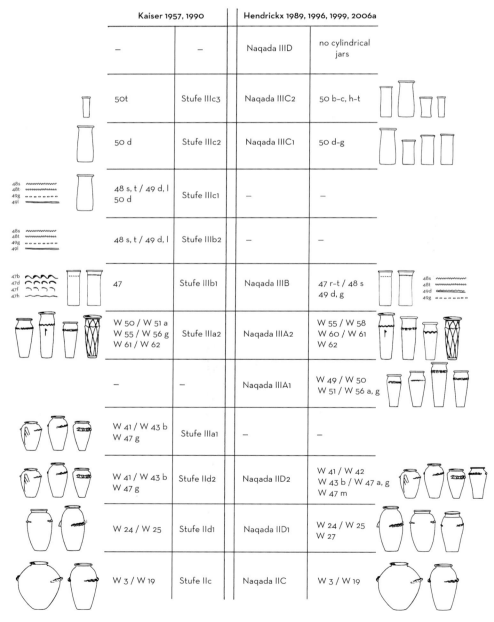

Figure 1.1. Comparison of Kaiser's and Hendrickx's division of the Naqada II–III periods

2. PETRIE AND THE DISCOVERY OF EARLIEST EGYPT

PATRICIA SPENCER*

William M. Flinders Petrie (fig. 2.1) is often credited with the discovery of Predynastic and Early Dynastic Egypt through his pioneering excavations of major sites such as Koptos, Naqada, and Abydos, and his invention of "sequence dating," a system of relative dating that enabled the earliest burials and tombs to be arranged chronologically. The origins of the distinctive culture of ancient Egypt had always held a fascination for Petrie and it is somewhat ironic, therefore, that when he started to encounter the evidence for which he had been searching, he did not at first recognize it as such. At the time Petrie started work, in the early 1880s, Egypt's early history and the origins of its distinctive culture were only poorly understood. As he remarked himself in the first edition of his *History of Egypt*: "The first three dynasties are a blank, so far as monuments are concerned; they are as purely on a literary basis as the kings of Rome or the primeval kings of Ireland" (Petrie 1894, p. 16).

FIGURE 2.1. Flinders Petrie (at upper left, holding pole) supervising excavations at Abydos (photo courtesy of the Egypt Exploration Society)

The kings of the first three dynasties, before the great pyramid builders of the Fourth Dynasty, were then known only as a series of names in badly preserved king-lists, Manetho's history, and on fragments of the Palermo Stone (Redford 1986; Wilkinson 2000b). There were no known monuments belonging to them and the origins of Egyptian civilization were still a matter of speculation. (For summaries, see Hoffman 1991, chapter 2; Spencer 1993, introduction; Wilkinson 1999, chapter 1; Wengrow 2006, pp. 127–50.)

Petrie was a devotee of the "dynastic race" theory, believing that the founders of Egyptian civilization came from outside the country. In 1893/1894, he obtained from the Service des Antiquités permission to excavate at Koptos, where he believed the "dynastic race" would have first settled in the Nile Valley after entering Egypt through the Wadi Hammamat from the Red Sea. He was rewarded with the discovery of three larger-than-life-size statues of the local god Min, decorated with emblems in low relief which were unlike typical "pharaonic" motifs (Petrie 1896; see further Kemp 2000). Petrie felt sure that these statues were very early in date — "prehistoric" as he described them — and was pleased when two of the statues were assigned to him in the "division" of antiquities at the end of the season. He offered them first of all to the British Museum, but they were rejected as being "unhistoric rather than prehistoric" (Petrie 1939, p. 153). They were then donated to the Ashmolean Museum in Oxford, forming the basis for that museum's pre-eminent collection of early Egyptian antiquities.

While working at Koptos Petrie had "eyed the hills on the opposite side of the Nile and heard of things being found there" (Petrie 1939, p. 155). In 1894 he started work at the site of Naqada, where he was finally to find the evidence he so desired of Egyptian culture before the pyramid age. Naqada turned out to contain an immense cemetery, in which Petrie and his team cleared over 2,000 graves in just over three months (fig. 2.2). The dead had been placed in graves covered over originally with brushwood and low mounds of earth that had collapsed onto the burials, many of which had been robbed in antiquity. Most of the bodies were in fetal positions — unlike the extended burials of the Dynastic period — but with their faces to the west, indicating that they shared the Egyptian theory of "the west" being the

FIGURE 2.2. Previously unpublished photograph of a Predynastic grave at Naqada (photo courtesy of the Petrie Museum of Egyptian Archaeology, University College London)

abode of the dead. They had grave goods which consisted of tools, slate palettes, cosmetic items, clay and ivory figurines, stone vessels, and an abundance of pottery of distinctive types (Petrie and Quibell 1896) (fig. 2.3). Petrie recognized straightaway that they were excavating an unusual cemetery that did not conform to regular Dynastic customs — there were no hieroglyphic (or any other kind of) inscriptions and no grave goods that were recognizably "Egyptian."

FIGURE 2.3. Predynastic pottery from Naqada, originally published as drawings in *Naqada and Ballas* (Petrie and Quibell 1896), pl. 29 (photo courtesy of the Petrie Museum of Egyptian Archaeology, University College London)

However, despite his interest in the origins of the Egyptian state, Petrie did not realize that he was excavating a Predynastic cemetery, preferring instead to see the burials as those of a "new race" which, he theorized, had entered Egypt during the instability of the First Intermediate Period and driven out the local inhabitants. As Margaret Drower (1985, p. 215) says in her biography of Petrie:

> It is odd that this essentially simple fact [the early nature of the burials] did not dawn upon Petrie, odder still that for two years, in the face of the scepticism of colleagues and increasing evidence to the contrary, he clung to his belief in the existence of his "New Race"; the explanation must lie in the very ingenuity and self-confidence that had made him what he was. Once he had seized upon a hypothesis it was sometimes difficult for him to envisage that he could be wrong ...

Petrie's excavation, including his identification of the graves as belonging to his "new race," was already in the press (Petrie and Quibell 1896) when news reached him that Jacques de Morgan, working for the Service at Naqada, had found a large mastaba, probably belonging to Queen Neith-Hotep, with similar grave goods to those of Petrie's "new race," and also the name of "Menes," known from the king-lists to be the first king of the First Dynasty. Having seen the material for himself, Petrie finally conceded that it was Predynastic rather than from the First Intermediate Period and in November 1901 he issued

a correction slip to *Naqada and Ballas* saying, "In the five years since Naqada was published the evidence has accumulated, showing that the people there described are predynastic, and constituted the oldest civilized people of the land, about 7000–5000 BC."

Now that he had recognized that his Naqada cemetery was Predynastic the meticulous records Petrie had made there, in particular his drawings of hundreds of different vessel shapes, took on a new importance and usefulness. In 1899 he excavated more Predynastic cemeteries at Hu and Abadiya (figs. 2.4–5), published in *Diospolis Parva* (Petrie 1901b), and he used the typology that he had devised for Naqada to date the new material. He then devised his "sequence dating" for Predynastic and Early Dynastic material, based on his work at the three sites, thus inventing the archaeological tool of seriation (fig. 2.6) (Petrie 1901b, pp. 4–12, pls. 2–4). Essentially Petrie realized that vessels evolve in shape and design over time — sometimes becoming simpler, sometimes more elaborate — and he devised a sequence of fifty "sections" in which evolving vessels were grouped chronologically with other types, enabling the latter to be assigned relative dates. Although it has been adapted over the years, this sequence is still the basis for dating anepigraphic artifacts of the Predynastic and Early Dynastic periods.

While Petrie's work in Egypt had been concentrated on finding Predynastic material, Émile Amélineau had been working (1894–1898) at Umm

FIGURE 2.4. Objects from tomb H9 at Abadiya (photo courtesy of the Egypt Exploration Society)

FIGURE 2.5. Objects from one of the richest Predynastic tombs at Hu/Abadiya. Tomb group from Abadiya B101 (photo courtesy of the Egypt Exploration Society)

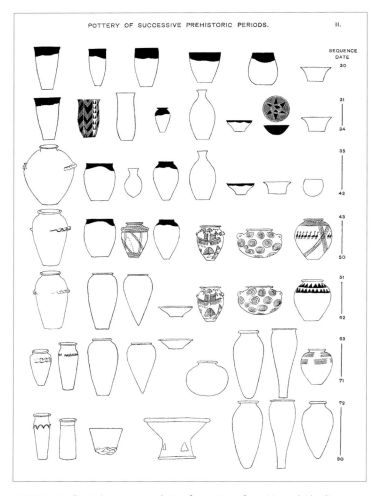

POTTERY OF SUCCESSIVE PREHISTORIC PERIODS.   II.

SEQUENCE
DATE
30
31
34
35
42
43
50
51
62
63
71
72
80

FIGURE 2.6. Petrie's sequence dating for pottery from Hu and Abadiya (Petrie 1901b, pl. 2)

(fig. 2.7). In three seasons of work (1899–1901) he re-excavated and mapped the royal tombs, finding some intact chambers, the contents of which he was able to record in their entirety. He drew and photographed the many fragmentary objects left behind by Amélineau, providing a mass of new inscribed and cultural material to the corpus of Early Dynastic finds.

One of the few sites where Petrie's desire to excavate was thwarted was Saqqara, which was reserved for Service des Antiquités excavations, and although he applied to work there on several occasions in the earliest years of the twentieth century, his applications were always turned down (Petrie 1931, pp. 189–91; Drower 1985 pp. 272–73). His wish to excavate at Saqqara seems mainly to have been related to his interest in the areas around the Step Pyramid and the Serapeum, but if he had been allowed to work there it would have been interesting to have seen if, with his almost uncanny ability to identify significant monuments, he would have discovered the tombs of the First and Second Dynasties, not revealed for another fifty years. Although thwarted in his request to work at one of the main Memphite cemeteries, in 1906 he excavated at Giza, hoping to find evidence for pre-Fourth Dynasty remains, and he was rewarded with the investigation of a large, previously discovered mastaba — usually known as G5 (fig. 2.8) — which is of similar construction to the royal tombs at Abydos and the Naqada mastaba of Neith-Hotep,

el-Qaab at Abydos, where he had located the tombs of the earliest kings of Egypt. Amélineau's work was described by Petrie as "scandalous" and when in 1899 he managed to obtain a concession to work there himself for the Egypt Exploration Fund, he fulminated: "It might have seemed a fruitless and thankless task to work at Abydos after it had been ransacked by Mariette, and been for the last four years in the hands of the Mission Amélineau. ... The results in this present volume are therefore only the remains which have escaped the lust of gold, the fury of fanaticism, and the greed of speculators, in this ransacked spot" (Petrie 1900, pp. 1–2; but see now Quirke 2010b, pp. 107–08). Amélineau had been interested only in fine antiquities, which he had taken back to France and which were sold at auction, but Petrie's interest in small objects, pottery, and the more mundane items buried in Egyptian tombs made him the ideal person to carry out a "rescue excavation" at Umm el-Qaab

FIGURE 2.7. The stela of Queen Merneith from her tomb at Abydos, as photographed by Petrie outside his excavation house at Abydos (photo courtesy of the Egypt Exploration Society)

FIGURE 2.8. Mastaba G5 at Giza, showing the paneled side wall (photo courtesy of the Petrie Museum of Egyptian Archaeology, University College London)

and contained jar-sealings of the First Dynasty King Djet (Uadji) (fig. 2.8) (Petrie 1907, pp. 1–7).

One of Petrie's last excavations in Egypt, before he transferred his attentions to the Palestine area, saw him return to Abydos in 1921 where he excavated what he called the "Tombs of the Courtiers," subsidiary burials around what had probably been the mortuary cult-places of the deceased kings (Petrie 1925).

Petrie's role in the discovery of early Egypt cannot be overestimated, even if he did not always realize at the time what it was he was finding. To the last he maintained that Egyptian civilization was the product of a "dynastic race" who had entered Egypt in the Predynastic period from Elam via Punt and the Red Sea and became her rulers, even though evidence for a direct evolution of civilization in the Nile Valley from Paleolithic time through Predynastic Egypt to the fully fledged monumental civilization was already well attested (Petrie 1939, pp. 77–78; Hoffman 1991). However, his meticulous attention to detail, his recognition of the importance of recording even the most seemingly insignificant of finds, and his sheer dogged persistence in the face of obstacles that would have deterred many a lesser excavator have rightly led him to be considered as one of the founders of scientific archaeology, and not just in Egypt. His methods and techniques, and in particular his invention of seriation with his sequence dating for early pottery, were ahead of his time and groundbreaking. By modern standards, however, though almost certainly an unfair comparison, some of his

excavation techniques and recording methods would be found lacking. He was not always present on the excavation himself, relying heavily on trusted workmen like Ali Suefi (fig. 2.9), with whom he worked for over thirty years (Quirke 2010a, pp. 6–7; Quirke 2010b), as at Naqada:

> Boys were set to hunt for soft places in the gravel; so soon as they had cleared round the edge of a tomb pit they were moved on. Then ordinary men were put to clear the pit until they should touch pottery in position. Next first-class men were put in to clear round the pottery and skeleton, but not to remove anything. Lastly the skill of Ali Suefi came in to remove every scrap of earth and leave the pits, bones and beads, all bare and exposed ... (Petrie 1931, p. 156).

A much longer, more detailed description of his work methods is given in *Naqada and Ballas* (Petrie and Quibell 1896, pp. viii–ix). After the workmen had cleared and cleaned the burial, Petrie or one of his students would record the burial in detail, although at this early period he was not yet using "tomb cards." Nor did the recording usually include photography because glass photographic plates were heavy and expensive. Photographs of objects found were carefully composed so that they would "suit the published plate in the final excavation report" (figs. 2.10–11); "... only later in Petrie's career, and only for the earliest burials, in which he was most

FIGURE 2.9. Ali Suefi (at center), who worked with Petrie for over thirty years on excavations in Egypt, shown during the excavation of the tomb of Khasekhemwy at Abydos. From Margaret Murray's photograph album (photo courtesy of the Petrie Museum of Egyptian Archaeology, University College London)

FIGURE 2.10. Petrie at Abydos, taking a photograph of copper dishes from the tomb of Khasekhemwy. From Margaret Murray's photograph album (photo courtesy of the Petrie Museum of Egyptian Archaeology, University College London)

FIGURE 2.11. The photograph Petrie is taking in figure 2.10 (photo courtesy of the Egypt Exploration Society)

interested, do we find many photographs of tombs as they looked to the recorder ... before the objects in the group had been removed" (Quirke 2010a, p. 7).

One of the main differences between a Petrie excavation and those today is that he followed the practice of paying "bakhshish" (monetary rewards) to workmen in proportion to the value or importance of objects which they found. Petrie justified this by saying, "In order to encourage the men to preserve all they find, and to prevent their being induced to secrete things of value, they should always be paid as a present the market price of such things at that place, and a trifle for any pottery or little scraps that may be wanted" (Petrie 1892, p. 162).

Petrie would undoubtedly have claimed that this practice paid off when, for example, a bandaged arm was found in the Abydos tomb of King Djer (fig. 2.12). "The lads who found it saw the gold, but left it untouched ..." (Petrie 1931, p. 175), and "... On seeing it, Mr. Mace told them to bring it to our huts intact, and I received it quite undisturbed" (Petrie 1901a, p. 16). It is interesting that neither Arthur Mace nor Petrie seem to have been present in the tomb at the moment when the arm was found, so, in this instance at least, Petrie's trust in the honesty of his workmen and/or the efficacy of the bakhshish system seems to have been repaid.

For Petrie and other excavators at the time, the acquisition of objects was desirable both academically, for the information which they could supply, and also economically, as virtually all fieldwork in Egypt was funded by donations either from private or institutional sponsors. The Service des Antiquités allowed a generous "division" of excavated finds

FIGURE 2.12. The arm from the tomb of Djer at Abydos, as found with bracelets (photo courtesy of the Egypt Exploration Society)

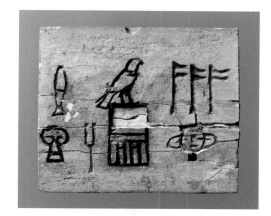

FIGURE 2.13. Part of an inscribed ivory box. From Umm el-Qaab, Abydos. Dynasty 1, reign of Djet. 3.3 x 3.9 x 0.6 cm. Catalog No. 83 (OIM E6105) (photo by Anna Ressman)

181

Chicago

Petrie (R.T. I) 1899-1900	sent 1900
Beads ф 70	prelist.
" green glaze X	"
" amethyst X27	"
Shell bracelets X51	"
A box of pottery from the Royal Tombs of the 1st dyn: (each piece marked with letter according to plan).	
Inscription XIII. 2.	Zet
Alabaster	"
Sealing	"
Inscription V. 2	Merneit
Ivory matwork	"
Sealing	"
2 Arrow heads	W
Abydos Inscription XIV. 9	Den
4 pieces ivory inlay	"
Piece of box	"

Petrie. (R.T. I) 1899-1900	sent 1900
2 Copper pins	Qa
8 model vases	"
Sealing	"
Steles, Nos 8, 25, 39, 46.	
Mirror, 2 alabaster vases Δ5. VI-XIIth dyn	
Beads, carnelian & blue glaz. Δ	" "
2 Jasper scarabs & beads. 9.	" "
Blue glazed beads 9.	" "
Abydos Glass beads G.	XVIIIth dyn
Bronze bag of Hegreshu; yoke & adze	" "
Ushabti of Pepenanhur	" "
Tomb D 14, clay boats	" "
Tomb D. 13	" "
" D. 14	" "
4 flint arrow heads	" "
Trial sculptures of heads	
Canopic jar heads	
37 Ushabtis	

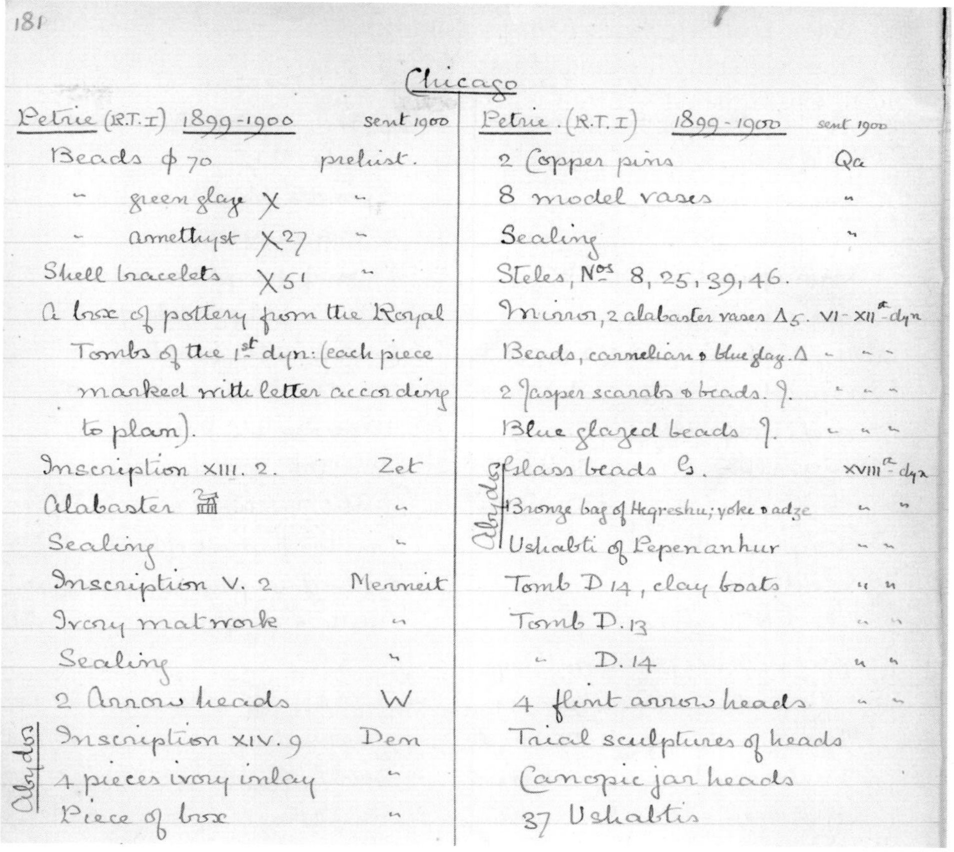

FIGURE 2.14. The Egypt Exploration Fund's distribution list for the Haskell Museum (now the Oriental Institute Museum) at Chicago showing OIM E6105, described as "Inscription XIII 2 Zet" (sixth object down in the left column). "XIII 2" is a reference to the line drawing of the object in Petrie 1901a (reproduced courtesy of the Egypt Exploration Society)

between the main Egyptian Museum (then at Bulaq) and the foreign excavator, with the result that expeditions such as Petrie's were able to take home a large number of objects of all sizes and descriptions to "divide" further among their supporters and to encourage them to continue funding fieldwork. The objects given to institutions went into their collections (figs. 2.13–14), while private donors passed their share on to local museums or, if they had collections of their own, retained them. In the late nineteenth century institutional donors to the Egypt Exploration Fund included, in addition to major museums worldwide, many smaller local museums, universities, public libraries, and schools within the United Kingdom, many of which have since transferred their Egyptian collections to major museums. This dispersal of objects throughout the world had a negative consequence in that objects were divided in proportion to the amount of funding received with little regard for keeping together, for example, a group of objects from a particular tomb. This practice in itself has generated a whole new field of research as Egyptologists try to track down all the antiquities from a particular site or tomb on which they are working. On the other hand, the scattering of finds throughout the world has undoubtedly helped to encourage and maintain a strong popular interest in ancient Egypt.

After having left the Egypt Exploration Fund in 1886 following fundamental disagreements with the governing committee, Petrie's ability to excavate, record, and preserve small objects was instrumental in his being recalled to work on the royal tombs at Abydos, since the Fund's other main excavator, Édouard Naville, was not renowned for his recognition of small objects. As Petrie himself wryly noted, "I was asked back because the Society was in low water and wanted to placate the American subscribers by having things found to distribute" (Petrie 1931, p. 164). In 1905, after Petrie had successfully re-excavated the royal tombs and provided donors with generous divisions of material, the Fund and Petrie parted company again; "I was told later, by a friend in the British Museum, that it was settled that as the Americans were now safely attached to the Fund, I was to be turned off" (Petrie 1931, p. 197).

Petrie is often criticized for publishing selectively and for producing his field reports so soon after the work had finished — often within a calendar year. Both were economic consequences of the time in which he lived and the conditions in which he had to work, with the expense of publication costs limiting the size of books and the number of illustrations, and rapid publication needed to satisfy donors on whom he relied to fund his next piece of work. Petrie did, however, make copious notes and most of these have survived, as have the majority of his photographic negatives — divided between the archives of the Egypt Exploration Society, the Petrie Museum at University College London, and the Griffith Institute in Oxford. All are available for further research and are frequently consulted by scholars working, for example, on particular sites or trying to identify objects in museum collections. If Petrie had published his fieldwork as slowly as do some archaeologists today, then his contemporaries might have remained in the dark about the early origins of ancient Egypt for perhaps another generation. As Margaret Drower wrote in her biography:

Too many excavators sit for years on their material, hoping to cross every T and elucidate every puzzle before they commit themselves to print, while their memory of their fieldwork fades, costs of production rise, and the world waits for the information only they can provide (Drower 1985, p. 432).

Fortunately, the world did not have to wait long for Petrie to reveal the results of his fieldwork in the 1890s and his rediscovery of Egypt's earliest history and culture must rank as one of the greatest of his many achievements.

NOTE

* I am grateful to the Egypt Exploration Society for permission to use images from the Society's Lucy Gura Archive, and to Professor Stephen Quirke, Susi Pancaldo, Ivor Pridden, and Katrin Swientek of the Petrie Museum at University College London for access to and permission to reproduce images from Naqada, Abydos, and Giza held in the Museum's Archive.

3. POLITICAL ORGANIZATION OF EGYPT IN THE PREDYNASTIC PERIOD

BRANISLAV ANĐELKOVIĆ

Archaeological finds, as the only surviving residues that constitute the record, or rather the remains of it, are burdened with many modern expectations — scientific, historical, aesthetic, to mention but a few. However, what we usually overlook is the fact that those barely visible ancient footprints of the human past do not lead down an abstract, long-gone, blind alley — they lead to human presence, to us. An integral part of this underlying archaeological naïveté, so to speak, is a tendency toward simplification and idealization, which is liable to "pacify the past" (see Carneiro in preparation), namely, to deprive ancient cultures of their essential political dimension and nature. Like parents who have learned to deny, or at least to postpone as long as possible, recognition that their children have become sexually mature, archaeologists still seem somewhat uneasy with use of the terms "prehistory" and "state formation" or "state politics" within one and the same context or explanatory model. Indeed, in such an innocent archaeological pastorale who would ever imagine that Narmer — the most powerful ruler and statesman of his era (ca. 3150 BC), famous for his palette showing decapitated and castrated enemies (fig. 3.1) — managed an army, spies, assassins, top secrets, and opposing interest groups at his court, or that he sometimes faced difficult political decisions as had, most probably, about eleven generations of Dynasty 0 rulers before him. Despite the fact that the outdated mantra of the unification of Upper and Lower Egypt at the beginning of the First Dynasty still echoes in many publications, what, along with the recent fieldwork, really stands at the cutting edge of Predynastic Egyptian archaeology is paleopolitics (see Anđelković forthcoming).

Although for a long time Egyptological "tacit agreement" rather arbitrarily used to equate state formation with the beginning of the Dynastic period, substantial archaeological evidence on which this assertion is to be based has hardly ever been presented. Moreover, the conceptual position between unattractive Predynastic potsherds and charming Dynastic marvels, along with the lack of relevant data, made, until relatively recently, the transition from prehistory to history a kind of scholarly no-man's-land. In other words, a constructive dialogue between Egyptian archaeologists (cf. Wendrich 2010), mostly experts in prehistory, and Egyptologists, mainly devotees of history, art history, and linguistics, both often subspecialized into some object type, was practically non-existent.

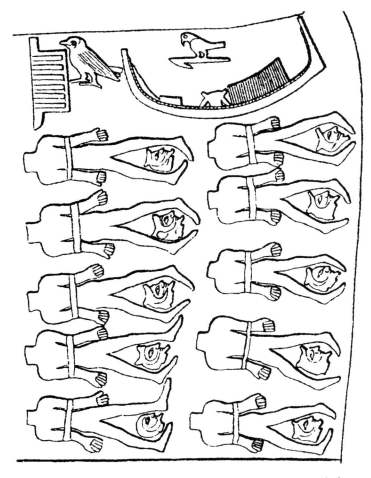

FIGURE 3.1. Narmer Palette, from Hierakonpolis, ca. 3150 BC. Detail of obverse showing decapitated and castrated enemies (after Wengrow 2006, fig. 2.2)

Did the remarkable Egyptian culture come from nowhere, or as Wilkinson (2003, p. 186) put it, had "the glories of ancient Egypt ... suddenly been switched on like a light-bulb at the beginning of the First Dynasty?" Most certainly not. Rather, Egyptian origins are to be traced along the trajectory of Predynastic social and political organization, with particular reference to factors of state formation, successive stages of "state seriation" that would put the formative events of the past in their correct order, parameters of statehood, monopoly of the means of violence, territoriality, sovereignty, taxation, bureaucratic administrative apparatus with implied authority and legitimacy, and subjection of the individual to bureaucratic authority (Anđelković 2008) — and finally an all-inclusive explanatory model. Our present level of knowledge makes it difficult to call such a complex assignment complete, and we should bear in mind that state formation is a multi-layered process and the synergic and cumulative result of a broad range of components operating together that cannot be fully explained either by environmental or social determinism.

THE PASSIVE NATURAL FACTORS

We have all heard Herodotus' famous remark that Egypt is the gift of the Nile. With the approximately 3,000-kilometer-long stretch of the Nile from Khartoum to the Mediterranean in mind, one cannot help but wonder why the gift was delivered only to a single short segment to the north and south of the Qena Bend, namely from Abydos to Hierakonpolis (some 150 km as the crow flies or approximately 250 km by the river) in the Naqada culture heartland — exactly where the first pharaohs of Dynasty 0 emerged — and nowhere else? Apparently, the factors for state formation are not to be seen in the favorable Nilotic environment present to some degree all along the river, but rather in very specific features of the Naqada culture itself.

To avoid misunderstanding — the Nilotic environment was of immense importance as a "stage set," for it is blessed, among other things, with an annual, fertilizing inundation and a high solar insolation level. Unique physical circumstances also included the "tube effect" of the Nile Valley, plenty of inorganic energy sources, the stimulatory possibilities

of low-cost riverine transport, and, last but not least, the gold (and also various mineral materials) of the Eastern Desert. Let us briefly comment on a number of mutually interacting natural components of such unprecedented "resource concentration" (cf. Carneiro in preparation; for additional details, see Anđelković in press).

The Nile Valley is a seasonally inundated river plain, not a swamp basin. The soluble salts and lime carried by the Nile drain off freely to the Mediterranean, rarely accumulating in the subsoil. The Nile floodplain belongs to the convex variety, accumulating primarily through bank overflow of suspended sediment. The sediment comes mostly from black clays of volcanic origin, and it is also rich in organic matter (Butzer 1976, pp. 15–16; Butzer 1995, p. 142). These characteristics enable free, natural fertilization annually and precluded soil exhaustion or salinization, presenting the ideal conditions for fruitful agriculture. The subsistence-friendly combination of the river, floodplain, and low desert ecosystems, including economically favorable biodiversity, enable easy exploitation of several complementary ecosystems at the same time. Flood-recession irrigation was probably an important factor in the initial development of population agglomerations in the alluvium, and at the same time the most productive form of agriculture known in terms of units of labor invested (Algaze 2001a, pp. 203–04; Algaze 2008, pp. 40–63).

The Nile Valley, a slender, continuous strip of arable land bounded by deserts, can be compared to a long "tube" that, in ancient times, did not allow for any substantial lateral dispersion of population or activities. As noticed by Wilkinson (2003, p. 162), in "some places the floodplain is less than half a mile wide, the cultivable land occupying an *impossibly restricted* strip between riverbank and desert edge" [emphasis added]. This fact amplified the sense of territoriality (cf. Anđelković 2008, pp. 1044–47), whereas reference of each village to its immediate northern or southern neighbor, be it ally or rival, significantly promoted social compacting.

Three inorganic energy sources — water, wind, and sunlight — are extremely rich in Egypt. Nile waters were a huge source of free kinetic power used for sediment deposition and transport. The stream provides energy in the downstream direction, whereas for upstream transport the energy of wind was exploited (the prevailing wind in the Nile Valley comes from the north) by use of the sail (Cottrell 1955). The outstanding solar energy amplifies evaporation of floodwaters from the floodplain, transforming ponds into fertile fields by enabling mud to produce nutritive nitrogen and phosphorus compounds. It is also essential for photosynthesis, which, in turn, is fundamental to the conversion of solar radiation into stored biomass energy.

The gold-bearing region of Upper Egypt stretches mainly between the Nile Valley and the Red Sea, extending south from Qena and Koptos. Gold mining started in Predynastic times with open pits to moderate underground workings (Klemm and Klemm 1998, p. 341). It is hardly accidental that the "gold town" of Naqada as well as Hierakonpolis — both Protodynastic centers of power — stood so close to the wadis that gave access to the gold mines of the Eastern Desert. This precious metal, sometimes called the flesh of the gods, was not only the main product of southern Egypt (Trigger 1985, p. 39) but was probably an important strategic currency of those power centers as well.

THE ACTIVE SOCIAL FACTORS

The active factors of state formation were encrypted in the cultural codes and concepts of the Naqada culture, specifically in the domain of an ideological, political, religious, social, symbolic, and mythological set of values, and in how this value system was organized, with sacred leadership as a stable axis of social configuration (Anđelković in press; Anđelković forthcoming). In other words, the social setting was dominated by the ideology of sacred power, fully blended with the concentration of economic, political, and military power. As stated by Wilkinson, "without the king as defender of order, chaos would triumph and everything would be lost" (2003, p. 194). The defense of order, that is, organized conflict, is depicted on quite a few objects of the Naqada culture, from White Cross-Lined pottery to rock tableaux. For example, a jar from Abydos, Umm el-Qaab grave U-239, dated to the Naqada IC period, depicts the ruler with his mace smiting a group of bound captives (fig. 3.2, left) (Dreyer et al. 1998, p. 114, fig. 13). A similar scene from the painted wall of the Naqada IIC Tomb 100 at Hierakonpolis is, according to Baines (1995, p. 97), "a central symbol of kingship, conquest, and domination" (fig. 3.2, center). It is obvious that even at this early developmental stage of the Predynastic period,

Naqada IC   Naqada IIC   Naqada III

FIGURE 3.2. Continuing iconography of power: (*left*) motif of smiting the defeated and often tied enemies represented on a Naqada IC jar from Abydos grave U-239 (after Dreyer et al. 1998, p. 114, fig. 13), (*center*) Naqada IIC wall painting from Tomb 100 at Hierakonpolis (after Case and Payne 1962, p. 13, fig. 4), and (*right*) late Naqada III Narmer Palette (not to scale)

"the ideology and imagery of political power were being actively developed" (Wilkinson 2003, p. 79). Many of the decorated palettes, mace-heads, knife-handles, and other monuments assuredly "focus on foreign relations, aggression, and the assertion of order" (Baines 1999). Indeed, below its pragmatic surface, the territorial expansion of the Naqada culture might have had deeper ideological and religious overtones, namely the subjugation of enemies (read: chaos) of cosmological order by the victorious divine ruler and his followers. Patricia Perry suggests an additional early and very successful amalgamation of ideological and political power: "It is likely that the Naqada IC–IIB Hierakonpolis elite employed ideological power [control over systems of meaning and belief, norm and ritual practices] as the principal means of political centralisation .... The Hierakonpolis ceremonial centre (HK29A) 'materialised' the role of the elite as intermediaries in an emerging ideological system" (Perry in press). As far as the concentration of economic power is concerned, it seems that the high elite were engaged in every domain or activity related to prestige and the acquisition, and then retention, of a better position in the Protodynastic power "food chain." The ruler's duty was to keep in check "the opposing forces of nature." The duty of the elite was to be his transmissive media, whereas the duty of the population was to obey. A breakdown in social order could be perceived as a breakdown in cosmic order. Therefore, as an ideological, religious, economic, and military focusing device for structuring society, the will to sacred power turned out to be the predominant and constantly intensifying active factor in the process of state formation in the Predynastic period (Anđelković in press). As noted by Wilkinson, this was "to prove so powerful an ideology that Egyptian kingship would survive as the sole model of government for 3,000 years" (2003, p. 194).

TIME LINE OF POLITICAL ORGANIZATION

The relatively rapid social and political progression from the earliest farming villages to Egyptian empire can be sequenced into six stages (Anđelković 2004; Anđelković 2008, pp. 1051–52).

1. Pre-nomes (about the beginning of Naqada IA, ca. 4000–3900 BC): Independent local villages of Upper

Egypt came to be characterized by political autonomy.

2. Proto-nomes (Naqada IA–B): The first composite political units of Upper Egypt were constituted from aggregations of previously autonomous local villages. According to Carneiro (in preparation), "welding together of several previously independent villages, [created] for the first time in human history supra-village polities ... the original chiefdoms .... As a matter of fact, the rise of even a single chiefdom spurred the formation of others, since the greater size of a chiefdom would, in itself, give it a distinct advantage when competing against societies that remained as autonomous villages. Natural selection would thus clearly have favored the emergence of chiefdoms and then their proliferation." With the tube effect of the Nile Valley in mind, we should stress that whatever made hundreds of small autonomous villages yield their sovereignty to proto-nomes, and made proto-nomes in their turn yield sovereignty to the next more complex and powerful polity (see below), the most manifest aspect of the power play was a fight over land and that is exactly why every subsequent political entity, from Upper Egyptian proto-nomes to the Egyptian empire, encompassed a larger territory in comparison to its precursor (Anđelković 2006, p. 600). This early territorial and political division of Predynastic Upper Egypt is probably reflected in the about forty-nine Naqada "standards" that have so far been identified. These are depicted as poles surmounted by cult images and are are known mainly from pottery (cf. Graff 2009, p. 173) and palettes of slightly later date[1] (Anđelković 2008, p. 1045).

3. Nome pre-states (Naqada IC–IIB): Large political entities of Upper Egypt constituted from aggregations of proto-nomes eventually became complex enough to approach the threshold of statehood. There were many fewer of these polities in comparison to the previous political units. Accordingly, the number standards, repeatedly represented on important Naqada-period objects and which may have some more official and public function, became significantly smaller, too. Out of a suggested eight Upper Egyptian centers with powerful local elites in late Naqada I (Abydos, Abadiya, Naqada, Gebelein, Hierakonpolis, Elkab, Edfu, and Elephantine) (Wilkinson 2000a, pp. 378–79, fig. 1; Hassan 1993, p. 554), only three — Abydos, Naqada, and Hierakonpolis

— prevailed, while the rest were either conquered or absorbed by their more predatory neighbors near the end of this stage. Since nome pre-states differed in size, power, and potential, we can assume, especially considering the motifs of victory, bound captives, and sacrifice that are widely represented, that rivalry, competition, and endemic conflict — manifestations of the will to power — were deeply interwoven within the Naqada culture itself. Perhaps we should not expect "absolute correspondences between these representations and patterns of economic or political interaction on the ground" (Wengrow 2006, p. 216), but in the light of the "stubborn fact that autonomous political units, be they tiny hamlets or large polities, simply do not willingly surrender their sovereignty" (Carneiro in preparation) we certainly should not expect anything far from it either.

4. The Upper Egyptian proto-state (Naqada IIC–IID1): An economic and political unit constituted from previous nome pre-states, ideologically, economically, and militarily "glued" to the most powerful polity, probably Hierakonpolis or Abydos (fig. 3.3). This short-lived political entity, sometimes termed the "Upper Egyptian commonwealth" (Anđelković 2004, pp. 537–40), was the crucial stage in the social alchemy that transformed the pre-states into the state. But instead of creating a sort of Upper Egyptian super nome, which would have happened if the process had remained within Upper Egypt itself, the Naqadian expansion and warfare agenda proceeded to the north. Sometime in the Naqada IIC period the cemetery of Gerzeh was founded, "far removed from the core of the [Naqada] culture in the south" (Stevenson 2009b, pp. 205–08). The subjugation of northern territories took place in the second half of Naqada IIC, along with the termination of Maadi, es-Saff, and probably several other northern settlements. As stated by Baines (1999), "it seems unlikely that a valid material culture like that of Maadi would have been eliminated peaceably." Soon, other sites with a so-called transitional layer, such as Buto, would be assimilated to Naqada culture, ideology, and values, probably by a mix of acculturation and coercion, along with further penetration and establishment of Naqadian sites such as Minshat Abu Omar in the Delta. As suggested by Frangipane (2001, p. 346), such "transitional" societies "were full forms of society per se, which took in and integrated new relations and traditional relational systems that, taken together, made up a new structure." In state formation archaeology one often gains the impression that certain dated finds are actually conceptual reflections

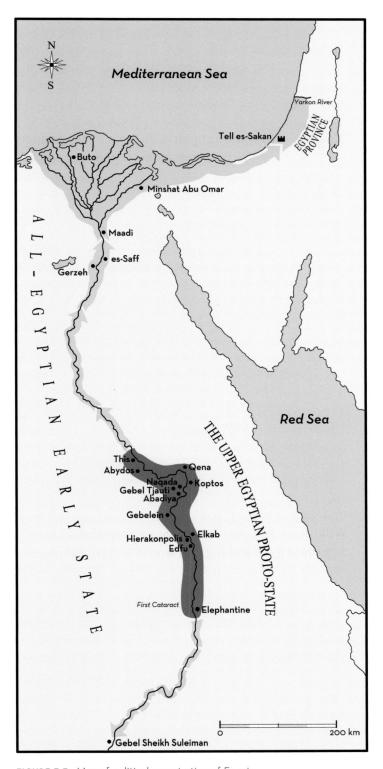

FIGURE 3.3. Map of political organization of Egypt in the Predynastic period

of some previous developmental step. Accordingly, we should bear in mind that the "fine line between complex chiefdoms and simple states is not always evident until a powerful state, with all its physical traits, has been in existence for some time, that is, post-dating by a sometimes considerable amount of time its emergence as a state" (Bard 1989, p. 243). The permanent expansion of Naqada culture to the north seems to confirm that Lower Egyptian culture, also known as Maadi-Buto, is a rather tendentious nomination since a compact regional cultural coherence was, judging from the data in hand, not extant in Lower Egypt at the time. In contrast to Naqada culture, the Delta communities (Midant-Reynes 2003, p. 114, map 3) comprise a few big villages still adhering to the Neolithic-minded logistic characterized by a somewhat "slower realization of the full potential" (Trigger 1985, p. 68). They were not organized in the same way. Apparently, the Delta communities were still on a chiefdom level while the Naqada culture already approached the threshold of statehood in Naqada IC–IIB (Anđelković 2006, p. 596). Along with the striking difference in the iconography of power and "power artifacts," Naqada culture and Lower Egyptian groups "were distinct in terms of the complexity and visibility of the material and ritual invested in burial" (Stevenson 2009b, p. 207), so typical and essential for emerging Egyptian civilization. All this, but not only this, makes very unlikely a scenario in which "the social, political, economic, logistical, administrative and ideological foundations" of state formation "had been laid in both parts of the country" (Köhler 2005; see also Köhler 2010). Note that the end of this and beginning of the next stage is exactly the point where Naqada culture is simply renamed Dynastic culture, or as Hendrickx put it (1995, p. 8), "the Dynastic culture evolved without interruption from the Naqada culture."

5. All-Egyptian early state (Naqada IID2–IIIB/IIIC1):

A large political entity encompassing both the south and north of Egypt ruled by a king with a highly centralized government appeared. (fig. 3.3). Politically, the term "Dynasty 0" can be applied to this stage, which still witnessed many conflicts including short-lived attempts by unsatisfied local elites to restore the old pre-centralized order or perhaps to establish a new one, as illustrated by the Gebel Tjauti rock tableaux (Darnell 2002, pp. 10–24; Anđelković

2004, p. 540). The number, names, and sequence of Dynasty 0 rulers, the first pharaohs, so to speak, are still not clear or easily distinguished, but so far we can consider Horus Narmer, Horus Scorpion II, Horus Crocodile, Horus Ka, Irj-Hor (Ro), Hat-Hor, Ny-Hor, "Double Falcon," Scorpion I, Pe-Hor, and two unidentified rulers (Anđelković 1995, p. 20, with references). With Naqadian (now Egyptian) expansion in mind it is hardly surprising that serekhs (a composite hieroglyphic symbol standing for the king/crown/state and the state's property) with the names of at least five Dynasty 0 pharaohs along with thousands and thousands of Protodynastic Egyptian objects have so far been unearthed in the southern Levant (see "Early Interaction between Peoples of the Nile Valley and the Southern Levant" in this volume). To be properly understood, the Egyptian presence in the southern Levant needs to be placed in the overall context of Egyptian development. It was a logical continuation of the northern advance of the Naqada culture that absorbed Lower Egypt and finally expanded into the southern Levant. Thousands of Protodynastic Egyptian artifacts have come from the forty or so Levantine sites known so far. Some five kilometers south of modern Gaza City, on the ancient route known as The Way of Horus, a large fortified site, Tell es-Sakan, characterized by almost exclusively Egyptian-related artifacts, was discovered (Miroschedji and Sadek 2008). A brief salvage excavation exposed parts of a fortified city roughly five hectares in area that had clearly been founded by the Dynasty 0 Egyptians about 3300 BC (fortified Dynasty 0 sites including Egypt proper are otherwise attested only by representations of crenellated walls on palettes and cylinder-seal impressions). Three successive defensive mudbrick walls, the latest 3.8 meters thick and at least 8 meters high, and an outer defensive tower or bastion did little to support the idea of "peaceful Egyptian settlement" in the southern Levant. When plotted on a map the peculiar arrangement and nature of Egyptian sites and finds makes the trade and migration models highly improbable and imply that even the colonial model can no longer be sustained (Anđelković 1995; Anđelković 2002). What emerges are the archaeological contours of the earliest known (Naqada IIIA1–C1) Egyptian Dynasty 0 province in the southern Levant, with the Yarkon River as its northern border (Anđelković 2009) (fig. 3.3). As stated by Algaze, "cases of pristine state formation, by their very nature, involve processes of external expansion. (2001b, p. 27). Province establishment was an Egyptian effort to control the southern Levant for the purpose of strategic extraction of resources, copper above all, needed by the Dynasty 0 state. Simultaneously, it was an attempt to settle and annex new territory — a recognizable modus operandi of Naqada culture since the very beginning. The southern Levant province was practically an extension of the Protodynastic Egyptian settlement in the Delta and along the northern Sinai coast. The fact that Narmer *serekh*s are the most numerous, about thirteen out of thirty-three discovered so far, hardly points to a single campaign, but rather suggests that during Narmer's time already well-established Egyptian activity was at its peak. Other identified *serekh*s belong to "Double Falcon," Ny-Hor, Irj-Hor, and Ka, and a single *serekh* of Narmer's immediate successor Aha (in whose time the Egyptian province in the southern Levant was abandoned). It is hardly surprising that another Egyptian foreign periphery, in Lower Nubia — and certainly a source of tax/tribute — also displays early Naqada III military activity, as illustrated among others by the Gebel Sheikh Suleiman rock tableau near the Second Cataract (but see "Relations between Egypt and Nubia in the Naqada Period" in this volume). The very same "subjugate and exploit" geopolitical pattern established during Dynasty 0 was to be restored in times to come, for the two territories annexed to Egypt to create its New Kingdom empire were again Canaan and Nubia.

6. Egyptian empire (Naqada IIIC1/IIIC2): A huge political entity starts at the beginning of the First Dynasty with Aha as the first king. It was the culmination of the process of formation of larger and larger political units, and the first predominantly solid and stable one. It should be stressed that since there is no obvious difference in archaeological material, "the Naqada culture as archaeologically defined, [also] includes the First and Second Dynasties" (Hendrickx and Bavay 2002, p. 58). Obviously, the material cultural and political chronology do not necessarily run in parallel, as well observed by Wilkinson (1996, p. 65). The overgrown volume, complexity, and extent of the entire social, economic, and political organization, which significantly exceeded the parameters of the initial Naqada culture as such, makes drawing the political border line between the all-Egyptian early

state and the succeeding Egyptian empire logical and necessary (Anđelković 2004, p. 541).[2]

MODELING THE PAST

In search of a model to explain political evolution and state formation in Predynastic Egypt, from the most popular but practically stillborn unification model, via the hydraulic model, the multivariate-multistage systemic interplay model, the trade model, and the cultural transplantation model, by far the best starting point is offered by the circumscription model — significantly modified to accent a conflict over power, not over scarce resources (Anđelković 2006, with references). Political organization in Predynastic Egypt was not a product of either ideology/religion or coercion taken separately, but of their joint effort embodied in the concept and person of a divine king — god, religious specialist, and victorious warlord all in one. The political compacting of Naqada culture was preceded by a "mortuary compacting" rooted in the powerful "ideology of afterlife" evident as early as the Naqada I period. Yet the ruler was not just a central figure in religious art; as a divine king he was also the defender of cosmic order in the world, brandishing a deadly mace and leading a mighty army.

Paleopolitics, as an analytical study of prehistoric politics, should be more substantially involved in archaeological debates, since it is crucial to the proper understanding of the actions of past complex societies and the reconstruction of ancient political geography. The real challenge lies in the fact that archaeology is a never-ending story that with every new find may be retold.

NOTES

[1] However, the inner wall of a Badarian bowl from grave 802 near Mostagedda bears a relief decoration in the form of a standard, thus suggesting that the use of similar insignias probably began as early as the Badarian period (Anđelković 2008, p. 1046, fig. 1).

[2] As has already been stated elsewhere (Anđelković 2002, p. 84 n. 33, with references), the finds of two clay sealings with royal names from Abydos do not unequivocally testify that Narmer was the first king of the First Dynasty. The concepts and terms such as "Dynasty 0" or "First Dynasty" were not established by contemporary ancient Egyptians but by modern scholars. The listings on the first seal — Khentamentiu (the god of Abydos), Narmer, Aha, Zer, Uadji, Udimu, and King's Mother Merneith), and the second seal (god Khentamentiu, Qa'a, Semerkhet, Anedjib, Udimu,

Uadji, Zer, Aha, and Narmer — are obviously not identical and represent a number of royal names and the god of Abydos, rather than some fixed and "canonical" list of the First Dynasty rulers. We do not know by which criteria the listings were originally made except that they contain various names of some deceased kings and queen plus a deity name. However, there are important reasons why an arbitrary, but nonetheless necessary line should be drawn between the archaeologically defined Dynasty 0 and First Dynasty, the dividing point between the Predynastic and Dynastic, between Narmer and Aha.

4. HIERAKONPOLIS

RENÉE FRIEDMAN

There was an immediate sensation when, in 1898, the Palette of Narmer was discovered on the low mound in the midst of a small village ten miles north of Edfu. This magnificent artifact, along with the oversized mace-heads decorated with images of Narmer, Scorpion, and other rulers, dedicated at the early temple, allowed the first glimpses at some of the earliest named kings of Egypt. They put Hierakonpolis, city of the falcon god Horus, on the map in modern times (fig. 4.1). Even more, they provided what appeared to be conclusive evidence for the unification of Egypt as the victorious act of Narmer, who issued forth from his capital at

Hierakonpolis, known in ancient times as Nekhen, to smite Lower Egypt, inaugurating the Dynastic age. Yet so accomplished were these depictions, with figures already equipped with the trappings that would define Egyptian kingship for millennia to come, it was hard to see the connection to the products of the preceding Predynastic culture, which had been first uncovered only five years earlier. In line with the thinking of the time, an invasion of a more advanced "dynastic race" coming from the north or east was proposed to explain the discrepancy (e.g., Emery 1961, pp. 30–45; "Petrie and the Discovery of Earliest Egypt" in this volume). This idea was eventually laid

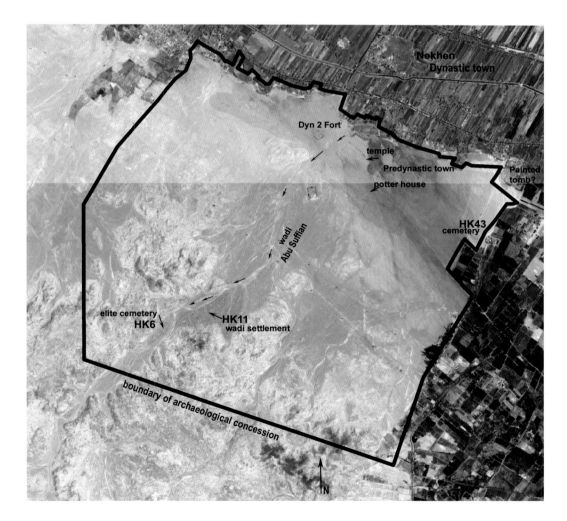

FIGURE 4.1. Map of Hierakonpolis with extent of Predynastic occupation indicated in yellow (satellite image courtesy of Digital Global)

FIGURE 4.2. A Predynastic brewery and pottery kiln installation at HK11 (left) with details of the brewing vats (above)

to rest as new discoveries throughout Egypt demonstrated that the "unification" of the land, both culturally and politically, took place before Narmer and that it was a far more complex process than the smashing of some heads could achieve. Nevertheless, for a view of the beginnings of this indigenous development and the origins of the distinctive form of Egyptian kingship, the best spot is still Hierakonpolis, where recent research can now place Narmer in a story that began five hundred years before he was born.

Evidence for this comes not from the deposits below the later Horus Temple in the cultivation, where the Narmer Palette and other objects of the so-called Main Deposit were found, but in the low desert to the west (Quibell 1900; Quibell and Green 1902). Here the ground is still covered with the remains of the largest Predynastic settlement still extant and accessible anywhere in Egypt. Continuously inhabited since the Badarian period (ca. 4500 BC) as deep coring 6 meters below the surface has shown, over time the site expanded and contracted and migrated to follow the ever-shifting course of the Nile (Hoffman et al. 1986). At its peak, from about 3800 to 3500 BC, Predynastic occupation stretched for over 2.5 kilometers along the edge of the desert and back almost 3 kilometers into the great wadi that bisects the site, extending for an unknown distance into the cultivated land, where it is now deeply buried beneath

the accumulated Nile silts (fig. 4.1). Clearly, in its day Hierakonpolis must have been one of, if not the largest urban units along the Nile, a regional center of power and capital of an early kingdom, composed of diverse neighborhoods, cemeteries, industrial zones, cult centers, trash mounds, and more (overview of older research in Hoffman 1982; Adams 1995).

Predynastic Heirakonpolis was divided into various sectors and quarters, each of which contributes to form a picture of a remarkably sophisticated society. On the north side of town was the industrial zone, where numerous installations were dedicated to the production of beer and porridge on what is clearly an industrial scale. Outfitted with six to ten large conical vats, each establishment was capable of yielding 100–200 gallons of the product per day (fig. 4.2) Nearby silos to store the grain prior to processing, and pottery kilns to make the jars to hold it afterward, indicate a highly organized and integrated production mode. Although ancient Egyptian beer was once thought to be made from partly baked bread crumbled in water and left to ferment, the analysis of the wheat-rich residue still adhering to the sides of the vats reveals a more complicated and labor-intensive process that involved the direct use of grain for a higher-quality beverage that must have been produced by specialists. Clearly, they took their beer seriously, and more than ten installations of this type have been identified across the site (i.e., HK24, HK11), some dating back to 3600 BC, making them the oldest breweries in the world (Geller 1992; Takamiya 2008; Baba 2008).

It is still unclear whether all this food was being produced for daily distribution or only for special occasions, or whether this pooling of agricultural resources was voluntary, perhaps as a hedge against shortages or coerced as tax. Nevertheless, control of the food supply and its surplus is a key step in the concentration of power into a small number of hands. Indeed, the lack of permanent storage facilities within the individual houses across the site suggests that the pre-eminence of Hierakonpolis may stem from the early development of a redistributive economy. Such a system is known from Dynastic times, when agricultural produce was centrally collected and then distributed, perhaps as wages (cf. Kemp 2006, pp. 163–79).

What the site's rulers could do with that surplus and the ideological power they used to justify its collection is demonstrated in the center of town. Here a palisade wall of large logs, traced for over 50 meters, likely enclosed an area of over 2.5 acres (Hikade et al. 2008), which included administrative or palace structures (HK34) and workshops for the fabrication of fine flint tools, semiprecious beads, and vessels

painstakingly drilled from a variety of exotic and decorative stones (Holmes 1992a). More importantly, it also contained an impressive ceremonial center (HK29A) composed in part of a walled, oval courtyard 45 meters long and 13 meters wide. On the south side was a monumental gateway framed by four enormous wooden pillars (fig. 4.3), a contemporary depiction of which may well be present on the unique decorated pot recovered from the Fort cemetery (fig. 4.4) (Logan 1990). In use for over five hundred years (Naqada IIA period–Dynasty 1), the ceremonial center underwent several renovations, but because its caretakers were fastidious housekeepers, it is the trash pits they dug around the peripheries that provide us with unique glimpses of actual cultic practices in the Predynastic age (Friedman 2009).

These pits contained thousands (37,500) of animal bones deriving from domestic livestock and fish as well as a diverse array of wild animals. The volume of bones, the presence of all elements of the skeletons, and the debris from the sharpening of flint knives combine to suggest that large numbers of animals were butchered at this site. The high-quality cattle, young sheep and goats, and the large fish, many over one meter in length, indicate feasting formed a large part of the festivities; however, the wild animals, including crocodile, softshell turtle, hippopotamus,

FIGURE 4.3. A view of the eastern half of the oval courtyard of the ceremonial center at HK29A with the emplacements for the huge wooden columns forming its monumental entrance and the trash pits which provide the best evidence of the ritual activities that took place here

FIGURE 4.4. Drawing of decoration on OIM E29871 (Logan 1990, fig. 3)

gazelle, barbary sheep, and various carnivores, imply something more than just fine dining. Making up nearly 17 percent of the faunal assemblage (compared to 1.5 percent in the general settlement), this collection of wild and often dangerous game had a much more important purpose — the control of chaos (Linseele et al. 2009). One of the fundamental themes of Predynastic iconography, the imposition of order over chaos, especially as embodied in the diversity of nature (see "Iconography of the Predynastic and Early Dynastic Periods" in this volume) continued to be the most important role of Egyptian kingship (Kemp 2006, pp. 92–99). Bringing this concept to life, the wrestling of these animals into submission and their ultimate sacrifice with ceremonial knives in this open court must have been a vivid demonstration of the containment of the chaotic and the victory of (human) order necessary to keep the cosmos in balance (Perry in press).

An incised potsherd also found among the temple debris further illustrates that domination was not limited to the animal sphere. On the obverse is the distinctive emblem of the cow goddess Bat, whose image also graces the Narmer Palette (Fischer 1962), while the reverse shows a stylized female held captive by an early symbol of royal authority, the bull (fig. 4.5) (Hendrickx 2002).

The seasonal availability of desert and aquatic fauna suggests that the rituals were associated with the coming of the Nile flood, an especially chaotic moment in the cosmic cycle of renewal that required extraordinary powers to negotiate. This mastery was such an important aspect of royal ideology, it may well be this specific time (or its corollary, the *heb-sed* jubilee or renewal of the king) and possibly even this actual place that is depicted on the Narmer Macehead, as the king presides over wild animals corralled in an oval court while large numbers of livestock and human captives are amassed for inspection. The temple both proclaimed and reinforced the authority of the king, but this was not the only way the established social order expressed itself, as work in the cemeteries has also shown.

THE ELITE CEMETERY (HK6)

In the early Naqada II period, in several locations throughout Upper Egypt, there began to emerge political centers whose rulers exhibited their power and status in the outstanding size and wealth of their burials. These elite tombs were eventually segregated

FIGURE 4.5. Incised potsherd from the ceremonial center at HK29A

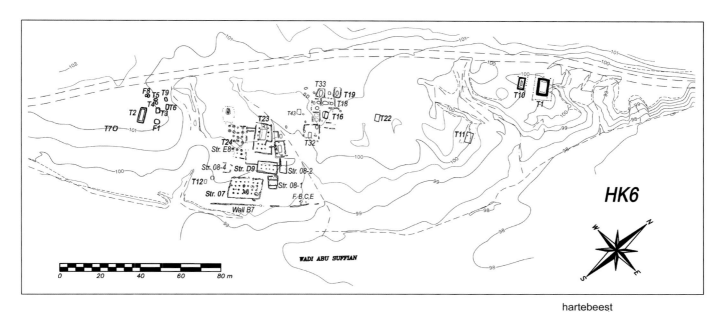

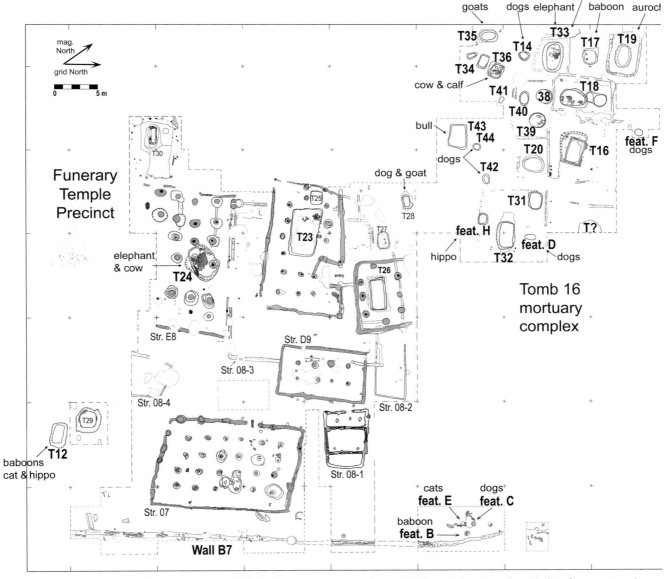

FIGURE 4.6. Above, overview of the elite cemetery HK6; below, map of excavated area at HK6 including the pillared hall or funerary temple precinct and the Tomb 16 mortuary complex

FIGURE 4.7. Tomb 16 with the later brick-lined tomb within it

FIGURE 4.8. Ceramic masks from Tomb 16 (photo by James Rossiter)

FIGURE 4.9. Possible reconstruction of the Tomb 16 mortuary complex

within a discrete section of the general necropolis or, in the most extreme cases, in entirely separate cemeteries, as seen at Abydos, Naqada, and Hierakonpolis (Wilkinson 2000a; Midant-Reynes 2003). The elite cemetery (HK6) at Hierakonpolis (fig. 4.6) is located in isolation 2 kilometers into the desert. Like other early sites, it also had large tombs (Adams 2000a), but it is only recently that excavations have revealed how much further the Hierakonpolis elite took the display of their status by placing their sizable tombs within impressive architectural settings and surrounding

them with subsidiary graves containing an intriguing array of human and animal associates (Friedman 2008a–b, 2010; Friedman et al. in press).

Recent excavations have concentrated around Tomb 16, a large tomb of the Naqada IC–IIA period (ca. 3650 BC) into which a brick-lined tomb of the Naqada IIIA2 period had later been inserted in what appears to have been an act of respectful renovation rather than usurpation (fig. 4.7). The original tomb measures approximately 4.3 x 2.6 meters and is roughly 1.45 meters deep, making it among the largest known from this period. In addition to its size, and despite plundering and reuse, it was a very rich tomb. More than 115 pottery vessels have been recorded from it, including one incised with the earliest known emblem of Bat, showing her close association with power from the beginning (Hendrickx 2008).

Two of the best-preserved and most remarkable of the ceramic masks known exclusively from this cemetery also originate from this tomb (fig. 4.8). Curved to fit over the human head and attached by means of a string passed through holes behind the ears, they are Egypt's earliest funerary masks. They stand at the beginning of a tradition whose origin has long been a matter of conjecture.

These grave goods, however, are only one indication of the owners' great power. More expressive still is the network of interconnected wooden enclosures containing the graves of associates which surround the tomb on all four sides in an arrangement that anticipates the rows of subsidiary graves around the tombs of the First Dynasty kings at Abydos (fig. 4.9) (overview in Vandou 2008 and "The First Kings of Egypt: The Abydos Evidence" in this volume).

Although all the satellite tombs have been heavily plundered and less than half the complex has been explored, enough remains of their contents to suggest that there was nothing arbitrary about their layout or their occupants. Near the front (east side) were young hunters with weapons and other gear, at the rear the women and children with ivory hair combs, semiprecious stone beads, and delicate pottery (fig. 4.10). The fine items with which they were buried already suggest that they were specially selected for the honor of accompanying their lord, but their demographic is even more revealing.

Of the thirty-six individuals found within the thirteen tombs directly flanking Tomb 16, no one is younger than eight years of age and no one is older than thirty-five; over two-thirds of them were juveniles under fifteen years of age and young women. The sample is still limited, but this is far from normal mortality. While there is nothing to prove that all the graves were created at the same time, or that all the bodies in them were interred concurrently, the fences around them could only have been erected after the graves had been dug and refilled, and the continuous foundation trench in which to bed the wooden posts indicates a single building phase (Friedman et al. in press).

For the animals, whose tombs form an outer perimeter around the entire compound, there is no doubt that they accompanied their master in death. Near identical radiocarbon dates from two of these animals indicate that both met their end at the same time — some point between 3660 and 3640 BC. These animals, buried whole, include an African elephant, a wild bull (aurochs), hartebeest, hippopotamus, three baboons, three domestic cattle (bull, cow, and calf), two large goats, twenty-seven dogs, and six cats — forty-six animals in all (so far), among which different levels of care and value are clearly evident. Perhaps not surprisingly the most prized appears to be the ten-year-old male African elephant (*Loxodonta africana*), and the aurochs or wild bull (*Bos primigenius*), both requiring extraordinary efforts to acquire as neither were locally available at that time (Van Neer et al. 2004). Both were found in large, fenced tombs of their own, wrapped in vast amounts of linen and matting (fig. 4.11). Whether they were endowed with additional grave goods remains unclear, but both were given a substantial final meal, a great deal of which was still present inside them. In addition to half digested items of settlement debris, detailed analysis of the botanical content of the elephant's final meal reveals that he also dined on river plants, acacia twigs, and emmer wheat, both chaff and grains, suggesting he was well maintained (Marinova and Van Neer 2009).

Although neither the elephant nor the aurochs show explicit evidence of long-term captivity, that the animals were sustained alive for some time is

FIGURE 4.10. Selection of objects from the subsidiary graves around Tomb 16

indicated by the hartebeest, who exhibited deformation of his dentition similar to that seen on wild animals kept in prolonged captivity in zoos today. Similarly, the baboons show healed fractures on the forearms (fig. 4.12), suggesting that violence was needed to keep these unruly creatures in check. Further evidence is supplied by the young hippopotamus that fractured the fibula of his hind leg, presumably while straining to free himself. That all of these injuries, fatal in the wild, were healed indicates captivity for a minimum duration of four to six weeks and significant efforts to maintain them (Linseele et al. 2007; Van Neer et al. in press).

The different levels of effort taken in the burial of these animals suggest that their meaning need not be the same. In general, the wide variety of taxa interred around the perimeter may have symbolically provided protection against the natural chaos they represented, but the burial of domestic animals may also have insured an eternal food supply and companionship, along with forming part of an ostentatious display of the sacrifice of valuable assets. However, the burial of the large wild animals was probably more than anything else a display of power. The ownership of these exotic animals would have been a strong visual statement to this effect. The creation and maintenance of royal menageries is known to have been a means of legitimizing pharaohs in the New Kingdom

(Müller-Wollermann 2003), and may also have served this purpose at this early time. Yet the power exhibited here was not simply the authority to control or kill these creatures, but also to become them, taking their formidable natural attributes for one's own. In this way, these graves reflect the physical reality behind the animal-based iconographies of power that dominate in the early periods of Egyptian history, as seen, for example, on the Narmer Palette and other documents, where royal power is manifest in several animal guises. The evidence from Hierakonpolis now suggests this royal symbolism can be traced back to actual physical mastery over some of the most powerful creatures of their world.

The full extent of the Tomb 16 complex is unknown, but it may be at least 60 meters long and 40 meters wide. Likewise, its likely appearance is still vague, but the range of fences may well have been modelled on the actual elite residence (or royal palace), perhaps in the same manner as Tomb U-j at Abydos (Dreyer 1998; "Tomb U-j: A Royal Burial of Dynasty 0 at Abydos" in this volume), but above ground, far larger, and much earlier.

The location of Tomb 16 itself was probably distinguished from its surroundings in some manner, but because of its later reuse (or renovation), what form that took is still unclear. The surviving traces indicate its superstructure was less elaborate than

FIGURE 4.11. The burial of an African elephant

FIGURE 4.12. Burial of a baboon with fractured forearm

entrance

burial chamber

posts of superstructure

enclosure wall

FIGURE 4.13. Tomb 23, the largest known tomb of the Naqada II period, with the posts of its superstructure and enclosing fence enhanced

FIGURE 4.14. The pillared hall of Structure 07

that of nearby Tomb 23, an enormous tomb (5.0 x 3.1 m) built just a generation or two later (Naqada IIB) (fig. 4.13). Its owners, if not borrowing an extant building, modelled the superstructure on the remarkable pillared halls, which like the temple in the center of town must have marked the focal point of this august necropolis (Friedman 2008a–b; Friedman 2010).

Concentrated in a special precinct in the center of the cemetery, these pillared halls not only provide the first examples of an architectural style (the hypostyle hall) previously only hypothesized for the Predynastic period, but also give ample evidence for the existence of developed mortuary temples and rituals from a very early time. These wooden buildings stretch back for generations, with at least three building phases as earlier buildings were replaced over time by even grander structures. Radiocarbon dating proves that at least one of the halls (Structure E8) from the later building phase was already present when the Tomb 16 complex was in use, serving as the location of the funerary rituals and cult. Fragments of red and green painted plaster, and some with figural designs in black, indicate that these structures, like the later mudbrick funerary enclosures of the Early Dynastic royalty at Abydos, were meant to impress (see "The First Kings of Egypt: The Abydos Evidence" in this volume). Together with the tomb complexes they provide a view of an elaborate

mortuary landscape on a scale hitherto unexpected for this period.

Of the eight structures known, the best preserved is Structure 07; 15.0 meters long and 10.5 meters wide, twenty-four wooden columns originally filled its interior (fig. 4.14). Although much denuded, as in all of the structures, a variety of objects were found at the corners. In the northeast were masses of ostrich eggshells attesting to the original presence of at least six rare and valuable whole eggs, one of which was incised with a hunting scene comparable to the egg in the Oriental Institute (Catalog No. 5) (Muir and Friedman in press). In the southeast corner were objects of different types, including a unique ivory wand carved with a procession of hippopotami along the top (fig. 4.15), a large collection of elegant

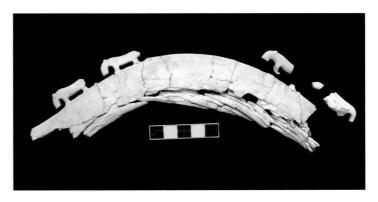

FIGURE 4.15. Ivory wand with a procession of hippopotami carved along the top. From Structure 07

FIGURE 4.16. Elegant hollow-based arrowheads from Structure 07 (photo by James Rossiter)

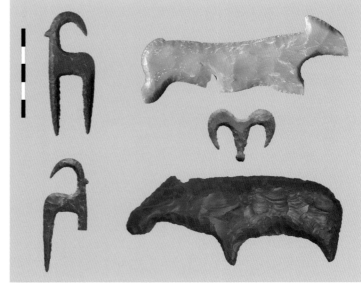

FIGURE 4.17. Flint animals from the HK6 cemetery

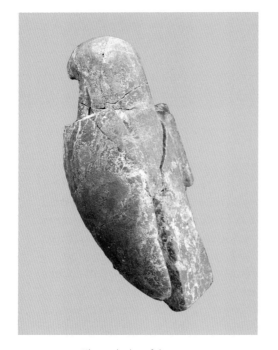

FIGURE 4.18. The malachite falcon from Structure 07

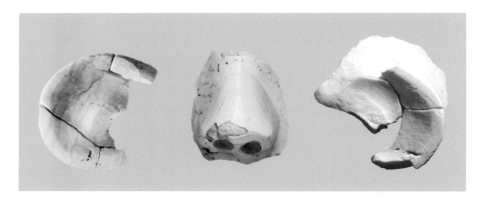

FIGURE 4.19. The nose and ears of the life-sized limestone statue from the Tomb 23 complex (photo by James Rossiter)

hollow-base arrowheads (fig. 4.16), some of large size anticipating the gigantism of the votive mace-heads and palettes of the Main Deposit. The skill involved leaves little doubt that the same craftsmen created the exquisite flint ibex also recovered nearby, as well as the numerous other flint animals found in the corners of other structures, always in association with arrowheads and weaponry, symbolic of control (Friedman 2008a–b and 2010). Members of a relatively rare class of artifact (only about sixty examples are known), these flint figurines from the HK6 cemetery now represents the largest single assemblage of flint animals with known provenance from anywhere in Egypt (fig. 4.17) (Hendrickx et al. 1997/98).

The quality of the objects is impressive, but the most remarkable artifact from Structure 07 is the falcon figurine masterfully carved from brittle malachite (fig. 4.18). This is Egypt's earliest falcon image, falcons only becoming common just before the First Dynasty, especially as markers of royal names. Whether this falcon already carried royal connotations is unknown, but given the elite context and the strong association of the local falcon god Horus with early kingship, it seems highly likely (Hendrickx et al. in press). However, the forces of the cosmos to be honored or appeased here were not limited to animal form. Fragments of a life-size stone statue were found in association with Tomb 23. Unfortunately only the ears and nose can be identified (fig. 4.19), while the rest has been reduced to six hundred small pieces, making it impossible to determine who (royal or divine) was being portrayed (Jaeschke 2004).

Although little remains above ground in the HK6 cemetery to help us, some idea of the pageantry, spectacle, and ritual that took place here can be gleaned from the decorated walls of the Painted Tomb 100, at the edge of the cultivation (Quibell and Green 1902; fig. 8.2 herein). Dating to the Naqada IIC period, when the elite cemetery had for some reason fallen into disuse, and elite burials throughout Egypt in general were rare, it seems that its owner (whether royal or just a pretender) still managed to take all the trappings with him to his burial place by painting them on the tomb's walls. Between the funerary or ritual barks we see animals being hunted and captured for ultimate burial, the ritual slaughter of animals and people, as well as displays of combat and domination, all to the accompaniment of female dancers, while a cohort of officials look on from an adjacent wall (see "Iconography of the Predynastic and Early Dynastic Periods").

HIERAKONPOLIS IN THE NAQADA IIC–III PERIOD

Naqada IIC was a period of many changes at Hierakonpolis. As the desert settlement began to diminish in size for reasons that are still unclear, but probably related to the movement of the river course, some sectors were abandoned forever and others changed function (Friedman 2008a). Part of the industrial zone became a cemetery, destined to be the main necropolis for the general population into the Dynastic age, and later still it became the location of King Khasekhemwy's mudbrick ceremonial enclosure (fig. 4.20), more generally called the Fort, giving its name anachronistically to the entire cemetery. Other than the graves excavated here by John Garstang (Adams 1987) and Ambrose Lansing (1935), our knowledge of the Naqada IID period at Hierakonpolis is a blank.

When the lights come back on again in Naqada III (Dynasty 0), power had shifted north to Abydos. How this occurred is a mystery. The continuity of royal imagery first attested at Hierakonpolis, like the falcon and Bat emblem, suggests a diplomatic alliance with Abydos rather than warfare and defeat (Hendrickx and Friedman 2003). Certainly Hierakonpolis was far from a broken reed. Returning to the ancestral cemetery, the elite undertook restoration of some of the earlier structures and also built for themselves the largest tombs in Upper Egypt outside of Abydos. Yet, in contrast to other sites, where mudbrick was

FIGURE 4.20. The "Fort," the ceremonial enclosure of King Khasekhemwy of Dynasty 2, the oldest freestanding mudbrick structure in the world

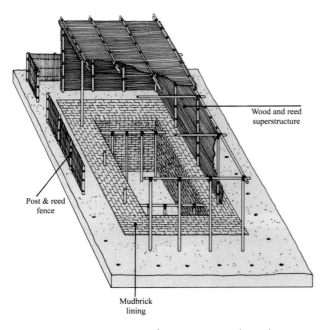

FIGURE 4.21. Reconstruction of superstructure above the Naqada III elite tombs at HK6 (after Fagan 1987, p. 74)

FIGURE 4.22. 1981 excavation photograph of the niched facade palace

used, the Hierakonpolis elite continued to mark their tombs with wooden structures modeled on the pillared halls and the superstructures above the graves of their ancestors (Adams 2000a) (fig. 4.21).

Furthermore, the temple of Horus in the new town center in the cultivation, with its oval mound of sand revetted with stone (McNarmara 2008) and the nearby palace with its niched or "palace" facade (fig. 4.22) — the only one to be found outside of a mortuary context (Fairservis 1986; Adams 1995) — indicate the site was still a location of significance. The hundreds of mace-heads (Catalog Nos. 93–94), stone vessels, ivory figurines, and enigmatic faience twists dedicated at this temple indicate special royal interest (Bussmann in press); however, whether the outstanding patronage by Egypt's earliest named kings shown by their palettes and mace-heads represents an actual connection to this site or recognition of its past greatness remains to be determined.

CONCLUSION

There can be no doubt that at about 3600 BC Hierakonpolis was far more than a local center of power. Although it is impossible to define the extent of the region it controlled, it probably spanned the southern part of Upper Egypt and into Nubia. The craft specialization seen at this surprisingly early date indicates that social differentiation was not limited to an elite-commoner dichotomy, but that a multi-tiered, stratified society was already in place by the beginning of the Naqada II period. This precocious development instigated by strong leaders able to marshal labor and exotic resources to express their authority in a variety of ways suggests that the idea of kingship in its dynastic form may well have originated at Hierakonpolis as the Narmer Palette first led us to believe — but just five hundred years earlier than previously imagined.

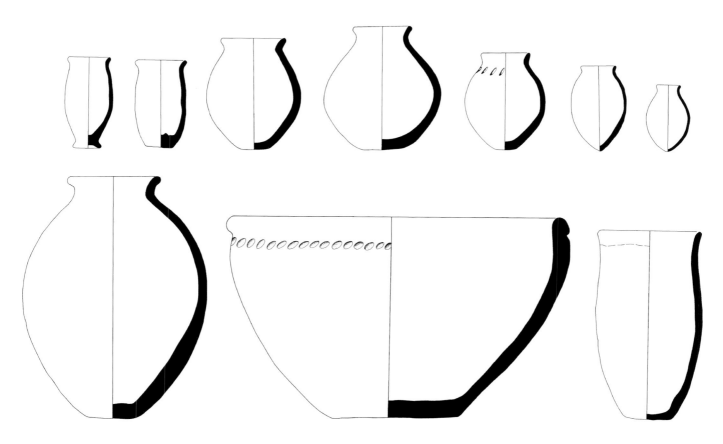

FIGURE 5.5. Ceramic forms characteristic from Maadi of the Lower Egyptian culture (after Rizkana and Seeher 1987, pls. 6, 7, 12, 15, 20, 35, 57, and 69). Various scales

FIGURE 5.6. Storage jars and postholes in the inhabited area of Maadi (after Rizkana and Seeher 1989, pl. 11.2)

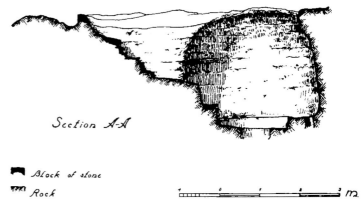

FIGURE 5.7. Subterranean dwelling, photograph and sketch. Maadi (after Rizkana and Seeher 1989, fig. 15, pl. 14.5)

(Perrot 1984), suggesting very close connections between Maadi and the Levant. Two cemeteries corresponding to two distinct phases of inhumation are associated with the site of Maadi, at nearby Wadi Digla. Bodies were placed in individual pits, on their sides and in contracted position (fig. 5.8), accompanied by a few pots and from time to time a shellfish valve (*Unio*). The inhabitants of Maadi practiced animal husbandry (cattle, sheep, goats, pigs, and dogs) and agriculture (different types of wheat and barley). They maintained commercial links with both southern Palestine and Upper Egypt. The peculiarity of the semi-subterranean houses, as well as the presence of copper and Levantine artifacts, suggest to some researchers that a Levantine colony was established in Maadi.

FIGURE 5.8. Burial WD38. Wadi Digla (after Rizkana and Seeher 1990, pl. 9)

The last phase of occupation at Maadi (the Digla I phase) corresponds to the oldest levels of occupation in Buto (phases I and II), in the northwest Nile Delta. The resumption of excavation work at the site by the German Institute of Cairo (Faltings 1998a; von der Way 1997–2007) has led to the identification of a later component of what used to be called the "Maadi-Buto" culture and is now preferably referred to as "cultures of Lower Egypt" (Faltings 1998b–c; Ciałowicz 2005). Vases of the Buto I phase are characterized by open shapes, with partly polished surfaces and thick walls. They are associated with a pottery of Ghassulian[3] inspiration, manufactured locally, as well as bowls or basins with thin walls decorated with painted bands (fig. 5.9) or sometimes a spiral motif, wide-mouth jars, bowls with a "V" profile and wavy-rimmed vessels called "pie-crust rims" (von der Way 1997). These shapes with a clear Levantine origin disappear during the Buto II phase in favor of bowls with concave walls manufactured with an alluvial clay fabric and a vegetal temper, sometimes decorated with incised motifs of small dots organized into rows or triangles, and "lemon-shaped" vases, an important cultural marker that is encountered in other Delta sites during the same period (Buchez and Midant-Reynes 2007). The links between Buto and the Near East are further emphasized by the presence of fired clay cones (von der Way 1993, pp. 34–35, 67–75) similar to those already known in the Uruk culture for creating decorative motifs on the walls of prestigious buildings (fig. 5.10), as well as by a large quantity of copper. As for the lithic material, it is closer to the material from Maadi, with large tabular scrapers of Palestinian origin, and in particular a twisted blade

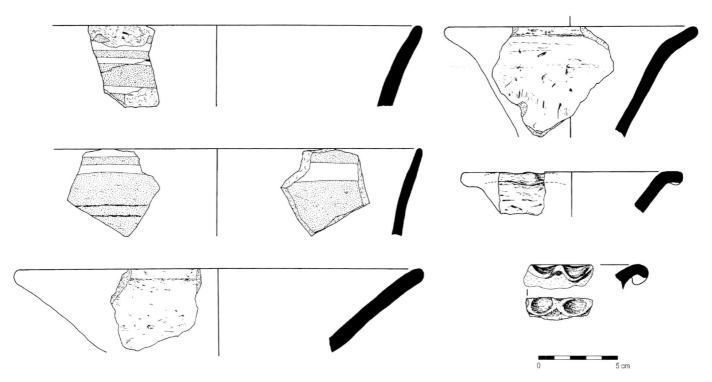

FIGURE 5.9. Ghassulian-inspired ceramic forms from Buto (after von der Way 1997, pls. 27–28)

and bladelet industry. Bifacial retouch is essentially unattested. The excavation, rendered very difficult by the remains being buried beneath groundwater level, revealed only a few small oval to rectangular domestic structures whose layout was identifiable by the presence of postholes.

The same type of structures are found in the Eastern Nile Delta. At the site of Tell el-Iswid (van den Brink 1989), hearths, pits, and postholes are, at this stage of the research, the only remains of settlement structures observed for the first half of the fourth millennium. The presence of small globular pots decorated with incised zigzags and bowls whose rims were adorned with fingerprints make them comparable to the Buto II phase. On the Western Kom at Tell el-Farkha, small rectangular light structures, of the same type as those at Maadi and Buto, are associated with pits and converted basins (Chłodnicki and Ciałowicz 2002–2008; Ciałowicz 2007a). More exceptional is the discovery of a brewery complex (Chichowski 2008; Kubiak-Martens and Langer 2008; "The Predynastic/Early Dynastic Period at Tell el-Farkhah" in this volume), associating baked clay vats lined with D-shaped bricks. This is considered to be the oldest construction of this type in northern

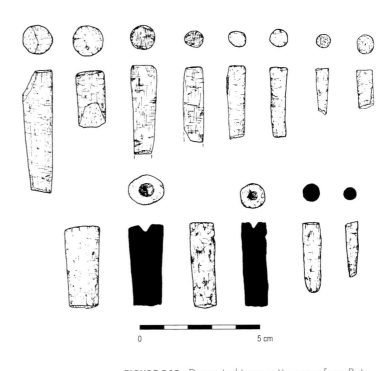

FIGURE 5.10. Decorated terra-cotta cones from Buto (after von der Way 1997, pl. 57)

Egypt. The ceramic material of the oldest levels of Tell el-Farkha is manufactured with local alluvial clay fabric and with vegetal temper. It includes small oval or ovoid "lemon-shaped" jars with round rims similar to those of Buto (Phase II), truncated bowls, different types of jars, and shallow bowls. Some containers are decorated with incised or dotted lines or zigzags (Mączyńska 2003–2008).

If Tell el-Farkha and Tell el-Iswid (South) have not yielded a cemetery corresponding to the oldest settlement, the neighboring site of Kom el-Khilgan (Midant-Reynes and Buchez in preparation) has offered to the trowel of the archaeologists a cemetery contemporary to the first two phases of occupation of Buto (I and II), the latest phase of the cemetery of Maadi (Digla II) and the first two phases of Tell el-Farkha (1 and 2). Around fifty tombs are associated with the first two phases of the site, KeK1 and KeK2. They are individual graves in which the body was placed either on its left or right side, in a contracted position, without preferential orientation (fig. 5.11). The funerary assemblages are not abundant and there is little diversity — the tomb containing a single vase in most cases, two to five baked clay vessels

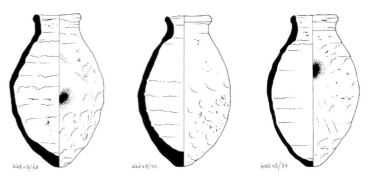

FIGURE 5.12. "Lemon-shaped" ceramic forms. Kom el-Khilgan. Various scales (drawings by C. Hochstrasse-Petit)

are present in only a third of the graves, sometimes associated with a valve of the *Unio* shellfish. Vases, manufactured with crude clay fabric with smoothed vegetal temper, offer a small variety of shapes, with a majority of them small ovoid "lemon-shaped" pots with a pointed or round base and with sub-vertical neck (fig. 5.12) (Buchez and Midant-Reynes 2007). A flint blade is also sometimes deposited in the grave. The same funerary traditions are attested in the cemeteries of Heliopolis north of Cairo and at Wadi Digla, near Maadi. The particularity of Kom el-Khilgan is

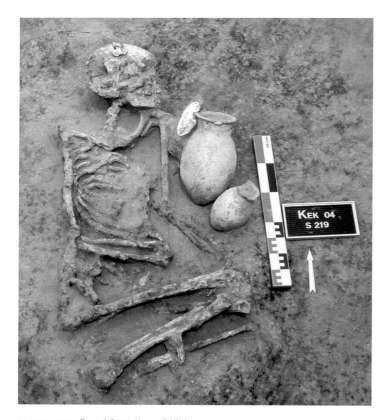

FIGURE 5.11. Burial S219. Kom el-Khilgan (photo by B. Midant-Reynes)

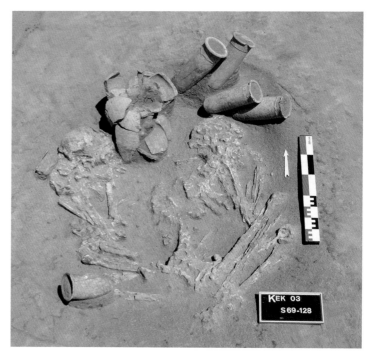

FIGURE 5.13. Lower Egyptian tradition burial S69 disturbed by more recent Naqadian burial S128. Kom el-Khilgan (photo by B. Midant-Reynes)

mainly that its cemetery has two cultural components, the later phase KeK3 having tombs with fully Naqadian characteristics, which have led to a better understanding of the acculturation process that marked the end of the Naqada II and III periods in the Nile Delta (fig. 5.13).

THE END OF THE PREDYNASTIC PERIOD (3600–2700 BC)

As early as the Naqada IIC–D phase, at Buto and at Tell el-Farkha, light structures built of perishable material give way to mudbrick buildings (Tristant 2004). Despite frequently incomplete data, one observes as early as Naqada III the development of important complexes, perhaps elite residences or storerooms (at Tell el-Farkha, for example; Ciałowicz 2009 and "The Predynastic/Early Dynastic Period at Tell el-Farkha" in this volume) located on the trade routes with the Levant, perhaps also with Mesopotamia. While in Abusir and Abu Rawash great Memphite tombs were being built, the Eastern Delta saw an unprecedented development of its necropoleis (Minshat Abu Omar, Beni Amir, Kafr Hassan Daoud, Tell el-Fara'in, Kom el-Khilgan, Minshat Ezzat [fig. 5.14], Ezbet et-Tell, Tell Abu Daoud, Tell el-Dab'a el-Qanan, Tell el-Farkha, Tell el-Mashal'a, Tell el-Samara, Tell Ibrahim Awad, and Mendes) where, starting in Naqada IIIA, and especially during Naqada IIIC, a significant transformation is visible (Tristant in press). Burials with the body placed on its left side become predominant, following a typically southern trait. Naqadian material takes over the local assemblage of Lower Egyptian tradition. Tombs built of bricks become standard while many great Naqadian cemeteries start dotting the Eastern Delta (fig. 5.15). This development takes place simultaneously with the full expansion of Levantine trade (see "Early Interaction between Peoples of the Nile Valley and the Southern Levant" in this volume). Furthermore, in addition to the cemeteries, large administrative and cultic centers appear, which can only be linked to the fundamental role played by the administration in the background, linked to royal power in full assertion. The over-representation of the Egyptian administration in the Eastern Delta must be taken into consideration, not only in view of natural factors (burying of structures by millennia of flood and silt), as well as the history of the research in the region, but also in light of historical facts, such as the presence of regional authorities, for example, representatives of royal power invested with administrative functions, like regional governors.

The new research carried out at Tell el-Farkha, Kom el-Khilgan, and Tell el-Iswid (South) has greatly modified the image that we had of Predynastic Egypt, which was too often limited to the large sites of Upper Egypt. In the Delta, as in the south of the country, the fourth millennium appears to have been a period of subtle evolutions. The data acquired during the most recent fieldwork have revealed that the societies of the Delta, more complex than we were first led to believe, evolved independently from those of Upper Egypt due to their privileged relationship

FIGURE 5.14. Flint knife with the name of King Den. Minshat Ezzat. Length 48.3 cm. Egyptian Museum, Cairo (photo by Y. Tristant)

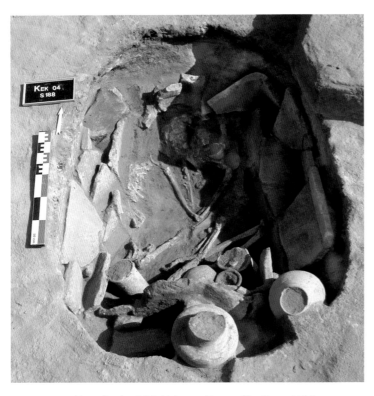

FIGURE 5.15. Naqadian burial S168 in a pottery coffin. Kom el-Khilgan (photo by B. Midant-Reynes)

with the Near East. The second half of the fourth millennium is a transition period during which phenomena of acculturation were clearly taking place, at Kom el-Khilgan, for example, thus suggesting that contact was maintained with the Naqadian region, which eventually, through repeated exchanges, led to the north's assimilation of Naqadian cultural traits and the disappearance of a distinct northern identity (Buchez and Midant-Reynes 2007). Recent work places the Nile Delta in a new research perspective, one which forecasts for coming years new advances in our understanding of the power structures which are at the heart of this evolution, as well as the more precise definition of the complexity of the cultures of Lower Egypt.

NOTES

* Translated by Rozenn Bailleul-LeSuer.

[1] Neolithic remains might also be present at the sites of Minshat Abu Omar (Krzyżaniak 1993) and Sais (Wilson and Gilbert 2003; Wilson 2006).

[2] "... the site which is being excavated possesses an essentially autonomous character. Its ceramic products, especially the smooth base-ring ware, its flint and limestone palettes, and its bold treatment of flint, all give the prehistoric civilisation revealed a stamp of its own, which justifies us to speak of a Maadi culture. The 'Maadian' should, therefore, be considered as a well defined group within the prehistoric evolution of Egypt" (Amer 1936, p. 69).

[3] Ghassulian is a Chalcolithic culture and archaeological stage of the southern Levant.

6. THE PREDYNASTIC/EARLY DYNASTIC PERIOD AT TELL EL-FARKHA

KRZYSZTOF M. CIAŁOWICZ*

In 1987, the Italian mission from the Centro Studi e Ricerche Ligabue in Venice, headed by Professor Rodolfo Fattovich, carried out a survey in the Eastern Nile Delta. During the survey, several dozen sites dating back to all periods of ancient Egyptian history were found. One of them was called the Chicken Hill (Tell el-Farkha) by the local people. It is composed of three hills (west, central, and east), called koms or tells, situated on the edge of the village of Ghazala, about 120 kilometers northeast of Cairo. These hills rise to the height of five meters over the level of the surrounding fields and cover an area of over four hectares. The Italian excavations lasted for three seasons (1988–1990). Four test trenches were dug and the preliminary chronology of the site was determined. Afterward, the project was abandoned (Chłodnicki et al. 1991).

In 1998, thanks to the courtesy of Italian colleagues, the Polish Archaeological Expedition started research in Tell el-Farkha.[1] From the beginning of the excavation, thanks to the complex geophysical and geological prospection, it was clear that the inconspicuous-looking hills concealed the remains of houses and workshops, as well as graves. The stratification survey confirmed that the site documents more than a thousand-year-long span, starting many centuries before the foundation of the Dynastic state, and divided into several distinct phases (Chłodnicki et al. 2002, pp. 66–67). The oldest period of the site is associated with the so-called Lower Egyptian culture of native inhabitants of the Delta who dwelled in a settlement at Tell el-Farkha from about 3700/3600 until about 3300 BC. Afterward, the first settlers associated with the Naqada culture from the south appeared, at the same time that the first political centers were evolving in Upper Egypt. The apogee of Tell el-Farkha is in the Protodynastic period (Dynasties 0 and 1, ca. 3200–2950 BC). In the middle of the First Dynasty, there was a sort of cultural collapse, and progressively poorer inhabitants occupied the site until the early Fourth Dynasty (ca. 2600 BC).

In the oldest layers of all three koms were found large residential structures made of posts connected by plaited walls (fig. 6.1). The buildings were divided into numerous rooms of various functions. Sometimes the buildings are grouped into distinct rows situated along relatively narrow streets. It is possible to observe the clear division of the settlement separated into parts, initially by wooden fences and later by brick walls. The brick walls start to appear already during the Lower Egyptian settlement.

These discoveries contradict a widely held opinion that the creators of the Lower Egyptian culture had been at a low stage of socioeconomic development. Further contradicting this theory is the sequence of breweries — the world's oldest known (ca. 3500–3350 BC) — unearthed on the Western Kom (fig. 6.2). They were made of a dozen big vats placed in recesses made of long narrow bricks (Cichowski 2008). Through evaluation of the plant remains it was possible to reconstruct the recipe for making this early beer (Kubiak-Martens and Langer 2008).

From the beginning, the inhabitants of Tell el-Farkha were very involved in trade exchange, as indicated by the presence of objects imported from the Near East and Upper Egypt. The presence of ceramics, tools, and raw materials from the Levant is not a surprise since they are present also at other sites in Lower Egypt. However, the presence of an unexpectedly large percentage of objects from Upper Egypt forces one to reconsider the nature of the relations between the Delta and the south of the country at the beginning of the second half of the fourth millennium BC. Imports from the south include decorated ceramics, stone vessels, mace-heads, and most important, beaded necklaces made from semiprecious stones and gold — the first examples of this metal in the Delta. The important role of trade is confirmed by remains of donkeys that were used as a means of transport.

It is not surprising that Tell el-Farkha, located on an important trade route, had drawn the attention

FIGURE 6.1. Remains of Lower Egyptian houses on the Central Kom

of Naqadians entering the Delta from the south. No doubt the agricultural land was of less interest to them than was taking control over trade. At this time in Upper Egypt the first political organizations were being established, and the leading elite stressed its position with luxury goods imported from the Levant and Nubia, making the trade routes through Tell el-Farkha even more important.

After a short time of coexistence, the Naqadians gained the clear advantage over the local inhabitants of the area, whose fate after this point is a mystery. There is no trace of war or destruction that could testify to the conquest of a "Lower Egyptian kingdom" by the herdsmen from the south. It is more probable that there was an assimilation and acculturation, in the course of which the native inhabitants of the Delta accepted the more attractive southern models of culture.

One of the first projects undertaken by the new settlers in Tell el-Farkha was erecting a huge building where previously there were breweries. So far,

the eastern part of this area has been examined (Chłodnicki et al. 2004, pp. 48–50). The western part will be the subject of exploration in the coming seasons. The new structure was a monumental complex, the largest yet known from this period in Egypt (ca. 3300–3200 BC). On its surface there was a mud layer, no doubt originating from the Nile inundation, which covered a thick layer of ashes indicating destruction by fire. Just under the ash there were traces of mudbricks forming an outline of the building. This sizable building (the examined part covers several hundred square meters) was divided into several rooms facing an inner courtyard. Walls over two meters thick separated the main rooms. Most of these rooms were apparently abandoned in a hurry.

One wonders what the function of the building was, and especially who its inhabitants were, and why it was erected at this very spot. Recovered storage jars, clay sealings, and numerous small objects that could be used to count, as well as the fragments of Palestinian ceramics, seem to indicate that trade was a significant feature in the life of the inhabitants. Perhaps we are dealing with a residence, adjacent to the storage rooms, that belonged to a Naqadian from southern Egypt who supervised the trade between Palestine, the Delta, and Upper Egypt. The resident was certainly associated with one of the early Egyptian rulers residing at Abydos or Hierakonpolis and controlling the whole Egypt or at least a substantial part of it.

It is difficult to assess whether the destruction of the building was a result of intentional human activity, or if it was a consequence of a natural cataclysm such as an earthquake. Taking the date of the fire (ca. 3200 BC) into consideration, it can be assumed that it was not a coincidence. It could have been related to the growing rivalry between the major political centers (although for now this is just a hypothesis). The rulers of these proto-kingdoms attached great importance to the trade with Sinai and Palestine. The acquisition of valuable natural resources (mainly copper) and products (wine, olive oil) was one of the main objectives of their policy. The hundreds of imported Palestinian vessels found in their graves at Abydos are substantive evidence (Hartung 2001). Tell el-Farkha, located at an important spot on the trade route, was undoubtedly the center of attention of the contemporary elites. Therefore, it can be assumed

that one of the early rulers wanted to control this region. Whether Tell el-Farkha was then independent or if it was the subject of another center is still difficult to determine. However, it might be assumed that the destruction of the residence at Tell el-Farkha is connected with an increasing competition within the Naqada culture, leading ultimately to the creation of the monarchy. In any case, the destruction has nothing to do with the conquest of the Delta by Upper Egypt, which was implied by the old theories on the origins of the Egyptian state (cf., e.g., Drioton and Vandier 1975, pp. 129–32).

Tell el-Farkha's peak of development was in the Protodynastic period during Dynasty 0 and the early First Dynasty. This is evidenced by the remains of an administrative-cultic center situated on the Western Kom (Ciałowicz 2009) and by the necropolis of the same period on the Eastern Kom, both of which provide new data about the origins of Egyptian architecture and historical development.

Examination of the administrative-cultic center on the Western Kom has revealed a complicated architectural structure consisting of two chapels. A votive deposit was discovered in each chapel. The first deposit consisted of figurines and vessels made of faience, clay, and stone. Of special interest are the representations of baboons and a figurine depicting

FIGURE 6.2. One of the breweries from the Western Kom

a naked prostrating man (fig. 6.3), perhaps a captive, as well as pottery rattles with incised decoration.

FIGURE 6.3. Figurine of a prostrating man, perhaps a captive. First deposit, Western Kom. Scale 1:1

The second chapel was examined in the seasons between 2006 and 2010. Numerous vessels of a ritual character were discovered, including jugs for ritual libation and distinctive stands that match the vessels. The latter were often depicted in Egyptian art as symbols of shrines (Ciałowicz 2001, pp. 203–04). The most important find was a deposit consisting of several dozen objects (fig. 6.4) made primarily of hippopotamus ivory. Most numerous are figurines depicting people and animals (Chłodnicki and Ciałowicz 2008).

Some of the figurines are unique works of art of a style previously unknown in such an early period of Egyptian history. The representations of women and children are among the most important. The former are depicted naked or dressed in long robes. Both types continued to be popular until the very end of ancient Egyptian art. Other figurines are women with children on their shoulders or laps. A figurine showing a mother sitting in a palanquin with a child on her lap is a representation hitherto unknown in Egypt (fig. 6.5). It has a clear connection with the

FIGURE 6.4. Votive deposit discovered in 2006. Western Kom

FIGURE 6.5. Ivory figurine of a mother with child in a palanquin. Second deposit, Western Kom

FIGURE 6.6. Ivory figurines of young boys. Second deposit, Western Kom

FIGURE 6.7. Ivory figurine of a male wearing a cloak, possibly representing a king. Second deposit, Western Kom

so-called *reput* — a statue probably depicting the divine mother of the king (Kaiser 1983, p. 262).

Small boys are often depicted seated with their knees drawn up and with the right finger in their mouth (fig. 6.6). This motif too continued to be a standard representation in ancient Egyptian art. It should be stressed that the figurines from Tell el-Farkha are among the best early examples of such depictions in terms of artistic quality.

The second deposit also includes several statues depicting males. The most important figure is clad in a cloak (fig. 6.7), probably one of the first representations of the Egyptian king during the *heb-sed* jubilee (Blaszczyk 2008). This ceremony was celebrated on the thirtieth anniversary of the king's accession to the throne and is known in Egyptian art from the middle of the fourth millennium BC. It stresses the role of the ruler as a guarantor of prosperity and the development of all aspects of life. Representations of captives of war depicted with one or two hands tied behind their backs are a separate category. These figurines fit very well into a very popular motif in ancient Egypt of the victory over external enemies, and more broadly, the taming of forces of chaos and disorder that threatened both the ruler and people of Egypt.

Thirteen dwarf figurines (fig. 6.8) were found at Tell el-Farkha, the largest group of such figurines so far discovered anywhere in Egypt (Buszek 2008). Dwarfs played an important role in the culture as indicated by images of them in art, but also by burials

FIGURE 6.8. Ivory figurine of a male dwarf. Second deposit, Western Kom

of dwarfs found in the immediate vicinity of the tombs of the kings and aristocracy. The depictions from Tell el-Farkha attract particular attention because of the high level of workmanship of most of them, as well as the realism of their facial expressions and the representation of their bodies. These are far more skillfully done than any of the previously known early dwarf sculptures.

The examples of fantastic creatures and the depictions of cobra uraei from the deposit in Tell el-Farkha are extremely interesting because they have no analogy in the corpus of Egyptian art. The depiction of a griffin with a feline body, female breasts, and a falcon's head holding a jug (fig. 6.9) is the most interesting. It is difficult to assess whether another small figurine depicting a snake with a face of a woman may be in some way connected with the goddess Wadjet. The cobra uraei, however, seem to indicate that they are derived from this Lower Egyptian divine patroness of the king. It is believed that, since the reign of King Den (middle of Dynasty 1), cobras became a characteristic element of Dynastic crowns. Meanwhile, the cobras from Tell el-Farkha, which predate the reign of Den, were probably attached to something, and they may have been part of a larger whole (perhaps royal crowns or sculptures depicting kings).

FIGURE 6.9. Ivory figurine of a griffin. Second deposit, Western Kom

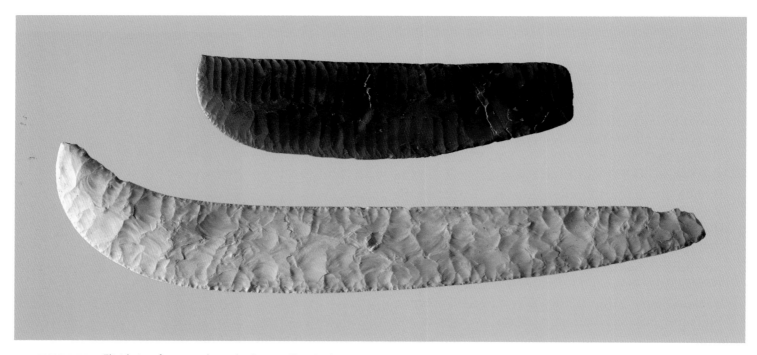

FIGURE 6.10. Flint knives from a cache in the Eastern Kom. Scale 1:3

Figurines of animals (lions, dogs, scorpions, fish, falcons) are known from many sites. However, they differ in details and in workmanship from the figurines of Tell el-Farkha. Representing a particular animal species probably mattered more than standardization of stylistic details. This diversity gives a good account of the contemporary artists and it shows that the art of this period is not monotonous and schematic. The same considerations also apply to the models of objects represented in the deposit of Tell el-Farkha: miniature boats of various types, granaries, boxes, mirrors, cylindrical seals, game pieces, and stone vessels, all of which appear at many other sites contemporary with Tell el-Farkha.

Other parts of the site provided equally interesting results. A very poor village, as well as a necropolis, was situated on the Eastern Kom. Even the former produced remarkable discoveries. A treasure, no doubt hidden intentionally, was found in one of the small rooms. It consisted of several dozen fragments of gold foil, carnelian and ostrich eggshell beads of a necklace, and two large flint knives (fig. 6.10).

The room in which the discovery was made is approximately one hundred years older than the beginnings of the Egyptian state. Poor archaeological context implies that all items were re-deposited here, and the site of their discovery was not the place for which they were originally intended. As it is apparent from the aforementioned results of the work at Tell el-Farkha that the period between about 3150 BC and the beginning of the First Dynasty was the time of the formation of Dynastic state and of the upheavals connected to that formation. It is not surprising that there must have been fights for control over our site. The discovery of the treasure suggests that the most valuable items from the equipment of a building in Tell el-Farkha were hidden before an impending invasion. It is tempting to say that the treasure was hidden from the same invaders who burned the residence in the Western Kom, but this is only one of the possible hypotheses. However, there is no doubt that these objects are older than the place where they were found.

Painstaking work on the reconstruction and conservation of some golden fragments from the Eastern Kom led to the conclusion that the remains belong to two statues. Both consisted of a core made of perishable material (probably wood), of which no traces survive. This core was then covered with a thin gold foil attached with gold rivets. The figurines represent standing naked men — one 57 cm high (fig. 6.11), the other 30 cm. The eyes of both statues were made of lapis lazuli imported from what is now Afghanistan. This may be further evidence for the important role that trade played for the ruling elite of the growing state. The eyebrows of the figurines were inlaid with material other than gold. Because it has not been preserved, it could be assumed that it was bitumen or ebony, both of which had to be imported to Egypt. The design of the figures and accentuated details — like large protruding ears, unnaturally large phalluses, and carefully modeled fingernails and toenails — fit well into the corpus of the art of Predynastic Egypt. The figurines, made of such precious materials, most likely represent the early ruler and his son and heir to the throne (Chłodnicki and Ciałowicz 2007).

The examination of the necropolis produced very important results. Almost 120 graves have been discovered so far, dated from the period between Dynasty 0 and the beginning of the Fourth

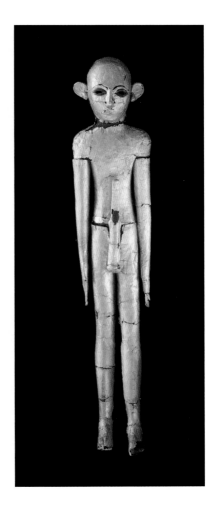

FIGURE 6.11. Golden figure of a Predynastic ruler from the Eastern Kom

Dynasty. It is possible to distinguish three groups among them differing in terms of design, quality, and quantity of the furnishings. The richest and oldest tombs (fig. 6.12) are the best in terms of their workmanship. The later structures are less carefully constructed, and the goods within them are of lesser quantity and quality. Among the last group we found only pit graves without equipment. This progression of gradual decline evidenced by the tombs confirms the increasing impoverishment of the inhabitants of "Chicken Hill" and the declining role it played.

A monumental building (over 300 square meters) is one of the most important discoveries in the necropolis (fig. 6.13). It is clearly earlier than the votive deposits found in the administrative-cultic center on the Western Kom. The origins of the cult center clearly overlap with the period of the erection of the buildings in the Eastern Kom. To date, it is the largest construction known in Egypt that can be dated to the period around 3200–3100 BC. The regular shape created by the few chambers separated by massive walls (up to 2.5 m thick), and the almost square main chamber with the descending shaft demonstrates the skill of the architects, and at the same time sheds new light on the beginnings of Egyptian architecture.

During the First and Second Dynasties and throughout the Old Kingdom, mastabas are considered to be the characteristic tomb type for the most important people in the country other than kings. The mysterious construction at Tell el-Farkha, which is much earlier than the First Dynasty, is probably a monumental tomb and therefore is the oldest mastaba known in Egypt. The work is ongoing, and full examination will take a few more years. Nevertheless, it can be concluded that the structure was connected with someone at the top of the contemporary hierarchy — perhaps a governor of one of the earliest Egyptian kings, or even the local ruler of the Delta.

Several other tombs at Tell el-Farkha dating to Dynasty 0 and the beginning of the First Dynasty no doubt should be regarded as mastabas as well. They are characterized by thick walls with distinctive

FIGURE 6.12. Example of a rich grave. Eastern Kom

FIGURE 6.13. Protodynastic mastaba. Eastern Kom

niches, covered on the outside by a kind of lime plaster (fig. 6.14). They contain, among other objects, jewelry, cosmetic palettes, tools, and up to several dozen pottery and stone vessels. Other graves from the beginning of the Egyptian state at other sites are equally well equipped.

Many vessels discovered in the tombs bore so-called pot marks, which some regard as the oldest hieroglyphs. The marks probably determined the place of origin or the direction of export of the goods stored inside the vessels (see also "Tomb U-j: A Royal Burial of Dynasty 0 atAbydos" in this volume). Some of them include the names of the rulers of the Dynasty 0. In two graves the name of Irj-Hor (fig. 6.15) was discovered, a king who hitherto was known only from the Abydos area. In the other graves names of other earlier rulers were discovered. The name of the first historical king, Narmer, appears twice.

The results of current research at Tell el-Farkha establish the uniqueness of this site. The division of the site into three large zones — residential-temple zone on the Western Kom, residential-business zone on the Central Kom, and the necropolis and village on the Eastern Kom — offers a unique opportunity to trace the reasons for the creation, development,

FIGURE 6.14. Mastaba dated to Dynasty 0. Eastern Kom

FIGURE 6.15. Name of King Irj-Hor (Dynasty O) inscribed on a wine jar. Eastern Kom

and decline of an important center dating back to the period of the formation of the Egyptian state. Such a complex site is unique in Egypt, and it is difficult to compare Tell el-Farkha with any other site (other than Hierakonpolis), because Predynastic–Early Dynastic sites usually consist of only a village or a necropolis.

It seems that our work finally disproved the theory that an armed raid on the Delta during the end of Lower Egyptian culture was responsible for the extermination of its population. Rather, it now appears that Naqadians slowly infiltrated northern Egypt, occupying empty areas and also settling in existing settlements. They brought with them new developments that were quickly adopted by the local people. Similar phenomena are also observed at the other sites in the Delta examined in recent years. What were the reasons for this expansion? A partial answer to this question is again provided by the results of the excavations at Tell el-Farkha. Among the many interesting findings, a particular group of relics represents imports from Palestine, including ceramic vessels and flint tools that were found in the oldest Lower Egyptian layers and also continued in the Naqadian occupation of the site. They testify to

a developed system of trade with Palestine and the Sinai throughout the whole Predynastic period that brought valuable products and raw materials to the Nile Valley. Security and control over the trade routes could be one of the reasons for the Naqadian expansion to the north. The elite born in Upper Egypt demanded more and more luxury goods imported from Southwest Asia.

From previous research at Tell el-Farkha, it can be also be assumed that the process of colonization of the Delta by settlers from the south was more complex than previously assumed (Ciałowicz 2008). Before arriving in the Delta, Naqadians did not create a single kingdom encompassing Upper Egypt. There still existed a few (at least two) centers that competed with each other in all areas. The cultural unification of Egypt from Elephantine to the Mediterranean Sea as documented by archaeological material was not the same as the political unity. Contemporary rulers, using the same language, script, and tools, competed for power and influence, and for domination over the Delta and its trade routes. This competition, however, took place within the Naqada culture. Therefore, it is not possible to sustain the theory based on the ancient written sources that there were kingdoms of Lower and Upper Egypt that were completely different from each other. Naqadian proto-kings competed with each other until one of them, who came from Abydos or Hierakonpolis, led to the creation of a single state on the Nile long before Narmer's accession to the throne.

NOTES

* Translated by Aleksandra Hallmann. All photos by Robert Słaboński.

[1] The research is carried out by the Polish Archaeological Expedition to the Eastern Nile Delta created by the Poznań Archaeological Museum and the Institute of Archaeology of the Jagiellonian University in cooperation with the Polish Centre of Mediterranean Archaeology of Warsaw. From the beginning, the work has been under the directorship of Dr. Marek Chłodnicki and the present author.

7. MATERIAL CULTURE OF THE PREDYNASTIC PERIOD

ALICE STEVENSON

Around 4500 BC, Neolithic communities in Egypt's Badari region began to return to the same locations in the desert behind the Nile's floodplain, generation after generation, to inter their dead. These represent the first large formal cemeteries in the Egyptian archaeological record. Not only do these cemeteries represent a new relationship between human groups and the landscape around the Nile, but they are also evidence for new forms of engagement with material culture. These graves were lined with reed mats on which the crouched body of the deceased was carefully placed. Surrounding the body could be pottery vessels, bone tools, ivory craftwork, thin strips of hammered copper, and stone palettes. This new vibrancy in the Egyptian archaeological record signals the beginning of a florescence of cultural expression.

During the fourth millennium BC an even greater diversity of objects was placed in tombs, most fashioned from local resources, but some from materials imported from far outside the Nile Valley. Artifacts were not made exclusively for funerals, but were usually drawn from the sphere of daily life as excavations of settlement areas have demonstrated. Early fourth-millennium Lower Egyptian communities created less elaborate forms of burial display, but their associated habitation areas reveal evidence for their own range of local objects in pottery, stone, ivory, and copper. By the later fourth millennium, material culture and burial practices were far more uniform across Egypt. Another key trend seen from the end of the Predynastic period is for elaborate forms of personal display to disappear as access to many types of artifacts became restricted to a privileged few. This was both a cause and a consequence of the development of the Egyptian state and the exclusive power of divine kingship.

POTTERY

Egyptian prehistoric pottery was produced long before the introduction of the potter's wheel. Each piece was thus almost entirely hand-made and many constitute some of the finest ceramics known from any period in Egyptian history. Such vessels are highly distinctive and come in many shapes and sizes. They are also the most prominent artifact type in burials (fig. 7.1). These factors allowed Flinders Petrie (1899) to develop his innovative and hugely influential sequence dating system. He achieved this by first distinguishing nine classes of pottery, within which he numbered different forms from bowls through tall

FIGURE 7.1. Naqada IIC burial H107 from Mahasna. Several pottery vessels now in Chicago can be seen (E8921, E26435–38, E26443, E26448). Courtesy of the Egypt Exploration Society

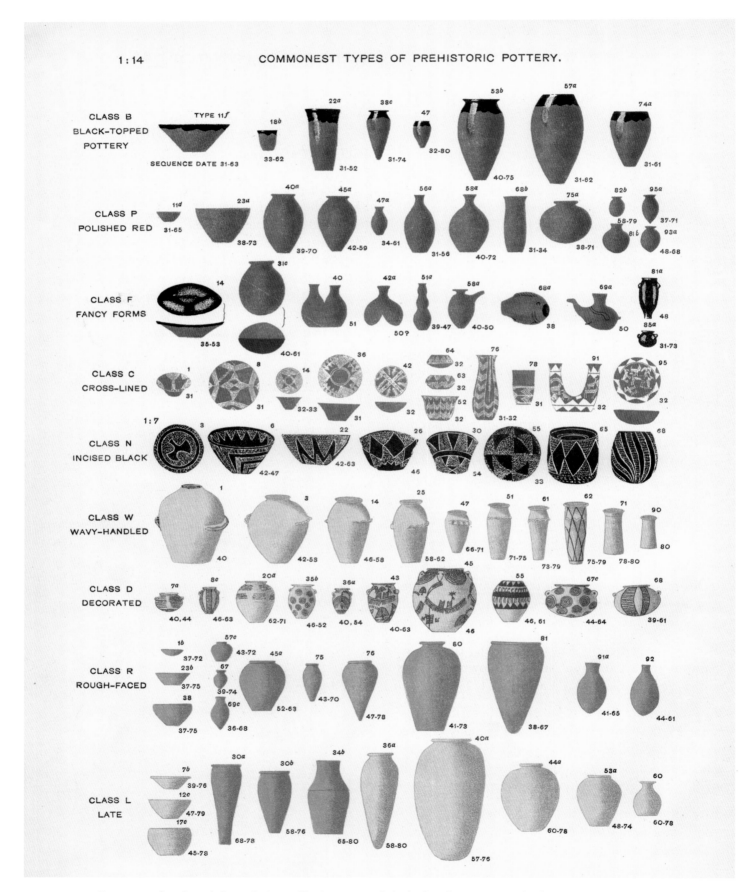

FIGURE 7.2. Frontispiece from Petrie's *Diospolis Parva: The Cemeteries of Abadiyeh and Hu, 1898-9* (1901b) illustrating his Predynastic pottery sequence (courtesy of the Egypt Exploration Society)

FIGURE 7.3. Examples of Black-Topped pottery (B-ware). OIM E9026, E5811, E905 (photo by Anna Ressman)

beakers (fig. 7.2). Although modern pottery specialists would not organize their corpuses of material in this way, the terminology introduced by Petrie remains the common reference point for Predynastic studies to this day. By comparing the presence and absence of types across thousands of grave assemblages, Petrie sorted them into a relative sequence, a process today referred to as seriation.

The earliest Predynastic assemblages of the Naqada I period were dominated by handsome red bowls and beakers that have a band of lustrous black around their rims which descends into the vessel interiors, a form Petrie dubbed "Black-Topped pottery" (B-ware) (fig. 7.3). Also appearing at this early date were glossy orange-red vessels, usually bowls and plates, but occasionally slender jars, adorned with creamy white designs. These constitute the earliest painted pottery in Egypt and are known as "Cross-Lined" vessels (C-ware) (Catalog Nos. 1, 28–29). Their decoration, which seems to be regionally variable (Finkenstaedt 1980), may imitate basketry or flora, but other vessels bear figurative scenes such as hunting. The third main pottery type in Naqada I assemblages are sleek Red-Polished vessels (P-ware).

All this early pottery was made with a type of clay called Nile silt, which was widely available. In the middle Predynastic period a new, harder type of clay was introduced — marl clay — procured from more restricted sources in the desert. Fresh pottery types were created in this medium, including jars with a wavy ledge handle feature adopted from

Levantine imports, called W-ware (fig. 7.4). It was these vessels that had given Petrie the vital clue that pottery could be used for dating. He hypothesized that over time there was a shift from globular vessels with pronounced ledge handles to cylindrical forms with a stylized wavy line (fig. 7.5). While many features of his chronological scheme have been refuted or refined, insightful observations such as this remain accurate.

Wavy-Handled W-ware never occurs in graves with Cross-Lined C-ware. Rather, a new type of decorated container, D-ware, also made in marl clay, now appeared alongside the W-ware. The shapes of such

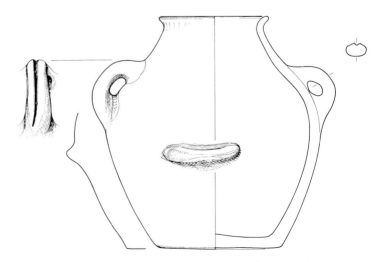

FIGURE 7.4. Imported Canaanite jar (W-ware) from Gerzeh in Lower Egypt (Naqada IIC), now in the Petrie Museum (UC10726) (illustration by Will Schenk)

FIGURE 7.5. Development of Wavy-Handled ware (W-ware). OIM E5816, E26815, E26112, E29255 (photo by Anna Ressman)

vessels often imitated those of stone and their adornment was the inverse of the C-ware, with red ochre motifs executed on a buff background. Gone too were the type of images that had featured previously and a new repertoire of geometric (fig. 7.6 and Catalog Nos. 35–36) and figurative scenes were created (Catalog Nos. 2, 31, 37–38).

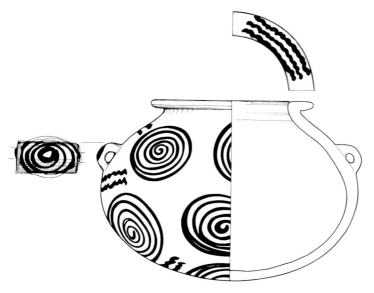

FIGURE 7.6. Decorated pottery from Gerzeh in Lower Egypt (Naqada IIC), now in the Petrie Museum (UC10751) (illustration by Will Schenk)

While W-ware signals relationships with the Levant to the north, a class of pottery Petrie named N-ware attests to networks extending southward. These dark vessels, usually bowls, bore impressed or incised white-filled decoration, a tradition associated with Nubia. Other foreign pottery is included among F-ware, Petrie's fancy-ware category (Catalog No. 13), a catch-all classification for unusual forms, both foreign and domestic. Late-ware pottery is a similarly heterogeneous grouping.

As time advanced, an increasing number of what Petrie referred to as Rough-ware vessels (R-ware) made from straw-tempered clay (Catalog No. 27) began to appear in burials alongside the fine F-wares. These straw-tempered ceramics had previously been seen only in settlement assemblages. As the occurrence of the coarser vessels increased, Black-Topped B-ware pottery became less frequent and by the Naqada III period had largely disappeared, along with P-ware and D-ware. In the closing centuries of the Predynastic period, pottery assemblages as a whole showed far more homogeneity. The scale of R-ware production increased markedly, as the vessels were now manufactured by specialist workshops (Köhler 1998, pp. 63–72), most noticeably seen in Delta settlement assemblages at Tell el-Farkha and Buto. In

8. ICONOGRAPHY OF THE PREDYNASTIC AND EARLY DYNASTIC PERIODS

STAN HENDRICKX

When W. M. Flinders Petrie excavated the Predynastic cemeteries of Naqada during the winter of 1895/96, he not only added a new chapter to the history of Egypt, but he also opened up a world of visual representations that could not be understood through the imagery of Dynastic Egypt. The new discoveries attracted much attention and the interpretation of Predynastic iconography was investigated mainly through ethnographic parallels which, in the opinion of those days, would allow this "primitive" art to be understood as both utilitarian and magical (Capart 1905). Its origin was considered African, whereas the "true"

Egyptian style would have originated only through influence from the Near East. This approach continued into the middle of the twentieth century when the available documentation was considered in a structuralist approach, allowing the concept of Predynastic representations as "primitive" to be discarded (Baumgartel 1955, 1960; Asselberghs 1961). Meanwhile, Predynastic iconography was considered, on the one hand, within its social and religious context, and on the other hand, as part of an evolution into the Early Dynastic and Old Kingdom representations.

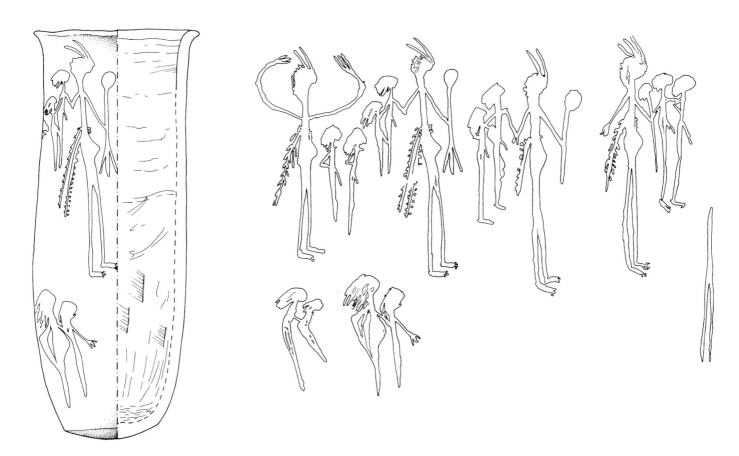

FIGURE 8.1. White Cross-Lined jar with victory scene. Abydos, Cemetery U, tomb 239. Vessel height: 30 cm (after Dreyer et al. 1998, figs. 12–13). Courtesy of the German Archaeological Institute

Pottery with painted decoration has always been a fundamental element for the study of Predynastic iconography. Petrie based his chronological work to a large extent on the difference between his White Cross-Lined and Decorated pottery classes, characteristic respectively for the Naqada I–IIA and Naqada IIC–IID periods. The chronological difference resulted in the search for different iconographic traditions and foreign influences, which hampered research for a long time. Meanwhile it became clear that a number

of iconographic themes were already present during the Naqada I period and that they continued into Dynastic times. This is especially obvious for scenes of military victory. The earliest examples of figures are on a few White Cross-Lined vessels from the elite Cemetery U at Abydos, at least for those with known provenance (fig. 8.1). The military aspect is not rendered through actual scenes of violence but through captives with their arms bound at their backs and in some cases "attached" to larger figures, sometimes holding maces, considered to be the victors. Raised arms are another expression of victory. The highly stylized manner of rendering indicates that such representations were easily understood and therefore common knowledge within Predynastic society, despite the fact that only five known White Cross-Lined jars show victory scenes. Furthermore, their composition is always non-symmetrical and does not appear to have been designed with the material features of the vessels in mind. This indicates that the original designs were made for flat surfaces such as walls, and they were only occasionally adapted for pottery. No such scenes can be found on Decorated pottery,

FIGURE 8.2. The painting from Tomb 100 at Hierakonpolis (after Quibell and Green 1902, pls. 76–78). Inset: detail of figure group at lower left.

human hunters and the Lycaon can be seen on the Hunters Palette (Spencer 1980, no. 575), where the hunters have tails attached to their belts that are identical in shape to those of the Lycaon. Apparently the hunters identified themselves to a certain degree with the animal. This may date back to early Predynastic times because the victors on the White Cross-Lined jars also wear tails, although the lack of detail does not allow us to state that Lycaon tails are intended. Another important theme on the decorated palettes is the palm tree with a giraffe on each side, but its interpretation remains problematic (Ciałowicz 1992; Köhler 1999). According to Christiana Köhler, the giraffe symbolizes the wild aspect of nature, and therefore chaos, and the palm tree the tamed aspect of nature, and therefore order. Be that as it may, there can be no doubt that the decorated palettes refer to control over chaos.

Although boats on Decorated pottery appear mainly in a funerary context, they also occur in large numbers in rock art at sites located far from the Nile where they can hardly be considered funerary. This is confirmed by a number of differences between boats on Decorated pottery and in rock art (Hendrickx and Eyckerman 2010). The rock-art boats are frequently occupied by large-scale people, often with raised arms. All of them seem to be male, in contrast to the dominance of females on Decorated pottery. In numerous examples, the occupants of the boats are armed with bows, throwing sticks, or maces. Occasionally they spear hippopotami, and roped animals are sometimes attached to the boats. These rock-art scenes are another aspect of the iconographic importance of hunting, and at the same time, they show that the boats are elements of power and symbols of status. During the early Naqada III period, boats occur also in royal contexts, as is seen on the Qustul Incense Burner (Catalog No. 10), which shows a king wearing the White Crown seated in a boat. In one of the two other boats, a seated captive is shown. The third boat is occupied by what appears to be a lion, which may very well symbolize the king. To the prow of this boat, another captive appears to be attached by a rope around his neck, although the rope does not touch the boat. However,

the characteristic bend of the arms behind the back hardly leaves any doubt about the identification of the man as a captive. The importance of boats is confirmed by the Gebel Sheikh Suleiman rock panel (fig. 9.15) (Murnane 1987), a scene of military victory in which a captive is attached to a boat, while below it are a number of dead enemies. The boat itself is empty, indicating that it must have had meaning by itself.

Williams and Logan (1987) showed that a number of elaborate late Predynastic representations, such as the Qustul Incense Burner, consist of interrelated and standardized series of themes and iconographic elements of the "greater pharaonic cycle." The principal idea behind them are the rituals of the elite and, in the end, of the king. The main elements are victory, hunt, sacrifice, and boat procession, all of which can be traced back to early Predynastic times. Although Williams and Logan may have overestimated the conceptual unity and premeditation of the greater pharaonic cycle, the link between the mentioned themes nevertheless remains fundamental. The process of state formation resulted in the development of a standardized art with the religious and political confirmation of divine kingship as the main objective. A number of previously existing iconographic elements, such as the falcon or the hippopotamus hunt, were integrated into formal Egyptian art, but many others disappeared from the repertoire, among which most of the iconography on Decorated pottery.

The development of and control over a formal iconography and its syntax was of fundamental importance for the elite, who had every reason to stimulate a strictly uniform iconographic language, confirming their own privileged position. Although some formal elements can be traced over an extended period, the definitive establishment of the formal principles that are fundamental for Early Dynastic art must have happened over a relatively short period, resulting in objects such as the Narmer Palette. But it can also be seen in far less spectacular objects such as a little ivory figure of a boy with his finger to his mouth (Catalog No. 74), a gesture that would become characteristic for identifying children throughout Dynastic times.

9. RELATIONS BETWEEN EGYPT AND NUBIA IN THE NAQADA PERIOD

BRUCE B. WILLIAMS

In the formative years of Egyptian civilization, relations with northern Nubia were strong and reciprocal. In the earliest stages, the Neolithic of Sudanese tradition strongly influenced the Tasian culture of Upper Egypt as illustrated by the famous calyciform beakers of the Sudanese Neolithic that appear also in the deserts, Lower Nubia, and at Deir Tasa (Brunton 1937, pl. 12.52–67; Friedman and Hobbs 2002, fig. 4; Darnell 2002, p. 162; Reinold 2000, p. 61). The Egyptian material culture soon diverged in the Badarian period and even more strongly in the early Naqada period. In this latter phase, local burials appear in northern Nubia that have Sudanese burial customs, but have objects mostly of Egyptian manufacture. Later, local Nubian objects appear, and the A-Group, as it is called, acquired a more distinctive appearance, belonging neither to the Sudanese Neolithic nor to Egyptian tradition, although it was influenced by them both and by the Abkan, a poorly known culture from the Second Cataract area. At the same time, the A-Group's center moved southward, expanding into the Second Cataract, and also extending deep into what is now the Libyan Desert. Materials related to the A-Group have even been found as far south as Khartoum (Gatto 2006–2007; Arkell 1953, pp. 82–89, pls. 40–42, 43.1–2). In its latest phase, the A-Group established a dynasty at Qustul, just north of the modern Sudanese border, elaborating a distinct version of the formal culture then emerging in Egypt.

Knowledge of A-Group Nubia is derived, even more predominantly than early Egypt, from burials. This is due to the fact that the region was largely explored in haste from areas to be flooded by impending dam construction during salvage excavations that had a limited scope for exploration (see Williams 1986, pp. 6–7). Much of the evidence was concealed by sand deposits or towns, or destroyed by changes in the river, wind erosion, excavation for fertilizer, and grave plundering. These took an immense toll, such that we must now reconstruct the culture and its career largely from fragments.

The beginnings of the A-Group are first distinguishable in cemeteries not far south of Aswan. We are primarily dependent on wealthy burials for evidence, and it is probable that the early Nubian settlement of the period is still undetected because the remains were simple and they were not published in detail. Both are phenomena that have plagued the study of later periods in Nubia, especially the Old Kingdom and the Napatan period (Williams 1989, pp. 121–23; Williams 1990, pp. 29–49; see Reisner 1910, pp. 134–37).

At Khor Bahan, an early cemetery contained a number of remarkably wealthy graves datable to the Naqada I period. Despite severe plundering and removal of soil for fertilizer, some one hundred early tombs remained. The largest, tomb 50, was, like many others, circular and well over two meters in diameter. Although quite plundered, it still contained fifty-five objects, and more from a neighboring deposit may have originally belonged to it. The pottery and objects are essentially derived from the early Naqada culture, but the burial in a circular tomb is not characteristic of the Naqada tradition, but typical of the Sudanese Neolithic. This burial shaft type was used for many of the tombs at Khor Bahan, especially in the earlier phases and in several of the richest interments. The use of Egyptian objects here thereby overlays a significant cultural distinction between Khor Bahan and Naqada I Egypt.[1]

The large number of Egyptian objects at Khor Bahan indicates that there was already enough economic potential in Nubia to result in substantial trade. Even though a complete list of goods transferred from Nubia is not available, red resin is already found at Khor Bahan, of a type found also in northern Sudanese graves.[2] In addition, stones such as carnelian were also probably traded, and possibly obsidian from Ethiopia.[3] There is also fairly strong evidence of conflict in Upper Egypt at this time,[4] and it should be considered quite likely that Nubians were enlisted in various forces, which could also account for some exported wealth. Finally, rock drawings in Lower Nubia depict many boats of Naqada type. Many are ceremonial or sacred barks, but many others are utilitarian, and instead of the cabins often shown on boats in Upper Egypt, many have low mounds with bands amidships that could represent cargo covered by a tarpaulin. Towing is also often depicted and that, as well as other support for traders, could well have provided a profitable local income.[5] A-Group pottery is found well north of Hierakonpolis, and settlements, burials, and even a cemetery are well known north of Aswan (Gatto and Giuliani 2006/07; Gatto 2006, p. 63; Gatto 2009). The interchange between the regions was reciprocal enough that Egyptians and Nubians must have had a thorough knowledge of each other.

A-Group relations to the south are more difficult to trace, apart from the frequent appearance of red resin, but black incised and white-filled pottery occurs in the earliest and richest Nubian tombs, and there is apparently at least one example of the distinctive Sudanese Neolithic calyciform beaker from an A-Group context. It is noteworthy that a number of pottery vessels have shapes similar to those of the pre-Kerma culture that developed in the Dongola Reach (see, for example, Engelmayer 1965).

As Egypt consolidated during the Naqada I and II periods, the A-Group expanded geographically toward the Second Cataract. A-Group manufactures, especially pottery, cosmetic implements, and larger grindstones, became more elaborate and clearly reflect southern traditions. The decoration of ripple-burnished pottery particularly became finer and more regular. Derived from burnishing over a rocker-stamped surface, this decoration is also part of southern connections (fig. 9.1).[6] It was in this middle phase, dating to the later Naqada II and IIIa1 (Kaiser; IID2 Hendrickx), that the A-Group culture reached the Second Cataract and social differentiation reached its peak.[7] In the early A-Group period, larger tombs had roughly twice the dimensions of the smallest, and rich tombs many times the number of pots, fifty-five in the richest (Khor Bahan tomb 17:50), versus two to five in ordinary tombs. In Middle A-Group the richest tomb known, Sayala Cemetery 137:1, was largely plundered and the rich remaining objects were only protected by a large fallen roof slab. It contained not only two mudstone (formerly called slate) palettes with two bird heads and a remarkable handled cup, but numerous high-quality copper implements, copper bars, weapons, local palettes, grindstones, and two gold-covered mace handles with (unmatched) heads. The Red-Polished black-mouthed (probably ripple-burnished) pottery clearly dates the tomb to Middle A-Group.[8] This tomb and another nearby have been considered to be those of local rulers (chiefs) based on the unparalleled presence of this accidentally preserved wealth, but they are not the largest tombs of the period. Those are found at Qustul (Cemetery L, tombs 28 and 29), far to the south, which have shafts and side-chambers that make tombs several times the size of Sayala 137:1.[9] The rich Sayala burials are easily explained as important deputies buried with great wealth, but not on the scale of rulers.

FIGURE 9.1. A-Group ripple-burnished jar. This form of surface treatment was refined to its highest degree in Sudan and Nubia and is found in Egypt as an influence or import. It is characteristic of the Badarian culture in Egypt. This example, from Cemetery Q at Qustul, was found in a cache, or deposit, not a tomb. Height: ca. 27.5 cm. OIM E21901 (photo by Anna Ressman)

FIGURE 9.3. Faience jars were among the vessels imported to A-Group Nubia in Naqada IIIA period. These two vessels come from Qustul, Cemetery L: (left) Height: 7.5 cm. OIM E24061; (right) height: 4.8 cm. OIM E24062

FIGURE 9.2. Imports were not just from Egypt itself, but sometimes even beyond. This Early Bronze Age I Levantine-type jug was recovered from Qustul, Cemetery L, tomb 24, and is a reflection of the large number of such imports at Abydos in Tomb U-j. Height: ca. 17 cm. OIM E23758 (photo by Anna Ressman)

FIGURE 9.4. Egyptian stone vessels are not common in A-Group assemblages, but over one hundred were found in Cemetery L at Qustul

FIGURE 9.5. Some imported pottery was unique, such as this tall vessel stand with three serpents in relief from Qustul, Cemetery L, tomb 5. Height: ca. 30 cm. OIM E24197 (photo by Anna Ressman)

FIGURE 9.6. This copper spearhead (OIM E23727; length 15.75 cm) and breccia mace-head (OIM E24159; height 6 cm) are Egyptian imports found in Cemetery L, tomb 24, but the gold bracelet (OIM E23666; diameter 5.25 cm) from Cemetery L, tomb 17, may have been locally made (photos of spearhead and mace-head by Anna Ressman; photo of bracelet by Jean Grant)

FIGURE 9.7. Incense burners were deposited in some A-Group graves. Some had not been used before burial, while others show definite signs of burning on the tops

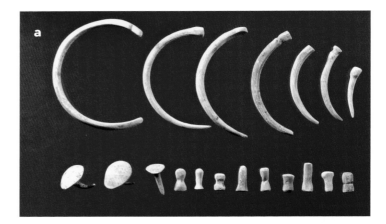

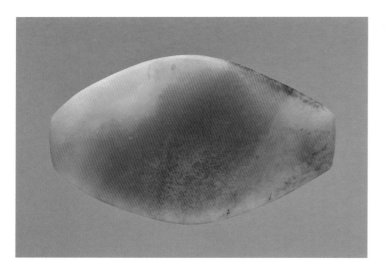

FIGURE 9.8. A-Group palettes manufactured for use had curved sides or were rhomboid and were generally made of quartz. Green malachite was ground on them with a pebble, moistened, and applied with a brush. From Qustul, Cemetery L, tomb 24. Length 8 cm. OIM E23726 (photo by Anna Ressman)

FIGURE 9.9. (*a, top row*) Shafts with heads at one end and points at the other appear in the Sudanese Neolithic and pre-Kerma cultures, often made from valuable stones. In A-Group assemblages, they were made of shell and often curved with the contour of the mollusk. They seem to have been worn on the forehead, and while possibly decorative, they could have been used to scratch the scalp through a tufted hairdo. There were other objects of shell also, such as ear-studs and plugs, for example (*a, bottom row*); (*b*) a single pile in Cemetery L, tomb 17, presumably from a bag or basket, contained over 1,700 shell hooks and other shell objects, a unique deposit

10. CRAFTS AND CRAFT SPECIALIZATION

STAN HENDRICKX

Craft specialization can be defined as investment of labor and means for the production of specific goods, with the intention to produce more commodities than needed for personal use, while others in the same community or elsewhere produce less than they consume, or even nothing at all. However, craft specialization is only possible when the economy at a given moment and place creates a food surplus that can be used for sustaining artisans, allowing them to invest most or all of their time in their crafts. This would have been embedded in a system of social relations that was organized by those controlling the food surplus. Therefore, the study of craft specialization offers the possibility to investigate sociopolitical structures of the past and it is particularly relevant for the case of early Egypt, as the earliest nation-state in the world.

Evidence for craft specialization can already be found in the Badarian period, around 4400–3900 BC. At that time, some of the pottery was of such high quality that it seems beyond the possibility that it was produced at a household level. This could still be questioned, but that can hardly be the case for the manufacture of stone vessels or ivory objects during the Badarian period. Yet, even predating the Badarian material is a remarkable stone bowl with handle found at the Tasian cemetery at Gebel Ramlah (Kobusiewicz et al. 2004, fig. 6.4), dated to around 4500 BC, whose high quality indicates a certain level of professionalism. Although these products certainly testify to craft specialization, the sociopolitical structure that allowed them to be produced may still have been relatively simple. Social complexity and differentiation have been demonstrated for the Badarian period on the basis of lavish burials that include goods not shared by all members of the society (Anderson 1992). Wealthy graves of sub-adults indicate that social position was at least partially hereditary, but on the other hand, no exceptionally rich tombs were found, demonstrating that a complex social system was not yet installed. The limited number of objects for which craft specialization is to be accepted, and

their presence in elite tombs only, shows that craft specialization during the Badarian period did not yet aim at mass production of objects accessible for a large part of society. This has been considered evidence for "part-time specialists" (Takamiya 2004, p. 1034), which indeed seems most likely.

From the beginning of the Naqada I period, a particular type of cylindrical basalt vessel with a high base (fig. 10.1) is certainly to be considered the production of specialized craftsmanship. More significantly, the basalt originates from the region between Cairo and the Fayum, while many such vessels were found in Upper Egyptian tombs (Mallory-Greenough 2002, p. 78, table 4. Besides centralized craftsmanship, this implies contacts over a considerable distance, which again would not have been at the disposal of all community members, but could be accepted as controlled by the elite.

During Naqada I times, social complexity increased, but it is difficult to define the moment when part-time specialization was replaced by "attached full-time specialization" as defined by Takamiya (2004, pp. 1034–35). Craftsmen were now attached to the elite, for whom they produced high-quality objects that demanded full-time specialization. The transition to this type of specialization of course would have been gradual, and most probably did not take place at the same moment for all sites, but it would have been concentrated at major sites, among them Hierakonpolis, which was of exceptional importance. At that site, the specialized production of stone vessels, specific types of flint artifacts, beads, and pottery has been identified, some of which date back to the early Naqada II period (Holmes 1992a; Friedman 1994; Takamiya 2008; Baba 2008; Hendrickx 2008). Of great importance is that workshops for producing bifacially worked flint artifacts, beads, and stone vessels were located close to the religious center at HK29A. Obviously, this indicates control by the religious — at the same time social — elite over production. Furthermore, professional workshops produced Black-Topped and Red-Polished pottery in the

FIGURE 10.1. Naqada I basalt vessels. OIM E10864, E10855, E10853 (photo by Anna Ressman)

neighborhood of the elite cemetery HK6 (Friedman 1994, pp. 608–858; Takamiya 2004, pp. 1030–31). Because this cemetery is located over two kilometers from the settlement area, the production must have been intended for the equipment of the tombs, and it clearly illustrates that the resources and craftsmanship were at the disposal of the elite. Furthermore, beer was produced in considerable quantities close to the elite cemetery and, as with the pottery production, this cannot have been for regular consumption in daily life but must have been served during funeral rituals. In the settlement area of Hierakonpolis, similar installations for producing beer and pottery have been found (Baba 2008), indicating that the specialized production for tomb equipment reflected the reality of the social structure at Hierakonpolis. All in all, there can be no doubt that already during the early Naqada II period a high degree of specialization existed. However, it remains an open question if this was unique for Hierakonpolis, which was at that time definitely a center of exceptional importance, if not the only site of such magnitude. Large-scale brewery installations are also known from Abydos, Mahasna, and Naqada (Peet and Loat 1913, pp. 1–7; Peet 1914, pp. 7–9), but as far as can be judged from the original excavation reports, these examples date rather toward the end of the Predynastic period. The large

brewery at Tell el-Farkha certainly dates to Early Dynastic times (Cichowski 2008).

Products of craft specialization such as bifacially worked flints, stone vessels, and, to some extent, Black-Topped pottery, have a decorative value that goes beyond the function of the actual objects. For example, the ripple-flaked knives (Catalog No. 79) are considered to have been prestige items rather than functional objects (Midant-Reynes 1987). Other objects such as beads, bracelets, or (decorated) ivory items are primarily decorative and their frequent presence in Predynastic tombs confirms the value attached to them. Although the relevance of the aesthetic aspect is difficult to evaluate for the Predynastic mind, it nevertheless is to be accepted as an aspect of craft specialization, if only because of the high technical skills required to produce these objects.

From the middle of the Naqada II period onward, marl clay was increasingly used for the production of pottery, among which are the well-known Wavy-Handled jars (fig. 10.2). The most important advantage of this type of clay is that it can be fired at higher temperatures than Nile silt and therefore allows for the production of less porous pottery. At first view, marl clay pottery seems less well done — more hastily made and finished — and not the result

of craft specialization. However, the preparation of the hard, almost petrified marl clay demands more work compared to Nile silt. Obviously the potters realized that the time investment for working marl clay resulted in a more interesting product. Also, marl clay pottery became more standardized, showing less variation within "types" distinguished by archaeologists (Hendrickx 1996a, pp. 44–47). The large number of marl vessels points toward mass production, indicating that not all of the specialized artisans were strictly dependent upon elite patrons. Otherwise, the mass production of pottery would have been organized through a system of redistribution, which seems rather unlikely. A difference has to be made between mass production of objects for daily use and the production of objects with great value due to their material, exceptional craftsmanship, or even intellectual implications such as the development of iconography. The second group, those objects of great value, therefore shows the characteristics of a "developed attached specialist stage" as defined by Takamiya (2004, p. 1035).

The production of stone vessels is particularly important when discussing craft specialization (cf. Stocks 2003). The often very thin walls, careful finishing, and polishing of the vessels bear testimony to sophisticated workmanship, while the procurement of raw materials from sites often at considerable distance from the Nile Valley is only possible in a well-structured logistic context, which was only at the disposition of the elite "patrons." The elite aspect is confirmed by the function of the stone vessels, among which luxury cosmetic vessels such as cylindrical jars (Catalog Nos. 16–19) are most frequent.

Stone vessels are probably the best example for considering the possibilities and differentiation of specialized production during the Naqada III period. At that time, they become a type of object that frequently occurs in tombs where they tend to replace pottery vessels. By the Naqada IIIC2–IIID period, stone vessels make up about 20 percent of funerary goods (Hendrickx 2006a, p. 73), but they are nevertheless not included in all tombs. For the royal tombs at Abydos, and also for the tombs of the highest officials at Saqqara, huge quantities of stone vessels were produced. The royal tombs contained tens of thousands of vessels in a wide variety of stones (cf. De Putter et al. 2000) (fig. 10.3). Many of them show no traces of use at all so they must have been made specifically for funerary use. The production must

FIGURE 10.3. Stone vessel fragments from the royal tombs at Abydos being inventoried at the Royal Museums of Art and History, Brussels (photo by Stan Hendrickx)

FIGURE 10.4. Fragments of stone vessel imitating a palm-leaf basket. Abydos. Width ca. 17.5 cm. Brussels, Royal Museums of Art and History E.4849 (photo by Stan Hendrickx)

have taken place in specialized workshops, which would have been under direct governmental control. Toward the end of the First Dynasty, the stone used gradually becomes of a less fine quality. This can be linked to the increased use of the "figure-of-eight" shaped drill, which required highly specialized craftsmen, but at the same time considerably facilitated the large-scale production of stone vessels (Hendrickx et al. 2001, pp. 87–88). The background for all this can be seen in the growing efficiency that must have been developed by the workshops that produced the funeral equipment for the royal tombs. In a more general manner, this bears testimony to the improving state organization throughout the Early Dynastic period. Finally, exceptional figurative stone vessels are to be mentioned. These are mainly complex plates in mudstone, most of which imitate floral elements or basketry (fig. 10.4) (Adams in press). These remarkable objects are transpositions in stone of rather common objects such as baskets, with the occasional integration of religious symbols, illustrating the elite manner of living (Hendrickx 1996b; Adams 2000b). The largest diversity of shapes comes from the royal tombs at Abydos (fig. 12.10 in this volume). They have also been found in the Saqqara mastabas, but hardly anywhere else. This last group of stone vessels provides a clear example of the "developed attached specialist stage" mentioned previously.

From the second half of the First Dynasty onward, and especially during the Second Dynasty, important changes occurred in ceramic technology and pottery types (Hendrickx et al. 2002). Meidum bowls (fig. 10.5), beer jars, and bread molds are the most obvious examples. They were affordable for everybody as is shown by their very large distribution in cemeteries as well as in settlement sites. Meidum bowls (Op de Beeck 2004) were used mainly as tableware, while bread molds and beer jars (Catalog No. 27) were for food production (Faltings 1998b). The technological innovations include modeling over a hump and the use of a slow turning device for shaping and finishing vessels. The latter was already in use from at least the early Naqada III period onward, but was now being used more frequently. The huge quantities of vessels produced, and their standardization, is only possible through professional production, but the reasons for this go beyond elite behavior. The new pottery types are the consequence of changes in the processing and preservation of food, both of which had an influence on the overall dietary patterns. It is obvious that different types of food required, among other things, different methods of cooking, and so forth, to which the vessels used would have to be adapted. The changes in food technology are to be considered a consequence of improved agricultural techniques resulting in higher surpluses which, in turn, increased the levels of social differentiation during the Early Dynastic period. The organization of the centralized state implies the presence of a growing number of professionals in the administration, religion, and crafts who had to be provided with food in an efficient manner. This is well illustrated by the production of beer made from fermented bread that was not only very nutritious but also whose alcohol

FIGURE 10.5. Meidum bowl. Sediment. 9.6 x 15.9 (max.) cm. OIM E28207 (photo by Anna Ressman)

FIGURE 10.6. Wine jar. Abydos, tomb M19. Dynasty 1. Height 68.7 cm. OIM E7774. Gift of the Egypt Exploration Fund, 1901–1902 (photo by Anna Ressman)

of, if not the most, prestigious food supplies for late Predynastic times. At that moment, wine was not yet produced in Egypt itself and it had to be imported from the southern Levant. Over seven hundred wine vessels from the southern Levant were found in the Naqada IIIA1 royal Tomb U-j at Umm el-Qaab (Abydos) (Hartung 2001). From the Naqada IIIB period onward, large storage vessels, with or without applied horizontal bands for reinforcement (fig. 10.6), occur in important quantities at the royal tombs. They are generally considered wine jars, although final proof for this is still lacking. If so, they indicate the local production of wine in Egypt, for which written evidence is available only toward the end of the Second Dynasty. Yet, also at that moment it was certainly beyond the possibilities of the large majority of the Egyptian population to afford wine, especially in Upper Egypt, where the characteristic jars have rarely ever been found outside Abydos. The production of wine is an aspect of specialization involving a completely different type of artisan compared to those involved with the production of pottery or stone vessels, but there can be no doubt that the origin of the craft of winemaking lies with the elite.

A particular aspect of craft specialization is the manner in which artisans dealt with the iconography of the representations on the objects they decorated. Iconography on Decorated pottery, characteristic for Naqada IIC–D (Catalog Nos. 2, 30–33, 35–39, and frontispiece), is far more structured compared to that on White Cross-Lined pottery, dating to Naqada I–IIA period (Catalog Nos. 1, 28–29) (see "Iconography of the Predynastic and Early Dynastic Periods" in this volume). Again, this suggests increased specialization, but although the intellectual concepts would have been developed by the elite, the contribution of the artisans to the visualization remains an open question.

It is difficult to identify tombs of artisans because personalized grave goods reflecting the occupation of the deceased are rare. Whitney Davis (1983, pp. 122–25) considers the occasional presence of copper tools in a very limited number of tombs as evidence for the deceased having been an artisan, more precisely a wood or ivory worker. This may very well be true for a number of examples, but copper objects occur regularly in very rich tombs, where they are prestige items that confirmed the status of the deceased — not his professional occupation. Also, the tools of potters

content, in combination with the slight acidity of the beer, slowly kills pathogenic bacteria that occasionally contaminate drinking water.

The increasingly sophisticated lifestyle of the Egyptian elite also played a role in the development of new pottery types, although not all aspects of this "sophistication" became accessible to the whole community. For example, ewers used for personal hygiene are only found in the wealthier tombs. More important are wine jars because wine must have been one

are well known from pottery workshops (Baba 2008), but they have never been found in tombs.

The social position of the artisans is hard to evaluate for the Predynastic and Early Dynastic periods. Davis (1983, pp. 127–28) considered most Predynastic crafts as household enterprises without direct dependence upon the elite. He accepts the presence of full-time specialists only from the First Dynasty onward, noting that at the same time, the social status of artisans would have increased strongly. This interpretation is no longer acceptable in view of the presented evidence and especially because of the discoveries made at Hierakonpolis over the last decade. As mentioned before, indications of professions are not a regular part of Predynastic burial equipment, although artisans' burials can be identified with a high degree of certainty for the Early Dynastic period (Davis 1983, pp. 128–32). For example, the Naqada IIID tomb of an adult found at Elkab (Hendrickx 1994, p. 222, pl. 66, graves 88–89) contained, besides a palette, only stone vessels, two of them unfinished. This tomb may very well be that of a stone vessel maker (fig. 10.7). However, this should be placed in the context of an overall evolution in burial customs from the end of the First Dynasty onward, when not only the number of objects tends to diminish, but also their character,

resulting in more beer jars and bread molds and fewer "luxury" items.

In summary, two aspects of craft specialization can be recognized. The first relates to the elite and concerns the most remarkable elements of Predynastic and Early Dynastic craftsmanship such as decorated ivories and palettes and exquisitely worked figurative stone vessels. For the elite, these objects would have held the potential to maintain and illustrate social inequality. At the same time, they allowed the development of a material culture that defined the manner of living of the elite and stimulated cohesion within the elite group. The earliest examples of such craftsmanship date back at least to the early Naqada II period.

The second aspect is mass production, which illustrates the growing impact of a structured society on the daily lifestyle of the population. The earliest examples date to the early Naqada II period, but these efforts seem to have been principally organized by and for the elite, with Hierakonpolis as the most obvious example. Specialized large-scale production for mass consumption became increasingly important during the late Naqada II period and it is an essential part of the economic production and social structure during Early Dynastic times.

FIGURE 10.7. Graves 88–89 at Elkab and the objects found within (photo at left by Stan Hendrickx; drawing after Hendrickx 1944, pl. 66; photo below by Roger O. De Keersmaecker)

11. THE INVENTION OF WRITING IN EGYPT

DAVID WENGROW

The world's earliest known writing systems emerged at more or less the same time, around 3300 BC, in Egypt and Mesopotamia (today's Iraq). At that time, both societies reached out far beyond their borders through overland and maritime trade networks, forming common frontiers of exchange around the Levantine coast and the shores of the Arabian peninsula (see "Early Interaction between Peoples of the Nile Valley and the Southern Levant" in this volume). They were not, however, in direct contact with one another, and despite their parallel development in these two regions, the two earliest writing systems do not appear to have been directly related (Woods 2010). Egypt and Mesopotamia, in the late fourth millennium BC, also had in common the fact that their respective societies were passing beyond a certain threshold of scale and integration, which anthropologists today recognize as the emergence of the world's first "complex societies." A critical feature of that process was the centralization of power and influence in the hands of ever-smaller groups (Baines and Yoffee 1998), and this provided a crucial context for the emergence of writing, not just in these regions, but also subsequently (and independently) in other parts of the ancient world such as the Indus Valley, the Yellow River Valley, and Mesoamerica (Trigger 2003; Woods 2010).

In Mesopotamia the process of centralization is most clearly documented by the rise of cities, such as Uruk (modern Warka) in southern Iraq, which achieved a size in the order of 200 hectares by 3300 BC (Algaze 1993). Uruk has provided the bulk of our evidence for the origins of the cuneiform script, which was impressed with a reed stylus onto tablets of damp clay and used initially for purposes of administrative bookkeeping (Nissen et al. 1993). In Egypt, the processes that led to the invention of writing appear on first inspection to have been very different, both in terms of the media on which early writing is preserved (which include royal monuments such as the Koptos Colossi; Kemp 2000), the range of functions that it served (some of which are clearly oriented toward ceremonial display; Baines 2007, pp. 281–97), and the kind of archaeological contexts from which inscriptions are usually recovered.

Urban centers, while no doubt present in Egypt by the late fourth millennium BC, are largely unavailable for archaeological inspection because of their location on the floodplain of the Nile and subsequent burial beneath the expanding alluvium. A growing number of exceptions from the Nile Delta are discussed elsewhere in this volume ("The Predynastic Cultures of the Nile Delta" and "The Predynastic/Early Dynastic Period at Tell el-Farkha"). They promise to transform our understanding of early Egyptian society, including the origins of the Egyptian writing system, in years to come. This overall pattern of urban (non-)survival contrasts with the situation in southern Mesopotamia, where the Tigris and Euphrates rivers have shifted their courses widely over the millennia, leaving the remains of cities — together with their archives of cuneiform texts — high and dry in the desert. In Egypt, by contrast, most of our evidence for the earliest development of writing derives from cemeteries located on the arid margins of the Nile Valley. The difference, however, cannot be solely attributed to factors of archaeological preservation. It also reflects the central importance of mortuary cults in the development of the Egyptian state (Wengrow 2006), which finds no ready parallel in Mesopotamia. The earliest Egyptian writing is also distinguished from that of Mesopotamia by its multiple forms and modes of execution. From its point of inception these included at least two main types: the hieroglyphic, carved or incised onto a range of high-status (and often durable) media; and the cursive, painted in ink onto the surfaces of more widely available objects. Of the latter, only pottery survives from these earliest phases of script development. But the contemporaneous use of papyrus cannot be ruled out and is directly attested by the First Dynasty (Baines 2004).

Given the central place of literacy in our own societies, it is easy to overestimate the scope and functions of writing at its point of invention. A generous estimate suggests that, even many centuries after its invention, only 1 percent of Egypt's population was literate (Baines 2007, pp. 64–67). Like the much more recent kingdoms of Europe, down to the inception of the printing press in the sixteenth century AD, these earliest states were — in the words of Benedict Anderson (1983, p. 15) — "tiny literate reefs on top of vast illiterate oceans." Moreover, writing itself took centuries to adapt to what we now regard as its primary function: the encoding of continuous speech.

The collections of the Oriental Institute house numerous examples of early writing from Egypt. Most were excavated in the late nineteenth or early twentieth century by Flinders Petrie (1900, 1901a) from royal burial grounds and associated ceremonial precincts at Abydos in the south of the country. The monuments of Abydos are discussed elsewhere in this book ("Tomb U-j: A Royal Burial of Dynasty 0 at Abydos," "The First Kings of Egypt: The Abydos Evidence," and "The Narmer Palette: A New Interpretation"). This chapter focuses upon the invention of the Egyptian script and our understanding of that process after a century of field research in Egypt.

THE PREHISTORIC BACKGROUND

The first writing in Egypt and Mesopotamia developed against a rich background of prehistoric visual traditions. Neolithic and Predynastic societies in the Nile Valley and Delta (ca. 5000 to 3300 BC) developed complex modes of cultural interaction that employed an elaborate repertory of signs and images. In the valley (extending as far south as modern-day Khartoum) these systems of interpersonal communication and display relied heavily upon the modification of the body with cosmetic paints, further enhanced by a striking range of miniature adornments such as beadwork, pins, combs, and bangles. By the early fourth millennium BC, in Egypt and Lower Nubia, everyday objects such as pottery came to bear a conventional range of imagery, both painted and modelled, figural and non-figural (Catalog Nos. 1–2, 28–39). By around 3400 BC, these elaborate modes of personal display — and at least some of their associated social institutions — had begun to spread northward into the

Fayum and the Nile Delta (Wengrow 2006, pp. 50–56, 99–123).

In non-literate societies, images are generally expected to fulfill a wider range of social functions than tends to be the case in highly literate ones, and with these functions go restrictions on their production and circulation (see examples in Coote and Shelton 1992). What we today call "Predynastic art" was a limited resource. Its cultural roles may have included the demarcation and transmission of property and the cementing of social contracts. Such roles are suggested, for example, by the remarkable concentration of painted images within one of the largest Predynastic tombs at Hierakonpolis, known as Tomb 100, dating to around 3400 BC (see fig. 8.2 in this volume). They comprise large-scale depictions of boats, animals, and humans in combat — including a "master-of-animals" motif likely of Mesopotamian derivation — which were executed within the course of the burial rite, almost certainly by a number of participants rather than a single painter. Already in prehistoric times, privileged access to images seems to have gone hand-in-hand with access to other key cultural resources, such as the labor required for building and furnishing large tombs, and the precious and sometimes exotic commodities placed within them as gifts to the dead (Wengrow 2006, pp. 120–23, 165–66).

In discussing the invention of writing, it is important to stress this extensive prehistoric background of image making and use. Throughout its millennia-long development, the Egyptian writing system (unlike the Mesopotamian) remained closely integrated with wider modes of pictorial composition and representation. It is striking, moreover, that the earliest development of writing in Egypt coincides with the decline of those conventional (prehistoric) modes of bodily display, as well as the virtual disappearance of decorative imagery from items of everyday use (Baines 1994).

Today we naturally tend to think of writing as something that enables and enhances the possibilities of information storage and circulation; but cultural innovation is rarely just a cumulative process. The initial appearance of writing systems, in both Egypt and Mesopotamia, is associated with simplification and standardization in many other areas of material culture. And this suggests a more complex interplay between innovation in some areas and a loss of competence in others (Wengrow 2006, pp. 151–75; Yoffee 2002).

THE NATURE OF EARLY EGYPTIAN WRITING

Egyptian uses of writing during the First Dynasty (ca. 3100–2800 BC) can be illustrated by a small wooden label, marked with the *serekh* of King Den, from the royal burial grounds of Abydos (fig. 11.1). By this time the *serekh* was established as a conventional framing motif for writing royal names. As on much larger monuments, such as the carved stelae placed above the royal tombs, the *serekh* is surmounted here by the Horus falcon, alluding to the divine persona embodied by the king and forming part of his official title.

Measuring about eight centimeters across, the label — like others discovered at Abydos and also at elite cemeteries farther to the north (notably at Saqqara) — is perforated for attachment to mobile goods. Inscriptions on the lower left-hand section of its surface allow us to identify those goods. They denote a specific quantity of "finest oil of Tjehenu," a region in the vicinity of modern-day Libya and therefore exotic to the Nile Valley, where the label and its associated products were deposited as part of a royal burial rite (Petrie 1900). As with other royal burials of the First Dynasty, that ritual also involved the carefully administered sacrifice of human life and many other material goods on a prodigious scale (see further Baines 1995; Wengrow 2006, pp. 231–58).

The label conveys its message through a combination of written and pictorial elements, as well as formalized divisions of space. These include the use of register lines, which became increasingly standard for royal display at this time. Among the captioned inscriptions is the name of a particular oil press. The top register on the right-hand side contains a complex pictorial scene: an abbreviated version of more monumental forms of depiction, of a kind perhaps already rendered in stone relief, but hardly preserved from these early periods (Alexanian 1998). It depicts part of a ceremony later enacted in the Step Pyramid complex of Djoser at Saqqara, during which the king's body (or some representation of it) circumambulated territorial markers signifying the extent of his political domain (Jiménez Serrano 2002). The hook-shaped sign that encloses the pictorial registers indicates that together they form the name of a year,

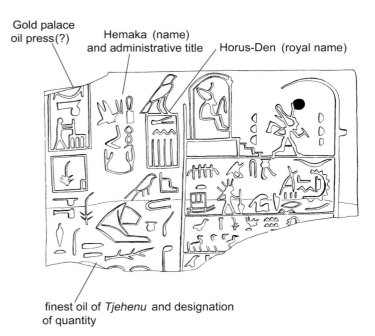

Gold palace oil press(?)

Hemaka (name) and administrative title

Horus-Den (royal name)

finest oil of *Tjehenu* and designation of quantity

FIGURE 11.1. Wooden label from Abydos with the *serekh* of King Den

constituting part of a larger series of annals that demarcated time according to designated royal actions. Compilations of such year-names are known from later Old Kingdom sources, such as the Fifth Dynasty Palermo Stone (Redford 1986; Wilkinson 2000b).

The core message of the scenes depicted on the Abydos label might be rendered in speech as something like "Kingship gives life to the land." This message, however, was not directly conveyed through writing, but through a combination of images and captions that refer to wider spheres of ritual activity. In the early stages of its development the Egyptian hieroglyphic script, like the scripts of other early states (Houston 2004), was not designed to convey the syntax or grammar of spoken language in visual form. Instead it was used to notate restricted elements of language such as the names of people, places, and things, which were combined in conventional ways with other, non-linguistic signs, images, and forms of communicative action. The use of hieroglyphs to write continuous discourse is not documented until some centuries after the script's invention (Baines 2007, pp. 33–62).

In addition to the official name of a king (Horus-Den), the upper part of the year-label also carries that of an administrator (Hemaka), part of whose title is written with a hieroglyphic sign that depicts

FIGURE 11.2. Cylinder seal with modern impression. The signs, from right to left, resemble the *šms*(.*w*), or "follower(s)," sign; a ram (possibly representing the god Chnum), and, to the extreme left, the early symbol of the goddess Neith. Stone, Dynasty 1. Provenance unknown (purchased in Cairo, 1920). 1.5 x 1.3 cm. OIM E10592 (photo by Anna Ressman)

a cylindrical seal. Hundreds of impressions from actual cylinder seals carrying the names of the king and his high official were found within the same tomb, rolled onto the clay stoppers of wine jars and other containers deposited there en masse (Petrie 1900; 1901a). Similar impressions and labels are documented in considerable numbers from other elite tombs at Abydos, and also at Saqqara and other major cemeteries to the north, suggesting a controlled movement of commodities for ceremonial purposes, and under royal patronage, across much of the country (Kaplony 1963; Endesfelder 1991).

The ceramic jars in which organic goods such as wine and oil were packaged were produced in large quantities to more-or-less standard sizes and volumes, suggesting centralized manufacture, most probably on royal estates (Adams and Ciałowicz 1997). The present exhibition includes a fine example of a cylinder seal impression on the clay stopper of one such commodity jar, from Abydos. It bears a royal name — perhaps that of Horus-Sekhemib, also documented on a seal impression at Elephantine to the south — as well as a high-ranking title: literally, "One Who Is Under the Head of the King" (Catalog No. 87).

Cylinder seals, of the kind that produced these impressions, were a Mesopotamian innovation (Collon 1988). They were imported in small numbers to the Nile Valley by no later than the middle of the

fourth millennium BC, where they were imitated and adapted by local craft workers in stone, wood, and ivory (Moorey 1987). Each bore a miniature intaglio design, applied (in reverse) to the sealing of a commodity vessel, or to the clay lock of a box or doorway, by rolling the seal across the malleable clay surface. Unlike their Mesopotamian prototypes, which at this time carry only pictorial images, in Egypt cylinder seals were used early on to transmit writing in the form of royal names and other brief inscriptions (fig. 11.2). As a method for mechanically reproducing and distributing complex signs, seals were highly exclusive objects, and their use was confined to an inner elite. In combination with year-labels, they illustrate an important function of the earliest Egyptian writing: the controlled dissemination of prestigious names, and associated imagery, on objects placed with the dead.

TOMB U-J AND THE ORIGINS OF THE EGYPTIAN SCRIPT

Whether the latter function of writing was central to its initial development, or is largely a reflection of the particular sources that have come down to us, cannot presently be known. At Abydos the use of writing in labeling high-status grave goods can now be traced back to the very earliest stages of script development, as a result of the remarkable finds from Tomb U-j, described in detail by the excavator (Günter Dreyer) in this volume. Here I focus on the inscribed material from the tomb, which includes the earliest known evidence for writing in Egypt, dating to around 3300 BC.

No less than three distinct techniques are attested for attaching signs to the objects found in Tomb U-j, each apparently being reserved for a particular category of object (Kahl 2001, p. 106). Especially important for the history of writing is a corpus of signs — painted at a large scale onto ceramic vessels, and incised in miniature onto perforated labels — that represent a formative stage in the emergence of the hieroglyphic writing system (Dreyer et al. 1998 and figs. 14.16–18 in this volume). Seal impressions found within the tomb may also be considered in this context (Morenz 2004, pp. 58–68). With regard to the content of the inscriptions, all that is generally agreed upon to date is that they notate prestigious names of some kind, perhaps including gods as well as kings and places, such as royal estates (Baines 2004). More specific readings are based upon partial analogies with later hieroglyphs and remain open to various interpretations (e.g., Breyer 2002; Kahl 2003).

It has been suggested that the inscriptions from Tomb U-j demonstrate the development of formal administrative structures used to command the flow of goods from one part of the country to the other, and even to control the conduct of foreign trade relations, notably with the Levant (Wilkinson 1999, pp. 41–44, 112; Hartung 2001). However, the jar stoppers associated with Levantine-style wine bottles — great numbers of which were placed in the tomb — are composed of local Nile mud (McGovern et al. 1997, p. 12). And despite their exotic forms, at least some of these vessels appear to have been made of clays available in the Abydos region, and may not have originated in the Levant (Porat and Goren 2002; but for an alternative view, see Hartung 2001). This does not exclude the possibility that locally made imitations of foreign commodity vessels, bearing prominent inscriptions, were represented as exotic items in the context of the burial rite. Other materials from the tomb, such as fragments from a cedar box and a magnificently carved obsidian vessel, have a more clearly foreign origin (Dreyer et al. 1998, pls. 10, 41). The nearest sources of these materials lie in Lebanon (cedar) and either Turkey or the Horn of Africa (obsidian). Neither object, however, is directly associated with inscribed material in the tomb.

In attempting to probe the functions of the inscribed tags from Tomb U-j, comparisons are often drawn with larger year labels of the First Dynasty, of the kind discussed above. Among the earliest known labels of the latter kind from the reign of Narmer (ca. 3100 BC; Dreyer 2000), whose palette is the subject of the essay "The Narmer Palette: A New Interpretation" in this volume. It contains a scene of royal victory that illustrates the close relationship between script development and pictorial representation in Egypt.

The king's name is rendered using the rebus principle, but the catfish sign that gives the sound *nar* is also equipped with human arms that make it an active participant in a pictorial scene, reaching out to grasp and smite a foreign enemy (see further Baines 2007, pp. 285–86).

It has been suggested that the inscriptions on year-labels had a primarily administrative (as opposed to ceremonial or ritual) function, recording the provenance of goods and their date of manufacture (Postgate et al. 1995). Similar interpretations have been extended back to the earliest writing at Tomb U-j. In evaluating them, it seems important to recall the scarcity of writing — and of visual signs in general — at this time, as well as the density of high-status imagery on the labels themselves. Had the recording of administrative details been their main purpose, would more economical forms of notation not have been used, as perhaps they were on ephemeral media that have not survived? It is also worth noting that, despite their small size, year-labels were complex artifacts, the manufacture of which demanded skilled and intensive labor, including the addition of colored pigment to miniature signs (Piquette 2004).

At the very least, the process of marking and labeling grave goods in this manner created an official and elevated biography for them, associating them with the performance of royal ritual, rather than the mundane world of human labor and exchange. Although the meaning of individual signs and sign combinations remains uncertain, the individuals responsible for creating the labels in Tomb U-j clearly drew from the same reservoir of symbols as the makers and users of ceremonial objects discussed elsewhere in this volume, such as the Koptos Colossi and the elaborately carved versions of cosmetic palettes, knives, and combs that appeared toward the end of the fourth millennium BC. In their coming together for an act of ritual commemoration, we can dimly perceive a centralized society taking shape.

12. EARLY INTERACTION BETWEEN PEOPLES OF THE NILE VALLEY AND THE SOUTHERN LEVANT

ELIOT BRAUN

This essay describes the long-term, albeit often intermittent, earliest relationship between sedentary denizens of the Nile Valley and their south Levantine neighbors in the well-watered zones east of Sinai. It is a story that began with desultory contacts and continued intermittently for well over a millennium (Kantor 1992; Braun 2002–2004). Scholars have been teasing evidence for it out of the archaeological record of both Egypt and the southern Levant for nearly a century, ever since W. M. Flinders Petrie first perceived what he thought to be "Aegean pottery" in the tombs of the kings of the First Dynasty (Petrie et al. 1912, pl. 8). The relationship, as we now understand it, began around the end of the fifth millennium and apparently came to an end sometime during the Second Dynasty, when it ceased altogether.

EARLY CHALCOLITHIC-BADARIAN PERIODS

In the southern Levant this period of initial contact is known as the Early and sometimes Middle Chalcolithic period. In Upper Egypt it is partially contemporary with early phases of the Badarian culture (ca. 4500–3800 BC; Midant-Reynes 2003, pp. 386–87). Initial contacts between sedentary peoples of these regions have been identified to date only from a handful of Egyptian potsherds, Nilotic shells prized for their mother-of-pearl surfaces (*Chambardia acruata*, formerly *Aspatharia rubens*; fig. 12.1a), and possibly flint tools and stone palettes in the southern Levant, either imported or Egyptian influenced (Commenge and Alon 2002, p. 144). The very sparse finds from this period may well reflect activities of desert dwellers moving across the landscape and bringing with

FIGURE 12.1. (*a*) Modern shell of the Nilotic bivalve *Chambardia acruata*, much prized in antiquity for its nacreous, mother-of-pearl interior; this type of shell was not found in the southern Levant, but was extensively imported. (*b*) Pendants made from *Chambardia acruata* (left to right: after Goren and Fabian 2002, figs. 7.1:6, 7.1:9, and 7.1:11)

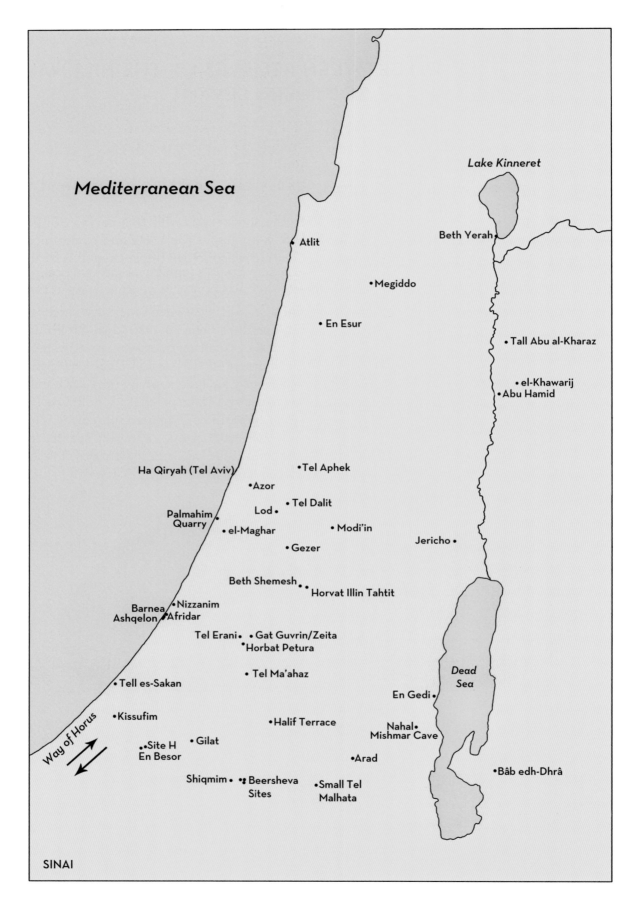

FIGURE 12.2. Map of the Levant with relevant sites and Way of Horus indicated

them artifacts from one green area to another of the Fertile Crescent, but that was to change in the next period.

LATE CHALCOLITHIC-TASIAN, BADARIAN, AND NAQADA[1] I–IIB PERIODS AND EARLY PHASES OF THE MAADI-BUTO CULTURAL COMPLEX

In the Late Chalcolithic period (ca. 4000–3500 BC) a trade network appears to have developed in *Chambardia acruata* shells, one that lasted until the end of the fourth millennium (Bar-Yosef Mayer 2002; Mienis 2007; van den Brink and Braun 2008). South Levantine Chalcolithic folk were fond of their mother-of-pearl surfaces, making them into beads and pendants (fig. 12.1b), which they often deposited in their tombs. Other imports include a calcite vessel from En Gedi in the Judaean Desert (for sites, see fig. 12.2) (Ussishkin 1980, fig. 12), flint tools from the Negev (e.g., Gazit and Gophna 1993, fig. 5; Rowan 2006; Rowan et al. 2006), a lentoid mace-head of Egyptian gabbro (fig. 12.3) from Gat Guvrin/Zeita (northern Negev), another of diorite from el-Khawarij in northern Jordan (Lovell 2008, p. 749, figs. 4–5), and a discoid stone mace-head from Modi'in (van den Brink and Kanias 2010, Area C1 east). Piriform mace-heads of hematite found in the Cave of the Treasure in Nahal Mishmar (Judean Desert; Bar-Adon 1980, p. 116) and Abu Hamid (Jordan Valley; Dollfus and Kafafi 1986, p. 517, pl. 86.3–5, 7–9) are also believed to be Egyptian in origin. Ivory statuettes from sites in the Beersheva region (Perrot 1959) resemble ivory figurines of the Badarian and Naqada periods (fig. 12.4). This movement of objects was probably not

unidirectional, although the evidence from Egypt for such movement has not yet been forthcoming.

Sporadic south Levantine finds at campsites on the coast of northern Sinai (Oren 1989; de Miroschedji 1998, pp. 21–22) indicate the route along which some objects in this period moved westward to the Nile Valley in both Lower and Upper Egypt. In Egypt, south Levantine wares from Stratum Ia of Buto in the Delta (figs. 12.5, 12.6:1; cf. fig. 12.6:2) and local production of similar types, has led scholars to convincingly argue for immigrants settling there (e.g., von der Way 1997, p. 107; Faltings 1998a, 2002; Porat 1997). Evidence for additional south Levantine influence in pottery is found in occasional occurrences of other pottery types, for example, vessels from Ballas (fig. 12.6:4) and Hierakonpolis (fig. 12.6:5). Copper for objects found in Egypt, likely originating in the Wadi Feinan in southern Jordan (Bourke 2002, p. 19), was possibly smelted at sites in the Beersheva Basin (Gilead 1992). Evidence, mostly from pottery, indicates imports and influence in Upper Egypt in this time period (Tutundžić 1989, 1993). A well-known south Levantine tool type, a tabular scraper from the Badari region, may also be a south Levantine import (Holmes 1992b, fig. 3; cf. fig. 12.9:2).

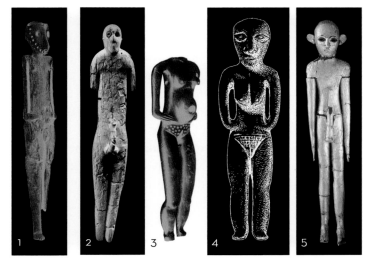

FIGURE 12.4. South Levantine Late Chalcolithic figurines and Egyptian comparanda: (1) Late Chalcolithic ivory male figurine from Beersheva (after Eldar and Baumgarten 1993, fig. 166, left side); (2) Predynastic ivory male figurine in the collection of the Musée du Louvre; (3) Late Chalcolithic ivory female figurine from Beersheva (after Levy 1986, fig. 93); (4) female figurine of the Badarian period, British Museum collection (after Brunton and Caton-Thompson 1928, no. 5107); and (5) wooden, gold foil-covered figurine from Tell el-Farkha, Late Dynasty O, in the same Egyptian iconographic tradition. Figurines not to scale

FIGURE 12.3. Half a lentoid mace-head of Egyptian gabbro found at the northern Negev site of Gat Guvrin/Zeita (courtesy of H. Khalaily, Israel Antiquities Authority). No scale available

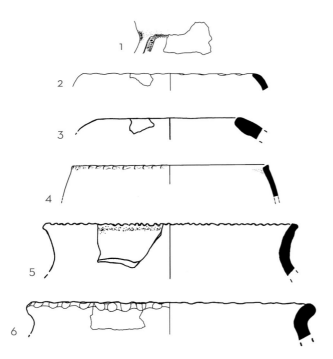

FIGURE 12.5. South Levantine pottery from Buto and south Levantine comparanda: (1) from Buto (after Faltings et al. 2000, fig. 1.5); (2) from Buto (after Faltings et al. 2000, fig. 1.6); (3) from Buto (after Faltings et al. 2000, fig. 1.7); (4) from Beersheva, Late Chalcolithic (after Commenge-Pellerin 1990, fig. 33.5); (5) from Ashqelon-Afridar, Early Bronze Age I (after Golani 2004, fig. 27.11); and (6) from Buto (after Faltings et al. 2000, fig. 1.1). Pottery is not to scale

These parallels indicate a chronological correlation between the Late Chalcolithic of the southern Levant and the Buto facies of the Maadi-Buto cultural complex of Lower Egypt that may also extend to an early phase of the settlement at Maadi. There, an unusual subterranean structure (Rizkana and Seeher 1989, figs. 15–18), similar to numerous structures associated with Late Chalcolithic types in the Negev (e.g., Perrot 1955, figs. 3–14, pls. 3–8) may be coeval with the Late Chalcolithic period in the southern Levant, although it seems the special culture of Maadi was primarily contemporary with the succeeding Early Bronze Age I, as may be discerned in south Levantine imports and influences.

THE EARLY BRONZE I PERIOD/ NAQADA IIC–IIIB (DYNASTY 0)

The chronology of the transition to the Early Bronze Age I period in the southern Levant is problematic, but once the period was in full swing evidence points to a slow but steady increase in contacts with Egypt (Braun 2001). In the early phases there is continued

evidence for acquisition of *Chambardia* shells at Ashqelon and remarkably, an Egyptian pot found on the seabed about 300 meters off the coast of Atlit, Israel (fig. 12.7:1 and comparanda: fig. 12.7:2–3) apparently contained live specimens of these bivalves, possibly intended as food for sailors. The special significance of this find is the suggestion it offers for early coastal maritime activity as an alternative to the north Sinai land route. Egyptian pottery, a calcite vessel, and spiny bones of Nile catfish and *Chambardia* from Site H in the Wadi Ghazzeh/Nahal Habesor (Macdonald 1932, pl. 26: left of 55, 61, pl. 40.53), in slightly later phases of Early Bronze Age I, suggest contacts increased slightly in this period, but were still limited in scope to virtually two sites in the northern Negev. Trade could still be attributed to the occasional wanderer across the landscape, especially

FIGURE 12.6. Fenestrated, pedestaled vessels, a south Levantine type: (1) typical Late Chalcolithic bowl type from Buto I (after Faltings and Köhler 1996); (2) typical Late Chalcolithic straight-walled (so-called "V-shaped") bowl from Beersheva (after Commenge-Pellerin 1990, fig. 23.2); (3) fenestrated, pedestaled goblet from Shiqmim (after Levy 1987, fig. 12.14); (4) fenestrated, pedestaled goblet from Ballas (after Baumgartel 1947, fig. 41.6); (5) south Levantine type jar from a grave at Hierakonpolis (after Friedman 1999, fig. 3: left); (6) south Levantine type jar from Azor (after Perrot and Ladiray, fig. 71.9); and (7) narrow-necked jar from a Late Chalcolithic mausoleum, Kissufim (after Goren and Fabian 2002, fig. 4.4:5). Pottery is not to scale

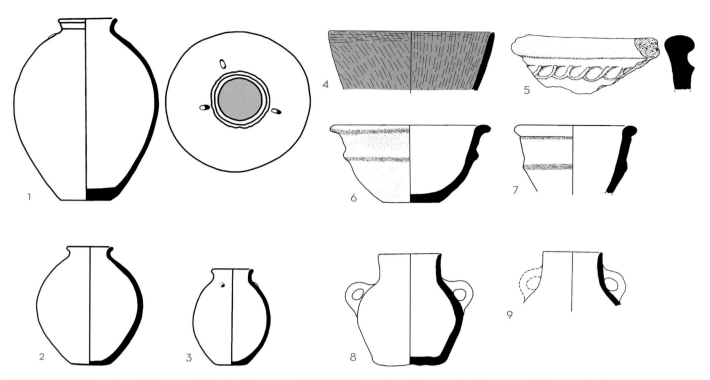

FIGURE 12.7. Pottery from En Besor and Maadi and comparanda: (1) Egyptian jar from the seabed off the coast of Atlit, Israel (after Sharvit et al. 2002, fig. 3a); (2) jar from Maadi (after Rizkana and Seeher 1987, pl. 18.2); (3) jar from Maadi (after Rizkana and Seeher 1987, pl. 39.3); (4) Egyptian red painted and burnished bowl from En Besor (after Gophna 1990, fig. 3.11); (5) krater from Maadi with south Levantine-style ropelike decoration (after Rizkana and Seeher 1987, pl. 59.3); (6) carinated bowl from Maadi (after Rizkana and Seeher 1987, pl. 55.3); (7) carinated bowl of gray burnished ware (Early Bronze Age I) from the East Slope of Megiddo (Oriental Institute Excavations 1925–1932), Collection of the Israel Antiquities Authority; (8) jar from Maadi (after Rizkana and Seeher 1987, pl. 74.3); (9) south Levantine two-handled jar from En Besor (after Gophna 1990, fig. 3:1.5). Pottery is not to scale

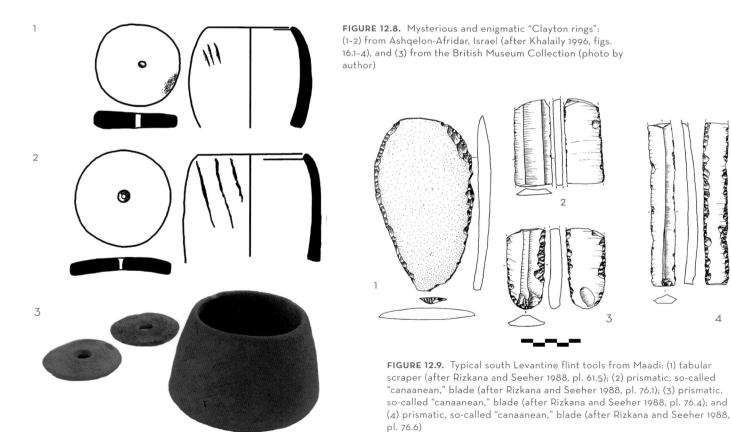

FIGURE 12.8. Mysterious and enigmatic "Clayton rings": (1–2) from Ashqelon-Afridar, Israel (after Khalaily 1996, figs. 16.1–4), and (3) from the British Museum Collection (photo by author)

FIGURE 12.9. Typical south Levantine flint tools from Maadi: (1) tabular scraper (after Rizkana and Seeher 1988, pl. 61.5); (2) prismatic, so-called "canaanean," blade (after Rizkana and Seeher 1988, pl. 76.1); (3) prismatic, so-called "canaanean," blade (after Rizkana and Seeher 1988, pl. 76.4); and (4) prismatic, so-called "canaanean," blade (after Rizkana and Seeher 1988, pl. 76.6)

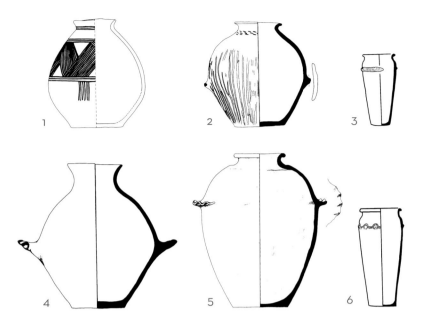

FIGURE 12.10. Pottery vessels from the Protodynastic Cemetery U at Abydos: (1) imported south Levantine vessel from Tomb U-j, painted in the "basket style" (red lines on a cream-colored background), typical of an advanced but not the latest Early Bronze Age I (after Dreyer et al. 1993, fig. 11.e); (2) imported south Levantine vessel from Tomb U-j, painted in the "pajama style" (red stripes on white coating), with oblique incisions ringing the neck, typical of the Erani C ceramic horizon, also of an advanced but not the latest phase of Early Bronze Age I (after Dreyer et al. 1993, fig. 11.f); (3) early type of Egyptian cylinder vessel from Tomb U-j with ledge-like handle (after Dreyer 1998, fig. 29.J5/16); (4) imported south Levantine vessel with ledge handle typical of the Early Bronze Age I (after Dreyer et al. 1993, fig. 11.g); (5) Egyptian-made vessel with ledge handle from tomb U-k similar to south Levantine types (after Dreyer et al. 1993, fig. 11); and (6) early type of Egyptian cylinder vessel from Tomb U-j with ledge-like handle (after Dreyer 1998, fig. 29.J10/175). Pottery is not to scale

in light of two intriguing finds of the same period. They are mysterious "Clayton rings" from Early Bronze Age I Ashqelon-Afridar (fig. 12.8; Riemer and Kuper 2000). These enigmatic, open-ended cylinders and their accompanying thin, pierced, circular disks were mostly found in remote outcrops in the eastern Sahara, which suggests long-distance contacts via desert dwellers and/or travelers, possibly through a Maadi connection, as the site appears to have been well positioned to act as an entrepôt.

The view from Egypt also indicates continued contacts. Excavations at Maadi have yielded south Levantine imports and local pottery (fig. 12.7:2–3, 5–6, 8) of similar, non-Egyptian forms (fig. 12.7:5, 9) as well as imported flint artifacts (fig. 12.8). Another semi-subterranean structure at Maadi (Hartung et al. 2003a, p. 166), stone-built and of sub-rectangular plan, also non-Egyptian, may be associated with a well-documented south Levantine tradition of construction (Braun 1989). A south Levantine import in tomb 26 at Hierakonpolis (Friedman 2006, p. 12) seems also to be of this same period, suggesting some interaction also with Upper Egypt.

A major south Levantine contribution to Egyptian material culture may well have begun in this period. The ledge (or wavy) handle was to have a long-lasting impact on Nile Valley potters, who rapidly co-opted this practical appendage (e.g., fig. 12.10:3, 5–6; Catalog Nos. 12, 15), making it their own. Early Egyptian potters were not fond of handles and they minimized the dimensions of these appendages and eventually, in later periods, transmogrified such handles into mere decoration (e.g., figs. 12.10:3, 6; Catalog Nos. 16–18).

THE "ERANI C HORIZON" IN THE SOUTHERN LEVANT

The following period, known as the "Erani C Horizon" (equated with Level C at the eponymous tell site; Kempinski and Gilead 1991; Braun and van den Brink 1998) witnesses a marked increase in contacts between the southern Levant and the Nile Valley, albeit not at that site. The evidence derives mostly from Sinai and Egypt, with only a modicum of information on Egyptian imports in the southern Levant.

"The Way(s) of Horus"

Campsites that have yielded both south Levantine and Egyptian pot types (Oren 1989; Oren and Yekutieli 1992; de Miroschedji 2000; fig. 12.11:3–9) offer direct evidence for continued use of a northern Sinai land route, which came to be known in historic times as "The Way(s) of Horus." That name, possibly deriving from a Dynasty 0 ruler represented by a falcon (Dreyer et al. 1998, p. 178), whose symbol came to be synonymous with kingship (Emery 1961, p. 106), may be almost of as great antiquity as the route itself (for an alternate view, see Wilkinson 1985). The route appears to have become important during the

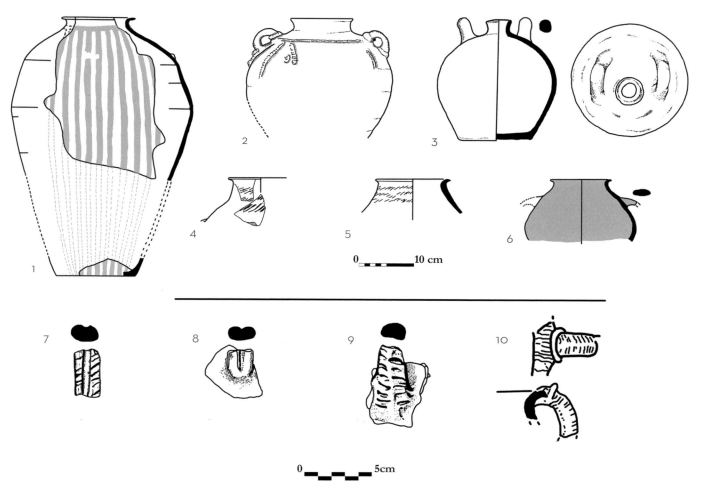

FIGURE 12.11. Pottery of the Erani C, advance Early Bronze Age I horizon and south Levantine imports from Abydos: (1) storage jar from a site in North Sinai (after Oren 1989, fig. 9.160); (2) small two-handled jar from Abydos (Amélineau excavations; after Watrin 2000, fig. 28.5a); (3) small jar with two basket handles from Abydos (Amélineau excavations; after Watrin 2000, fig. 28.5c); (4) neck of jar of the Erani C horizon from Sinai (after Oren 1989, fig. 9.14); (5) neck of jar of the Erani C horizon from Sinai (after Oren 1989, fig. 9.15); (6) neck of jar of the Erani C horizon from Sinai (after Oren 1989, fig. 8.13); (7) handle of a small vessel of the Erani C horizon from Sinai (after Oren 1989, fig. 8.5); (8) handle of a small vessel of the Erani C horizon from Sinai, after Oren 1989, fig. 8.6); (9) handle of a small vessel of the Erani C horizon from Sinai (after Oren 1989, fig. 8.7l); and (10) decorated handle from the site of Har Tuv near Beth Shemesh (after Mazar and de Miroschedji 1996, fig. 18.7)

Erani C horizon, as may be discerned not only from remnants of this distinctive style of pottery found there, but also from similar finds, mostly in Upper Egypt. The domestication of the donkey increased the possibilities of trade and may have been in some part responsible for utilization of this land route (van den Brink and Gophna 2004; Milevski 2010).

Erani C Pottery Styles

Two highly distinctive pottery styles, types found in Egypt, are associated with the Erani C phase, although the eponymous occupation and a large, contemporary, neighboring settlement, Horbat Petura, have failed to yield definitive Egyptian finds (Yekutieli 2006; Gorzalczany and Baumgarten 2005;

Baumgarten, personal communication 2009), with the possible exception of some bullae (Kempinski and Gilead 1991, p. 187, figs. 14–15). No motifs were preserved on the bullae from Level C, but their presence may hint at the beginnings of intense contacts, as these objects may be associated with some early aspect of Egyptian administration. Notably, exposure of later occupations at this same site have yielded significant quantities of Egyptian and Egyptianized objects (Brandl 1989).

One Erani C style is identified by a bright white, lime slip over which narrow, red, vertical stripes were painted, and necklace-like decorations of short, oblique incisions on jars (figs. 12.10.2; 12.11:3–4, 6). The other is identified with narrow bands of clay surrounding handles and spouts, while handles of such vessels, sometimes with two or even three strands, were often incised with lines of horizontal or oblique marks (fig. 12.11:1, 7–10). Examples of these, and another contemporary south Levantine style of decoration known as the "basket style" (a mode of painting in thin red stripes on a light-colored background in imitation of woven basketry; fig. 12.10:1), have been found, for example, in Upper and Lower Egypt at Hierakonpolis (Adams and Friedman 1992, pp. 322, 332) and at Tell el-Farkha (Mączyńska 2006, fig. 8.6).

ROYAL TOMBS AT ABYDOS: CEMETERY U

Many south Levantine vessels in Tomb U-j (fig. 12.10:2; Hartung 1993; Hartung et al. 2001) of King "Scorpion" at Abydos/Umm el-Qaab (early Dynasty 0), and other sepulchers of that cemetery (Adams and Porat 1996) and elsewhere in Upper Egypt indicate the elite valued such imports enough to have them entombed with themselves. However, there is disagreement among scholars (Porat and Goren 2001; 2002; contra McGovern 2001) as to how many of the between 450 and 700 non-Egyptian-type vessels in Tomb U-j that originally contained wine were truly south Levantine imports (e.g., fig. 12.10:1–2), and how many might have been made locally (e.g., fig. 12.10:3). However, it is certain that at least a modicum of those vessels was imported, probably via the Way(s) of Horus, as an array of broken pots strewn over campsites in northern Sinai indicates (e.g., fig. 12.11:3–4, 7–9). In the contemporary southern Levant, by contrast with Egypt, imported Egyptian vessels remain virtually unreported in the literature. As far as this writer has been able to ascertain, they are represented by only a handful of examples from Barnea Ashqelon (A. Golani, personal communication).

LATER PHASES OF EARLY BRONZE AGE I

The following period to the end of the Early Bronze Age I sees remarkable developments in interaction with Egyptians. What interested the early rulers and elites buried at Abydos in Cemetery U appears to have drawn their successors into an extraordinary and unusually Egyptian venture, the establishment of a large colonial outpost near modern-day Gaza City, as well as two smaller settlements and probably several enclaves of Egyptians settled within south Levantine communities.

Evidence suggests a four-tiered hierarchy of Egyptian activity in the southern Levant, with Tier 1 type settlements exhibiting primarily Egyptian material culture and associations such that it is obvious they were peopled by settlers from the Nile Valley. Tier 2 sites exhibit primarily south Levantine material culture, but have sizable increments of Egyptian and Egyptianized material culture. Sites of primarily south Levantine character with a modicum of Egyptian and Egyptianized material culture can be characterized as Tier 3, while communities exhibiting primarily south Levantine characteristic, with only rare or no Egyptian and Egyptianized artifacts, are considered as Tier 4.

AN EGYPTIAN COLONY IN THE SOUTHERN LEVANT

In the Early Bronze Age I an Egyptian colony of unparalleled size and importance was established at Tell es-Sakan on the south bank of Wadi Ghazzeh/ Nahal Habesor, near where it debouches into the Mediterranean. Four levels at the site, the last three apparently fortified, suggest a thriving community overwhelmingly associated with Egyptian or Egyptianized material culture. Primary publications indicate Nilotic peoples settled there (de Miroschedji 2001) and apparently fortified the site by building successive phases of massive mudbrick walls. What is truly extraordinary is that such fortifications are unknown in contemporary Egypt, and the use of mudbrick was only beginning to be popular (Chłodnicki and Ciałowicz 2002, pp. 69–71, fig. 4). Although some south Levantine communities may have already constructed massive defenses, most of those sites are farther to the north and show virtually no evidence of contact with Egyptians. Thus, a fortified Egyptian settlement outside the borders of Egypt remains, at least for the present, a unique phenomenon and one that is not well understood.

The size and scope of the Tell es-Sakan enterprise suggests highly organized activity, presumably under royal aegis, an interpretation further bolstered by evidence for Egyptian administration found at south Levantine sites. Bullae of local clay found at two sites,

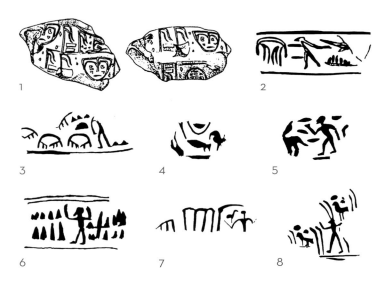

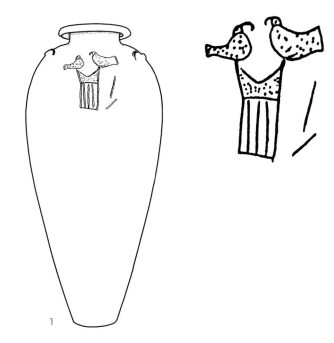

FIGURE 12.12. Objects from the southern Levant associated with Egyptian administration: (1) two sides of a locally made, Egyptianized bulla from the Halif Terrace (after van den Brink 1998, fig. 3a); (2) rendering of motif on cylinder seal found at Gezer (after Brandl 1992, fig. 1.2); and renderings of motifs on bullae from En Besor: (3) after Schulman 1976, fig. 1.2; (4) after Schulman 1976, fig. 1.5; (5) after Schulman 1976, fig. 1.6; (6) after Schulman 1976, fig. 1.14; (7) after Schulman 1976, fig. 1.8; and (8) after Schulman 1976, fig. 1.9

FIGURE 12.13. Jar incised with a *serekh* from el-Beidah (after van den Brink 1996, fig. 1: IIa.5)

as well as a cylinder seal from Gezer (fig. 12.12:2), all bearing Egyptianized motifs, argue for orderly administration of goods, most likely foodstuffs. One large group of bullae (fig. 12.12:3–8; Schulman 1976) used to seal sacks was found at En Besor (a Tier 1 site), a small way station that appears to have been a depot for transshipment of goods, perhaps to Tell es-Sakan, which lies farther to the west on the same stream bed. Several additional bullae were recovered at the Halif Terrace (fig. 12.12:1) where they seem to have been associated with an Egyptian enclave (Levy et al. 1997) within a primarily south Levantine, Tier 2 type settlement. Significant Egyptian-associated finds from Tel Ma'ahaz indicate it was another Tier 1 site, but virtually nothing of its physical character is known as most artifacts from it derive from looting activities (Beit-Arieh and Gophna 1999).

THE BEGINNING OF AN EGYPTIAN ROYAL ENTERPRISE?

A jar found at el-Beida near Ismailia on the Way(s) of Horus, incised with a royal *serekh*[2] flanked by two falcons (fig. 12.13) associated with a protodynastic king known as "Double Falcon" (Hassan et al. 2006, pp. 688–91), is likely an indication of an Egyptian royal association with south Levantine interaction. Two uniquely south Levantine finds, *serekh*s from two sites incised prior to firing on locally made vessels, may be associated with the same ruler. That from Palmahim Quarry (fig. 12.14:1A–C), in which the upper, horizontal register (analogous to the "name compartment" in later *serekh*s) is filled with a simple punctate design, is paralleled in the el-Beidah *serekh* (fig. 12.13) and may also signify "Double Falcon" (Braun and van den Brink 1998). Another from contemporary Horvat Illin Tahtit (fig. 12.14:2A–C) may well be of the same ruler as it is on the same vessel type, but unfortunately the incised *serekh* was only very partially preserved.

THE WAXING OF EGYPTIAN INFLUENCE

Fragments of cylinder vessels, dated by their net-painted decoration to the post-Erani C period (Gophna 1972, fig. 2.3; Braun 2009, fig. 6.1), are additional evidence of Egyptian activity during Dynasty 0, prior to the reign of Narmer. The Egyptian relationship began in this period to wax quite strong as witnessed by the virtual flood of imported and Egyptianized objects found at a number of select

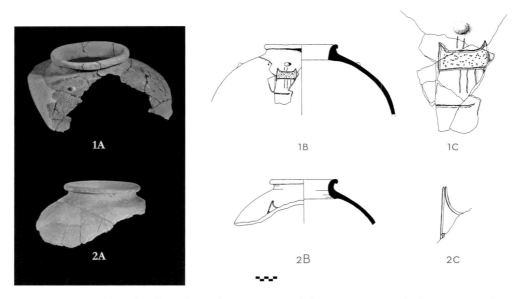

FIGURE 12.14. *Serekh*s on locally made, south Levantine jars: (1) from Stratum 2 at Palmahim Quarry and (2) from Stratum IV at Horvat Illin Tahtit

south Levantine sites in the following, latest phases of Early Bronze Age I.

EGYPTIAN ROYAL ASSOCIATIONS

Of foremost interest in the latest phases of Early Bronze Age I in the southern Levant are more than twenty *serekh*s found incised on imported Egyptian vessels from a number of sites. The earliest, preserved on a "wine" jar fragment from Lod, has an upraised arm and hand incised into its "name compartment" identifying it with Ka, either the last or next-to-last king of Dynasty 0 (fig. 12.15:3). Other *serekh*s with identifiable names, from Arad (fig. 12.14:1; Amiran 1974), Tel Erani (fig. 12.15:2; Yeivin 1960),

Tel Halif (Levy et al. 1995), and other sites are all of Ka's successor, Narmer (fig. 12.16), whose highly schematic catfish hieroglyphs are easily identified in their name compartments. Unfortunately the name compartments of additional serekhs from Lod, Horvat Illin Tahtit, Small Tel Malhata (Amiran et al. 1983), and Tel Maʻahaz are not preserved and so cannot be identified with one or another ruler.

What does this royal symbol signify on these jars, and why were they imported to the southern Levant? One intriguing potter's mark on such a jar fragment from Lod (fig. 12.17), possibly a determinative for wine (*irp*), suggests they were indeed for that beverage. Were they for wine from royal Egyptian stores for export to the southern Levant, perhaps to the colony or an armed contingent at Tell es-Sakan?

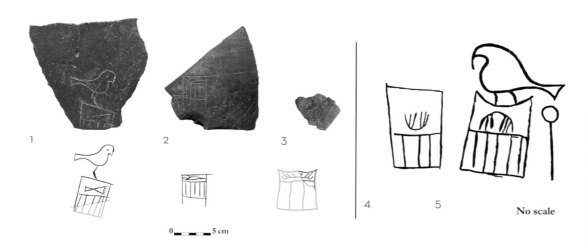

FIGURE 12.15. *Serekh*s of Narmer and Ka from the southern Levant and Egypt; (1) Narmer *serekh* from Arad, Israel; (2) Narmer *serekh* from Tel Erani, Israel; (3) Ka *serekh* from Lod, Israel; (4) rendering of Ka *serekh* from Kafr Hassan Daoud, Egypt (after van den Brink 1996, fig. 27); and (5) rendering of Ka *serekh* from Helwan, Egypt (after van den Brink 1996, fig. 28)

0 ▬▬ 5 cm

No scale

FIGURE 12.17. Fragment of an Egyptian "wine jar" from Lod, Israel, with a potter's mark incised prior to firing, possibly the determinative for wine (*irp*)

FIGURE 12.16. *Serekhs* of Narmer from Lod, Israel

If so, then it was the equivalent of sending coals to Newcastle, as wine is believed to have appeared in the southern Levant earlier than it did in the Nile Delta, where early texts indicate the presence of wine estates. However, by this time Egypt was most likely a wine producer as the number of these jars and seal impressions suggests (Kaplony 2002). Were the contents of these imported jars, provided they had contents when exported, intended for Egyptians in the Levant who might not care for the local vintage, or was imported wine intended for locals with exotic tastes (van den Brink and Braun 2002)? Could these large, heavy jars, so much better for transporting than any local vessel, have been sent as empty containers for transporting south Levantine wines back to the Nile Valley, perhaps to the king's stores? And what is the significance of the royal insignias?

The answers to these intriguing questions are far from clear, and scholars do not agree on how to interpret the evidence. Some are wont to construe it as an Egyptian sedentary presence, a colony with specific borders (i.e., a province) that encompassed the northern Sinai route with its campsites (de Miroschedji 1998, 2000) and the Mediterranean littoral up to the region of Tel Aviv. Others (e.g., Brandl 1992; Anđelković 1995; Yekutieli 1998, 2004) argue for models of colonial activity analogous to colonies of ancient Rome and the Western European experiences in Asia and Africa in the modern era. However, the evidence is unclear as to the true nature of the relationship between Egyptians in Egypt, Egyptians in their south Levantine enclaves, and the indigenous peoples of the southern Levant. Did transplanted Egyptians maintain some degree of hegemony over their indigenous neighbors, and if so, was it based on force of arms? That might explain the existence of a fortified Tell es-Sakan, but is that in sync with the tiny, unfortified way station at En Besor or Egyptian enclaves within local communities? How can the existence of Tier 3 and 4 type sites, all well within a zone of intense Egyptian activity, be explained with such paradigms?

Was the relationship between Egyptians and locals one of complete domination, with tribute and possibly slaves collected and sent to the Nile Valley, where presumably they enriched and nurtured a nascent Egyptian polity as it embarked on unification, or was there a more equitable arrangement based on trade? Perhaps this latter explanation is suggested by the significant quantity of Egyptian objects found in the southern Levant. Such a scenario suggests Tier 1 settlements maintained strong contacts with select local communities of Tier 2 (e.g., Tel Erani, Halif Terrace, Small Tel Malhata, Ashqelon-Afridar, Nizzanim, el-Maghar, Lod, and Azor), while evidence of Tier 3 communities is explained by lesser or even spillover contacts (e.g., at Palmahim Quarry, Horvat Illin Tahtit, el-Maghar, En Esur, Arad). Tier 4 sites (e.g., Beth Shemesh, Tel Dalit, Tel Aphek, Megiddo, Beth Yerah, Tall Abu el-Kharaz, Bâb edh Dhrâ³), either with nothing to offer or lying beyond the immediate Egyptian sphere of influence would, in such a paradigm, have been virtually ignored. The presence of Egyptian objects and influence at Megiddo, farther to the north and outside the primary zone of contact, may be due to its pre-eminence as a shrine, indicated by the monumental nature of the J4 temple located there (Finkelstein et al. 2006); that at widely exposed Beth Yerah, marked by only a few Egyptian objects, remains obscure (Greenberg and Eisenberg 2002; Greenberg et al. 2010).

This period of Egyptian settlement in the southern Levant, according to the stratification of Tell es-Sakan, must have lasted for at least three generations. However, the Egyptian episode at En Besor, which apparently displaced an earlier settlement of local people, and was in turn resettled by south Levantines, seems to have been of short duration. The details leave us with a very incomplete picture of this period of interaction, but the wealth of Egyptian and Egyptianized goods in the southern Levant indicates its intensity and the variability of the experiences they represent.

Included are objects of prestige such as finely made bottles, large and small (fig. 12.18), cylinder vessels (fig. 12.19), and rare vessels decorated in reed patterns (fig. 12.20; Kansa et al. 2002 and parallels). Other objects of particular value, mostly from tombs of locals, include a beautiful rippled, pressure-flaked Egyptian knife (fig. 12.21:1; cf. fig. 12.20:2), bull amulets (fig. 12.22), a faience statuette (Gophna 1993), and stone palettes (fig. 12.23) exhibiting greater and lesser skills. More quotidian imported, functional types include wine jars and locally made, exceedingly coarse ware (e.g., fig. 12.24:1, 4, 6), often with straw temper, jars, bottles, and baking bowls.

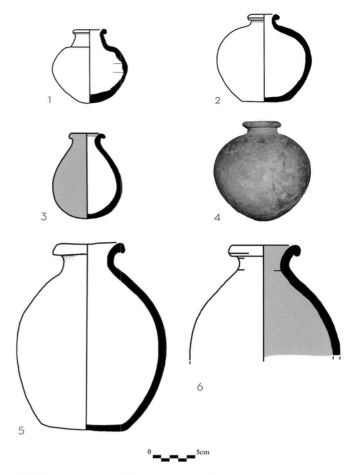

FIGURE 12.18. Imported Egyptian bottles: (1) from a tomb at En Esur (after Yannai 2002, fig. 22.1:12; (2) from a tomb at En Esur (after Yannai 2002, fig. 22.1:13); and (3–6) from Lod

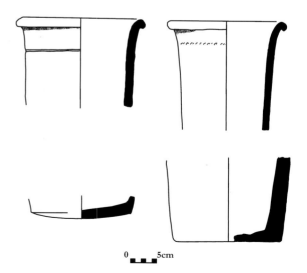

FIGURE 12.19. Imported Egyptian cylinder vessels from Lod (Yannai 2002)

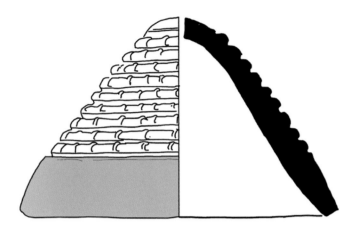

FIGURE 12.20. A reed-decorated, conical, ceramic lid from Halif Terrace. 10.8 x 7.1 cm (based on Kansa et al. 2002, fig. 2)

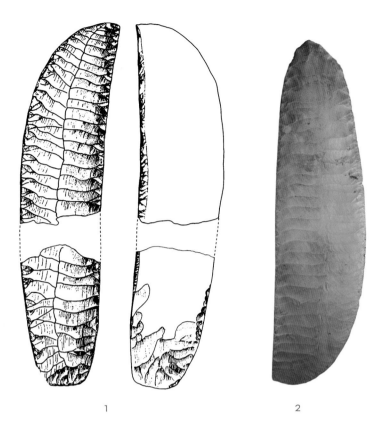

FIGURE 12.21. Egyptian rippled, pressure-flaked flint blades: (1) from a tomb at Azor. Length 25.2 cm (after Ben-Tor 1975, fig. 13.15) and (2) unknown provenance (purchased in Luxor, 1920). Length 23 cm (see Catalog No. 79)

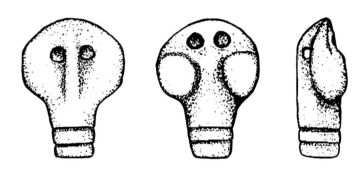

FIGURE 12.22. Bull's head amulet from a tomb at Azor. Height 3.3 cm (after van den Brink et al. 2007, fig. 10.1)

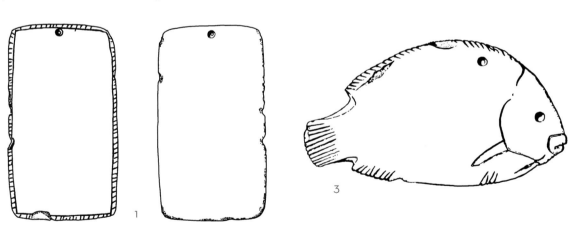

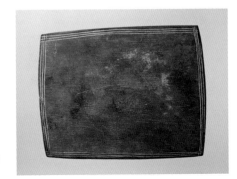

FIGURE 12.23. Imported Egyptian palettes: (1) from a tomb at En Esur (after Yannai 2002, fig. 22.1:22); (2) Rectangular palette from Abadiya (Catalog No. 51); (3) from Gaza (after Brandl 1992, fig. 1.1); and (4) fish palette from Abadiya (Catalog No. 6). Palettes not to scale

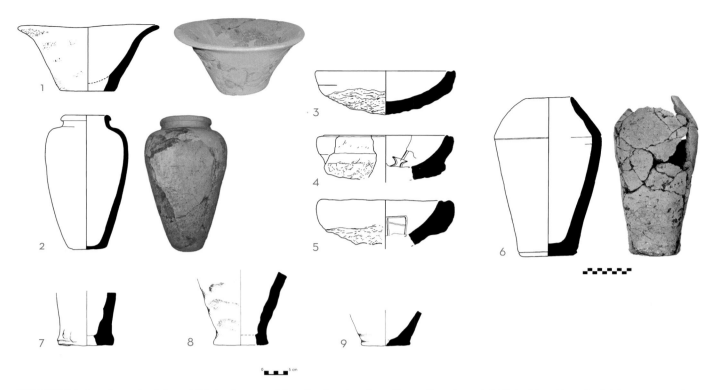

FIGURE 12.24. Locally made plain and "kitchen" wares of Egyptian typology from the southern Levant: (1) "lotus" bowl from Lod; (2) coarse ware jar from Lod; (3) baking bowl from En Besor (after Gophna 1990, fig. 2.4); (4) baking bowl from En Besor (after Gophna 1990, fig. 2.5); (5) baking bowl from En Besor (after Gophna 1990, fig. 2.6); (6) "granary jar" from Megiddo, East Slope (Oriental Institute Excavations 1932); and (7–9) coarse ware jar from Lod

EVIDENCE FROM EGYPT-LEVANTINE IMPORTS AT THE END OF DYNASTY 0

Concurrently in Egypt there appears to have been a trickle of south Levantine goods and influence at many sites. The ledge handle, earlier co-opted by Egyptian potters, had truly entered the repertoire of accepted forms as both a functional and a decorative element, even in stone vessels (fig. 12.25:1; van den Brink and Braun 2006). Evidence for imports and influence comes mostly from sites in Middle Egypt, for example, el-Gerzeh (Petrie et al. 1912, pl. 11:185, 33, 94) and Abusir el-Meleq (Möller and Scharff 1969: pl. 9.5–6); and Lower Egypt, for example, Minshat Abu Omar (fig. 12.26) and Tell el-Farkha (fig. 12.25; Jucha 2008, figs. 1–2), but whether that is due to the vagaries of discovery in Upper Egypt or a true picture of the archaeological record remains unclear. One small jar of south Levantine morphology was found at Adaïma in Upper Egypt, but it is believed to be an import from Lower Egypt (Midant-Reynes et al. 1997, fig. 2). Finds in the Delta suggest that royal influence was already felt there in this period, which may explain something of this relationship with the southern Levant (see "The Predynastic/Early Dynastic Period at Tell el-Farkha" in this volume). One notable type of south Levantine import, several examples of which were transshipped from Egypt to Qustul, Nubia, was left to grace a royal tomb there (fig. 12.27). It is especially noteworthy as the imported, coarse-ware vessels were used by a non-south

FIGURE 12.25. South Levantine import and influence at Tell el-Farkha in the Delta: (1) small stone bottle from Tell el-Farkha, courtesy of Kyzysztof Ciałowicz, Institute of Archaeology, Jagiellonian University, Krakow; and (2) small ceramic bowl with knobs from Tell el-Farkha (after Sobas 2009, pl. 4.12)

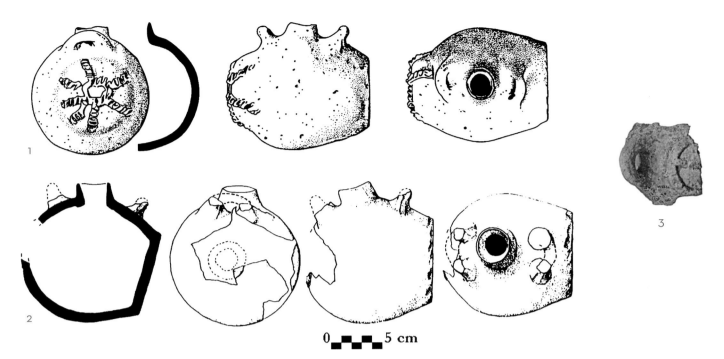

FIGURE 12.26. "Waterskin"-type ceramic vessels from Egypt and the southern Levant dated to late phases of Early Bronze Age I: (1) from Minshat Abu Omar, courtesy of Karla Kroeper; (2) from Horvat Illin Tahtit, courtesy of the Israel Antiquities Authority; and (3) from Jericho (Garstang's 1930s excavation), courtesy of the Israel Antiquities Authority

Levantine potter as a morphological template to produce a slipped and finely burnished, orange-colored example (fig. 12.27:2).

THE END OF EGYPTIAN ACTIVITY IN THE SOUTHERN LEVANT

The Early Bronze Age I in the southern Levant came to an end about 3000 BC, sometime between the end of the reign of Narmer and prior to the death of Djer (Braun 2009), more or less the time when Upper and Lower Egypt were undergoing final unification. Did that cause the communities of Middle and Lower Egypt to cease foreign activities, bringing about new economic conditions? The coincidence is intriguing, but the sparse evidence does not allow for a really serious interpretation of that ancient reality. Suffice it to note that Egyptian sites in the southern Levant were all abandoned at the end of Early Bronze Age I and coevally imports to the southern Levant ceased abruptly. That coincidence does, however, suggest a direct, causal relationship. Egyptian–south Levantine interaction was dormant then for a period of perhaps several generations, after which it was renewed in

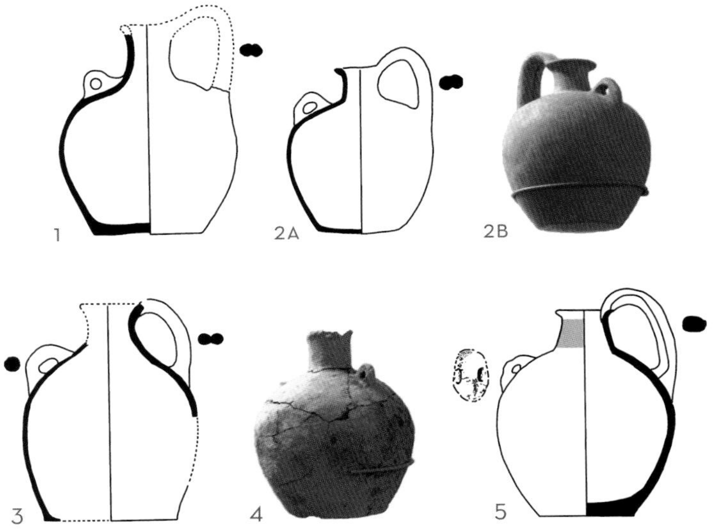

FIGURE 12.27. Jugs from the southern Levant and Qustul, Nubia: (1) jug from Qustul, probably a south Levantine import (after Gophna and van den Brink 2002, fig. 18.3:6); (2) jug from Qustul, probably locally made, slipped, and burnished orange (after Gophna and van den Brink 2002, fig. 18.3:7); (3) jug from Qustul, Nubia, same as no. 2; (4) jug from tomb, Azor, Israel (after Gophna and van den Brink 2002, fig. 18.3:3); (5) jug from Qustul, Nubia, probably a south Levantine import; and (6) jug from tomb, Palmahim Quarry, Israel (after Gophna and van den Brink 2002, fig. 18.3:1). Pottery is not to scale

the initial phase of Early Bronze Age II, albeit apparently on a very different basis.

EARLY BRONZE AGE II/DYNASTIES 1 AND 2 — A NEW PARADIGM FOR INTERACTION

Levantine ceramic imports, some definitively from the southern Levant (fig. 12.28), and others of more obscure Levantine origin, are found in Egypt, foremost in the First Dynasty royal tombs at Abydos beginning with that of Djer. The appearance of that pottery may be related to a hypothesized special relationship with the urban center of Beth Yerah and an Egyptian polity (Greenberg and Eisenberg 2002; Eisenberg and Greenberg 2006, fig. 8.79). A potter's mark on a typical south Levantine jug (fig. 12.29) found at that site, interpreted as a hieroglyph (Kaplony 2002), may be the key to understanding that relationship. In addition, vessels of a type called light-faced painted ware (i.e., Petrie's [1902] Aegean ware) from somewhere in the Levant, appear in the tombs of several rulers from the time of Den (fig. 12.30) and in small quantities at sites in the northern

FIGURE 12.29. Jug from Beth Yerah with what is believed to be an Egyptian hieroglyph. Height 29.7 cm (after Kaplony 2002, fig. 29.3)

reaches of the southern Levant. As there is no evidence to date of analogous Egyptian imports in the southern Levant, the evidence may be of a one-way relationship or, at least, of some type of reciprocity that left no impact whatsoever on the archaeological record of the southern Levant. Interaction appears to have wound down during the Second Dynasty, and by the time of the Third Dynasty it was once again in hiatus.[4]

SUMMARY

Egypt's first major experience in the southern Levant took place prior to Dynasty 0 after more than a millennium of casual and desultory contacts. It began with small enclaves of south Levantines settled in Egypt at Buto and later at Maadi, possibly whetting locals' appetites for imports, especially wine from grapes not yet cultivated in the Delta. Contacts developed slowly over time to when it behooved an Egyptian polity to establish Tell es-Sakan on the Way(s) of Horus: a colony and its satellites at the very gateway to the well-watered zones of the southern Levant. That interaction left considerable quantities of Nile Valley imports and local replications at select

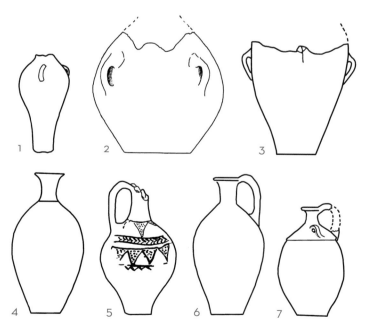

FIGURE 12.28. Levantine imports: (1) jug from royal Cemetery B, Abydos (after Petrie 1902, pl. 6.7); (2) jar ("combed ware") from Royal Cemetery B, Abydos (after Petrie 1902, pl. 8.7); (3) jar from royal Cemetery B, Abydos (after Petrie 1902, pl. 8.8); (4) jar from Royal Cemetery B, Abydos (after Petrie 1902, pl. 8.2); (5) jug (light faced painted ware), Saqqara (after Amiran 1969, pl. 17.10); (6) jug from Royal Cemetery B, Abydos (after Petrie 1902, pl. 8.4); and (7) jug from Royal Cemetery B, Abydos (after Petrie 1902, pl. 8.5). Pottery not to scale

FIGURE 12.30. Light faced painted ware imports from Abydos: (1a) sherd from Royal Cemetery B, Abydos, First Dynasty (after Petrie 1902; pl. 8.15); (1b) photograph of sherd marked "tomb of Den-Abydos" (Ashmolean Museum Collection); (2) sherd from Royal Cemetery B, Abydos, First Dynasty (after Petrie 1902, pl. 8.18); (3) sherd from Royal Cemetery B, Abydos, First Dynasty (after Petrie 1902, pl. 8.16); (4) photograph of a sherd, probably from Abydos (British Museum Collection); (5) sherd from Royal Cemetery B, Abydos First Dynasty (after Petrie 1902, pl. 8.17); (6) photograph of a sherd, probably from Abydos (British Museum Collection); (7) photograph of a sherd, probably from Abydos (British Museum Collection); (8) sherd from Royal Cemetery B, Abydos, First Dynasty (after Petrie 1902, pl. 8.19); (9) photograph of a sherd, probably from Abydos (Ashmolean Museum Collection); (10) photograph of a sherd, probably from Abydos (Ashmolean Museum Collection); and (11) photograph of a sherd, probably from Abydos (Ashmolean Museum Collection). Not to scale

south Levantine sites. Quite possibly that nascent relationship created some of the wealth that allowed for the eventual aggrandizement of the power of a line or lines of Abydene rulers known from Cemetery U, which resulted in the gradual unification of Upper and Lower Egypt (Köhler 2008). Perhaps full unification tolled the death knell for the Egyptian south Levantine colony, as the two events appear to have coincided. After a brief hiatus in interaction from perhaps as early as the end of the reign of Narmer, to sometime prior to the end of the reign of Djer, the relationship resumed, albeit on a different, possibly unidirectional basis. During the First and Second Dynasties south Levantine imports appear in royal and elite tombs at Abydos and elsewhere, but by the onset of the Old Kingdom (Third Dynasty), the relationship seems to have run its course as interaction shifted to Byblos until sometime in the second millennium. But that is a tale beyond the scope of this essay.

NOTES

* I wish to express my special thanks to Edwin C. M. van den Brink for his valuable comments on earlier drafts of this paper and to Silvia Krapiwko for her invaluable instruction in the arts of computer illustration. The following institutions are owed my thanks for generously supplying photographs of objects or allowing me to photograph artifacts in their collections: The British Museum, Israel Antiquities Authority, Institute of Archaeology, Tel Aviv University, and Jagellionian University, Krakow. Thanks are also due to Yaakov Baumgarten, Amir Golani, and Hamudi Khalaily (of the Israel Antiquities Authority) for allowing me to mention finds from Horbat Petura, Ashqelon-Afridar, and Zeita, respectively. I'm also grateful to Emily Teeter and Thomas Urban (Oriental Institute) for their help and forbearance in bringing this essay to press.

[1] As defined by Kaiser (1957) and Hendrickx (1996).

[2] *Serekh* is an Egyptian transliterated word from the hieroglyphs 𓊁 used to signify kingship in proto-historic and Early Dynastic times in Egypt (Hassan et al. 2006: pp. 691–93). In its earliest form this symbol was a rectangle divided into several vertical registers believed to represent inset-offset outlines of a facade of either a temple or palace. A horizontal register or registers above this facade was used to designate the Horus (sacred falcon) name (one of five official names) of a king, usually written in an abbreviated form. Sometimes, an image of this bird was perched atop the symbol.

[3] Each of these sites has yielded either one or a very few Egyptian imports.

[4] Discovery of that same type of pottery in the Amuq Valley (Braidwood and Braidwood 1960) and at Tell Um Marra, Syria (Curvers and Schwartz 2007, fig. 2, painted sherds), admits of the possibility of it ultimately deriving from the northern Levant.

Approximate Correlations for the Southern Levant and Egypt

Southern Levant Cultural Phase	Southern Levant Type Sites	Upper Egyptian Cultural Phase	Lower Egyptian Cultural Phase
Early–Middle Chalcolithic	Gilat	Tasian-Badarian	Fayum A-Merimda-el-Omari
Late Chalcolithic	Beersheva (Abou Matar, Horvat Beter)	Naqada I–IIA/B	Buto I(a)
Early Early Bronze Age I (initial phase)	Ashqelon-Afridar (Area G)	Naqada IIC/D–IIIA	Buto I(b)
Early Early Bronze Age I (advanced phase)	Site H, Wadi Ghazzeh	Naqada IIIA1	Maadi
Erani C	Tel Erani (Level C)	Naqada IIIA2–B	Naqada IIIA2–B
Late Early Bronze Age I (early phase)	Palmahim Quarry 2	Naqada IIIB	Naqada IIIB
Late Early Bronze Age I (late phase)	Horvat Illin Tahtit III Arad III (early phase)	Naqada IIIB-C/late Dynasty 0-early Dynasty 1 (between reigns of Narmer and Djer)	Naqada IIIB–C/late Dynasty 0-early Dynasty 1 (between reigns of Narmer and Djer)
Early Bronze Age II	Arad III (late phase) Arad II Beth Yerah, period C*	Naqada IIIC/First Dynasty (reign of Djer)	Naqada IIIC/First Dynasty (reign of Djer)

* In Eisenberg and Greenberg 2006.

13. THE RISE OF THE EGYPTIAN STATE

E. CHRISTIANA KÖHLER

From the earliest days of Egyptology, the emergence of the ancient Egyptian state has been a topic of great interest, but of little agreement among scholars. This is probably because its complexity has been consistently underestimated. Unlike many other events in world history, there does not seem to be a single narrative that can be universally applied to the various processes that occurred in different regions of Egypt and that eventually led to the creation of a politically unified territorial state around 3100 BC.

The modern concept of state formation in ancient Egypt is often equated with the Dynastic notion of the "unification of the two lands" (*smȝ tȝ.wy*), which suggests that prior to its materialization, there were two divided lands. This idea of Egypt's division into two lands is certainly one of the most consistent aspects pursued in past research as it is deeply embedded in royal ideology expressed, for example, in the king's later titulary, "King of Upper and Lower Egypt." In the past, it has often been suggested that territorial unity was therefore the result of warfare and territorial competition between two parts of the country, as is often narrated in ancient Egyptian mythology. This point, however, has only recently received more focused attention by scholars, and many today agree that this does not necessarily have to be the case. Although conflict cannot be entirely excluded as a form of inter-polity contact, there is no evidence for extensive warfare in early Egypt other than pictorial, often very abstract, representations of persons fighting and being subjugated. These representations can often be found in the wider context of an imagery that tries to convey a leader's role in protecting the subjects under his care and in creating order over chaos, both topics that are later central to royal ideology.

Further, it is evident that ideology, religion, and symbolism played an important role in the legitimization of kingship, and it is therefore very possible that this dual concept of the "Two Lands" was one that the Egyptians only regarded as their idea and ideal of the state, but not as a reflection of reality. This suggestion is supported by the observation that prior to the creation of political unity across Egypt, state formation occurred in several different parts of the country and resulted in numerous small "proto-states." One should therefore consider the emergence of the state not on the background of prior duality, but plurality, and this in more sense than one.

Modern research has moved away from finding a common narrative that describes the rise of the Dynastic state. Instead it has been intensively focusing on a variety of key questions. It appears as if several essential factors, such as craft specialization, long-distance trade, political economy, centralization, urbanism, social complexity, and bureaucracy, which in combination are often recognized as signs of a society's imminent development toward statehood, were already in place or emerging in different, autonomous regions prior to territorial unity. These factors are interdependent and they individually assist in investigating just how, why, and exactly when, they came into existence in the different regions of Egypt, and how they mutually stimulated the others.

In many prehistoric societies, as in Neolithic Egypt (ca. 5000–4000 BC), the majority of people were engaged in agriculture and animal husbandry. Objects of daily use, such as pottery, stone tools, and baskets, were made at the household level for its own consumption, a pattern that is often referred to as primary production. Under certain circumstances, it is possible that the manufacture of such goods exceeds that of the household's own needs and results in exchange for other goods for the household's benefit. If this production develops into a full-time occupation, and the manufacturer now specializes in this production and is no longer engaged in agriculture or animal breeding, it can develop into a full-time industry (see "Crafts and Craft Specialization" in this volume) whose main purpose is to supply the producers with income that in turn allows them to purchase food and other goods. In Egypt, this process took place during the Chalcolithic period (ca. 4000–3200 BC), which can be ascertained on the basis of archaeological evidence at sites such as Maadi and Hierakonpolis. At Maadi, the conditions seemed to have been favorable for the emergence of a basalt vessel industry that produced high-quality vessels that were traded throughout Egypt (Catalog No. 40). At Hierakonpolis, the remains of early potters' workshops suggest that ceramic industries had developed and that they supplied pottery at least at a regional level. Moreover, there seem to have been ceramic workshops in other parts of Upper Egypt that specialized in the manufacture of painted pots made of marl clay (Petrie's Decorated ware, see Catalog Nos. 2, 31–39) that were found all over Egypt and even as far away as the southern Levant (see "Early Interaction between Peoples of the Nile Valley and the Southern Levant" in this volume). By the end of the Predynastic period, there is sufficient explicit and implicit evidence to suggest that specialized craft production was the main mode of production for a variety of commodities including flint and cooper tools, pottery, stone vessels, and textiles, and that these industries continued to flourish well into the historical period. In isolation, craft specialization is not an indicator of state formation. However, it is when found in association with the other factors described next.

Prehistoric trade can have many forms and appearances, but interregional trade and especially trade that reaches exchange partners at great distance from a commodity's source or place of manufacture are complex forms of interaction between societies. Although there is always the possibility that a commodity may have ended up at a distance by way of indirect or down-the-line trade, there is evidence to suggest that intentional long-distance trade between Egypt, Mesopotamia, the Levant, and Nubia was practiced already in Chalcolithic Egypt and that it intensified with the emergence of the early Egyptian state. Commodities in this exchange include pottery, wine, resin, cedar wood, oils, obsidian, lapis lazuli, copper ore, elephant ivory, gold, and various other materials that either Egypt or her trading partners did not have locally. Some of these raw materials were imported into Egypt via boat and donkey caravan and then manufactured into highly valued goods by the local craft industries who supplied their clientele with the desired merchandise. It is very possible that key interest groups in this long-distance trade were the emerging elites in the regional centers

such as Hierakonpolis, Naqada, or Abydos, where the population was denser and where local craft industries could find the necessary demand. These elites not only consumed many of these prestigious goods to demonstrate their higher status, but they also gave active support to the trade and industries in order to control the flow of raw materials and commodities as a means of peer competition between neighboring polities, a pattern that can be described best as political economy. It is possible that economic advantage played an important role just prior to and during the process of political unification when the proto-states tried to enlarge their polities and thus competed for control over trade routes, resources, and ultimately dominion over greater regions.

Part and parcel of this process is the necessity to centralize resources and industries in order to enhance distribution and control — factors that not only benefitted the Predynastic elites and proto-states for their political interests, but also the craft industries for their economic interests. It is therefore not surprising that those places where early craft specialization has been observed also exhibit signs of higher population density as well as increasing social complexity.

Demand and a solid population base are preconditions for an industry to be economically viable. Increasing craft specialization combined with higher population density is often a sign of growing social differentiation, both horizontally as well as vertically. The thousands of Predynastic graves associated with the early commercial centers of Hierakonpolis, Naqada, Abydos, and other areas have provided the opportunity to study social differentiation and structure, particularly with regard to vertical differentiation or social hierarchy. This form of social structure can often be ascertained archaeologically on the basis of a society's mortuary expenditure, that is, the effort that is invested in constructing and furnishing a person's tomb, which in turn reflects differential access to resources and thus social inequality.

This concept can be applied when there is a contrast between many small graves with only a few grave goods (= poor) and a small number of graves with large quantities of grave goods (= wealthy). The greater and the more differentiated the wealth groups in a community are the greater is its social complexity. This concept, together with other factors described above, helps in determining the level of social complexity and if a society qualifies as a pre-state (for example band, tribe, or chiefdom) or state society. The small states of Protodynastic Egypt already exhibited high levels of social complexity. A perfect example is Abydos, where Cemetery U concentrates much diverse evidence for long-distance trade, specialized craft production, centralization, and social complexity. These culminate in Tomb U-j, which is most probably the grave of a Protodynastic ruler who, at around 3250 BC, also commanded early hieroglyphic writing as a means of economic management (see "The Invention of Writing in Egypt" and "Tomb U-j: A Royal Burial of Dynasty 0 at Abydos" in this volume). This new tool of administrative control was quickly adapted and modified by the other polities along the Nile Valley, and soon writing also served as a means of political, ideological, as well as religious expression. It is through these early forms of hieroglyphic writing that we are aware of the various proto-states across Egypt because their rulers used a common language in expressing their personal identity, namely via the so-called Horus name, which is the first step in the development of royal titulary. A large number of such Protodynastic Horus names have been found across Egypt, for example, inscribed on ceramic vessels and on seals (Catalog No. 89), and, depending on their provenance, they sometimes may assist in locating the geographic location of their polities.

It is interesting to note that at the end of the Predynastic period there does not appear to be a single polity that emerged as a dominant center and subsequently grew into the primary center of the early unified state. Instead, it seems as if one dominant polity in the south, most probably Abydos, saw the necessity to move north and develop another already highly populated center as the capital of their new territorial state. This center was located at the apex of the Nile Delta, where the river approached from the south and divided into the numerous branches and a wide alluvial plain, giving access to agricultural land and the Mediterranean Sea in the north as well as to the land bridge to the Levant in the east. Such favorable conditions were probably recognized by the early kings of Egypt as the ideal environment to build their capital and center of government and from where the territorial state of Egypt that now stretched along the length of the Nile from the First Cataract in the south to the Mediterranean coast in the north, could be ruled. They named this new center the White Walls (*inb.w ḥḏ*) and it quickly grew into a major city that was later to be known as *Mn-Nfr* or Memphis.

Although there is very little surviving evidence of the actual city, much information can be derived from the numerous Proto- and Early Dynastic cemeteries that surround it. These allow for a reconstruction of the city's population size, and its social and economic structure. There are currently about 12,000 early graves known from the region around Memphis, the majority of which cluster along the eastern edge of the valley between modern-day Maadi and Helwan, suggesting that the urban center could not have been far away. These vast cemeteries exhibit a high level of social complexity and economic diversity, especially in contrast with the smaller elite cemetery on the west bank where the socioeconomic status of occupants appears much higher than in the east. The evidence from the cemeteries (including the quantitative mortuary data as well as qualitative data derived from inscriptions and artifacts) thus indicates that Memphis was indeed a primary center and that the regional centers of the former proto-states now played a secondary role, at least in economic terms. Although the archaeological evidence comes from funerary contexts and must therefore be regarded with caution, it is possible to conclude that Memphis also housed the necessary administrative units and infrastructure of government in order to collect, store, and redistribute revenue from the regions' major sanctuaries where the kings paid tribute to the gods and thereby validated their political supremacy and, of course, all the other aspects that were initially discussed as necessary factors to identify a society as a state system.

In conclusion, the rise of the Egyptian state cannot be described in one single narrative, but must be observed from many different angles and in a dynamic interplay of factors that mutually stimulated or influenced each other at different times and in different places.

14. TOMB U-J: A ROYAL BURIAL OF DYNASTY 0 AT ABYDOS

GÜNTER DREYER

Tomb U-j at Abydos represents one of our most important sources for early Egypt. Its architecture and tomb furnishings provide new insight into a stage of the Predynastic period that had hitherto remained obscure. The tomb was discovered in 1988 during the course of the investigations carried out since 1977 by the German Archaeological Institute in Cemetery U, the oldest section of the royal necropolis of Umm el-Qaab at Abydos.[1]

This cemetery comprises approximately seven hundred graves dating to the Naqada I–III period (ca. 3700–3050 BC). Initially a place of interment with mainly simple pit graves, apparently by the Naqada IId period only members of the elite were buried there. In Naqada III the architecture of the graves becomes more sophisticated, all of them being outlined with brick walls and covered with a roof of wooden beams. Nine tombs are subdivided

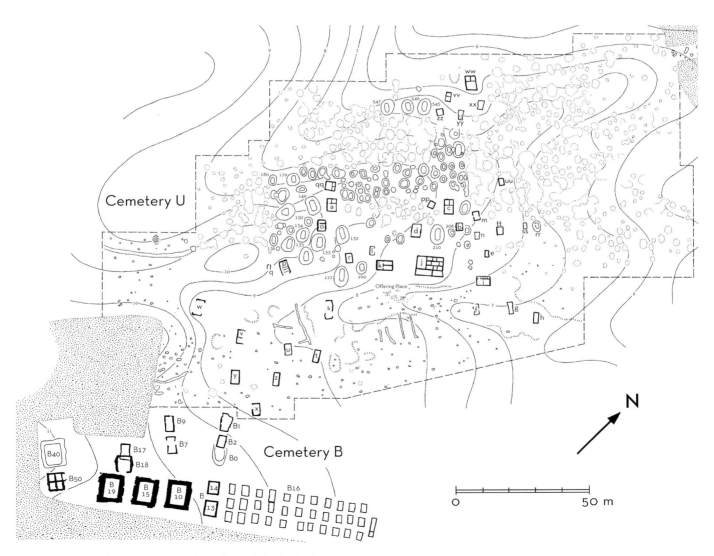

FIGURE 14.1. Plan of Cemeteries U and B at Umm el-Qaab, Abydos

into several chambers. Most of these multi-chamber tombs, as well as the large single-chamber tombs in the southern section, which are to be dated somewhat later, can probably be assigned to Predynastic rulers. These graves are succeeded by the double-chamber tombs of the last Predynastic rulers Irj-Hor, Ka/Sekhen, and Narmer in Cemetery B (fig. 14.1). Cemetery U thus forms the predecessor of the royal necropolis of the First and Second Dynasties.

Tomb U-j is not only the largest but was also the most richly equipped tomb of a Predynastic ruler that has hitherto been discovered. Based on the ceramics, it can be dated to the Naqada IIIa2 period. Radiocarbon tests show that it dates from roughly 150 years before the beginning of the First Dynasty (ca. 3200–3150 BC). Compared to the picture that is derived from several hundred graves in various cemeteries of the Naqada III period, a far higher degree of development is seen in Tomb U-j. The architecture and the finds create a new basis for understanding the Early Dynastic period and it shifts the transition from "prehistoric" to "historic" by about two hundred years.

ARCHITECTURE OF TOMB U-J

Tomb U-j lies at the southern edge of the plateau of Cemetery U, roughly in the middle, between the multi-chamber tombs U-i and U-k, immediately before the edge of the terrain that drops by approximately one meter toward the southeast. The corners of the tomb are oriented roughly to the cardinal points of the compass. In the following description, the longitudinal axis of the burial chamber is taken as the direction north. The tomb is in the shape of a slightly distorted rectangle. It is subdivided into twelve chambers of different sizes. The two southern chambers (11 and 12) were added in a second stage of construction (figs. 14.2–3).

In the first stage of construction the exterior side lengths are north 10.10 m, south 10.30 m, west 5.20 m, east 5.25 m. Presumably 20 x 10 cubits were intended as the dimensions. In the second construction stage the tomb measured north 10.10 m, south 10.60 m, west 8.25 m, and east 8.00 m.

The masonry is approximately 1.53 m (3 cubits) deep. Its upper edge now lies about 0.6 m below the

FIGURE 14.2. Tomb U-j, looking north

desert surface. The exterior walls are two bricks thick (0.44 m). In contrast, the partitions between the chambers (with the exception of the original south wall of the first construction stage) are only 1.5 bricks (0.35 m). A few remnants of roofing were preserved on the north wall and on the west wall of chamber 11 and on the east wall of chambers 7 and 10. This roofing consisted of residues of wood and mats with a mud coating that was preserved up to approximately 10 cm beyond the upper edge of the masonry. Fragments of beams of acacia wood 15–20 cm in diameter were found in chambers 6 and 11. As with the other brick chamber tombs of Cemetery U, the roof seems to have consisted of beams covered with mats and a further layer of brick with a finish coat that extended beyond the masonry on all sides. Most likely a tumulus made of material excavated to create the grave pit was erected above the tomb to provide protection and to mark the place of interment. As in the case of later tombs, it may have symbolized the primordial mound, which, according to ancient egyptian belief is where all life began and which guaranteed the resurrection of the deceased. South of the tomb, a place of sacrifice at which over one hundred small clay dishes and other vessels, two offering plates, and the fragment of a large alabaster basin with an inscription of Narmer were found,

bears witness to a cult establishment lasting into the First Dynasty.

The large chamber (1) in the northwest certainly served for the burial. Remains of a wooden shrine 2.10 x 3.15 m were still identifiable on the floor of the chamber. The nine small chambers (2–10) adjoining the burial chamber to the east are arranged in three rows approximately 2 cubits wide in the north and approximately 3 cubits wide in the middle. In the south the chambers are of different lengths. This group of nine chambers seems to have been intentionally arranged so that the larger central chamber (6) had smaller chambers on its sides and medium-sized chambers at its corners. In contrast, the long chambers (11–12) added on the south side in the second building stage have no relationship to the older subdivision. They were also executed with somewhat less care and with an irregular outline.

All the chambers, including those of the second building stage, are connected to one or more adjacent chambers by slit-like wall openings that take two different forms. In the north–south direction, they are only 0.85 to 1 m high and 0.15 to 0.20 m wide. In the east–west direction they are narrower at 0.10–0.15 m, but taller (1.00–1.20 m), and they have a board embedded at the top much like a door lintel. About 10 cm below this feature is a round wooden crosspiece (now broken out) with a diameter of 2 cm that certainly served the purpose of suspending doormats (which are not preserved). These wall openings resemble features of Old Kingdom false doors with

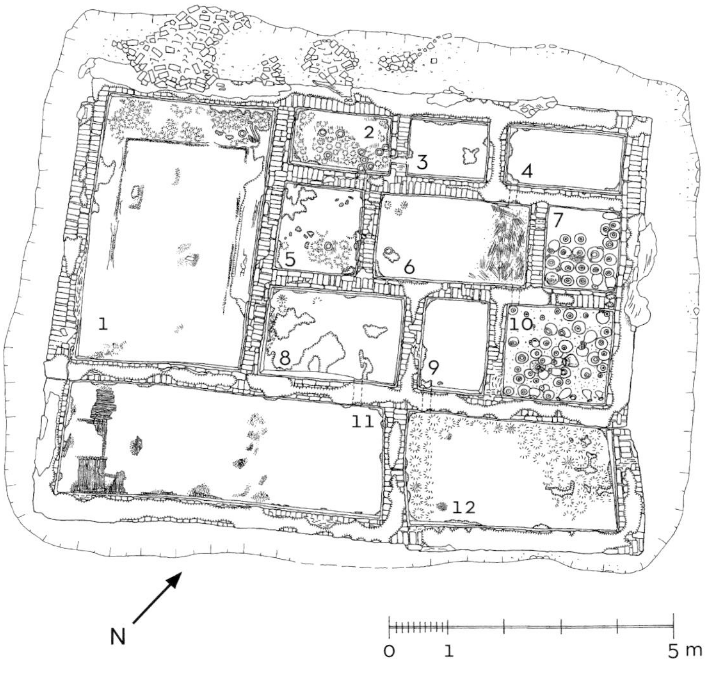

FIGURE 14.3. Plan of Tomb U-j

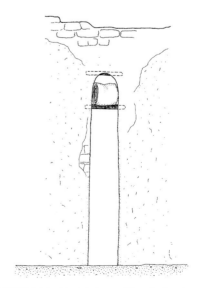

FIGURE 14.4. Model door with rolled mat

The arrangement of the rooms and passages indicates a function-adapted structuring of the building that anticipates the form of a "tripartite house," one that is divided into three sectors: an entranceway, the reception rooms, and the private rooms.

Architectural features of the tomb chambers that correspond to rooms of a house or palace include:

a) Room 5 allows access to room 2 and to its adjacent room 3, both of these having no direct connection to the central hall 6, which suggests that they represent storage rooms;

b) Room 8 is the only one that has a separate entrance and is thus clearly distinguished from all others. This room may represent the living quarters of the domestic staff;

c) Room 6 represents a room for official purposes, functioning as a reception hall;

d) Rooms 4, 7, and 10, which can only be reached via the central hall 6, probably correspond to private rooms, such as a bedroom. Room 9 represents a space that could have been used as a kind of service room for dignitaries or servants.

There are two possible explanations for the different forms of the openings. On the one hand, the east–west passages, which could be blocked by unrolling the doormats, may have been used to separate the different sectors of the building from each other whenever necessary. On the other hand, they may reflect features of daily life: The north–south passages are wider and were left open in order to allow

FIGURE 14.5. Central chamber 6 of Tomb U-j, looking west

their representation of rolled-up mats fixed under the door lintel (fig. 14.4).

These openings were intended to give the owner of the tomb symbolic access to the grave goods. The position and the differing forms of the openings are hardly arbitrary. Just like the groundplan of the tomb, they can be explained by the fact that chambers 2–10 are a model of a house or palace that the deceased would inhabit in the afterlife. The central chamber (6), which would represent a hall, has seven openings (fig. 14.5). The lateral openings in chamber 6 give access to side chambers (4, 9, and 10) that cannot be reached directly. The three openings in its west wall could be interpreted as referring to the three longitudinal tracts of the building. They may have also have been assigned to different ranks of people on official occasions.

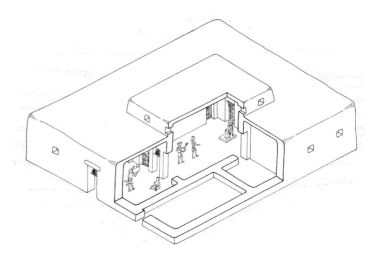

FIGURE 14.6. Reconstruction of a palace

the cooling north wind to sweep through the house (which, however, presumes window openings that, naturally, could not be made in the model house represented by the tomb), whereas the narrower east–west passages could be closed for protection against the sun's heat. Obviously, the tomb is deliberately laid out to reflect the features of a princely residence like that in which the tomb's owner presumably dwelt during his lifetime.

In the attempt to relate the layout of the tomb to a small residential palace (fig. 14.6), a width of 8 cubits (ca. 4 m) has been assumed for the rooms in the middle row, this being still narrow enough to be covered with palm trunks yet leaving enough room for the three passages into the central hall. In order to achieve a harmonious exterior appearance of the roof raised over the central hall in the middle, the rooms of the side tracts were made of equal width at 6 cubits. The proportions of the rooms and the position of the passages approximately correspond to the conditions in the tomb chambers. The wall thicknesses of 2 or 2.5 bricks would suffice to support walls 6 or 8 cubits in height (3.14 or 4.10 m). The overall size of the building was approximately 24 x 30 cubits (ca. 12.6 x 15.7 m).

TOMB FURNISHINGS

The tomb was probably plundered early on, and it was also presumably at least partially uncovered and emptied during the hasty excavations of Émile Amélineau.[2] Nearly all the contents of the chambers were robbed or ransacked and scattered throughout the area of the tomb. Of the original equipment, it is mainly large numbers of ceramics that have remained in situ because they were of no interest to grave robbers, whereas very little is preserved of what was most probably numerous costly grave goods. However, the distribution and the scope of the grave goods can be largely inferred on the basis of individual finds in the chambers and from the environs of the tomb, as well as from the impressions of clay vessels on the floor and walls.

The contents of the tomb include:

Chamber 1: A large wooden shrine with burial in a wooden coffin(?); personal possessions such as a scepter (see fig. 14.9), jewelry, cosmetic utensils, and presumably clothing and weapons. North of the shrine were five rows of Wavy-Handled vessels in three to four(?) layers, and south of the shrine, further rows of wavy-handled vessels, approximately five hundred overall;

Chamber 2: Approximately 190 to 250 Wavy-Handled vessels stacked in three to four layers;

Chamber 3: Coarse Egyptian ceramics (beer jars, etc.) of Nile clay;

Chamber 4: Coarse Egyptian ceramics (beer jars, etc.) of Nile clay;

Chamber 5: In the northern section, presumably Wavy-Handled vessels, and in the southern section, marl jars, perhaps in two layers;

Chamber 6: In the western section, marl jars; in the eastern section, coarse beer jars, plates, baking platters, etc., and plates of Nile clay, some with foodstuffs(?);

Chamber 7: Approximately 120 Canaanite import vessels with wine stacked in four layers;

FIGURE 14.7. Imported wine jars in situ. Tomb U-j, chamber 10

Chamber 8: Presumably only marl jars;

Chamber 9: Presumably coarse Egyptian ceramics;

Chamber 10: Approximately 173 Canaanite import vessels with wine stacked in four layers (fig. 14.7);

Chamber 11: Various grave goods, probably in fourteen or more wooden chests; several sets of ivory game pieces, lengths of fabric, stone vessels, grain, furniture(?);

Chamber 12: Approximately 400 Canaanite import vessels with wine stacked in four layers.

The division of the objects among the chambers was apparently related to the value of the goods. The most important objects were located in the royal chamber (1) and in adjacent chamber 11. Chambers 2–10 and 12 contained only ceramics, sorted according to their type.

The quantity of clay vessels (about 2,000) is striking. The Wavy-Handled vessels that contained oil or fat were apparently especially important for the sustenance of the deceased in the afterlife. They were piled one on top of another in several layers in the burial chamber (1) around the wooden shrine. The

quantity of imported vessels from Palestine/Canaan is also striking, being about seven hundred overall. All of these vessels were sealed with small bullae made of Nile mud (fig. 14.8). According to analyses of the residues of the contents, they contained resinated wine which, allowing for a 6 to 7 liter capacity of each vessel, would total about 4,500 liters in

FIGURE 14.8. Seal impression on imported pottery. Scale of photo 2:1

FIGURE 14.9. Ivory scepter. Tomb U-j. chamber 1. Scale 1:2

FIGURE 14.10. Gold nails. Tomb U-j, chamber 1. Scale 2:1

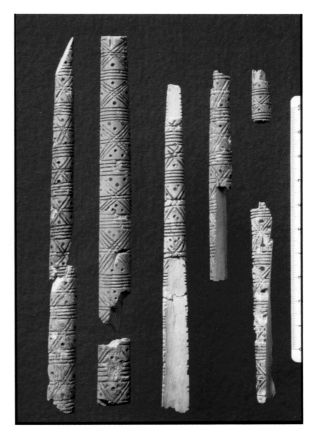

FIGURE 14.11. Obsidian bowl. Tomb U-j, chamber 11. Length 23.6 cm

FIGURE 14.12. Ivory game sticks. Tomb U-j, chamber 11

all. These wine jugs, however, seemed to have been worthless to grave robbers, so that two of the three chambers (7 and 10) filled with them remained largely undisturbed.

In addition to a few fragmentary Wavy-Handled vessels, the nearly empty royal chamber (1) also yielded a scepter (fig. 14.9), a comb, several decorative ivory pins, an obsidian blade, two small gold nails (fig. 14.10), a piece of gold leaf, a spathe shell probably used as a cosmetic bowl, a few particles of galena, small carnelian and turquoise beads, and various ivory fragments.

Chamber 11 served as a sort of treasury with special grave goods, most of which were packed in wooden chests made of cedar. This chamber also yielded fragments of several stone vessels of rose quartz and smoky quartz, dolomite, and a large obsidian dish with a human hand carved in relief on its outer surface (fig. 14.11). The raw material for the dish was probably imported from Ethiopia. Numerous fragments of large game sticks[3] used like dice as well as game pieces were also recovered from that chamber (figs. 14.12–13). Fragments of several cedar chests preserved on the floor probably held lengths

FIGURE 14.13. Ivory game pieces. Tomb U-j, chamber 11

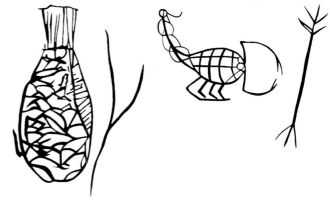

FIGURE 14.15. Two reconstructed ink inscriptions from pottery vessels. Left, fish and tree; right, scorpion and tree

FIGURE 14.14. Inscribed pottery from Tomb U-j

of cloth. Most of the small bone and ivory tags with indications of quantity and notations regarding the source of the goods (see below) were likewise recovered from this chamber. They probably originally belonged to these chests or to other containers.

The most important group of finds from Tomb U-j are the approximately 125 clay vessels and fragments of vessels with ink inscriptions and the approximately 160 small tags of bone or ivory with incised characters. The ink inscriptions are found only on so-called Wavy-Handled vessels that contained oil or fat (fig. 14.14). The inscriptions are composed of one or two large-scale characters, usually a tree or a plant and an animal (scorpion, fish, the pteroceras [*lambis*] shell (figs. 14.15). The key to understanding these notations is the consideration that the only things that can be meaningfully conveyed by them

are the contents of the vessels, their origin, or their disposition (consignee/owner). Since the vessels all contained the same substance — oil or fat — the different inscriptions can hardly refer to the contents. Given the same findspot, an indication of different owners or destinations for the jar is just as unlikely. On the basis of parallels from later periods, the best explanation is that the inscriptions indicate a place of origin, specifically economic establishments (tree = agricultural estate) that were founded by various kings (animal = royal name). The domain that occurs most frequently by far, the "Estate of Scorpion," was certainly founded by the tomb owner himself, whose name can thus be identified as "Scorpion."[4] His estate supplied the principal quantity of grave goods, whereas only lesser quantities were derived from the still-functioning estates of his predecessors (Shell,

FIGURE 14.16. Tags with numbers from Tomb U-j. Scale ca. 2:1

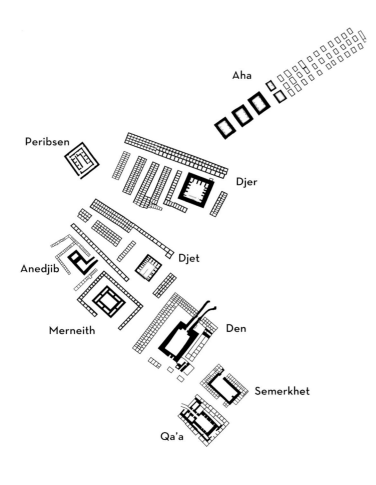

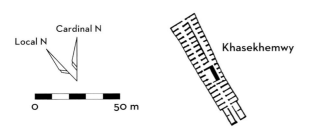

FIGURE 15.2. Plan of Umm el-Qaab showing the subterranean chambers of the Early Dynastic royal tombs (after Dreyer et al. 1996, fig. 1; Dreyer et al. 2003, fig. 1)

all the individuals buried in them died at the same time. Sacrifice is the most plausible explanation.

The royal chambers, while plundered, were all originally equipped with luxury goods. Classes of artifacts are similar to those from the subsidiary graves (Catalog Nos. 19, 83, 91, 102, 112). One unique find from the tomb of Djer was a linen-wrapped arm wearing bracelets; this had been stuffed in a hole and was overlooked for millennia. The bracelets had beads of turquoise, amethyst, lapis, and gold, and in one case the beads were carved in the form of *serekh*s. It seems most likely that this was the arm of Djer himself — the earliest known royal remains from Egypt (fig. 2.12 herein; Petrie 1901a, frontispiece and p. 16).

Despite these similarities, there are also notable differences in these four tombs. Aha was unique in constructing three main tomb chambers. This was in contrast to his predecessors, who had built small double-chambered tombs, and his successors, who built very large single main chambers. Aha's subsidiary graves are also unique, being singly constructed and arranged on only one side of his tomb. Djer's reduction of the number of royal chambers and his arrangement of lines of contiguous subsidiary graves on all sides established traditions that would continue for the rest of the dynasty, though the number of such graves he included would never again be equaled. A feature observed at Djet's tomb was a brick retaining wall that seems to have enclosed a mound of loose sand. This mound was entirely subterranean. It is possible that an additional similar mound would have formed the superstructure of the tomb, and probable that other tombs at Umm el-Qaab would have had similar features now destroyed (Dreyer 1990). Merneith's tomb is simpler than those of her immediate predecessors, without the complicated banks of subsidiary graves at Djer and Djet's tomb.

The four early First Dynasty rulers built their cult structures, usually now called funerary enclosures, in the North Cemetery (fig. 15.3). Again there are both similarities and differences among these monuments. The funerary enclosures seem to have remained quite static in basic form. They had massive mudbrick walls and would have looked from the outside similar to private mastaba tombs of the period: they were simple rectangles in plan, always oriented north–south.[1] Their exterior walls were decorated with a complex pattern of niching on their local east face and simpler niching on their other sides. At the exterior base

the subsidiary population from Aha's tomb complex and is reinforced by the architecture of subsidiary graves from Djer and later kings. Here we see numerous graves — 318 for Djer — constructed in contiguous rows, each grave sharing a wall or walls with others. It would have been difficult if not impossible to roof such graves selectively, making it probable that

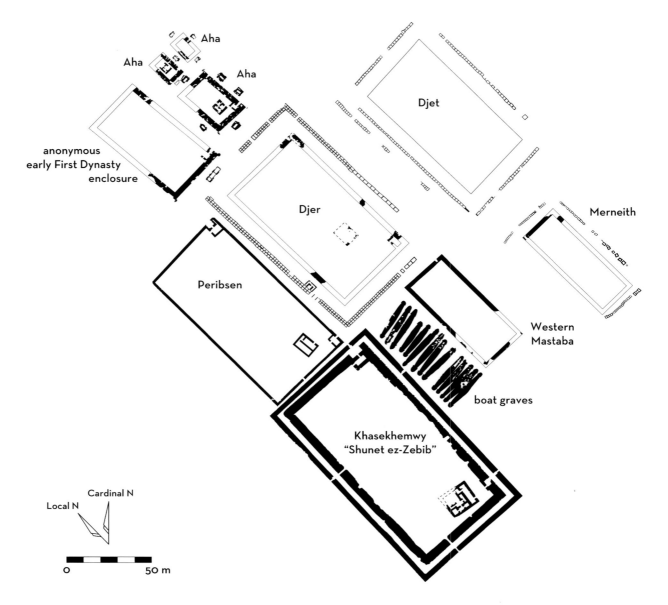

FIGURE 15.3. Plan of the Abydos North Cemetery showing all known funerary enclosures. Courtesy of the Pennsylvania-Yale-Institute of Fine Arts, New York University Expedition to Abydos

of the walls ran a low brick bench. The enclosures had two doorways, one at the southeast and one at the northeast. The southern door was the larger and was usually augmented by a gateway chamber built in the interior of the enclosure. The northern door was blocked with a brick wall in every early First Dynasty example that has been preserved and excavated (O'Connor 2009, p. 171). The interiors of the enclosures were largely open space, though small cult chapels with ceramics and remains of organic offerings were found in some cases; they almost certainly were built in every enclosure. The offerings found

in these chapels clarify the role of enclosures as cult structures. Additional activities may have taken place in temporary structures erected in the open space as indicated by the possible remains of one such structure from the reign of Aha (Bestock 2009, pp. 72–73). All the early First Dynasty enclosures are associated with subsidiary graves.

Interpreting the precise function or functions of these enclosures is difficult. That they were places of cult offering is clear, and they likely housed important royal ceremonies. That they are in some way related to the mortuary establishment of the kings is also clear, both from their location at Abydos and from their use of subsidiary graves. They do not appear, however, to have functioned like later mortuary temples. Most notably, many of the early First Dynasty enclosures show clear evidence of deliberate destruction fairly early in their history, perhaps either when the king died or when his successor built his own enclosure. This suggests that unending mortuary cult was not the point of these monuments, which rather probably served a cultic function for living kings. Perhaps their destruction indicates that they, like the inhabitants of the subsidiary graves, were ritually killed and buried to accompany the deceased king (O'Connor 2009, p. 176; Bestock 2008, p. 47).

The differences between the enclosures of the early First Dynasty rulers in large part mirror the differences in the tombs of this period. Aha was the first to build a positively identified enclosure, though it is possible that earlier ones existed. Aha built three enclosures, one larger than the other two. The larger enclosure had six subsidiary graves, many of which were quite rich, while the smaller enclosures had three graves each; all these graves are constructed separately, like those at Aha's tomb. Though one of these was intact, it was notably poorer than those of the large enclosure (fig. 15.4). It seems likely that the large enclosure was for Aha himself while the smaller two were for others, perhaps queens (Bestock 2009, pp. 98–102).

Djer has one known enclosure. While he thus built fewer than his predecessor Aha, he massively expanded the size and number of subsidiary graves provided, parallel to his innovations at Umm el-Qaab. As at his tomb, Djer's 269 subsidiary graves here were built in contiguous rows. Petrie noted that some of the bodies in these graves showed signs of having been alive at the time of burial (Petrie 1925, p. 8). Djet's enclosure had 154 subsidiary graves; its walls have not yet been found though there is no reason to doubt its existence. Merneith's enclosure is somewhat smaller and narrower than her predecessors', and has seventy-nine known graves.

One further enclosure from this period is known but cannot be attributed to a specific reign on current evidence (but see Bestock 2009, pp. 102–04, for a discussion). This monument is somewhat smaller than Djer's enclosure, to which it is near. Remarkable

FIGURE 15.4. An intact but relatively poor subsidiary burial from one of the small funerary enclosures of Aha in the North Cemetery (photo by Laurel Bestock)

features of this building are the ten donkeys discovered in its southern subsidiary graves — the only subsidiary graves it is known to have had — and the numerous seal impressions found in its southeast gate. These seal impressions provide the relative date of the building and also show that this door was repeatedly closed and sealed, then reopened (O'Connor 2009, pp. 166, 170). This again highlights the important ritual nature of the enclosures.

THE LATER FIRST DYNASTY

The monuments of the later First Dynasty at Abydos appear somewhat different from those of preceding generations, though rapid innovation continued to be the rule. These four kings, Den, Anedjib, Semerkhet, and Qa'a, all built subterranean mudbrick tombs at Umm el-Qaab. These are by and large more tightly centralized around the main chamber than were earlier tombs, with the exception of Merneith's. Stairwells to the royal chamber were built in all these tombs, allowing for the complete construction of a roof and perhaps superstructure before the interment of the king. The number of subsidiary graves also continued its uneven decline from the high of Djer's reign. An even sharper contrast is clear in the North Cemetery, where only one late First Dynasty enclosure is known. This has no human subsidiary graves at all, and cannot be attributed to a particular king.

The first tomb of the second half of the First Dynasty belongs to Den, son of Merneith. Den's tomb complex at Umm el-Qaab is one of the more remarkable of the First Dynasty royal tombs, and indeed his reign as a whole seems to have been a long and important one. Den's tomb has the first of the stairways leading down to the main chamber. The main chamber itself is the largest at Umm el-Qaab and was partly lined in red granite (Petrie 1900, p. 11). The arrangement of the 135 subsidiary graves is dissimilar to earlier kings' tombs; here they are primarily in banks, three deep, on the northwest and northeast sides (fig. 15.2). Many private stelae, often with titles, came from these graves. A unique element of Den's tomb is an enigmatic suite of rooms at the south corner of the complex. This consists primarily of a staircase leading down to a small room that abuts the outside of the main chamber. This room has been convincingly interpreted as a type of serdab designed to hold a statue of the king (Dreyer 1990, pp. 77–78). It has further been suggested that the absence of similar features at earlier and later First Dynasty royal tombs is because a chapel with similar function may usually have been a surface feature (O'Connor 2009, pp. 154–55).

Anedjib's small tomb appears to have been built in haste. It is somewhat irregular, and its sixty-three subsidiary graves have narrow walls. These are arranged in banks somewhat analogous to those of Djer and Djet. Semerkhet and Qa'a built tombs that are more impressive, and which incorporate the new feature of subsidiary graves directly abutting the royal chamber. Semerkhet had sixty-nine such graves, and Qa'a, the last king known to have subsidiary graves at all, only twenty-six. Den, Semerkhet, and Qa'a all have known royal name stelae. In the case of Qa'a, one of his two stelae was found near the surface on the east of the tomb, possibly close to the place it was originally erected. Dozens of pieces of stone bowls suggested to Petrie that a place of offering was located here (Petrie 1900, p. 15).

Only one funerary enclosure from the later First Dynasty is known, probably due to an accident of preservation or discovery rather than a failure of these kings to build such monuments. Called by Petrie the Western Mastaba, it lies some distance southwest of Merneith's enclosure, very close to the southwest of Djer's enclosure (fig. 15.3). The Western Mastaba is similar in scale and proportions to Merneith's enclosure, but the absence of a low bench at the exterior base of the walls and the absence of surrounding rows of subsidiary graves distinguish it from most earlier enclosures. A unique feature probably to be associated with the Western Mastaba is a line of fourteen buried boats along its western side. The wooden hulls of these boats were about 25 meters long and each was given its own low, boat-shaped superstructure. These may be seen as a kind of subsidiary grave holding important things rather than people in this instance being buried to accompany the king in his afterlife, much like the donkeys of the earlier anonymous enclosure (O'Connor 2009, pp. 185–94).

THE SECOND DYNASTY

King Hetepsekhemwy of the Second Dynasty was responsible for the burial of Qa'a, as shown by seal impressions from the latter's tomb (Dreyer et al. 1996, pp. 71–72). Despite this, Hetepsekhemwy and his immediate successors were buried not at Abydos but at Saqqara, far to the north. It is only at the very end of the Second Dynasty that royal tombs are again constructed at Abydos, and this during the perhaps tumultuous reign of Peribsen. Peribsen and his successor, Khasekhemwy, built tombs and enclosures at Abydos, in the same areas used by the First Dynasty kings. Their tombs are still subterranean mudbrick constructions, but they differ significantly from the earlier royal tombs. They have relatively small main chambers that do not appear to have had inner wooden rooms. They have sets of small storage chambers — a very large number in the case of Khasekhemwy — but do not have the subsidiary graves seen in the First Dynasty. Subsidiary graves are also absent from the Second Dynasty funerary enclosures, though in plan these are otherwise more similar to their forebears.

The tomb of Peribsen is unusual for Abydos in having had only a single construction phase; this and its poorly applied plaster seem to indicate hasty construction (Dreyer et al. 2006, pp. 98–99). The form of the tomb is a small central chamber defined by brick walls. A passageway runs around this chamber, separating it from small rooms on the sides that are also defined by mudbrick walls. A further corridor lies between these small rooms and the outer wall. Inscriptions naming Hetepsekhemwy, Raneb, and Ninetjer were found in the tomb, as well as vessels of copper and seal impressions. Two stelae with Peribsen's name and the unique Seth-topped *serekh* were found somewhat out of context on the southwest of the tomb (Petrie 1901a, p. 12).

Peribsen's enclosure, despite its relatively thin walls, is largely similar to those of the First Dynasty. It has the expected niching, gateways, and cult chapel, the latter with substantial remains of offering pottery and seal impressions. It differs from earlier practice in the inclusion of an additional door in the south wall, the elaboration of the north gate, and the absence of any subsidiary graves, human or otherwise.

Peribsen was succeeded by Khasekhemwy. Khasekhemwy's tomb, in contrast to Peribsen's, went through several iterations, starting as a small, almost square construction on a similar plan to Peribsen's tomb. Expansions to both north and south led to corridors flanked with small rooms, apparently for

FIGURE 15.5. The Shunet ez-Zebib, funerary enclosure of Khasekhemwy (photo by Laurel Bestock)

storage. An intriguing feature of Khasekhemwy's tomb is the flattening of the walls of the central part of the tomb to barely half their original height, apparently due to the pressure of a massive weight. Dreyer has suggested that this is due to a superstructure mound, potentially stone reveted, and above ground in this case (Dreyer et al. 2003, pp. 108–11). Some elements of this tomb are familiar to anyone aware of Djoser's Step Pyramid complex: a stone-lined main chamber, an astonishing wealth of stone vessels, and fragments of faience tiles that resemble the well-known subsequent djed pillars. Indeed, Djoser's name itself is found on seal impressions both here and at Khasekhemwy's enclosure, following the common pattern that is taken to indicate the burial of a dead king by his immediate successor (Dreyer 1998, pp. 31–34). Additional artifacts recovered here include copper vessels, copper tools, flint knives, jars filled with grain, beads, basketry, and sealings.

Khasekhemwy's funerary enclosure is the only standing feature in the Abydos North Cemetery, the only Early Dynastic monument at the site to be largely intact (fig. 15.5). It dominates the landscape. With walls five meters thick and ten meters tall, its niches throwing patterns of light and shadow, it gives some sense of the imposing presence that the other enclosures must have had during the brief periods they stood. Khasekhemwy's enclosure, now known as the Shunet ez-Zebib, is both typical of this monument type and unique. In general plan, location, orientation, and features it is entirely familiar. Differences include the presence of additional doorways to the west and south, the construction of a perimeter wall around the entire enclosure, and a much more complex chapel than known previously. The northern gate of Khasekhemwy's enclosure is also unique in not being bricked closed.

That the Shunet ez-Zebib was left standing also marks it as different from its predecessors. Perhaps, as Djoser began the process of erecting a monument in stone intended to stand for eternity, the old practice of burying temples with their kings became obsolete. In its lonely monumentality, Khasekhemwy's enclosure at Abydos marks the end of one era and the beginning of another.

NOTE

[1] In fact, the Abydos enclosures are oriented substantially off a perfect cardinal axis, as can be seen in figure 15.3, but this is because the Nile in the region of Abydos flows from southeast to northwest. The enclosures are oriented parallel to the Nile, even though the river is many kilometers away. As such, these monuments are notionally rather than cardinally aligned to a north–south axis. Notional directions are used in this discussion.

16. THE NARMER PALETTE: A NEW INTERPRETATION

DAVID O'CONNOR

Round about 3000 BC, King Narmer, one of Egypt's earliest rulers, dedicated to the temple of the god Horus at Hierakonpolis a cosmetic palette richly decorated on both faces with representations in low relief (fig. 16.1). While utilized, or at least displayed, before the god in his sanctuary for an extended period, the palette was eventually ceremonially buried in the vicinity of the temple, along with other items of sacred furniture that were considered otiose. Almost 5,000 years later, excavators recovered Narmer's Palette (Quibell 1900; Quibell and Green 1902), which is now on permanent display in the Egyptian Museum, Cairo. The Egyptian authorities consider it so unique that, unlike many of Tutankhamun's treasures, it is never permitted to leave the country for exhibit abroad.

Ever since its discovery and initial publication the Narmer Palette has stimulated much discussion among Egyptologists who are attracted by its aesthetic qualities — it is superbly carved in terms of the craftsmanship of its day — and by the challenge presented to any attempt to read or interpret the scenes upon it (fig. 16.2). Many theories have been put forward, but they remain inconclusive because,

FIGURE 16.1. The Narmer Palette, recto and verso, reign of King Narmer, Dynasty 0, before ca. 3150 BC. OIM C209

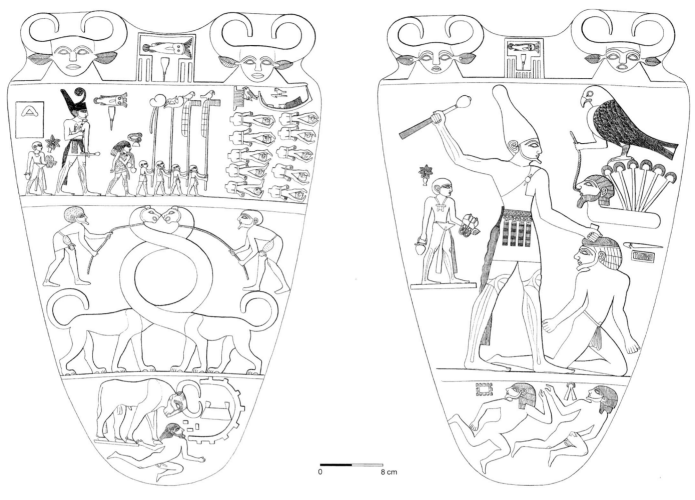

FIGURE 16.2. Line-drawing of the Narmer Palette (after Wengrow 2006, pp. 42–43, figs. 2.1, 2.2)

to modern observers at least, the actions and beings depicted on the palette are highly ambiguous so far as their possible meanings are concerned (O'Connor 2004; Köhler 2002). In fact, when asked to provide an essay on the palette, I assumed that I would simply sample some of the theories, and point out the problems associated with them. However, to my surprise I discovered that recent scholarship seemingly related only peripherally to the Narmer Palette actually opened up a major and apparently hitherto unsuspected perspective as to its possible meaning! I expand upon this point below, hopefully justifying the ambitious subtitle of this essay, "A New Interpretation."

First, however, some preliminary observations are needed. In terms of context, and insofar as the difficult archaeological circumstances at the site permit interpretation, the temple at Hierakonpolis seems to have long antedated the reign of Narmer

(Adams 1999; O'Connor 1992). Scanty but significant remains of the early temple were found in situ, most importantly a stone threshold for a gateway or doorway leading into the temple or its court. Nearby rose a massive mound of sand, encased in stone masonry; some scholars believe the main temple at Hierakonpolis was situated on the mound, but the site with the in situ threshold is more likely, especially as a series of later temples were built in exactly the same place. Originally, temple and mound were not shielded from the surrounding town, but at some point a massive brick enclosure was built around them, perhaps in Narmer's time or thereabouts, although some would prefer later dates.

The Narmer Palette is relatively small. Shield-shaped, and made of fine-grained, dark gray-green siltstone, the palette is only 63.5 centimeters long, quite tiny compared to the high, relief-carved walls that survive in some later Egyptian temples. Yet the

FIGURE 16.3. An early form of cosmetic palette. Height 25.3 cm (after Spencer 1993, fig. 24)

for the grinding and mixing of minerals used as cosmetics (fig. 16.3).

Conventionally, the two faces of the Narmer Palette are referred to as the obverse and the reverse. On the obverse face a circular, undecorated area was intended for manipulating cosmetics; this circular space was outlined by two magnificently carved "serpopards" who are each apparently restrained by a leash grasped by a human attendant. Serpopards are mythical creatures found on some earlier palettes and other items and ultimately were derived from the iconography of contemporary Mesopotamia. However, most of the subject matter on Narmer's Palette is thoroughly Egyptian in character, including Narmer's crowns, costumes, and regalia; the birds and animals depicted; and the pictorial references to the marshy environments fringing the Nile Valley and extending more widely throughout the Egyptian Delta.

Above the area utilized for cosmetics is a complex scene (fig. 16.4). King Narmer is shown in procession, perhaps having emerged from a palace, indicated schematically by a rectangle containing a symbol, on the far left. Narmer is preceded by standard bearers and followed by a sandal bearer. The emphasis on the king's bare feet on both obverse and reverse suggests that the ground he trod on was in some sense sacred, perhaps associated with a temple at one level, but at a higher, parallel one perhaps part of the divine world itself. The processing king is approaching a scene that likely looked as grisly to the ancient Egyptians as it does to us. In two rows are

representations on it have a monumental quality; boldly modeled figures of men and other creatures, some on a comparatively large scale, are arranged in formally well-organized compositions. And in fact the palette itself is a monumentalization in that — like a few earlier palettes — it is a much enlarged version of the small, often undecorated palettes of the same or similar stone used by prehistoric Egyptians

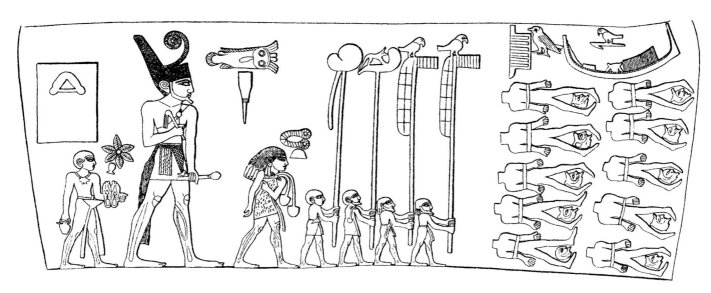

FIGURE 16.4. Enlargement of the upper register, obverse face of the Narmer Palette (after Wengrow 2006, p. 43, fig. 2.2)

depicted ten headless corpses; prostrate on their backs, bound at the elbows, each has his head neatly placed between his legs, and each head — save one — is neatly topped by its owner's severed penis (Davies and Friedman 1998). Mysteriously, a boat seemingly floats over the corpses and is in turn surmounted by a harpoon-holding hawk, certainly to be identified as the god Horus, already tutelary deity of Egyptian kings. In front of the boat is yet another bird and what looks like the leaf of a door or gate, intended to be swung on its pivots.

A scene at the bottom of the obverse depicts a walled settlement ravaged by the horns of a magnificent bull, perhaps a visual metaphor for the king himself, and expressive of his aggressive power against foreign foes. And indeed, also trampled by the bull is the corpse of an alien, perhaps a personification of the community decimated by the bull's power.

The top of Narmer's Palette displays the same configuration on both faces. On either side of each face rear up two horned heads, whose ears are bovine but whose features are human. They represent the goddess Bat and in this context signify "heaven." Between each pair of heads, the upper edge of the palette declines in height.

On the reverse face of the palette is an eye-catching representation, all the more so in that it occupies most of the palette's surface. King Narmer menacingly raises a mace, and with his other hand grasps the hair of a kneeling man of un-Egyptian type, who is seemingly paralyzed with terror as he anticipates a deadly blow. Above the alien is a complex, somewhat emblematic group. A handsome hawk (again, the god Horus) with beautifully rendered wing feathers sprouts a hand holding a rope leading down to an alien head projecting from an area of marshy land in which papyrus stalks grow. The rope, attached to a nose ring, signifies that Horus has brought the people of this personified marsh or "papyrus land" in subjection to the king, rendering them open to the king's domination as expressed by the smiting pose.

Below this visually striking scene, at the bottom of the reverse face, are two males, seemingly nude, and again un-Egyptian in appearance. The two may be corpses, one of whom has had his penis and scrotum removed; the other may be depicted as circumcised, respected as a custom acceptable to Egyptian norms.

Interesting efforts have been made to construct a narrative, linking both faces, from the representations described above, including theories that require the assumed viewer or audience to keep moving around the palette (supposedly held in place vertically with both faces displayed) in order to follow the story (Davis 1992) (fig. 16.5). Such theories, however, involve assumptions that are hard to prove, and in any case the primary audience for the palette was probably the god in whose sanctuary the palette was displayed — and such a divine being could instantly comprehend any meanings the palette was intended to convey without having to engage in the movements of a human viewer around the object.

Instead of tracing a narrative around the palette, the imagery employed on the two faces may be discrete but complementary entities (O'Connor 2002–2004). On Narmer's Palette and earlier ones (when decorated on both faces; some were not) the imagery on the reverse face was structured so as not to cross the central vertical axis, and to convey the message that the frontier between order and chaos (Maat and Isfet, in later Egyptian usage) had to be sharply defined. The apotropaic or protective nature of this imagery was appropriate, since the reverse face was subject to pollution, as it would be handled during rituals and be laid down on surfaces when not in use; the potential pollution had to be prevented from passing through to the obverse face, used for the cosmetics ultimately applied to the divine image.

On the obverse face, around the circular, undecorated space dedicated to cosmetic preparation, imagery was structured by a circularized compositional structure, in which the figures of animals or humans substantially overlapped with the vertical central axis. Here, another aspect of the relationship between chaos and order was celebrated; the anarchic energy of the former was the essential potential for life, but had to be transformed into the actualized life that would sustain the cosmos. This theme was appropriate to the obverse, upon which unattractive minerals were transformed into colored cosmetics utilized in rituals that empowered divine images.

More generally, debate about the Narmer Palette has been sharply divided as to whether any of the events depicted on it referred to historical ones that had actually occurred, or instead to ceremonies, repeated from one reign to another, celebrating the king's capacity to coerce and dominate in general.

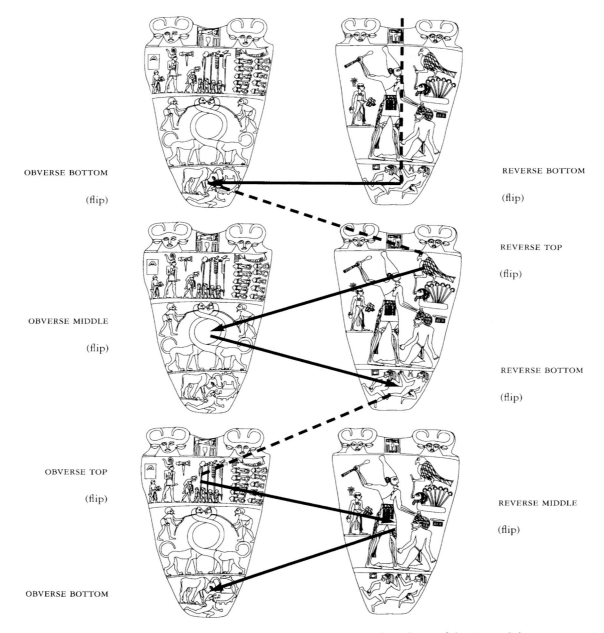

OBVERSE BOTTOM

(flip)

REVERSE BOTTOM

(flip)

REVERSE TOP

(flip)

OBVERSE MIDDLE

(flip)

REVERSE BOTTOM

(flip)

OBVERSE TOP

(flip)

REVERSE MIDDLE

(flip)

OBVERSE BOTTOM

FIGURE 16.5. Diagrammatic representation of a suggested narrative sequence through part of the Narmer Palette representations (after Davis 1992, fig. 42, bottom 3 images)

On the one hand, scholars such as John Baines suggest the types of representation in question "may not record specific exploits of the rulers who commissioned them, but rather may express general aspirations and conformity to norms of rulership" (2007, p. 122). On the other hand, others suggest the reverse-face scene references an actual "victory over an enemy based in the delta," the ruler of which was named Wash, according to the phonetic reading of the signs placed next to the kneeling alien (Kemp 2006, p. 84);

or that scenes on both faces celebrate Narmer as the first attested unifier of all Egypt (Yurco 1995; see also Schulman 1991/92).

An ivory label, used to date the storage of artifacts to be deposited in a royal tomb, was recently discovered at Abydos and displays imagery similar to that on the obverse face of Narmer's Palette (fig. 16.6). The label imagery provides the name assigned to a specific year in Narmer's reign and to some scholars refers to a "definite historical event" (Dreyer

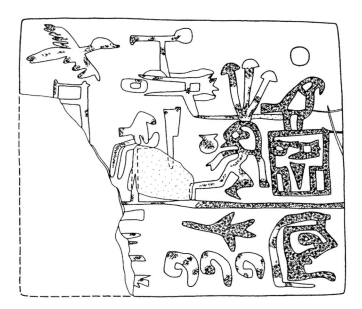

FIGURE 16.6. Ivory label commemorating Narmer, who is represented directly as a catfish (an element in his name as written) preparing to smite an alien who has papyrus stalks projecting from his head. Width 7.5 cm (after Wengrow 2006, p. 205, fig. 9.13)

2000), but the imagery remains ambiguous enough that a major royal ceremony of only a generalized nature might have been involved.

As noted above, recent research on aspects of royal regalia, including crowns, has opened up new perspectives on the Narmer Palette, perspectives which appear not to have been explored in depth up to this point. Before I do so, some preliminary remarks are necessary.

Like any artifact or artwork, the Narmer Palette should be studied in its own right, in terms of its specific form and representational program, and of what we know about the context in which it was used. But the Narmer Palette had a past when it was made, and a long future extended before it as well; both its past and future are involved in the interpretation of the palette's possible meanings. On the one hand, Narmer's Palette, as regards its material, form, and representations, relates to a series of earlier and similar palettes (Petrie 1953; Davis 1992) (fig. 16.7). However, certain aspects of Narmer's Palette relate to images and concepts that were to continue to be viable for virtually the entire course of traditional Egyptian culture. For example, the smiting scene on the obverse face (which had simpler antecedents; Köhler 2002) is repeatedly used thereafter on temple pylons and elsewhere, and as late as the Roman period (see Hall 1986) (fig. 16.8). I intend to show below

that other imagery on the palette also resonates powerfully with later materials, materials which vary widely in date and style, but which can legitimately be used to interpret Narmer's Palette. As Katja Goebs (2008) has shown, the diverse themes involved go back as early as the Pyramid Texts inscribed on the walls of Old Kingdom royal burial chambers, which in turn may well incorporate ideas that go back another seven centuries, to the time of Narmer.

The scene most impacted upon by reference to recent research is the upper one on the obverse face (fig. 16.4) showing the king processing toward two rows of decapitated corpses. Diana Patch (1995) has pointed out that here Narmer wears a most unusual and rare costume, all or much of which appears occasionally on subsequent kings as late as about 1250 BC. Called by Patch the "Lower Egyptian" costume, it involves representational symbols such as references to marshy environments, net-like containers, and an amulet in the form of a swallow (fig. 16.9). Later, these elements in their totality symbolize the daily (re-)birth of the sun god Re; Re is not definitely attested at this time, but he or another form of the sun god are likely referred to here. In addition, Narmer is wearing the Red Crown, which is later associated with Lower Egypt, the northern of the "Two Lands" ruled by Egyptian kings, but also has other, more

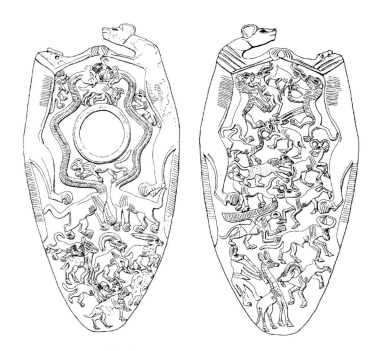

FIGURE 16.7. An earlier decorated palette, also found at Hierakonpolis (after Wengrow 2006, p. 180, fig. 9.3)

FIGURE 16.8. Ptolemy XII depicted striking enemies on the pylon of the Temple of Edfu (photo by Emily Teeter)

the continuation of the solar cycle (sunrise – sunset – sunrise) upon which that vitality depended. Moreover, the corpses of Re's enemies are subsequently cooked or otherwise treated so he can consume them, and combine the power each opponent represented into a single great entity, the "one who makes himself out of millions" (Goebs 2008, p. 371).

Thus, I would suggest that here in this scene Narmer, via his crown and costume, is assuming the identity of one of Re's divine defenders, and perhaps, at another level, of Re himself, in the context of a royal ceremonial which is seen as analogous to and supportive of these cosmos-shaking and -shaping events. This in turn suggests the slaughtered men represent Re's defeated enemies, laid out neatly as prepared foods for his consumption. Their appearance in fact evokes later descriptions of these maltreated foes, who are described as beheaded, and bled-dry as a result, or as beheaded fish (cf., e.g., Goebs 2008, pp. 222–23, 258). Moreover, the net-like aspect of the "hip-drape" which is part of the "Lower Egyptian" costume recalls the many references to Re's enemies being literally ensnared in a net before their destruction and consumption (Patch 1995).

generalized meanings. Specifically, the Red Crown is a symbol of blood, slaughter, and destruction and its red color was intended to equate with "fresh or dark shimmering light or color, appertaining, for example, to blood" (Goebs 2008, p. 163 and passim).

Goebs does not discuss the Narmer Palette in detail, but has demonstrated that, in general, the Red Crown is not only a symbol of sunrise, but refers to the bloody battles (reflected in the red-filled dawn sky) that had to be fought against the enemies and competitors that needed to be slain in order for the sun god Re to achieve, via tremendous effort, his daily rebirth. His reappearance in the morning sky commemorated the original creation of the cosmos and simultaneously ensured that each repeated sunrise would revitalize the cosmos and guarantee

FIGURE 16.9. Enlarged figure of Narmer wearing the "Lower Egyptian" costume; note the beaded apron (including papyrus and marsh-plant motifs), net-like hip-drape, and swallow amulet (after Wengrow 2006, p. 43, fig. 2.2)

The linking of the decapitated corpses to the dramatic events associated with sunrise is reinforced by the assemblages of signs immediately above them. These have been interpreted in various ways, but in fact they seem to form an unusually early version of the later conceptualization of the "morning bark" that carries the reborn sun god into the sky. The vessel on the Narmer Palette is provided with the appropriately high prow and stern, and preceded by a swallow, a bird whose distinctive behavior associates it strongly with sunrise in later iconography (fig. 16.10). On the Narmer Palette, the door leaf in front of the swallow may signify the doors which, in later sources, open to permit the reborn sun to enter the sky.

The upper register on the obverse then seems to be a rendition both of the drama of solar rebirth, and of royal ceremonials that are analogous or parallel to this process. This possibility would support the notion that the palette's overall iconography records generalized ceremonies rather than specific historical events. More importantly, however, it also seems possible that this re-reading of this particular register might influence our interpretation of all the representations on both faces. It is generally recognized that the imagery is cosmologically structured, with the semi-bovine goddesses at the top signifying sky or heaven, and the lower registers on each face relating to earth, and possibly even the netherworld as well. However, it is striking that the distinctive shape of the palette's top recalls the twin-peaked mountain that in later iconography is part of the word for *akhet* (horizon), the liminal zone between day and night, and the locale for solar death (sunset) and rebirth (sunrise). This latter meaning is especially appropriate if the upper register on the obverse does indeed celebrate the solar rising.

Moreover, the smiting king on the palette's reverse wears the distinctive White Crown, emblematic of southern Egypt, but also symbolizing generalized and brilliant light of both the moon and stars, and also of the full daytime sun (Goebs 2008). In either case, reference may be being made to a cosmological rather than historic event. Perhaps here the king's generalized victories over his enemies on earth are depicted as paralleling that of the sun god over his on the obverse; and perhaps Narmer's victims on the reverse are directly equated with the sun god's enemies. "Marsh" or "Papyrus Land," for example, may evoke not the Egyptian Delta, but the danger-filled marshes and wetlands associated with the sun god's morning struggles and later said to cluster around the Akhet. In this context, the signs next to the kneeling alien's head may not be a name, but instead a description of an act — "striking down the wetlands," for example. It is worth noting that the single barbed harpoon utilized here is exactly paralleled by the one held by the falcon figure hovering over (and defending?) the apparent solar bark on the obverse (Kaplony 1958).

These are all issues requiring further research. However, it is a testimony to the protean strength of the imagery on Narmer's Palette that it can continue to generate yet further hypotheses (as all of our interpretations must be) as to its meaning.

FIGURE 16.10. (*a*) door leaf; swallow, sun god's morning bark, with harpoon-grasping Horus hawk above (from Wengrow 2006, p. 43, fig. 2.2); and (*b*) line-drawing from the coffin of Pasebakhaemipet (Brooklyn 08.480.2B), showing a representation of the sun god's morning bark, with swallow on prow (after Patch 1995, p. 111, fig. 14)

CATALOG OF OBJECTS

THE PHYSICAL SETTING: THE NILE VALLEY

The Nile Valley was especially suited to incubate a rich civilization. The river provided food and transportation, and its silt ensured an endless supply of fertile land to grow crops. The narrow floodplain compacted settlements and attracted wild game.

The early Egyptians were careful observers of their environment, and animals and hunting scenes are common artistic motifs. They also exploited the abundant natural resources; using clay from the banks of the Nile or from the desert to make pottery, quarrying stone for vessels and palettes, and carving bone, ivory, and shell into personal ornaments. ET

1

1. JAR WITH HUNTING SCENE

Baked clay (Nile silt)
Naqada I, ca. 4000–3800 BC
Abydos, Cemetery C
Gift of the Egyptian Exploration Fund, 1908–1909
H: 32.2 cm
OIM E8923

Although limited in number of examples, hunting scenes are the most important group of figurative scenes on White Cross-Lined pottery. This jar, found in a tomb at Abydos just over a century ago, is exceptional because of the orientation of the scene. Despite the poor preservation of the jar itself, one can easily recognize three rows of animals on its neck. Normally, the decoration encircles the vessel oriented to its horizontal plane, making it difficult to recognize whether or not the scene has a beginning and an end. In this case, the organization of the scene is obvious, but the order of the animal rows becomes the problem, especially if one assumes that it represents a continuous line of animals divided into three registers. When following the drawing in the original publication (fig. C1), the upper animal row consists of two gazelles or ibexes, followed by two dogs. The first dog bites the hind leg of the second gazelle/ibex. The row below shows one gazelle/ibex followed by two dogs. Below this are three hippopotami preceded by a single dog. The position of the dogs is significant. In the two upper rows with desert animals, they clearly refer to hunting with dogs, but dogs have no part in hippopotamus hunting. In whatever order the rows are considered, the dog preceding the hippopotami will always follow a row ending with another dog, suggesting that the row with hippopotami is also a reference to hunting.[1]

Remarkably, the human hunters are not represented. This is also the case for nearly all the desert hunting scenes on White Cross-Lined ware. In scenes of hippopotamus hunting, the hunters are occasionally depicted, but often only the harpoons with their floaters are shown. For the arrangement of the composition on this jar neither of them apparently were suitable, which may have been the

reason for the combination of the dog preceding the hippopotami.

Because hunting had hardly any economic importance during Predynastic times but was an event of social display in a ritual context (see "Iconography of the Predynastic and Early Dynastic Periods" in this volume) the dogs on this jar can by themselves be considered symbols of power.   SH

NOTE

[1] For another White Cross-Lined vessel with the combination of desert animals, hippopotami, and a single dog, see Hartung 2010.

PUBLISHED

Ayrton and Loat 1911, pl. 27.12

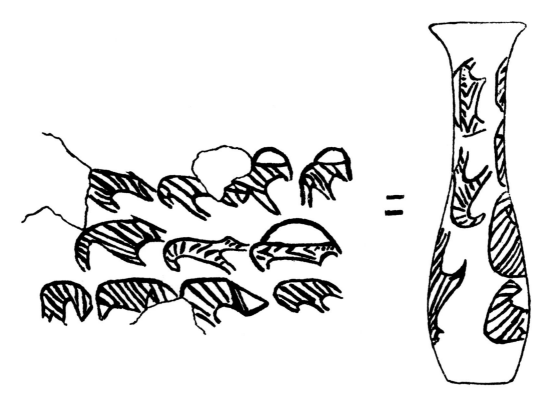

FIGURE C1. Sketch of the vessel from the original publication, Ayrton and Loat 1911, pl. 27.12

2, view a

2, view b

2.   PAINTED VESSEL

Baked clay, pigment
Naqada II, ca. 3800–3300 BC
Purchased in Luxor, 1920
H: 19; D: 13 cm
OIM E10762

The buff-colored, painted pottery of the Naqada II period preserved scenes of the Nilotic environment. This tall, ovoid jar has a flat base, short neck, everted rim, and two horizontally pierced cylindrical lugs. Between the lugs are two curved river craft with blunt ends being rowed to the left, although the oars slant from the right. Each boat has two simple cabins and three large fronds in the bow. Each vessel has a standard attached to the rear cabin with streamers trailing behind. Each standard is a combination of horns and possibly bows. The lug handles are covered with panels of horizontal wavy lines that extend above and below. Below each lug is a large plant with curved, drooping fronds that is probably a palm. Below one boat is a row of tall birds, either flamingoes or ostriches, above a row of triangles. On the other side below the boat is a hide or apparatus suspended from a pole by a double cord. A pair of wavy lines circle the bottom of the vessel and there is a panel of them below one of the plants. The vessel bottom has two pairs of wavy lines crossing in the center, while the rim has a band of cross-hatching.   BBW

3

3. CARVED TUSK

Ivory
Naqada II or earlier, ca. 3800 BC
Purchased in Cairo, 1920
L: 13.0; W: 1.3 cm
OIM E10688

Hippopotamus hunting is an important element of Predynastic iconography that continued into Dynastic times. Hippopotamus tusks must have been an important visual result of the actual hunt, and as trophies they may have become symbols of the power of their owner. Actual hippopotamus tusks are already present in a few Badarian graves and presumably from this, different types of amulets are developed during the Naqada I and early Naqada II periods (Hendrickx and Eyckerman in press). Among them, tusks decorated with geometric patterns and perforations allowing attachment. Furthermore, many imitations of tusks are known, not only in hippopotamus ivory but also in bone and different kinds of stone. These "tags" are generally smaller in size and often flat instead of round. Tusks and tags are frequently found in cemeteries but also in settlement sites, indicating that they have no specific funerary intentions but were objects used in daily life. This points in a general manner to an apotropaic, magical function. SH

4

4. BRACELET

Shell
Dynasty 1, ca. 3100–2890 BC
Abydos, Umm el-Qaab, tomb X 51
Gift of the Egypt Exploration Fund,
1900–1901
D: 6.3; T: 0.5 cm
OIM E5912

Shell, with its iridescent surface, was highly prized for jewelry. Of special importance was mother-of-pearl from *Chambardia acruata* (formerly *Aspatharia rubens*). As early as the mid-fourth millennium BC this shell was traded from Egypt to the Levant (see "Early Interaction between Peoples of the Nile Valley and the Southern Levant" in this volume).

Many examples of these shell bracelets are very small and could fit only a child, suggesting that they were either heirlooms preserved from one's youth, or that they were votives made for the tomb (Bagh 2004, p. 599). This bracelet was recovered from one of the subsidiary burials surrounding the tomb of Anedjib. ET

5. DECORATED OSTRICH EGG

Egg, pigment
Naqada I, ca. 3800–3300 BC
Purchased in Luxor, 1925
L: 16.4; W: 12.7 cm
OIM E12322

Ostrich eggs were occasionally used as containers and also for making beads. Recently, a significant number has been found at Hierakonpolis in elite funerary contexts dating to the early Naqada II period (Muir 2009). At least some of them had been blown and they were obviously not intended as food for the afterlife. The deposition of ostrich eggs must have been ritualistic and might be part of rites that include symbols of rebirth.

Decorated ostrich eggs are rare and this example is one of the very few complete ones. The decoration consists of two main parts, a desert hunting scene and an enigmatic zigzag motif. In the hunt scene, the large animal chased by a relatively small dog is most probably to be identified as an oryx because of its long, backward-curving horns. The identification of the two other animals is

more problematic. The larger with the smaller on top is considered by Kantor (1948, p. 49) to be a female with her young. However, it might also be another hunting scene in which a dog is on top of a chased gazelle(?), for which parallels can be found in rock art (Storemyr 2009, fig. 8). Between the large animals are two enigmatic objects that can be compared with animal skins on poles known from decorated pottery, considered to be funerary symbols (see "Iconography of the Predynastic and Early Dynastic Periods" in this volume, and Catalog No. 2). This might confirm the interpretation of the eggs themselves as referring to rebirth in the afterlife.

The meaning of the zigzag motif is far less obvious because it is unparalleled in Predynastic iconography. However, the curved ends of the lines

5, side a

are most probably to be seen as bird heads, most of them probably ostriches, a frequent theme on a variety of Predynastic objects. Furthermore, ostriches are often shown in closely packed rows, comparable to the overall effect of zigzag lines. It can be suggested that the strange design represents an attempt to make the idea of a row of ostriches visible from different viewpoints because an egg has no fixed point for viewing.

The linear filling of the animal representations can be compared with that of White Cross-Lined pottery, which is an important argument for attributing this object of unknown provenance to the early Predynastic period.   SH

PUBLISHED

Kantor 1948

5, side b

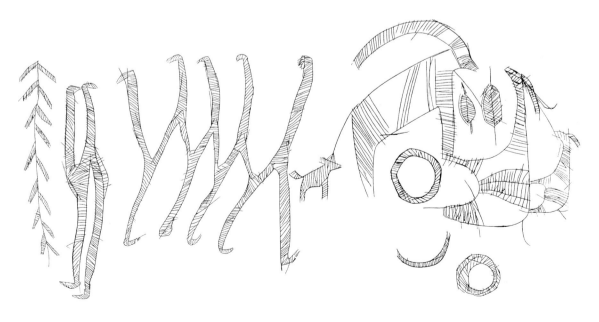

6

6. FISH-SHAPED PALETTE

Siltstone, shell
Naqada IIA–IIIA, ca. 3800–3200 BC
Abadiya, grave B424
Gift of the Egypt Exploration Fund,
1898–99
L: 10.5; W: 7.2 cm
OIM E5256

Of all the zoomorphic forms taken by palettes in the mid-fourth millennium BC, it is fish that were the most popular. The design of such pieces makes it difficult to tell which species of fish is represented, but the tilapia fish seems to be the most frequently portrayed. Palettes resembling the genera *Mormyrus* and *Tetraodon* are also known (Brewer and Friedman 1989, p. 9). Upon the smooth surface of the palette colored materials were ground together with fat or resin, and this pigment was then applied to the body, most likely around the eyes. Such artifacts

have been recovered from habitation sites, but it is from Predynastic graves that palettes are best known, from small, quite sparse tombs to large, well-furnished ones.

The choice of the tilapia fish in this latter context might be understood in relation to the later Egyptian association between this fish and eternal life (Gamer-Wallert 1970). One of the names for tilapia was *wadj*, which was connected with the notion of youthfulness and greenness, as well as being the same term for the green pigment — malachite — most often prepared on the palette itself in mortuary arenas (Brewer and Friedman 1989, p. 9). In Predynastic burials, malachite is frequently found between the hands of the deceased, sometimes in a leather pouch or reed basket. AS

PUBLISHED

Marfoe 1982, p. 22

12

12. JAR WITH WAVY HANDLES

Baked clay
Naqada IId1, ca. 3400 BC
Abadiya, tomb B160
By exchange with the Metropolitan
Museum of Art, 1950
H: 19; D: 13 cm
OIM E26072

The wavy handles on this Egyptian-made jar were copied from vessels imported from the Levant. The wavy handles on Egyptian vessels became increasingly abstracted until they were simplified to represent a rope or string around the upper part of the vessel.   ET

13.   STRAIGHT-SPOUTED JAR

Baked clay
Naqada IIC–D/Middle Uruk period,
ca. 3500 BC
Naqada, tomb T 1108
Excavated by Petrie and Quibell, 1895
H: 17.5; D: 16.0 cm
OIM E858

13

This red-slipped and vertically burnished spouted jar was used to pour liquids, perhaps filtered water, beer, or wine. It is one of a group of objects that suggests Predynastic Egyptians were in contact with the growing urban civilization of Mesopotamia as early as 3500 BC (Stevenson in press).

The jar itself was made by Egyptian potters using local Nile clay and in the local ceramic tradition of Red-Burnished ware, but its form, particularly its spout, was unusual in Predynastic Egypt. However, similar vessels were commonly made and used in the early cities of Mesopotamia like Nippur or Uruk (e.g., Hansen 1965). This contrast of local manufacture and foreign style suggests that Egyptian potters were familiar with elements of the Mesopotamian ceramic tradition from having seen Mesopotamian vessels that were brought to Egypt.

When Petrie excavated the cemetery at Naqada, he identified this pot and other material as non-Egyptian and suggested that the assemblage was made by a "new race" or "Dynastic race" that had migrated into the Nile Valley and developed what became Dynastic Egypt. This theory has been rejected by archaeologists for many reasons and instead today these cultural borrowings — which also include use of cylinder seals, elements of figural art, and perhaps niched mudbrick architecture — suggest trade connections with Mesopotamia and subsequent local imitation.

This particular jar was placed in a tomb on the southeastern edge of the Naqada cemetery. The other objects found in the tomb include two other pots — a painted Decorated ware jar and a Rough ware pot (Payne 1987) — and a polished pebble (Baumgartel 1970), perhaps used for grinding pigment or for burnishing ceramics. Petrie distributed these four objects after the excavation to four different museums.   GE

23

23. BOTTLE

Baked clay
Naqada II, ca. 3800–3300 BC
Naqada
Gift of Petrie and Quibell, 1895
H: 20.7; D: 10.9 cm
OIM E1826

24. JAR

Baked clay
Naqada II, ca. 3800–3300 BC
By exchange with the Metropolitan
Museum of Art, 1950
H: 12.40; D: 0.85 cm
OIM E18253

24

25. BLACK-TOPPED JAR WITH POT MARK

Baked clay
Naqada I, ca. 3800–3300 BC
Naqada, Main Cemetery, tomb 1426
Gift of the Egypt Exploration Fund, 1895
H: 23.4; D: 11.0 cm
OIM E1814

25

In 1895, Flinders Petrie excavated thousands of graves in the Main Cemetery at the site of Naqada. In tomb 1426, he found a skeleton in a contracted position, three carved ivory tusks, and a large quantity of Black-Topped pottery. Vessels such as this represent an early stage of ceramic production, at which time pottery was hand-made. Similar Black-Topped vessels are found at many sites in Egypt at this time, indicating widespread uniformity in their production.

This particular vessel, like some of the other vessels in the tomb, bears a pot mark. Incised into the baked clay, this pot mark resembles the later hieroglyphic number "10" — an inverted "U"-shaped sign. EVM

PUBLISHED (SELECTED)

Baumgartel 1970, pl. 42; Petrie and Quibell 1896, pp. 28, 43–44; pls. 19.27d, 55.387; MacArthur 2010, p. 122

26. POLISHED RED-WARE DISH

Baked clay
Naqada Ic–II, ca. 3800 BC
Naqada, tomb T 1507
Gift of Petrie and Quibell, 1895
H: 6.7; D: 17.4 cm
OIM E1708

Polished Red-ware is contemporary with Black-Topped vessels and it appears in the same range of forms. It was once thought that the Black-Topped vessels all originated as Red-ware which were then transformed in a secondary firing. ET

PUBLISHED
Petrie and Quibell 1896, p. 29

26

27

27. ROUGH-WARE JAR

Baked clay
Naqada II, ca. 3800–3300 BC
Abadiya, grave B 217
Gift of the Egypt Exploration Fund, 1898–1899
H: 19.7; D: 9.3 cm
OIM E5330

Petrie's category of Rough-ware (R-ware) is made of buff-colored Nile silt with heavier straw temper. Forms include jars, bottles, bowls, and large basins. Rough-ware became very common in mid-Naqada II and it appears in great numbers in tombs alongside Black-Topped and Red-Burnished vessels.

This style of pottery is so distinctive and different from the finely worked Black-Topped and Red-Burnished wares that it was once thought it was introduced by a "new intrusive cultural element" that may "represent infiltration of an ethnic strain from the northwest" that "was quickly assimilated" (Needler 1984, p. 189). It is now recognized that the proliferation of this style of pottery is related to the rise of baking and brewing, both of which activities required great numbers of bread molds and vessels that could be rapidly made (Wengrow 2006, pp. 39, 87–88). This example is a beer jar. ET

DECORATED POTTERY

Painted pottery is a hallmark of the Naqada period and each phase of the Naqada period had a distinctive kind of painted decoration. Despite obvious differences between the phases, the motifs of each are related to each other and to the overall art of ancient Egypt. The art of painted pottery shared subjects and designs with rock art of the period as well as other media, notably painted textiles of Naqada I, a painted tomb in Naqada II, and relief-decorated palettes and ivories in Naqada III. A few subjects were even shared with three-dimensional sculptures.

In all periods, painted figures were simple and summarized in a definite style. Animals were shown with significant features that allow them to be identified in most cases, and humans always, but plants were so summary that they are difficult to identify with any precision.

In Naqada I (ca. 4000 BC), the painting was almost always white on a red background (Catalog Nos. 1, 28–29), and animal figures were generally filled with cross-hatching, zigzags, chevrons, or other linear decoration that suggests the texture of a coat or hide. In Naqada II, the red-on-buff figures of humans and animals were generally solid, while plants were linear or had simple suggestions of some internal structures. Large objects, such as boats, cabins, and hide-frames, were also outlined and sometimes had internal details suggested by texture. Simple elements of landscapes, such as triangles for cliffs at the edge of the valley, were also added. They were textured in Naqada I, but were solid in Naqada II and III. In Naqada II, groups of zigzags were added in various orientations to depict water, and small rows of Z-shaped lines, probably for sand.

The simplest decoration might consist only of a single figure or even an almost abstracted design, but the art generally consisted of tableaux of varying complexity. Scenes of the hunt, a river procession, or plants predominate, with varying combinations of supporting figures and elements. The interpretation of many scenes and elements remains a matter of discussion, or controversy, but it is widely agreed that the painting on pottery had meaning that was well understood. In the broadest sense, scenes on the White Cross-Lined pottery of Naqada I were dominated by the hunt and, to a lesser extent, victory (see "Iconography of the Predynastic and Early Dynastic Periods" in this volume). They were mostly found on cups or beakers, bowls, narrow jars, and vases.

In Naqada II times (ca. 3500 BC), painted vessels were in the form of jars. Subject matter changed so that the larger-scale scenes were mostly of processions of large river craft being rowed. These almost always have cabins, and they almost always have standards that carry symbols that largely appear later as symbols of deities and nomes. A frequent composition on a lug-handled jar, for example, would consist of large, curved boats stretching between the lugs, alternating with large plants, probably date palms, made up of curved fronds arranged on either side of a short trunk and one large curved frond ending in a pod protruding from the top. Often these alternated with smaller fan-shaped plants or oblong structures that may be hides mounted on poles. Summary solid human figures often appear, placed on or above the boat's cabins or away from the vessels. Most prominent is a woman, shown face front, with both arms raised above the head in curved arcs generally considered to invoke the appearance of a bovine (Catalog No. 30). Men also appear, shown in the semi-profile view later typical of Egyptian art, most often holding a small crook in one hand.

Often, groups of long-legged birds are interspersed with the other elements of the decoration and sometimes other animals (Catalog No. 37), normally some kind of oryx, addax, or gazelle, sometimes a dog. A number of other elements and details occur more rarely, but this style of painted pottery is remarkably consistent. In fact, a large body of evidence exists from the period in another medium — rock art — but the subjects are quite different. For example, the boats are shown less often with cabins, and less often rowed, and the plant life is missing. The same is true of the Hierakonpolis Painted Tomb 100 that dates to the Naqada II period (fig. 8.2 in this volume). In the tomb painting, the boats are more detailed, but they are not depicted being rowed, and the tableaux as well as the entire composition are far more complex. Naqada II painting on pottery was closely related to art in other media, but it was not just a selection from larger-scale works — it included elements not present in other art forms.

Generally, above the main tableaux a row of solid triangles might depict the cliffs at the edge of the valley (Catalog Nos. 31, 37–38), while variously arranged groups of zigzags or jogged lines are probably water and Z-shaped lines may be sand. To be added to this simple repertoire of landscape elements are bands of vertical or horizontal cross-hatching. These usually appear with animals or long-legged birds, and they may represent some kind of net structure used to enclose animals at the end of a hunting drive.

While this is not a thorough discussion of Naqada II pottery, it suffices to indicate its simplicity, repetition, and consistency, such that it clearly communicated a restricted number of well-understood and controlled themes.

Late in Naqada II or early in Naqada III, this painted pottery changed enough to be identified as a new style. While some jars were still decorated, some of the most elaborate compositions were on large bowls. The processions of curved boats and the fan-shaped plants were abandoned. Animals and people were often shown with rudimentary details, and the suggestion of landscape was reduced to a band of triangles (Catalog No. 38). Groups of zigzags continued, but were sometimes very elongated and grouped even more irregularly. Crocodiles, scorpions, serpents, and possibly amphibians appear, sometimes shown top-town and sometimes in profile. Palm trees, sometimes quite stylized, appear and are relatively easily recognizable. Boats appear twice, both times as the sacred bark known from Egyptian religious scenes. Also new are scenes at shrines, one showing the *imy-wt* sacrificial pole, another a somewhat enigmatic presentation at a pole-shrine of a crocodile and a plover with a palm(?) and vultures attacking serpents. This last is connected to carved ivory representations. A third major scene shows giraffes flanking palms that have vultures attacking fallen men, a theme that appears on mudstone palettes just before King Narmer. BBW

MANUFACTURE

The pottery first designated "D-ware" by Petrie all belongs to the class of hard, pink pottery that became dominant in Naqada II. It was made in Upper Egypt of a local material, called marl by most archaeologists, probably from an indurated clay deposit known to geologists as marlstone or mudstone and a filler or temper of sand, often with fragments of limestone. Built by hand, the vessels were fired in a closed kiln rather than a firing pit or stack, which allowed the control over atmosphere necessary to achieve the light surface color. BBW

28. PAINTED BOWL

Baked clay, pigment
Naqada Ic, ca. 3700 BC
Naqada, tomb 1592
Gift of the Egypt Exploration Fund, 1895
H: 8.2; D: 19.3 cm
OIM E940

This bowl is an example of C-ware, White Cross-Lined pottery with decoration that is characteristic of Naqada I. ET

28

29

29. PAINTED BOWL WITH ANIMAL HEAD

Baked clay, pigment
Naqada I, ca. 4000–3800 BC
By exchange with the Metropolitan Museum of Art, 1950
L: 15.0; D: 5.2 cm
OIM E18243

The interior and exterior of this whimsical C-ware bowl are painted with spots in imitation of the animal's hide. ET

30, view a

30. PAINTED VESSEL

Baked clay, pigment
Naqada IIC–D, ca. 3400 BC
Purchased in Cairo, 1920
H: 11.5; D: 14.9 cm
OIM E10581

Boats are an essential part of Predynastic representations and they occur most frequently on decorated pottery. As a means of transport, they would have been beyond the means of the sedentary life of the farmers who made up the very large majority of the Egyptian population. Boats are furthermore expensive objects, certainly made

of wood, another indication of their association with the lifestyle of the elite. On contemporary rock art, human representations can often be found on boats, but they are not portrayed doing expected activities such as rowing; rather, they have their arms raised and often carry bows or maces. Their male gender is generally emphasized,

30, *view b*

30, *view c*

and they are to be seen in the context of hunting and military power, two strongly related concepts (see "Iconography of the Predynastic and Early Dynastic Periods" in this volume and Hendrickx and Eyckerman 2010).

On this vessel, humans also occur above the boats, but they are different from those found in rock art. Above each boat is one large figure, which can be identified as female only because the smaller figures are clearly identified as males by their sex, although it is a penis sheath that is represented and not the penis itself. The male figures are directed toward the females, touching them or presenting curved objects and are obviously subordinate.

Similar scenes occur rather frequently on Decorated vessels and they are part of a standardized visual language. The very large majority of these vessels have been found in tombs and the meaning of their decoration is generally considered to be funerary. The dominating position of females on Decorated vessels can be contrasted to that of males in rock art. While the male representations refer to political and economic power, the female images are almost self-evident symbols of life and birth. In both contexts this is to be integrated in a religious

framework and a structured visual language. The boats are representations of power on both rock art and decorated vessels, but on the vessels they are in the context of regeneration and hence can be considered the predecessors of the Dynastic funerary barks.

Between the boats are two addaxes, easily recognizable by their long, undulating horns. A strong statistic relation between these animals and female representations above boats has been shown (Graff 2003) and the addax must have been a funerary symbol of some sort, but the exact meaning and the reasons for this remain unknown.

The shape of the jar is well known for Decorated pottery, but the five appliques, unfortunately broken off, are not. At least two of them were lug handles, but the others may have been figurative appliques but are too damaged to allow identification. Plastic additions occur only exceptionally on Decorated vessels of this period and when they occur, do not seem directly related to the syntax of the painted decoration. SH

PUBLISHED

Graff 2009, p. 355, no. 485; Kantor 1974, p. 244, no. 202

31.   PAINTED VESSEL

Baked clay, pigment
Naqada II, ca. 3800–3300 BC
Abadiya, tomb B 248 N.D
Gift of the Egypt Exploration Fund, 1898–1899
H: 29.4; D: 14.9 cm
OIM E5189

This convex-sided jar with a flat base has an
everted rim and three vertical triangular lugs
pierced horizontally. Its shoulder is painted with
three wavy lines, below which a band of triangles
continues over the lugs. The scene below centers
on a curved-hull boat. The rest of the decoration is
largely floral, consisting of two small, fan-shaped
plants; what is probably a large date palm with a
trunk, a semicircular cascade of fronds, and a large,
probably reproductive frond above; three more fan-
shaped plants, also with reproductive fronds; and
a set of ten jogged lines below, and finally a second
large plant. The boat has a bumper or mooring
rope suspended from the bow and a tall frond
curving above. Amidships are two small cabins, the
rearmost one holding a standard with streamers
topped by the zigzag symbol widely considered
to be that of the god Min. The number of oars
shown on these boats indicates that they were very
large.   BBW

31, view a

31, view b

31, view c

32. PAINTED FUNNEL

Baked clay, pigment
Naqada II, ca. 3800–3300 BC
Abadiya, tomb b 325
Gift of the Egypt Exploration Fund, 1898–1899
H: 5.7; D: 5.0 cm
OIM E5230

This funnel was made from a small, convex jar with
a flat base. The rim was ground around the vessel
about halfway down the side and the base pierced.
The painted decoration consists of two fan-like
plants alternating with two long-legged wader birds
with long, lowered beaks. BBW

32

33, view a

33. PAINTED VESSEL

Baked clay, pigment
Naqada II, ca. 3800–3300 BC
Abadiya, tomb b 93
Gift of the Egypt Exploration Fund,
1898–1899
H: 23; D: 24 cm
OIM E5234

33, *view b*

33, *view c*

This ovoid jar with a flat base has a short neck and everted rim. Three pierced, triangular lugs are attached vertically to the shoulder. Decoration above consists of a band of wavy lines below the shoulder, large swags of wavy lines between the lugs, and narrow lines on the edges of the lugs. Below one lug is a row of five long-legged birds, either flamingos or ostriches. Below another lug is a pair of fan-shaped plants with a row of short, Z-shaped lines above, possibly representing a sand bank. Between the birds and the plants are two single zigzag lines, shown at an angle. The area below the third lug is empty and the decoration may not have been completed. BBW

181

34

34. PAINTED VESSEL

Baked clay, pigment
Naqada II, ca. 3800–3300 BC
Naqada, tomb 1869
Gift of Petrie and Quibell, 1895
H: 7.0; D: 9.6 cm
OIM E768

This squat, sub-globular jar has a round base, flattened, everted rim, and two horizontally pierced cylindrical lugs. Large spirals and a vertical wavy line are painted on the body. On and near the handles are short, horizontal wavy lines. The shape of this vessel was also used for stone vessels. Some painted vessels have textures that indicate an attempt to imitate the naturally occurring patterns in such stones as breccia or granite. Some stone vessels of this type have gold covers for the handles, which could explain the wavy lines on the handles here. BBW

35. PAINTED VESSEL

Baked clay, pigment
Naqada II, ca. 3800–3300 BC
Mahasna
Gift of the Egypt Exploration Fund,
1908–1909
H: 16; D: 21 cm
OIM E8922

35

This squat, globular jar has a round base, short neck, everted rim, and two horizontally pierced cylindrical lugs. The painted decoration on the body consists of large spirals scattered over the surface. Interspersed among the spirals are single long, wavy lines. Groups of wavy lines cover the lugs and the rim has a band of cross-hatching. Irregular decorative patterns of this type have long been considered interpretations of patterns in stone, especially breccias. The cylindrical lugs and rims of stone vessels in this shape (see fig. C3) were often covered with gold foil, which the wavy lines seen on the lugs of this example may emulate.   BBW

PUBLISHED

Ayrton and Loat 1911, pl. 25.5

FIGURE C3. OIM E8922 (right) and E10862 stone breccia (left) for comparison

36

36. PAINTED VESSEL

Baked clay, pigment
Naqada II–III, ca. 3800–3100 BC
Gift of David and George Hillis, 1916
H: 14.2; D: 16.2 cm
OIM E9345

This convex jar has a flat base, everted rim, and three vertical pierced lugs. The painted decoration consists of horizontal groups of wavy lines between the lugs, a continuous band of four wavy lines around the waist, and simple lines on the lugs. BBW

37.   PAINTED VESSEL

Baked clay, pigment
Naqada II, ca. 3800–3300 BC
Purchased in Luxor, 1920
H: 31.5; D: 27.0 cm
OIM E10758

This convex jar has a flat base,
everted rim, and four vertical
lugs pierced horizontally. The
decoration on the upper part
of the vessel consists of two
large swags made up of wavy
lines alternating with two rows
of solid triangles that continue
onto the lugs. The decoration
on the waist is arranged around
two boats located below the rows
of triangles. The curved hulls,
blunt ends, simple cabins, and
broad fronds are quite typical.
With two cabins and more than
forty oars on a side, the vessels
must have been quite large.
The standards on each boat
are difficult to interpret. They
may consist of four horns tied
together, which might indicate
one Delta deity, or it could be
a package of two or four bows,
which might indicate the goddess Neith. Between
the boats are two curious objects. They could
be either animal skins, possibly hippopotamus,
stretched and suspended from a pole, or some kind
of apparatus, such as a bird trap. On one side of the
jar is an unusual painting of a bird. The long legs,
short, curved wings, and heavy body indicate that
it is an ostrich. Below the bird on either side are
groups of spots that seem to represent eggs, which
in nature ostriches lay in communal nests of from
eight to twenty. Below the bird is a row of four
triangles.   BBW

37, view a

PUBLISHED

Graff 2009, 348, no. 463; Kantor 1974, p. 244, no. 203;
MacArthur 2010, p. 117; Marfoe 1982, p. 20, fig. 6; Wilson
and Barghusen 1989, no. 9

37, view b

38. PAINTED VESSEL

Baked clay, pigment
Naqada II, ca. 3800–3300 BC
Purchased in Luxor, 2910
H: 29.1; D: 28 cm
OIM E10759

38

This convex jar has a flat base, low everted rim, and three vertical, roughly triangular pierced lugs. Below the neck is a continuous row of solid triangles. On the shoulder are two large swags of grouped wavy lines, one painted around and over a lug, the other opposite, between the other two lugs. Two long pairs of wavy lines curve down from the triangles and the swags onto the vessel body, enclosing areas that contain rows of small zigzags and short rows of triangles that are also painted below the lines. If the interpretation of long wavy lines as water and triangles as rocky cliffs along the Nile is correct, this representation could be explained as a scene in the First Cataract, well known to the Naqada-period Egyptians. The row of triangles at the top would then show the rocky valley edge, while the shorter ones would indicate rocky islands. Narrow zigzags could represent bars of sand that appear in the cataract on and among the islands. The long wavy lines would then show narrow braided channels, while the great swags would be the rushing waters of the cataract. BBW

186

39

39. PAINTED VESSEL

Baked clay, pigment
Naqada II–III, ca. 3800–3100 BC
Naqada, tomb 401
Gift of Petrie and Quibell, 1895
H: 18.2; D: 16.2 cm
OIM E734

This small, convex-sided jar has a flat base and everted rim. The body is painted with groups of three hooked strokes. The groups of strokes are very carelessly applied, and the number was probably determined by the amount of paint held by the brush. This decoration was unique at Naqada, although scattered strokes and splotches sometimes occur in combination with organized designs in the later phase of Decorated pottery. BBW

STONE WORK

STONE VESSELS

Among the most impressive and beautiful of the Predynastic and Early Dynastic crafts are the vessels made of stone. A wide range of materials was used, including limestone, basalt, porphyry, breccia, calcite (Egyptian alabaster), serpentine, rock crystal, gabbro, and granite.

The earliest vessels were made of very hard stone such as basalt (see Catalog No. 40). These were already being made by specialized craftsman (see "Crafts and Craft Specialization" in this volume). Stone vessels became more common in the Naqada II period, perhaps due to the development of better tools.

Stone vessel manufacture reached its apogee in Nadaqa III–First and Second Dynasties, during which period royal and elite tombs contained huge numbers (an estimated 40,000 examples were recovered from the subterranean chambers of the Step Pyramid of Djoser). Many of them were empty, underscoring their role in the display of power and consumption of resources as opposed to their functional value. The fact that less labor-intensive materials could be used to make containers likewise indicates the prestige value of stone vessels.

The bases and handles of early stone vessels imitate the styles seen on contemporary pottery. By Naqada II, the reverse is seen, with pottery vessels painted with spiral patterns that imitate the large-scale veining of breccia vessels (Catalog Nos. 34, 42).

Stone-working tools of the Predynastic period were made of sandstone, flint, or copper (Arnold 1991, p. 265). Drills with tubular bits aided by abrasives, probably powdered quartz, were used to bore out the interior of vessels. Workshop scenes from the mid-Old Kingdom show craftsmen using a "wobbly drill" (see fig. C4 [left]), a bent wood axis fitted with a bit. Downward force and momentum were created by weights attached to the upper part of the axis. Parallel lines on the interior of some vessels (Catalog No. 41) suggest the use of some sort of rotary tool. Recent experiments making stone vessels with replicas of ancient tools showed that it required 22 hours and 35 minutes to create a limestone vessel 10.7 cm tall and 10 cm in diameter (Aston et al. 2000, p. 65), presumably without the final polishing. ET

FIGURE C4. Craftsmen making stone vessels. The workman to the left uses a "wobbly drill" to bore out the interior of a cylindrical stone vessel. The two men before him are using stone polishers to finish the exterior and interior of vessels. Dynasty 5. Saqqara (photo courtesy of Emily Teeter)

40. STONE VESSEL

Basalt
Naqada I, ca. 4000–3800 BC
Purchased in Cairo, 1920
H: 21; D: 12 cm
OIM E10853

40

Footed stone vessels with two lug handles such as this are almost always made of the hard volcanic stone basalt. Since there is a limited regional distribution of such rock along the Nile Valley, and because the chemical composition of each basaltic lava flow is unique, it has been possible to source the stone used in the production of these vessels. Of the five known basalt sources in Egypt, only the Haddadin basalt flow near modern Cairo has provided a direct mineral and chemical composition match to Predynastic stone containers like this

one. This correlates with the typological form of these vessels, since footed specimens in pottery are a hallmark of the Maadian communities that lived in this part of Egypt. Thus jars that show this type of base in Upper Egypt can be regarded as exports from Lower Egypt and demonstrate the interaction of these two areas of Egypt. The lug handles may have allowed the vessel to be suspended or permitted cords to pass through so that a lid could be secured over the vessel mouth.   AS

41.   JAR WITH LUG HANDLES

Mottled limestone(?)
Naqada II, ca. 3800–3300 BC
Purchased in Cairo, 1920
H: 14; D: 11.5 cm
OIM E10609

Marks from the craftsman's rotary tool can be seen in the interior. The walls of this jar are extremely thin considering its overall size.   ET

41

41, detail of tool marks

42

42. SQUAT JAR WITH LUG HANDLES

Porphyry
Naqada II, ca. 3800–3300 BC
Purchased in Luxor, 1920
H: 15.6; D: 33.5 cm
OIM E10790

This form of squat, round-bodied jar with lug handles and a flat, often wide rim, was popular in Naqada II and III. As in this case, they are often made of a boldly patterned stone that added to their prestige. They were made in a wide range of sizes, from small to even larger than this impressive example. During Naqada II, inexpensive copies of patterned stone vessels were made of pottery that was painted with circles to imitate the patterning of the stone (see Catalog No. 35).   ET

43. JAR

Diorite
Naqada II–III, ca. 3800–3100 BC
Purchased in Cairo, 1920
H: 14.0; D: 11.4 cm
OIM E10610

43

44. BOWL

Schist(?)
Naqada III, ca. 3200–3100 BC
Purchased in Cairo, 1920
H 7.6; D: 33.2 cm
OIM E11063

44

45. JAR

Red breccia
Naqada III, ca. 3200–3100 BC
Purchased in Cairo, 1920
H: 21.8; D: 12.8 cm
OIM E11085

The shape of this vessel imitates a
Rough-ware beer jar (compare to
Catalog No. 27).   ET

46

46. BIRD-SHAPED VESSEL

Red breccia
Naqada III, ca. 3200–3100 BC
Purchased in Cairo, 1920
L: 29.0; D 16.2 cm
OIM E10859

Theriomorphic stone vessels such as this are rare, but containers in the shape of fish, hippopotami, and birds are known both in stone and in pottery. This example takes the form of a sitting duck with two indentations made for eye inlays that were probably ring-shaped shell beads, but are now lost. The body has been hollowed out to make the vase. Such vessels demonstrate the Predynastic Egyptian's great skill in working with stone, which developed further in the Early Dynastic period and ultimately led to the supreme sculptural and architectural achievements of the following period.

This vessel's original findspot is not known, but similar types of vessels were excavated by Petrie at Naqada in one of the large tombs within Cemetery T (Petrie and Quibell 1896, pl. 12) and at least two were found in the Hierakonpolis Main Deposit. These are notable contexts that suggest that vessels like this were restricted to elite contexts of consumption.   AS

PUBLISHED

Glubok 1962, p. 48; Marfoe 1982, p. 21

PALETTES

A "palette" is a stone object, often in a decorative shape, whose surface was originally used to grind cosmetics. By the Naqada III period they became ceremonial objects of display, their front and back surfaces carved with ritual scenes (fig. 16.1, Catalog No. 80).

In the early phases of the fourth millennium BC, all palettes took the form of a rhomboid (Catalog No. 47). Occasionally these would have a stylized bird's silhouette or a pair of horns carved at one end, but most are plain. These palettes tend to be much thicker in cross section than later palettes and they were often very heavily worn. Palettes with two bird's heads (Catalog No. 48), like the fish-shaped examples (Catalog No. 6), were popular in the mid-Predynastic period. The style of these can vary, with some examples depicting stylized feathers between the heads. In contrast, those with the profile of an elephant are rare. An elephant-shaped palette from Naqada grave 268 dates to Naqada IIB, while other examples are more ambiguous and may represent hippopotami (see Friedman 2004a, p. 153).

Toward the end of the Predynastic period palettes became a less frequent feature of grave assemblages. By this time they were more likely to be found in larger, more elaborately furnished tombs. Those that have been found in early Naqada III contexts also tend to be simpler in shape than had been the case previously. Rectangular forms (Catalog No. 51) are the most commonly encountered shapes, some with a border incised on one face of between one and three lines. Oval and circular palettes, with and without border lines, were also in use during the later Predynastic period. Palettes in the form of a falcon (Catalog No. 51) appear in Late Predynastic and Early Dynastic contexts, such as at the cemeteries of Tarkhan (Petrie 1914, pl. 22). They might conceivably, therefore, refer to early royal iconography, with the falcon used in a similar way as on the early *serekhs*. Such palettes are rare. AS

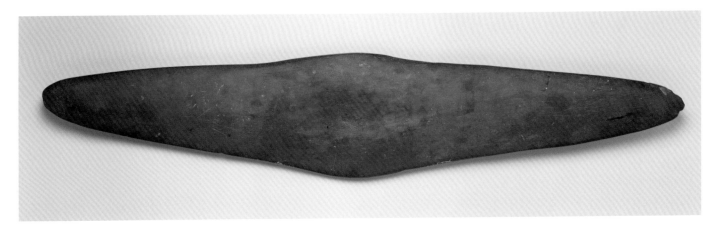

47

47.   RHOMBOID PALETTE

Siltstone
Naqada IC–IIA, ca. 3700–3600 BC
Hu, grave U252
Gift of the Egypt Exploration Fund, 1889
L: 41.8; W: 3.5; T: 14.5 cm
OIM E5283

A noticeable, lengthwise depression can be seen on this palette, the result of repeated acts of grinding. Also visible on the surface are the remains of what was last ground on its surface before it entered the archaeological record: a dark-red pigment that was determined to be an iron-based substance through elemental analysis using a JEOL scanning electron microscope with energy dispersive spectroscopy (SEM-EDS) at the Department of Geophysics, University of Chicago. AS and AW

48

48. DOUBLE-BIRD PALETTE

Siltstone
Naqada IIC–D, ca. 3400 BC
Purchased in Cairo, 1920
L: 34.6; W: 6.7 cm
OIM E11473

49

49. "PELTA-SHAPED" PALETTE

Siltstone
Naqada II, ca. 3800–3300 BC
Purchased in Cairo, 1920
L: 13.0; W: 7.1 cm
OIM E11054

This "pelta-shaped" palette was so called on account of its resemblance to shields carried by Amazonian Indians (Petrie 1920b, p. 37), although it more readily resembles a boat with a cabin on top. Like many palettes, it has a suspension hole in the central portion drilled from both faces. What it was attached to is unclear. They have not been found tied to a body and there is no proof they were a form of adornment, which is, in any case, unlikely for the much larger and heavier examples. One possibility is that they may have been suspended within structures. In two Naqada III burials at Tarkhan, for instance, rectangular palettes were found affixed with mud to the wall of the burial chamber. The second hole on the pelta palette is likely to have been decorative. AS

50

50.   ELEPHANT PALETTE

Siltstone, shell
Naqada II, ca. 3800–3300 BC
Purchased in Luxor, 1920
L: 12.7; W: 84.0 cm
OIM E12170

51. RECTANGULAR PALETTE

Siltstone
Naqada IIIA–B, ca. 3200–2950 BC
Abadiya
Gift of the Egypt Exploration Fund,
1898
L: 12.2; W: 10.0 cm
OIM E5279

The green residue on the
surface of this palette was
determined to be a copper-based
pigment through elemental
analysis using a JEOL scanning
electron microscope with
energy dispersive spectroscopy
(SEM-EDS) at the Department
of Geophysics, University of
Chicago.   AW

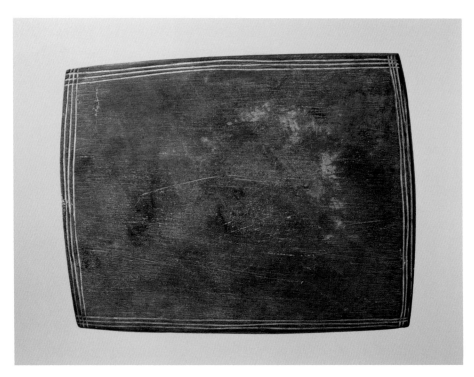

51

52. FALCON PALETTE

Siltstone
Naqada IIIB, ca. 3100 BC
Purchased in Cairo, 1920
L: 17.0; W: 12.5 cm
OIM E11463

52

53

53. COMPOSITE ANIMAL PALETTE

Graywacke
Dynasty 1, ca. 3100 BC
Purchased in Cairo, 1920
H: 13.5; L: 22.5; T: 1.8 cm
OIM E11470

On this most interesting object, the head of a bull can easily be recognized, not only because of its general shape but especially by the sinuous line on the head which is also found in representations of bulls on, for example, the Narmer Palette (figs. 16.1–2) and the Bull Palette (Paris, Louvre E 11255). The damage at the top of the head indicates that horns and ears were originally present. But the palette does not render the full representation of a bull, for the "body" consists of a rather shapeless rectangle with rounded corners. Most remarkable is the absence of legs and tail. Where the tail should be, a tailfin can be seen, most probably that of a

tilapia. Although partially broken off, two other fins can easily be recognized on the "back" of the animal. Damage to the areas where the legs would be supposed makes it impossible to say for certain whether or not these were also replaced by fish fins.

Although this combination of bovine and fish elements is unique for Predynastic times, composite animals are not (see "Iconography of the Predynastic and Early Dynastic Periods" in this volume). Take for example the ibex-tilapia hybrid identified by Dirk Huyge on a knife handle preserved in Berlin (Inv. 15137; Huyge 2004, fig.

3). That strange creature has a fin on its snout, a feature that the Chicago palette shared, as suggested by traces of an element, now missing, at the same location.

The highly artificial combination of animals of very diverse nature must have had symbolical significance, but its precise meaning is hard to define. Two lines of interpretation are possible. On the one hand, the symbolism of the animals involved can be taken as starting point. The bull is already a well-known symbol of (royal) power in the Predynastic period. During Dynastic times, the tilapia is a symbol for renewal of life and fertility, presumably mainly because of the peculiar way it incubates its offspring by holding them in its mouth. The combination of the bull and tilapia may refer to the renewal of royal power but expressed in a visual manner that did not continue into Early Dynastic iconography. This is, for example, also the case for the dog as a symbol of power in hunting scenes, or the rosette identifying the king on the Narmer Palette, both motifs which were not included in the visual language of the Dynastic period.

On the other hand, hybrid animals can be elements of chaos, as is the case for the serpopards and griffins on late Predynastic decorated palettes, for example. The ibex-tilapia hybrid figures on decorated knife handles in combination with desert animals arranged in orderly lines, some of which end with a dog or a rosette as an element symbolizing domination and control. The establishment of order over chaos expressed in this manner is a fundamental ideological concept throughout Egyptian history.

That the two options are not necessarily mutually exclusive is shown by the example of the lion that is an element of chaos on the Hunters Palette (London, British Museum EA 20790 and Paris, Louvre E 11254), but which also appears as a royal symbol on the Battlefield Palette (Catalog No. 80). Depending on the context, the meaning of hybrid animals may equally differ. SH

LITHICS

In ancient Egypt, flint or chert was used for knapped stone tools from the Lower Paleolithic down to the Dynastic period. The raw material was available in abundance on the desert surface, and it could be mined from the limestone formations along the Nile Valley. While the earliest lithic industries of prehistoric Egypt resemble the stone tool assemblages from other parts of Africa, as well as Asia and Europe, the later prehistoric stone industries in Egypt had very specific characteristics, producing some of the finest knapped stone tools ever manufactured in the ancient world. Throughout Egypt's history, butchering tools such as knives and scrapers, and harvesting tools in the form of sickle blades made of flint underlined the importance of stone tools for the agrarian society of ancient Egypt. While a great deal of stone tools were made by professionals many were also produced by ordinary people on the spot. The specialized craftsmanship of flint knapping in ancient Egypt probably came to an end in the first millennium BC.

The flint objects in the exhibition cover a wide variety of functions and time. Some are prestige objects intended for the elite or even a single ruler such as the fish-tail knives (Catalog Nos. 77–78) and the ripple-flaked knives (Catalog No. 79), while others speak of the life of hunters, like the barbed projectile points (Catalog Nos. 7–9), or farmers, as the examples of sickle blades show. Some of the objects were clearly made by highly skilled, specialized craftsmen who served the elite of their community. These knives are among the finest stone tools ever made in ancient Egypt and indeed the world. Some tool categories were very common in the agriculture-based society of ancient Egypt. For example, the sickle blades (Catalog Nos. 55–58), once inserted into a sickle bow made of wood, were probably the standard tools in many households. These blades show a high level of standardization and conservatism in regards to their shape. Why change a perfectly well-balanced and suitable tool? Other tools, such as the bi-truncated regular blade implement were mass products of the third millennium BC, manufactured in special workshops and then distributed throughout the country. They were a standard implement in the stone tool kit of every household as well. The use of stone tools was depicted in many tombs and even the re-sharpening of the implements can be seen, but there are only a few scenes from ancient Egypt that show flint knappers at work (see figs. C5–6). TH

FIGURE C5. Flint knife manufacturing shown in Middle Kingdom tombs in Beni Hassan (Griffith 1896, pl. 7). Courtesy of the Egypt Exploration Society

FIGURE C6. Flint knife manufacturing shown in Middle Kingdom tombs in Beni Hasan (Newberry 1893, pl. 11). Courtesy of the Egypt Exploration Society

54.   BI-TRUNCATED REGULAR BLADE TOOL

Caramel-colored flint with white lines
Mid-Dynasty 1, ca. 2950 BC
Abydos, Umm el-Qaab, tomb of Den
Gift of the Egypt Exploration Fund, 1900–1901
L: 6.4; W: 2.5; T: 0.5 cm; weight: 12.3 g
OIM E6151

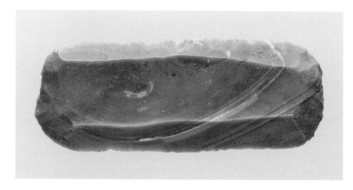

54

One of the most common standardized tool classes of the Early Dynastic period to the Old Kingdom is without any doubt the implement labeled here "bi-truncated regular blade tool." In the past this type of tool was initially called a "razor blade," implying a cosmetic function. The shape is rectangular and it was manufactured using a large, regular blade as a blank with straight edge and in some cases the two dorsal ridges are quite parallel. The terminal and basal ends were truncated by semi-steep retouching. The retouch size can be medium to large. The cross section of the bi-truncated regular blade tool is trapezoid and the long section is generally thicker toward the terminal end. The chronological development shows that the early forms of the First Dynasty have an oval contour while those from the Second Dynasty to the Fifth Dynasty these tools were rectangular (see fig. C7).

The tools were highly standardized and generally have a length-to-width ratio of around 2.7–2.8:1. With an average length of around 6.5 cm for the finished tools, it can be assumed that the blanks measured more than 10 cm in length with a corresponding even larger core size. This also means that the core exploitation ended in a rather early stage indicating that the flint knappers either discarded them or produced smaller blanks and tools. These tools must have been made by highly qualified flint knappers in centralized workshops. So far, however, no production site for these tools has been found in Egypt.

The big question in regards to the bi-truncated blade tools is of course their function. Initially placed in the domain of personal hygiene, no further proof for a use as a razor blade or any

type of cosmetic tool has been put forward. Use-wear analyses have been rather inconclusive, with the result that fine abrasion as well as larger use wear can be detected along all margins. Any task of slicing or scraping is possible. Even scaling fish could be an option as one needs for this task a tool which is not too sharp yet strong and short enough to apply some force. Perhaps it can be best described as the Swiss Army Knife of Egypt in the third millennium BC.   TH

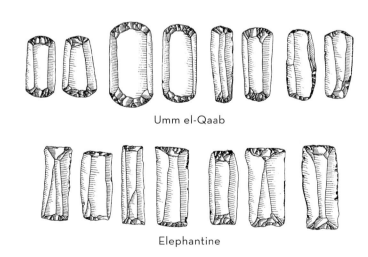

Umm el-Qaab

Elephantine

FIGURE C7. Chronological sequence of bi-truncated, regular blade tools based on finds from the Royal Cemetery at Umm el-Qaab at Abydos (Dynasty 1) and from the settlement on Elephantine Island (Dynasties 2–5) (drawing by T. Hikade)

SICKLE BLADES

Sickle blades were one of the most common flint implements in the tool kit of ancient Egypt. The segmented sickle inserts already appear in Upper Egypt during the fourth millennium BC. Only the manufacturing process seems to have changed during the Old Kingdom with more and more segmentations made by snapping off the terminal and basal ends. Together with end pieces that may have had one pointed tip they were inserted into wooden sickle bows (fig. C8). The use of sickles is depicted in many harvesting scenes in tombs from the Old Kingdom on. The men are leaning forward, resting their weight on the forward leg, grasping a bundle and cutting the grain with a swinging movement of the sickle bow. This cutting results in sickle sheen on the blade and the resulting sheen depends very much on the quality of flint. Depending on the raw material the gloss can be seen with the naked eye sometimes after only 200 strokes but in other cases it can take up to 2,500 strokes to produce a visible sheen. TH

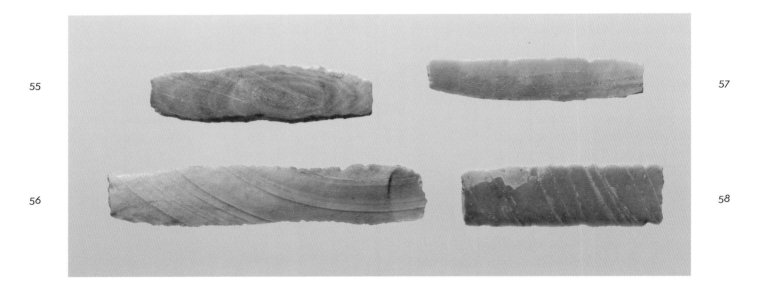

55

57

56

58

55–58. SICKLE BLADES

Light to mid-brown banded flint
Early Dynastic to Old Kingdom, ca.
3100–2160 BC
Abydos, Temenos of Osiris(?)
Gift of the Egypt Exploration Fund,
1901–1902

A note on provenance: As the sickle blades were a gift of the Egypt Exploration Fund in 1901–1902, it is possible that they belong to the same batch of finds as scraper Catalog No. 59 and thus would come from the Temenos of Osiris at Abydos.

55. OIM E7538
L: 4.8; W: 1.3; T: 0.4 cm; weight: 3.0 g

56. OIM E7535
L: 67; W:14; T: 0.4 cm; weight: 4.3 g

57. OIM E7558
L: 4.6; W: 1.0; T: 0.4 cm; weight: 2.5 g

58. OIM E7354
L: 4.3; W: 1.4; T 0.4 cm; weight: 2.9 g

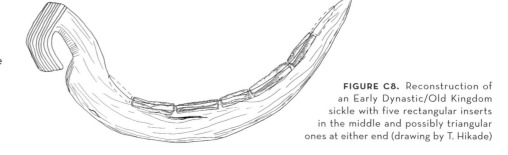

FIGURE C8. Reconstruction of an Early Dynastic/Old Kingdom sickle with five rectangular inserts in the middle and possibly triangular ones at either end (drawing by T. Hikade)

59. SPIKED FLINT TOOL

Flint with remains of chalky white cortex on dorsal side
Dynasty 1, ca. 3100–2890 BC
Abydos, Temenos of Osiris, level 34
Gift of the Egypt Exploration Fund, 1901–1902
L: 7.6: W: 7.5; T: 1.0 cm; weight: 38.3 g
OIM E7411

The father of Egyptian archaeology W. M. F. Petrie once called stone implements like this "comb flints." He assumed that they had developed from round flint scrapers and possibly were used for scaling fish. Today we know that there was a great variety of flint scrapers in use in Egypt during the fourth and third millennia BC, which all seem to have had different functions rather than developing from each other. What the spikes were really used for remains unknown, but the comb tools represent a rather rare shape and might have been used by a specialized craftsman. TH

PUBLISHED

Petrie 1902, pl. 26.323 (dorsal face only)

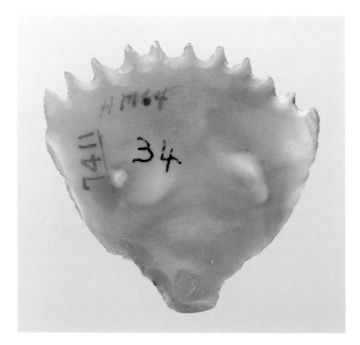

59

59, dorsal face

60. BLADE

Light-brown flint
Abydos, tomb 485, tomb of Mernesut
Dynasty 1, ca. 3100–2890 BC
Gift of the British School of Archaeology in Egypt,
1921–1922
L: 10.0; W: 2.1: T: 0.8 cm, weight: 14.1 g
OIM E11917

60

The first step of a flint knapper's task is to find good-quality raw material and then begin the process of primary production. This means that the flint nodule has to be prepared for the extraction of blanks that are either flakes or blades. Once the length-to-width ratio is greater than 2:1 we generally refer to a blade. While a blade can be used as it is since it already has a pointed tip good enough for drilling soft materials, often the blanks, flakes, and blades alike are further altered by retouching to produce a stone tool such as scrapers, drills, knives, and arrowheads. TH

61

61. PEBBLE STONE

Flint with mid-brown, shiny cortex
Date undetermined
Naqada, Cemetery T
Gift of Petrie and Quibell, 1894–1895
L: 4.3; W: 2.9 cm
OIM E805

Pebble stones have been frequently found in connection with slate palettes. On these palettes minerals such as green malachite, galena, hematite, and red ocher were ground with such pebbles. The ground cosmetic could then be applied as eye makeup. Slate palettes were made in zoomorphic and geometric forms and were very popular throughout the Predynastic and Early Dynastic periods after which their importance declined rapidly. TH

EARLY DYNASTIC RELIGION

GODS

With the transition to the Early Dynastic period and the increase in the number of texts, the importance of certain gods and goddesses can be documented. One prominent goddess is Neith, a war-like goddess whose emblem is crossed arrows. Texts from the Old Kingdom indicate that she was especially associated with the protection of the king and the defeat of his enemies (el-Sayid 1982, p. 238). Her cult center was located at Saïs in the western Delta. The affinity of the kings to the goddess is documented by a text of King Aha of the early First Dynasty that records his visit to her shrine. EVM/ET

62. BOWL FRAGMENT WITH INSCRIPTION

Serpentine
Dynasty 1, reign of Merneith, ca. 2950 BC
Abydos, Umm el-Qaab, tomb Y, tomb of Merneith
Gift of the Egypt Exploration Fund, 1902
L: 7.0; W: 4.9 cm
OIM E6168

The devotion to the goddess Neith among members of the royal court and the elite is reflected in the compounding of personal names with the name of the goddess. This fragment of a bowl bears the name "Merneith." The name, translated as "Beloved of Neith," is written with a hieroglyph in the form of crossed arrows, the emblem of Neith, and the hoe sign "beloved [of]." Petrie, who excavated this piece, had long thought that Merneith was a king, but later recognized her status as a queen. She was probably the wife of King Djet and the mother of King Den. Seal impressions found in the tomb of King Den list Merneith with the other rulers of the First Dynasty where she is given the title "mother of the king," suggesting that in some circumstances, she had the same status as a king. This foreshadows the high social status of women throughout Dynastic period, during which time several women were proclaimed king.

62

Merneith's name is attested on numerous stone vessels and objects from Abydos. The use of hard stone, which was a luxury product, is a reflection of the royal family's access to the finest resources. EVM/ET

PUBLISHED

Petrie 1901a, p. 23, pl. 5A.21

63. CYLINDRICAL VESSEL

Ivory

Dynasty 1, reign of Djer, ca. 2950 BC

Abydos, Umm el-Qaab, subsidiary tomb of Djer, O2

Gift of the Egypt Exploration Fund, 1902

H: 5.4; D: 3.6 cm

OIM E5954

63

This miniature cylindrical vessel is incised with the name of a woman interred in a subsidiary grave of King Djer. Her name is Neith-Hotep "Neith is Satisfied," perhaps a reflection of the woman's desire to honor the goddess. The popularity of Neith can be judged by the prevalence of the deity's name in personal names of the First Dynasty, especially on the funerary stelae from the subsidiary burials at Abydos.

The tiny vessel with a wavy band below the jar rim imitates larger stone examples (Catalog No. 19). EVM/ET

PUBLISHED

Kaplony 1963, p. 589, no. 11; MacArthur 2010, p. 128; Petrie 1901a, pp. 20, 33, pl. 2.12

VOTIVE OFFERINGS

Deposits of votive objects dating to the Early Dynastic period have been recovered in, or near, temples at Abydos, Hierakonpolis, and Elephantine in the south, and Tell Ibrahim Awad and Tell el-Farkha (see "The Predynastic/Early Dynastic Period at Tell el-Farkha" in this volume) in the north. Presumably, these deposits are made up of objects that were left in temples as offerings that were later gathered up and buried. Although each deposit has its own characteristics, the presence of votive deposits in both the north and the south suggests that offering cults were a feature of early cult practice throughout

Egypt. However, localized cults probably existed as well, judging from the existence of types of votive objects that are present at one site but not at another.

Most Early Dynastic votives are made of glazed faience, stone, or ivory. There is no contemporary textual evidence to explain the rituals that must have required votive objects. However, the presence of these deposits suggests an organized cult that involved craftsmen who made the objects, some sort of distribution system, and a set of beliefs that required the deposition of votives. Presumably, animal figurines are references to deities, and model vessels are

69. BABOON

Limestone
Dynasty 1 or later, ca. 2800 BC
Abydos, Osiris Temple, deposit M65
Gift of the Egypt Exploration Fund, 1902–1903
H: 6.2; W: 5.4; T: 3.9 cm
OIM E7960

This baboon is more naturalistic with more modeling. He sits on the ground, his hands between his legs.   ET

PUBLISHED

Petrie 1903, p. 27, pl. 10.221

69

69, back view

69, side view

70. VOTIVE PLAQUE

Faience
Dynasty 1, ca. 3100–2890 BC
Abydos, Temenos of Osiris, deposit M69
Gift of the Egypt Exploration Fund, 1902–1903
H: 13.4; W: 9.7; T: 1.7 cm
OIM E7911

70

This votive offering was probably deposited in the temple to gain favor from Osiris. The man who presumably dedicated it is depicted in profile, his hair cropped short. He wears a kilt wrapped around his waist with a belt tied at his navel and he holds a long staff — a symbol of rank. He strides forward with his left foot. This striding pose is the typical two-dimensional representation of a man of rank that continued to be used well into Roman times 3,000 years later.

The text gives the man's name and title, the exact translation of which is disputed. The name appears in the bottom most line of text. It seems to be *Tri-nṯr* "The One Who Worships the God." This name emphasizes the man's devotion to the deity. The connection of worshipper to god expressed by personal names continued through Egyptian history with later theophoric names such as Meresamun ("Amun Loves Her"), Thutmose ("Thoth Bore Him"), and Djed-Khonsu-Iws-Ankh ("Khonsu Said She Will Live"). Above his name is his title,

which seems to indicate his status as an important person, perhaps a director of a economic institution called *Nḥn.w* in the town of *Mnḫ(.t)*. The recording of the personal name along with the title was a form of egocentric commemoration and also an indication of how the individual fit into the overall society. This continued to be a feature of Egyptian culture through the Dynastic period.

Faience plaques such as this were made in specialized workshops that served the temples. The plaque must have been expensive, another indication of the perceived value of votive objects. EVM/ET

PUBLISHED (SELECTED)

Kaplony 1963, p. 553; Klasens 1956, pp. 26, 32, no. 136; MacArthur 2010, p. 136; Petrie 1903, p. 25, pls. 1, 5.33; Petrie 1939, p. 68, pl. 37.9; Teeter 2003, pp. 11–12; Weill 1961, vol. 1, pp. 145–46

MODEL OFFERING VESSELS

Small copies of ritual vessels found in temple deposits provide good evidence for the continuation of rituals from the Early Dynastic through the Dynastic era because containers with these shapes continued to be standard equipment for cult activities for the next three thousand years. Model offering vessels have been recovered from Abydos, Hierakonpolis, Tell el-Farkha, and Elephantine.　ET

71　　　　　　　　　72　　　　　　　　　73

71.　MODEL *HES* JAR

Faience
Dynasties 1–2, ca. 3100–2685 BC
Abydos, Osiris Temple, deposit M69
Gift of the Egypt Exploration Fund, 1902–1903
H: 5.5 cm
OIM E8315

72.　MODEL *HES* JAR

Faience
Dynasties 1–2, ca. 3100–2685 BC
Abydos, Osiris Temple, deposit M69
Gift of Egypt Exploration Fund, 1902–1903
H: 10.6; D: 3.7 cm
OIM E7900

These two model vessels were part of a larger group discovered in deposit M69 at Abydos. The slender *hes* jar was used to pour liquids in funerary and temple ceremonies of purification. The silhouette of the *hes* is the word "to honor" in hieroglyphic writing, so the act of pouring from the vessel, or leaving a model of the vessel in the temple, was an act of venerating the god. *Hes* jars usually have a broad, flat lid and a curved spout, neither of which elements are reproduced on the models. Large-scale *hes* jars of faience were used in offering rituals of the New Kingdom and later, and an example in gold was recovered from the tomb of Amenemope at Tanis. *Hes* jars continued to be an essential part of cult ceremonies, and they can be seen in the hands of priests well into the Roman period, more than three thousand years after these models were left in the temple.　ET

PUBLISHED

OIM E8315: Petrie 1903, p. 26, pl. 7.112
OIM E7900: Petrie 1903, p. 26, pl. 7.110

73.　MODEL *NW/NEMSET* VESSEL

Faience
Dynasties 1–2, ca. 3100–2685 BC
Abydos, grave Q 22
Gift of the Egypt Exploration Fund, 1900–1901
H: 5.2; D: 4.8 cm
OIM E6651

Round jars, called *nw* or *nemset*, were used in funerary and temple rituals. They are usually shown with a bent spout and a domed lid, the latter feature being reproduced on this model. Such jars are frequently shown in scenes where the king, holding a round jar in each hand, adores the god. Examples of functional jars in this shape are preserved in bronze from the fourth to second century BC (Green 1987, p. 58).　ET

PUBLISHED

Randall-MacIver and Mace 1902, pl. 99

74. FIGURINE OF A YOUTH

Ivory
Dynasties 1–3(?), ca. 3100–2613 BC
Abydos, Osiris Temple, deposit M69
Gift of the Egypt Exploration Fund, 1902–1903
H: 6.4; W:1.7; T: 1.9 cm
OIM E7910

When Petrie excavated the early layers of the
Temenos of Osiris at Abydos in 1903, he found
several deposits of votive objects. Deposit M69 was
constructed during the Sixth Dynasty rebuilding
of the temple and the objects found in it may
therefore date as late as the late Old Kingdom.
Among the votive objects are an important number
of ivory and faience figurines (see also Catalog Nos.
68, 72). The most remarkable is an ivory figurine
of an anonymous Early Dynastic king (London,
British Museum EA 37996), but beside that there are
representations of both adults and children. The
male children are characterized by the finger at the
mouth (see also fig. 6.6 in this volume), a manner
of representing youth that continued throughout
Dynastic times. Dating the figurine is difficult, and
although it certainly does not predate the Early
Dynastic period and it might well be attributed
to that period, a date in the Old Kingdom is also
possible.

The delicately made little figurine testifies to
the excellent craftsmanship reached at an early
date in Egypt. The tiny curls of the hair most
probably do not indicate that the boy is to be
considered a Nubian, but rather they are part of an
elaborately worked hairstyle, perhaps part of a wig.

Although the general concept of votive
figurines as elements for religious demands or
dedication seems obvious, the precise meaning
of these figurines is hard to define. They may be
intended for protection of children while growing
up. SH

PUBLISHED

Petrie 1903, p. 24, pl. 2.7

74

74, back view

TOMB OFFERINGS

75. STYLIZED TAG

Ivory
Naqada IC, ca. 3700–3600 BC
El-Amrah, grave a 45
Gift of the Egypt Exploration Fund, 1900–1901
L: 8.4; W: 2.2; T: 0.7 cm
OIM E5653

This tag was found as one of a set of three in a Naqada I tomb at el-Amrah. Although tusks and tags are important evidence of hippopotamus hunting, their shape can also be linked to female representations because of the well-known female figurines and the female representations on decorated pottery (fig. C10) have similar cone-shaped legs. The same shape can also be seen as the central element in many examples of the so-called Naqada plant, allowing one to relate the female representations with plants, which is paralleled in the tree goddesses of Dynastic times (see "Iconography in the Predynastic and Early Dynastic Periods" in this volume). In this case, the cone shape may refer to religious forces supporting a positive afterlife.

The relation with such concepts as hippopotamus hunting and plants as aspects of the afterlife seems unlikely, but accords well with the Predynastic visual language, in which elements can be combined in different manners allowing specific concepts to be visualized. For the tusks and tags, this implies that on a more abstract level, the visual element of the "cone" has a semiotic meaning of protective power that only obtains its specific meaning through the context in which it is used.

In tombs, tusks and tags are generally found as sets of two or three, placed by preference in front of the body near the hands or lower arms. Although leather straps have been found attached to them, they are never attached to the body or to any other type of object. Clearly they were not worn on the person, and examples found in baskets, boxes, or vessels indicate that they were not intended to be worn or hung on a constant basis, but instead carefully stored until needed. This agrees well with a ritual use. The rites themselves cannot be reconstructed, although it seems obvious that more

75

than one of these amulets was needed for them. SH

PUBLISHED

Randall-MacIver and Mace 1902, p. 17, pl. 7.2

FIGURE C10. Detail from Catalog No. 30

76. AMULET IN FORM OF A MAN

Hippopotamus ivory
Naqada II, ca. 3800–3300 BC
Purchased in Cairo, 1920
H: 6.0; W: 2.8; T: 7.0 cm
OIM E10695

76

Human-headed tags are part of a much wider variety of amulets for which the human head can be replaced by a pointed end, bull horns, bird heads, or a combination of the last two (Hendrickx and Eyckerman in press). The simplest shapes are amulets with one pointed end, derived from the shape of hippopotamus tusks (see Catalog No. 75). Hippopotamus tusks are symbolically related to hippopotamus hunting, which must have been an explicit male event. The combination of tusk-shaped amulets with human heads, of which the male character is stressed by impressive beards, therefore comes as no surprise.

In the past, some human-headed tags were described as representing females on the basis of slender "waists" which were considered to be a female characteristic. However, this necessitated ignoring their very long "chins" and considering the double lines parallel to them as the rendering of garments or jewelry. Their identification as female is contradicted by a number of large tusks showing detailed representations of human heads with long triangular beards, proving beyond doubt that the pointed "chins" and parallel lines on the human-headed tags represent beards. The male identity of the tags is further confirmed by the fact that pointed chins never occur on figurines that are beyond doubt female because of the presence of breasts. Further corroboration is found in the stylistic continuity from the human-headed tusks and tags into more detailed representations such as the MacGregor man (Oxford AM. 1922.70) or the Koptos Colossi (Oxford AM. 1894.105c–f, Cairo JdE 30770), for which beards are an important visual element. Beards themselves are therefore to be seen as symbols of male power, the echo of which is found in the royal and divine false beards of Dynastic times. SH

RITUAL KNIVES

Skillfully flaked flint knives are one of the hallmarks of the Predynastic and Early Dynastic periods. Most of these had a ritual function rather than an everyday use. ET

77

77.   FISH-TAIL KNIFE

Dark-gray flint
Naqada I–IIA, ca. 4000–3600 BC
Purchased in Cairo, 1920
L: 11.5; W: 7.9; T: 0.6 cm; weight: 141.97 g
OIM E11252

Fish-tailed flint knives are known from Naqada I to IID. This example is an early type: it has a wider fork than later examples and a broader, more gently curved notch in comparison to the V-shape of mid-Naqada II pieces. It is made of dark-gray flint, which contrasts with the lighter caramel-colored material used for later specimens (Hikade 2004b). Both sides of the knife display retouch and there is a very fine serrated edge around the forked end, demonstrating a high standard of craft specialization. The edges show very little sign of wear and the practical function of these implements is unknown. Petrie regarded them as lances used for short-distance hunting. Another suggestion is that they are related to the *psš-kf* knife that in the Dynastic period played an important role in the ritual of "the Opening of the Mouth" (Roth 1992).

Most examples are found without handles, but a recently excavated knife from Hierakonpolis proves that such knives could be hafted in reed and bound with leather. It was found in burial 412 of cemetery HK43 and, like most other fish-tail knives known from graves, it accompanied the interment of a male (Friedman 2004b). AS

78. FISH-TAIL KNIFE

Dark-brown flint
Naqada II, ca. 3800–3300 BC
Purchased in Cairo, 1920. Possibly
from Abydos, based on a pencil note
on the object
L: 18.3; W: 6.1; T: 0.8 cm;
weight: 38.3 g
OIM E11250

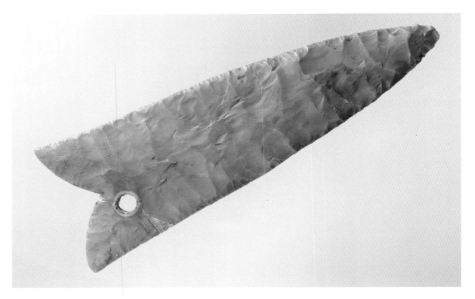

78

In Egyptological literature, fish-tail knives have been linked with an implement known as a *psš-kf*. The term is known from many sources from the Old Kingdom to the Ptolemaic-Roman period and has been the subject of many interpretations. Early on it was associated with the Opening of the Mouth ritual. This ritual was usually performed by an heir of the deceased and through it the deceased, and his or her statue, were brought back to life. Based on the Pyramid Texts the *psš-kf* has also been linked to simply strengthening the jaw of the deceased. In another interpretation, the implement is seen as the tool to cut the umbilical cord of a newborn baby. All interpretations see the Predynastic fish-tail knives as the forerunners of the *psš-kf* in form and sometimes also in function. A more archaeological perspective has also been put forward suggesting that the bifurcated tool was a lance or simply a table knife. Fish-tail knives are well documented for the Naqada I to possibly early Naqada III period (ca. 4000–3200 BC). They are usually made on a core, seldom on a large flake, that has been worked into a shape that remotely resembles the letter "Y." There are two major variants. The older fish-tail knives (Catalog No. 77) have at one end a broad fork with a wide notch and date to about 3800–3600 BC. The younger form, as this example, has a narrow V-shaped fork and dates to about 3600–3200 BC. Both kinds of knives were completely retouched on the dorsal and ventral aspects and, in some cases, traces of grinding from

an earlier stage of manufacture are still visible. Along the forked end a very fine denticulation was often applied which, in most cases, never shows damage, as if the knives were actually never used for cutting. The handle could have been of an organic material such as ivory, bone, or wood. Although complete studies of the raw material of both types have not been carried out, it seems very likely that most of the early fish-tail knives were made of a dark, brownish gray flint, whereas caramel and brown flint seems to dominate the younger artifacts of this group.

Although the exact function of the fish-tail knives has yet to be determined, their quality in respect to the flint-knapping process and their rarity (fewer than 200 are known today) places them in the realm of the elite. The stratification of society became more complex during the fourth millennium BC and a class of specialized workmen was being created with links to the ruling elite, who therefore had access to a broader range of material goods and, notably, also knowledge, that separated them from the majority of the population. Thus, the demands of the ruling elite and the producers of the fish-tail knives were very strongly intertwined and linked the latter with the prestige (power, knowledge, etc.) of those who ultimately used them.

A drilled hole in the upper part of this knife caused a fracture of one part of the fork. TH

79. RIPPLE-FLAKED KNIFE

Light-brown flint with pinkish
discolorations
Late Naqada II–early Naqada III,
ca. 3400–3100 BC
Purchased in Luxor, 1920
L: 23.0; W: 5.8; T: 0.7 cm;
weight: 141.9 g
OIM E10533

79, obverse

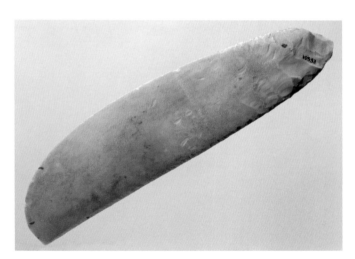

79, reverse

Ripple-flaked knives are among the finest flint tools
from anywhere in the world. They show the distinct
ripple flaking on one side while the opposite side
of the knife features a ground surface with only
marginal retouching at the back of the blade. A
very fine denticulation occurs along the cutting
edge of the knife which, in many cases, shows no
use wear or damage. Original handles of the ripple-
flaked knives could be of ivory or bone and with
depictions of rows of animals, but also scenes of
warfare and hunting as shown on the famous Gebel
el-Arak knife, today in the Louvre in Paris (E 11517).
The handles also possess a knob for a string that
allowed the attachment of the knife to a belt, for
example. Modern reproductions of ripple-flaked
knives have shown that the ripple effect with its
parallel and lamellar appearance is the result of
removal of broad, ellipsoid flakes through pressure
flaking. Ripple-flaked knives date from late Naqada
II to early Naqada III (ca. 3400–3100 BC). Their raw
material is often a light-brown flint with pinkish
discolorations like this piece. Their function was
purely ceremonial. Finds in the late Predynastic
cemetery at Abusir el-Meleq near the Fayum
indicate a belief that ripple-flaked knives were the
carriers of magical powers. There, several of these
knives had obviously been deliberately broken
before they were placed inside the tombs.   TH

THE RISE OF THE STATE

THE BATTLEFIELD PALETTE

80. THE BATTLEFIELD PALETTE

Siltstone
Naqada III, ca. 3100 BC
Acquired at Abydos, presented to the Ashmolean
Museum, 1896
H: 28; W: 20 cm
Ashmolean AN1892.1171

Cosmetic palettes are characteristic products of
the Predynastic period. Their shape changed over
time, and by Naqada III, they evolved into large
commemorative pieces carved with elaborate and
often enigmatic scenes. Some of these decorated
palettes, including this one, have a circular
depression that reflects their original use as a
surface upon which cosmetics were ground. The
decorated palettes are made of a fine-grained,
dark-gray siltstone (also called slate, mudstone, or
graywacke) that comes from the Wadi Hammamat
in the Eastern Desert (Nicholson and Shaw 2000,
p. 58). The complex iconography of the decorated
palettes comprises some of the most important
evidence for the growth and development
of political and religious ideology of the late
Predynastic period, before the advent of writing.

Three fragments of the Battlefield Palette are
known; this one from the Ashmolean, a larger piece
now in the British Museum, and a smaller fragment
in a private collection.

The decoration on this palette, as on many
others, refers to the control of chaos (see
"Iconography in the Predynastic and Early Dynastic
Period" in this volume) that is equated with the
Egyptian king's domination over his enemies. The
British Museum fragment shows a lion, a symbol
of the king, mauling foreigners. The "otherness" of
the enemies is expressed by their hair and beards;
their lack of status is underscored by their nudity;
and their defeat, by the ravens and vultures that
peck at their bodies. The sense of chaos is conveyed

80, obverse

80, reverse

by the confused sprawl of the enemy's bodies which seem to float free of any organizing groundline. This general composition is seen on other decorated palettes, where an animal, a bull or lion, may be shown goring, trampling, or biting enemies. The bull, like the lion, was a symbol of the Egyptian king and his power.

The obverse of the Ashmolean fragment likewise shows the contrast between chaos and order. In the upper section, men's legs flail. Below, enemies, their arms bound behind them, are seized and driven forward by anthropomorphized standards topped with a falcon and an ibis, both of which presumably represent Egyptian deities. Here, the conquest of chaos is represented by the binding and subjugation of the enemy.

On the reverse, long-necked animals, perhaps giraffes or long-necked gazelles, flank a palm tree.

A guinea fowl(?) stands above. As summarized by Hendrickx ("Iconography in the Predynastic and Early Dynastic Period" in this volume), "the giraffe symbolizes the wild aspect of nature, and therefore chaos, and the palm tree the tamed aspect of nature, and therefore order," yet the further interpretation of this composition remains "problematic."

These large decorated palettes were probably commissioned as temple offerings. EVM/ET

PUBLISHED (SELECTED)

Capart 1905, pp. 238–41, figs. 178–80; Midant-Reynes 2000, pp. 242–43, fig. 20; H. Müller 1959, pp. 68–70, pl. 3; Petrie 1953, pp. 10, 14, pls. D13, E14; W. Smith 1949, p. 112, fig. 27; Spencer 1980, pp. 79–80, pl. 64.576; Spencer 1993, pp. 54–55, figs. 34–35; Whitehouse 2009, p. xii

80, joined with the British Museum piece

STATUE OF KING KHASEKHEM

This limestone statue of Khasekhem is one of two closely similar figures of the last king of the Second Dynasty (the other, carved in siltstone, is now in the Cairo Museum) excavated at Hierakonpolis within an area of the later temple enclosure that may have been used originally for performances of ceremonies associated with kingship. Among the earliest surviving examples of royal stone statuary from Egypt, these masterpieces exhibit many of the conventions that were defined during the Early Dynastic period, encapsulating elements of royal iconography that continued in an unbroken tradition into the Roman period.

Both statues show the king seated on a block throne with a low back and plain recessed panels on each side. The king wears the White Crown of Upper Egypt and he is wrapped in a long robe with a thick collar, similar to that worn in the *heb-sed* festival, a jubilee during which the king's authority was reaffirmed through rituals of rejuvenation. His left arm is held across his body and his right arm is stretched out along his thigh. The clenched right fist is pierced with a small hole, possibly for attaching an item of regalia such as a mace handle or scepter.

Lightly incised on top of the base, in front of the king's bare feet and facing toward him, is the name "Khasekhem," written inside the stylized motif of the niched palace facade (the *serekh*) surmounted by the falcon of the deity Horus. This was the oldest name in a king's elaborate titulary. The *serekh* symbolized the center of royal administration and power, identifying the king as a living manifestation of Horus, the god of Egyptian kingship.

Around the base of the throne on both statues, the bodies of slain enemies are depicted in contorted poses that may evoke the aftermath of a battle. The style of incision of the figures is unusual. The lines are created by series of short, retouched strokes, contrasting sharply with the formal, almost geometric pose of the king seated above. The front edge of the plinth is inscribed with a total for the number of defeated foes: 47,209 on the present statue and 48,205 on the one in Cairo. This statue identifies them as "northern rebels" by means of a prostrate bearded figure on the right, bound at the elbows and struck down by a mace, with a clump of papyrus — emblem of the marshy Delta — on top of his head.

This theme of military conquest occurs on other objects inscribed with Khasekhem's name found at Hierakonpolis, including a fragmentary stone stela mentioning "foreign lands" and a group of large, stone vessels inscribed with a motif for the "Union of the Two Lands" recording the "Year of fighting the northern enemies." This has led to the suggestion that the king waged a military campaign to regain control of the north after which he reunited the country and changed his name to Khasekhemwy (meaning "He Who Shines Forth [with] the Two Powers").

Whether these objects record historical events in a reunification of Upper and Lower Egypt at the end of the Second Dynasty, or whether Khasehem(wy) was conforming to one of the norms of Egyptian kingship, the meaning of the two statues is plain: positioned below the king's feet, the enemies of the state are subject to his power and dominion. Containment of unrule — here represented by the rebellious northerners — was one of the main duties of the king, who maintained the order of the cosmos by eradicating chaos on earth. The image of the triumphant king subjugating his fallen enemies was essential to Egyptian art for the next three thousand years. LM

PUBLISHED (SELECTED)

Junker 1955; McNamara 2008; Quibell 1900, p. 11, pls. 39–41; Quibell and Green 1902, p. 44; Whitehouse 2009, pp. 38–40

81

81, side of base

81. STATUE OF KING KHASEKHEM

Limestone
Dynasty 2, ca. 2685 BC
Hierakonpolis, temple enclosure
Excavations of Quibell and Green,
1897–99
Gift of the Egyptian Research Account
H: 62.4 cm
The Visitors of the Ashmolean Museum,
Oxford AN1896–1908 E.517

81, front of base

THE INVENTION OF WRITING

The first examples of writing appear in Tomb U-j at Abydos dated to Dynasty 0 (see "The Invention of Writing in Egypt" and "Tomb U-j: A Royal Burial of Dynasty 0 at Abydos" in this volume). Until recent years, it had been thought that writing developed in Egypt as a result of contact with Mesopotamia. However, now this diffusionist theory has been superseded by the idea that writing was developed independently in both areas and at about the same time, about 3300 BC. The earliest texts from Egypt are geographic and personal names, the names of commodities, and numerals. Several centuries would pass until narrative texts appeared. ET

82. FRAGMENT OF INSCRIBED STORAGE VESSEL

Baked clay
Dynasty 1, reign of Qa'a, ca. 2890 BC
Abydos, Umm el-Qaab, tomb of Qa'a
Gift of the Egypt Exploration Fund, 1902
H: 7.9; W: 13.7; T: 1.2 cm
OIM E5899

82

This fragment of a large storage vessel, probably for wine, is incised with the name of an economic institution that supplied goods for the tomb of King Qa'a at Abydos. The partially preserved inscription consists of the upper half of an oval surrounded by a wavy line that represent a geographic location surrounded by a wall. Within the oval is the top of a *serekh,* of which only the falcon, the top of the rectangle, and a single partially preserved hieroglyph remain. The composition denotes an area controlled by the king. However, because the lower part of the *serekh* is lost, the name within cannot be definitely matched with other known *serekh*s, but it is probably to be read Semerkhet (*s[mr-ḫt]*). Since some tombs, like U-j, were found to have jars with different markings, Günter Dreyer has concluded that such notations denote the origin of the contents, not their destination ("Tomb U-j: A Royal Burial of Dynasty 0 at Abydos" in this volume).

The text was incised on the jar before it was fired, attesting to close coordination between the managers of the pottery workshop where the vessels were made, the overseers of the vineyards

that supplied the contents, and those who were in charge of furnishing the tomb — an interlocking system of responsibilities that is evidence of a sophisticated administrative system. EVM/ET

PUBLISHED (SELECTED)

MacArthur 2010, p. 124; Petrie 1900, pp. 29–30, pl. 46.103

83. INSCRIBED IVORY

Ivory, pigment
Dynasty 1, reign of Djet, ca. 2950 BC
Abydos, Umm el-Qaab, tomb of Djet
Gift of the Egypt Exploration Fund,
1902
L: 3.3; W: 3.9; T: 0.6 cm
OIM E6105

83

Many examples of early writing functioned as more than simple communication. Some tags from Tomb U-j, as well as some from First Dynasty royal tombs, were incised with hieroglyphs that were laboriously filled with pigment, suggesting that early writing also conveyed a sense of prestige.

This object bears the name and title of an official who worked for the royal administration. His title (at left) is "Chief of the Servant(s) of the Royal Beard," perhaps a reference to an attendant for the official regalia of the king that would have included a false beard. The official's name (at right) is Hery-netcherw. By prominently placing his name and title on either side of the *serekh* of King Djet, he stressed his association with the king, thereby claiming elite status. The object was recovered from the tomb of Djet, and so perhaps it was a gift to the king by his loyal official.

Grooves and holes on the back of the piece allowed it to be attached to another surface, perhaps to a small box.   EVM/ET

PUBLISHED (SELECTED)

MacArthur 2010, p. 129; Petrie 1900, p. 40, pls. 10.9, 13.2; Vandier 1952, p. 850, fig. 567.2; Weill 1961, vol. 1, p. 119

84

FIGURE C11. Reconstructed cylinder seal with the seat/throne and duck sign combination and the *serekh* of King Aha (after Kaplony 1963, fig. 80)

84. INSCRIBED JAR FRAGMENT

Calcite
Dynasty 1, reign of Aha, ca. 3100 BC
Abydos, Umm el-Qaab, Cemetery B
Gift of the Egypt Exploration Fund, 1902
H: 7.6; W: 5.4 cm
OIM E5933

The surface of this vessel fragment is incised with two hieroglyphic signs. The first is a seat or throne ⌐. The other sign, probably 🦆, is a pintail duck. Scholars agree that they represent a personal name. Since this sign combination appears on some objects in conjunction with the *serekh* of King Aha (fig. C11), some scholars have interpreted

the notation as the name of a son of King Aha. However, as on this jar fragment, the name occurs in isolation, suggesting that the signs may refer to a courtier. In either case, this individual was closely connected to the king, but exactly in what manner remains unknown. EVM

PUBLISHED (SELECTED)

Helck 1987, p. 179; Kaplony 1963, p. 610; Petrie 1901a, pp. 20, 48–49, pl. 2.13

85, obverse

85, reverse

85. TAG

Ivory
Dynasty 1, reign of Qa'a, ca. 2890 BC
Abydos, Umm el-Qaab, rubbish heap
Gift of the Egypt Exploration Fund, 1902
H: 2.5; W: 2.3 cm
OIM E6192

This double-sided tag was originally square with a hole perforated in the upper corner. Perforated ivory tags such as this were attached to bags, boxes, and jars of commodities that were left in tombs. These inscribed tags presumably had a ceremonial or ritual function beyond simple identification, as expressed by the precious material — ivory — and the time-consuming process of incising, rather than inking, the inscription.

The text is an "annals label" that records special ceremonies or occurrences during a specific year of a king's reign. Most commemorate religious ceremonies or military actions, but this example is more mundane.

The obverse has three columns. Using another, better-preserved example the text can be reconstructed. The right column is the name of the year ("... acacia wood by the two carpenters of the King of Upper and Lower Egypt ..."). This probably refers to the delivery of material to a royal workshop (Wilkinson 1999, p. 218). Although not on the same scale of other year names that refer to seemingly more important events, this delivery warranted its own special mention.

The middle column has the ceremonial *nbty* name of King Qa'a, "Sennebty," that associated him with the goddesses Nekhbet and Wadjet, followed by a notation of a "fine quality" oil called the "fighter scent." The left column has the *serekh* of King Qa'a followed by the name of two economic domains, "Ḥwt p-ḥr-msn" and "Ḥwt-ʾIt." The reverse of the tag reads "bird fat," presumably the source of the oil.

The text on the whole thus identifies a commodity (bird fat-based oil) that was transferred from two economic institutions of King Qa'a in the year that a delivery of acacia wood was made. EVM/ET

PUBLISHED

Kaplony 1963, pp. 298–301, 312, fig. 847B, Qa'a a,1–2, pl. 145; MacArthur 2010, p. 127; Petrie 1901a, p. 26, pl. 8.2; Petrie 1902, p. 7, pl. 11.11

86. LABEL WITH INKED INSCRIPTION

Ivory, pigment
Dynasty 1, reign of Aha, ca. 3100 BC
Abydos, Umm el-Qaab, Cemetery B
Gift of the Egypt Exploration Fund, 1902
H: 1.9; W: 1.7; T: 0.2 cm
OIM E5929

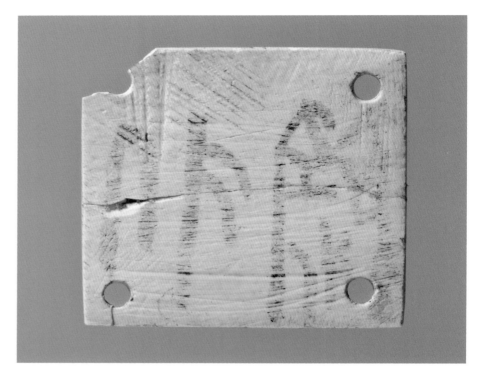

86

Petrie found this object in the vicinity of the tomb of King Aha at Abydos. The black and red pigment inscription is badly worn, but one can still identify the *serekh* of King Aha (at right), and two hieroglyphic signs 𓊞 and 𓏤, rendering the possible translation *šms.(w?)* ꜥ*ḥꜣ* "the follower(s) of King Aha." Another, smaller label in the collection of the Oriental Institute Museum (OIM E6198) bears the same text and perforations. The function of this piece is unclear, but presumably the four holes allowed it to be attached to another object.

Even the earliest examples of writing in Egypt include phonetic signs rather than purely pictographic one. The early writing system was very complex, incorporating different kinds of signs: logograms, alphabetic signs, single signs that stand for two or more phonetic values, and non-phonetic determinatives. The earliest texts record the names of kings, economic institutions associated with the kings, and commodities deposited in the tombs, indicating that one of the primary purposes of early writing was to express the power of the king.   EVM/ET

PUBLISHED (SELECTED)

Helck 1987, p. 147; Kahl 1994, p. 732 n. 2281; Petrie 1901a, p. 20, pl. 3.17

87. SEALING

Clay
Dynasty 2, reign of Sekhemib,
ca. 2690 BC
Abydos, Umm el-Qaab, tomb of
Peribsen
Gift of the Egypt Exploration Fund,
1902
H: 5.1; W: 5.1; T: 2.2 cm
OIM E6252

Some of the best documentation
for early writing and for the
growth of the administration
comes from inscriptions left by
cylinder seals on clay that was
used to seal jars and boxes. This
seal bears the title "One Who Is
Under the Head of the King" (*ḥry-
tp ny-sw.t is-ḏfꜣ*). The king referred
to is Sekhemib.   ET

PUBLISHED (SELECTED)

Emery 1949, p. 95, fig. 55; Helck 1987,
p. 200; Kaplony 1963, p. 1128, fig. 267,
pl. 72; Naville 1914, p. 49, pl. 9; Petrie
1901a, p. 31, pl. 21.165; Quibell 1904–
1905, pl. 8.165

87

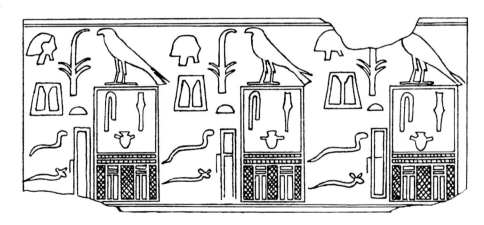

SYMBOLS OF ROYAL POWER

From the end of the Predynastic period to the Early Dynastic period, a series of artistic and iconographic features were formulated to differentiate the kings from their subjects. Most of these features continued to be part of royal ideology and iconography for the following three thousand years. The status of the kings was also proclaimed by their near monopoly over resources such as hard stone and crystal and their access to the best craftsmen. ET

88. RIM OF BOWL WITH *SEREKH*

Dolomitic limestone, pigment
Dynasty 1, reign of Aha, ca. 3100 BC
Abydos, Umm el-Qaab, Cemetery B
Gift of the Egypt Exploration Fund, 1902
H: 4.1; W: 3.7 cm
OIM E5930

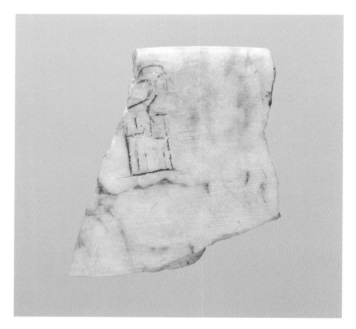

88

Egyptian kings differentiated themselves from their subjects by setting their names within a distinctive frame, called a *serekh*. In the Early Dynastic period, the name was placed in a rectangle that represented the niched facade of a palace surmounted by a falcon, the representation of the god Horus. This name, later called the "Horus name," expressed the nature of the king as the earthly manifestation of the god (Wilkinson 1999, p. 200). The *serekh* graphically illustrated that association as well as the idea that the palace was the residence of the god-king. The use of *serekh*s was a perogative of the king. In a culture with very limited literacy, the *serekh* was an unmistakable visual marker of the king's presence.

This fragment of a bowl is incised with a *serekh* with the name of King Aha. A reddish pigment has been rubbed into the incision to make the *serekh* stand out against the veining of the bowl. ET

PUBLISHED

Petrie 1901a, p. 20, pl. 3.7

89. SEALING OF KING NARMER

Unbaked clay
Dynasty 1, reign of Narmer, ca. 3100 BC
Abydos, Umm el-Qaab, tomb B17, tomb of Narmer
Gift of the Egypt Exploration Fund, 1902
H: 11.4; W: 11.0 cm
OIM E6718

89

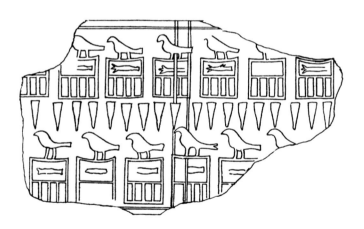

Storage jars were sealed with large lumps of clay over which a carved seal was rolled leaving an impression. This sealing bears the repeating *serekh* of Narmer, who is now believed to be the first king of the First Dynasty. He is best known as the triumphant king on the ceremonial Narmer Palette (see "The Narmer Palette: A New Interpretation" in this volume) and the Narmer Mace-head. His *serekh* has been found at numerous sites in Egypt, the southern Levant (see "Early Interaction between Peoples of the Nile Valley and the Southern Levant" in this volume), and in Nubia, documenting the range of his activities.

His name, written with the sign for a catfish (*nˁr*) and the *mr*-chisel, shows the fluidity of early Egyptian writing. The *serekh* may contain both signs, or as here, the catfish alone with the chisel outside and below the *serekh*, repeated again and again as a decorative pattern. Sealings are among the best documentation for the names of the Early Dynastic kings and the order of their succession. EVM/ET

PUBLISHED (SELECTED)

Kaplony 1963, pp. 60, 1094, fig. 26A; MacArthur 2010, p. 131; Petrie 1901a, pp. 30, 51, pl. 13.91

90

90. FRAGMENT OF A LABEL

Ebony
Dynasty 1, reign of Djer, ca. 2950 BC
Abydos, Umm el-Qaab, tomb of Djer
Gift of the Egypt Exploration Fund, 1902
L: 5.9; H: 2.1 cm
OIM E6058

The kings recorded special ceremonies or events as a history of their reign. This fragment of such a record lists types of oil and an event from which the year took its name. The oil quality marks include: ☒ ḥ3.t, "high-quality [oil]"; ☒ pḥ(.w), another quality designation; and ○ nw, following Helck, perhaps for ⦚/○ ṯḥn.w or "Libyan oil." To the right of the oil designations an enclosure containing three bound captives is a reference to an event for which the year was named. The bound prisoner(s) motif continued to be used by kings to express their royal authority and dominance for the rest of Egyptian history. EVM

PUBLISHED

Helck 1987, pp. 173; Petrie 1901a, p. 23, pl. 5A.13

91. LABEL WITH IMAGE OF KING DEN

Ivory
Dynasty 1, reign of Den, ca. 2950 BC
Abydos, Umm el-Qaab, tomb of Den
Gift of the Egypt Exploration Fund, 1902
H: 3.6; W: 3.0 cm
OIM E6146

91

This label, or ornament for another object, bears an image of a king standing behind a tall thin pole (most now lost) topped with an image of the jackal god Wepwawet, whose name means "Opener of Ways." It appears in scenes of the king smiting enemies, especially Libyans, here alluding to the power of the king over his foes. Wepwawet was also a protector of the necropolis, and so he was especially appropriate to be portrayed on objects from the royal tombs. Standards topped with figures of gods or with geographic emblems are shown in rituals where they were carried (see reverse of the Narmer Palette (figs. 16.1–2), fixed in the ground, or attached to the cabin of ships (see Catalog Nos. 30, 31, 37).

The king wears a long wig that falls down his back but leaves his ears uncovered, a (false?) beard, bands that cross his chest, and a kilt tied at the waist. He is shown striding forward with a mace in his right hand and a long staff in his left — a motif that lasted for thousands of years. In the reign of Den, the king acquired another title and name in addition to the Horus name that was in a *serekh* (see Catalog No. 88). This new name was linked to the title, *nsw-bity* "King of Upper and Lower Egypt." It specifically proclaimed the king's domination over the entire country, rather than just the area in the south around Abydos and Hierakonpolis. Although kings before Den ruled the north and the south, this authority was now expressed by the newly introduced title.

Here, the *nsw-bity* name in front of the king can be read either *Ḫꜣs.ty* or *Smy.ty*. Interpretations differ, but regardless of the reading, the name refers to the deserts, hill countries, or foreign lands. It has been thought to be related to the king's military campaigns in the northeast which are also documented by materials from Syria-Palestine found in Egypt that can be dated to the reign of Den (Wilkinson 1999, pp. 76–77). The combination of the *nsw-bity* name and the cult standard of Upper Egypt on this label stresses the power of the king.

The development of a series of formal names of the king (the "titulary") demonstrated the refinement of royal ideology. By the middle of the Old Kingdom, the king had five elements to his name that expressed his association with the gods Horus and Re and the goddesses Wadjet and Nekhbet, who respectively represent the north and south.   EVM/ET

PUBLISHED (SELECTED)

Kahl 2004, p. 344; Petrie 1900, p. 38, pls. 10.14, 14.9; Vandier 1952, p. 852, fig. 852, upper right

92. FRAGMENT OF A CRYSTAL VESSEL

Rock crystal
Dynasty 1, reign of Semerkhet,
ca. 2890 BC
Abydos, Umm el-Qaab, tomb U, tomb
of Semerkhet
Gift of the Egypt Exploration Fund,
1900–1901
H: 5.1; W: 3.8 cm
OIM E6446

92

Although the tombs of the first kings were plundered and even burned in antiquity, and crudely excavated by early archaeologists, Petrie was able to recover many spectacular objects during his work at the turn of the last century. The splendor of the objects interred with the kings is demonstrated by this fragment of a rock crystal vessel. Crystal was obtained from the Western Desert and Sinai peninsula, making it a rare and precious material. Petrie recovered this bowl fragment and others like it from the tomb of King Semerkhet. The use of such lavish, and impractical, materials was largely restricted to tombs of royalty and high officials. The fragile nature of such a vessel suggests that it was not intended for routine use, but rather it was a luxury item that reflected the prestige of the king. This fragment is incised with a cross-like sign at its upper edge (center). [Petrie inked a "U" on the fragment to record its provenance (Tomb U).] Petrie found examples of this mark on vessels from the tombs of the rulers Djer, Merneith, and Qa'a. EVM

MACE-HEADS FROM THE MAIN DEPOSIT AT HIERAKONPOLIS

The Main Deposit at Hierakonpolis was a collection of ceremonial objects most of which reflected the power of the king. The deposit was located in a part of the temple that has been described as an "arena for rituals of kingship ... used by successive kings" (McNamara 2008, p. 928), a further indication of the materials' symbolic nature. Objects from the deposit include some of the most famous works of Early Dynastic art — the Narmer Palette (fig. 16.1) and the Narmer and Scorpion mace-heads (Quibell 1900, 1904–05).

Among the objects in the deposit were "hundreds" of small mace-heads. On the Narmer Palette, the king is shown smiting enemies with a pear-shaped mace-head, a scene that continued with variations throughout the Dynastic period. These smiting scenes function on a more cosmic level far beyond any reference to actual martial activity, for one of the primary obligations of the king was to maintain the order of the world and to forestall the forces of chaos.

By the First Dynasty, mace-heads were purely ceremonial, having evolved from actual weapons to symbols of the power and prestige of the king. A carved ivory cylinder (now in the Ashmolean Museum) shows large-scale mace-heads like those of Narmer and Scorpion set up on poles, perhaps in a "court of royal appearances" (McNamara 2008, p. 928). The variety of different stones employed to make mace-heads, and the friability of some of those materials, only underscores the ceremonial nature of these objects. The most common shapes for mace-heads are the disk and pear shape, but they were also made in the form of falcons and hippopotami, references to Horus, with whom the king was associated, and perhaps to slaying hippos which was an allusion to the king conquering chaos.   ET

93.   DISK-SHAPED MACE-HEAD

Porphyry
Naqada II, ca. 3800–3300 BC
Hierakonpolis, Main Deposit, 471
Gift of the Egypt Exploration Fund, 1897–1898
D: 10.9; H: 1.6 cm
OIM E4725

Disk-shaped mace-heads were replaced by pear-shaped mace-heads in Naqada II (Needler 1984, p. 258).   ET

PUBLISHED
Quibell and Green 1902, pl. 27.2–7

93

94. PEAR-SHAPED MACE-HEAD

Limestone
Dynasty 1, ca. 3100–2890 BC
Hierakonpolis, Main Deposit, 471
Gift of the Egypt Exploration Fund,
1897–1898
H: 4.5; D: 5.7 cm
OIM E4739

The perforation through this
mace-head, which would
have allowed it to be hafted
to a handle, is incomplete,
underscoring its symbolic, rather
than functional, role.   ET

PUBLISHED

Quibell and Green 1902, pl. 27.25

94

WEAPONS

ARROWHEADS FROM THE ROYAL TOMBS

Arrowheads of the Early Dynastic period were made of various materials. Flint is quite frequent, but the use of bone (see Catalog Nos. 97–101), ivory, wood, or crystal is not uncommon. Catalog No. 96 is made of transparent crystal and features a pointed leaf shape with a small stem for hafting. Both faces are pressure flaked. Catalog No. 95 is made of ivory and is from the tomb of King Djer, in which hundreds of these arrowheads were found (fig. C12).   TH

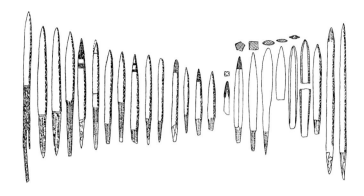

FIGURE C12. Selection of bone and ivory arrow tips from the tomb of King Djer (after Petrie 1901a, pl. 34)

95

96

95. ARROWHEAD

Ivory
Dynasty 1, reign of Djer, ca. 2950 BC
Abydos, Umm el-Qaab, tomb of Djer
Gift of the Egypt Exploration Fund, 1900–1901
L: 5.8; W: 0.6 cm
OIM E6015

PUBLISHED
Petrie 1901a, pl. 34

96. ARROWHEAD

Crystal
Dynasty 1, reign of Djer, ca. 2950 BC
Abydos, Umm el-Qaab, tomb of Djer
Gift of the Egypt Exploration Fund, 1900–1901
L: 4.5; W: 0.9; T: 0.4 cm; weight: 1.6 g
OIM E6096

PUBLISHED
Petrie 1901a, pl. 6.6

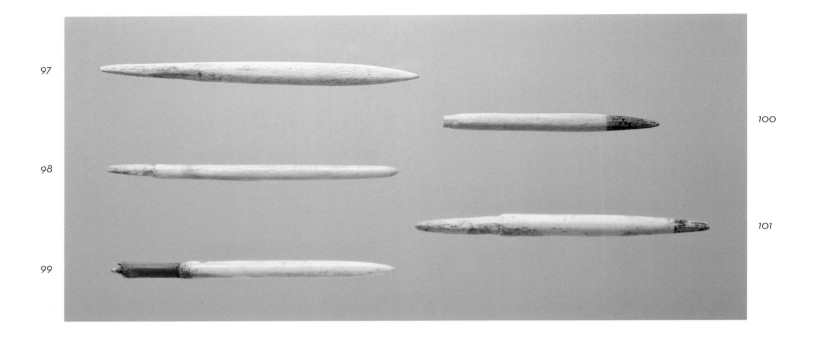

97

100

98

101

99

97–101.   GROUP OF ARROWHEADS

Bone
Dynasty 1, reign of Djer, ca. 2950 BC
Abydos, Umm el-Qaab, tomb of Djer
Gift of the Egypt Exploration Fund, 1900–1901
Range of length: 5.8–8.0 cm
97. OIM E6002
98. OIM E6008
99. OIM E6009
100. OIM E6004
101. OIM E6007

Petrie recovered "hundreds" of bone arrowheads from the tomb of Djer. He suggested that they had originally been inserted into reed shafts. The ends of the arrowheads are tipped with red ocher, which Petrie speculated could be poison, or it could be a form of sympathetic magic alluding to the blood of the animal that the arrow would kill. Petrie states that this style of arrowhead was common in the earlier part of the First Dynasty, but fell out of use by the end of the dynasty. Many different shapes of arrowheads were found in the tomb of Djer.   ET

PUBLISHED

Petrie 1901a, pp. 34–35, pl. 34

102. PEAR-SHAPED MACE-HEAD

Dolomite marble
Dynasty 1, reign of Djer, ca. 2950 BC
Abydos, Umm el-Qaab, tomb of Djer
Gift of the Egypt Exploration Fund,
1900–1901
H: 6.3; D: 5.6 cm
OIM E6046

Pear-shaped mace-heads were
the ceremonial weapon par
excellence. Although obsolete as
a weapon in the First Dynasty,
they were symbols of prestige and
power. This example is blackened
and cracked by fire, perhaps
from the fires that destroyed the
royal tombs in antiquity, or in the
further destruction of the tombs
and their contents at the end of
the nineteenth century AD (Petrie
1901a, p. 2).   ET

102

102, bottom

241

103

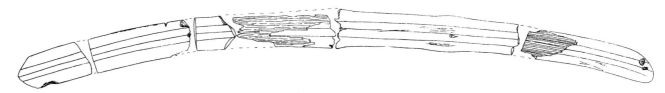

FIGURE C13. Wood fragments of a throwstick. Scale 1:2 (after Petrie 1901a, pl. 36.14)

103. THROWSTICK

Wood
Dynasty 1, reign of Djer, ca. 2950 BC
Abydos, Umm el-Qaab, tomb of Djer
Gift of the Egypt Exploration Fund, 1900–1901
Maximum dimensions: L: 13.0; W: 3.1; T: 1.1 cm
OIM E6439A–D

One of the most primitive weapons in the Egyptian arsenal, the throwstick acquired conflicting symbolic status in Egyptian practices. On multiple jar sealings from the tombs of the First Dynasty kings Djer, Djet, Den, and Queen Merneith, the common hieroglyph of upraised arms ⨆ (Gardiner Sign-list D28, *k3*) was modified to include a throwstick held in the right hand: 🖑.[1] Parallel and later writings lack this feature, so that the modification probably reinforced the sign's primary significance as the "vital force" of an individual.[2] As a traditional instrument of military prestige, throwsticks were included among royal tomb furnishings at least until the New Kingdom. Many pieces of such throwsticks were found in the tomb of King Djer, and the selection of fragments now in the Oriental Institute are among the earliest surviving examples of these weapons.[3] The arrangement of pieces in the catalog photograph is intended only to suggest the general shape, as precise joins are not possible. Further throwstick fragments were found in mingled debris discarded from the plunder of the adjacent tombs of the last kings of the First Dynasty, Semerkhet and Qa'a (see fig. C13).[4] Throwsticks would again appear in quantity in the tomb of Tutankhamun.[5]

Although used by Egyptians "from the earliest to last dynasties" (Carter 1933, p. 142) (fig. C14), the throwstick was early adopted as a hieroglyph (⟩, later ⟩) to designate foreigners with less sophisticated weaponry. As an ideogram, it is used to spell both "Libya" and "Asiatic," and as a determinative the sign was later applied to all foreign lands and peoples (Gardiner 1957, p. 513 [Sign-list T14–15]). Distinct types of Egyptian, Libyan, and Syrian throwsticks are represented in relief, and scenes of foreign combatants using throwsticks are readily attested.[6] The bivalent throwstick thus symbolizes royal might and foreign weakness. RKR

FIGURE C14. Egyptian holding a throwstick (Rosellini 1977, pl. 117)

NOTES

[1] See Petrie 1900, pp. 25 (nos. 10 and 12–18) and 43 (nos. 10 and 12), and pls. 19.10 and 20.12–15, 18); and Petrie 1901a, p. 31 and pl. 16.121, 123–24.

[2] Griffith (in Petrie 1900, p. 43) suggests with hesitation "thrower of the boomerang" for the modified *k3*-arms in sealing no. 10, but treats the same sign as a simple variant in no. 12 (*k3 3ḥ* "spiritualized ka"). For parallel sealings with and without the modified *k3*-arms, cf. Petrie 1900, pl. 20.20 (Merneith) and Petrie 1901a, pl. 16.124 (Djer). This distinction is not noted in the comments on parallelism in Petrie 1901a, pp. 31 and 52.

[3] For examples and discussion, see Petrie 1901a, p. 37 and pl. 36.1–2 and 14.

[4] See Petrie 1901a, p. 39, and pl. 44.2 and 22.

[5] Carter 1933, vol. 3, pp. 141–42 and pls. 76–77. Among the "missile-weapons" found in the Annexe and Antechamber, Carter distinguishes boomerangs used for hunting from throwsticks used for warfare. In shape, both types may be simple curved pieces of hard wood. Among the thirty-four projectiles were ceremonial throwsticks of faience, gilt wood, or ebony. For the distribution, see Reeves 1990, pp. 175–76 and p. 29 (additional fragmentary faience examples from the tomb).

[6] Gardiner 1957, p. 513 (Sign-list T14–15).

[7] See Petrie 1917, p. 36 and pls. 43 (drawings of Syrian, Libyan, and Egyptian types) and 69 (preserved wooden Egyptian types). Canaanites carrying throwsticks appear in paintings at Beni Hassan, see Yadin 1963, vol. 1, pp. 167–69 ("hurling-sticks").

OBJECTS FROM THE ROYAL TOMBS

104–107. FURNITURE INLAYS

Ivory, pigment
Dynasty 1, ca. 2950 BC
Abydos, Umm el-Qaab, tombs of Den (E6147) and Anedjib (E6184, E6185, E6186)
Gift of the Egypt Exploration Fund, 1899–1901
104: OIM E6147: L: 4.0; W: 2.1 cm
105: OIM E6184: L: 6.2; W: 0.9 cm
106: OIM E6185: L: 4.4; W: 1.6 cm
107: OIM E6186: L: 5.1; W: 2.8 cm

105

106

107

104

The tombs of the First Dynasty kings at Umm el-Qaab were heavily disturbed at different occasions in antiquity. The tombs were discovered at the end of the nineteenth century by Émile Amélineau and only a few years later they were excavated again by W. M. F. Petrie (see "Petrie and the Discovery of Earliest Egypt" and "Tomb U-j: A Royal Burial of Dynasty 0 at Abydos" in this volume). During the last decades, the site has been systematically investigated by the German Archaeological Institute. Fragmentary objects are all that remain of the once rich funeral equipment. Many fragments of ivory inlays were found by Petrie and presented to different museums. They must once have been part of the decoration of furniture such as chairs and boxes. Although figurative decoration also occurs, these fragments show only finely cut geometric patterns into which dark-brown pigment has been introduced. At least some of them are based on imitations of wickerwork or basketry, and they show how common utensils were turned into elite objects through the use of prestigious materials. SH

PUBLISHED

OIM E6147: Petrie 1901a, pl. 11.57
OIM E6184: Petrie 1901a, pl. 42.55
OIM E6185: Petrie 1901a, pl. 42.47
OIM E6186: Petrie 1901a, pl. 42.44

LEGS FROM FURNITURE

Bovine legs take a particularly important place among the furniture elements found in the Early Dynastic royal tombs. The best-preserved example Catalog No. 108) represents a back leg while the other (Catalog No. 109) may have been a front leg. The two objects were found in different tombs and obviously do not belong to the same piece of furniture, but they nevertheless show the standardization of the production. The legs stand on ribbed cylinders, another standardized characteristic of this type of object. Although beds are the most frequently attested furniture for the Early Dynastic period, the two objects seem too small to have been parts of beds and so are probably from chairs. Nearly all remains of furniture have been found in elite tombs, showing that furniture as a part of funerary equipment illustrates the high social status of the tomb owner.

Creating legs of beds and chairs in the shape of bovine or lion legs is of course of symbolic significance. There can hardly be any doubt that these two impressive and powerful animals have been chosen as protectors, or originally perhaps, even as personifications of the individuals using the furniture.   SH

108. FURNITURE LEG

Ivory
Dynasty 1, ca. 2890 BC
Abydos, Umm el-Qaab, tomb of Semerkhet
Gift of the Egypt Exploration Fund, 1899–1901
H: 10.5 cm
OIM E6901

PUBLISHED
Petrie 1900, pl. 12.8; Petrie 1901a, pl. 43.1

108

109, front

109, back

109. FURNITURE LEG

Ivory
Dynasty 1, ca. 2890 BC
Abydos, Umm el-Qaab, tomb of Djer
Gift of the Egypt Exploration Fund,
1899–1901
H: 10.4; W: 3.9; T: 3.0 cm
OIM E5952

The back view shows the
complicated drilling and mortises
that allowed the craftsman to join
pieces of ivory.   ET

PUBLISHED

Petrie 1901a, pl. 34.16

111. MODEL HARPOON

Copper
Dynasty 2, ca. 2685 BC
Abydos, Umm el-Qaab, tomb of Khasekhemwy
Gift of the Egypt Exploration Fund, 1899–1901
L: 11.3; W: 1.7 cm
OIM E6229

110. MODEL CHISEL

Copper
Dynasty 2, ca. 2685 BC
Abydos, Umm el-Qaab, tomb of Khasekhemwy
Gift of the Egypt Exploration Fund, 1899–1901
L: 12.9; W: 3.7 cm
OIM E6224

The royal tombs were furnished with a wide array of model tools. Presumably, these were deposited in the tomb for the king to use in the afterlife. However, because it is very unlikely that a king would use craftsmen's tools, the deposition of model tools may be compared to the allegorical scenes in much later royal tombs that show the king reaping the fields, or similar scenes in private tombs that show high officials working in the field. The tradition of leaving model tools in tombs continued through the Dynastic period, and a set of tools was found in the tomb of Tutankhamun that is some 1,500 years later than this example. ET

Model harpoons were associated with the hippopotamus hunt. Throughout the Dynastic period, the hippopotamus was a symbol of evil and chaos. Scenes that show the king spearing the animal symbolize his power and guardianship over the land. This link between the king and the hippopotamus hunt continued into the Ptolemaic era, during which time it was prominently portrayed in the Edfu Temple. ET

PUBLISHED
Petrie 1901a, pl. 9A.5

PUBLISHED
Petrie 1901a, pl. 9A.4

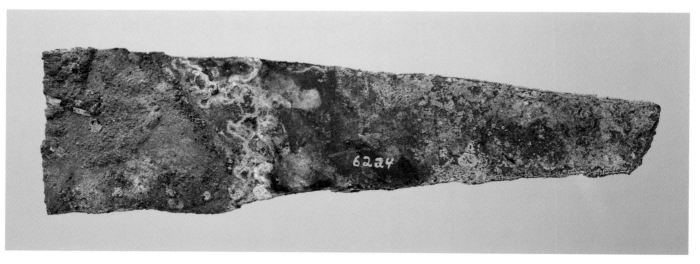

110

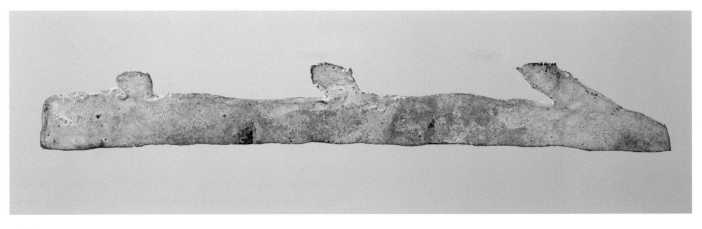

111

112. AX HEAD

Copper
Dynasty 2, ca. 2685 BC
Abydos, Umm el-Qaab, tomb of
Khasekhemwy
Gift of the Egypt Exploration Fund
1899–1901
W: 14.6; L: 10.7; T: 0.9 cm
OIM E6240

112

This heavy, cast copper ax head may have been a functional tool. The hole allowed it to be hafted to a handle. It was one of several found in the tomb of Khasekhemwy. Axes may have been placed in the tomb because the value of the copper reflected the wealth of the king and his ability to take such valuable material to the tomb, and they may, like mace-heads, symbolize the power of the king.   ET

PUBLISHED

Petrie 1901a, pl. 45.76

113

113. GAME PIECE

Indurated limestone(?)
Dynasty 1, ca. 2950 BC
Abydos, Umm el-Qaab, tomb of Djer
Gift of the Egypt Exploration Fund, 1899–1901
H: 3.1; D: 1.7 cm
OIM E6057

Game pieces were recovered from the royal tombs, the tombs of courtiers, and from temple deposits at Abydos, indicating the popularity of board games. Scenes of kings as well as courtiers playing board games continued to be an enduring theme in Egyptian art.   ET

PUBLISHED

Petrie 1901a, pl. 35.73

114. LIONESS GAME PIECE

Ivory
Dynasty 1, ca. 2950 BC
Abydos, Osiris Temple, deposit M69
L: 5.7; W: 2.0; H: 3.0 cm
Gift of the Egypt Exploration Fund,
1902–1903
OIM E7895

114

This elegantly carved figure of a feline sits in a serene recumbent pose with its forepaws outstretched in front of it and its tail curved around its haunch. Both the incised detailing of an embroidered collar and the lack of a conspicuous mane make it clear that this piece represents a lioness. Most artifacts such as this have been found as individual finds in graves of the Early Dynastic

114, front view

114, back view

period, such as in the retainer burials around the royal tombs and enclosures at Abydos. This example, however, was recovered from the Osiris Temple at Abydos in deposit M69, which Petrie interpreted as a rubbish hole into which damaged temple offerings were thrown (Petrie 1903, p. 23).

The lioness may originally have been part of a set for the ancient Egyptian game *mehen* or "serpent game" (fig. C15) (Kendall 2007). In later tomb scenes, such as that of Hesy-Re of the Third Dynasty at Saqqara (Emery 1961, fig. 150), the game is depicted as comprising three lions and three lionesses, together with thirty-six marbles and a set of rods that were probably used as throwsticks. The *mehen* board took the form of a coiled snake and although the rules of play are unknown it seems that pieces would be moved around the segmented coils of the snake's body toward the head in the center. In funerary contexts, these game pieces may have taken on magical properties that aided the deceased, for in later Egyptian times there is evidence that victory in such games could be symbolic of attaining life after death (Kendall 2007, pp. 41–42). AS

FIGURE C15. *Mehen* game board. Calcite. Old Kingdom, Dynasties 3–6, ca. 2707–2219 BC. 38.0 x 4.5 cm. OIM E16950

115. FRAGMENT OF A BRACELET

Diorite(?)
Dynasty 2, ca. 2690 BC
Abydos, Umm el-Qaab, tomb of Peribsen
Gift of the Egypt Exploration Fund, 1899–1901
L: 4.5; W: 1.6; T: 0.8 cm
OIM E6213

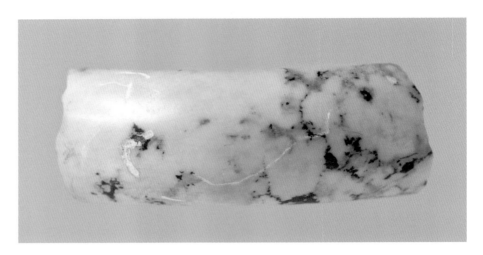

115

The material recovered from the royal tombs, as fragmentary as it is, suggests the splendor of the lifestyles of the early kings. This fragment of a bangle bracelet is made of a hard stone, an expression of the king's monopoly on the time of craftsmen and his access to the finest materials. ET

PUBLISHED

Petrie 1901a, pl. 45.7–17

SUBSIDIARY BURIALS OF THE FIRST DYNASTY

Hundreds of subsidiary burials surrounded the tombs and funerary enclosures of the kings of the First Dynasty (see "The First Kings of Egypt: The Abydos Evidence" in this volume; figs. C16–17). The phenomenon of subsidiary burials began with the second king of the First Dynasty, Aha, who was accompanied in death by two women — Sema-nebty and Bener-ib — and some thirty-four additional, unnamed individuals. The height of this phenomenon came during the reign of King Djer, whose grave complex contained some 318 subsidiary burials. After his reign, however, fewer and fewer individuals were buried with kings, and the last ruler to have subsidiary burials was Qa'a, the final king of the First Dynasty.

Subsidiary burials consisted of small tombs into which either wood coffins or hide-wrapped bodies were placed. Some of these chambers have been identified as magazines for storing goods, not bodies. Others, such as those at the so-called Donkey Enclosure at north Abydos, contained donkeys, not humans. Within the graves was a wide range of funerary goods, including game pieces, furniture, weapons, and jewelry. The graves were arranged around the tomb of the deceased king, often in contiguous rows, whereby graves shared common walls and perhaps even roofing.

Small funerary stelae, carved with the name and sometimes the title of the deceased, marked the graves. These document that both men and women were buried alongside the king. These stelae appeared first in the reign of King Djer. The upper part of each was carved and the lower part left blank, so that it could be securely embedded in the ground to mark the identity of the individual interred below, not unlike modern tombstones. Unfortunately, only a few of the stelae recovered from the royal cemetery can be associated with a particular grave or area.

The burial of so many individuals alongside the king has excited the imagination of scholars, and

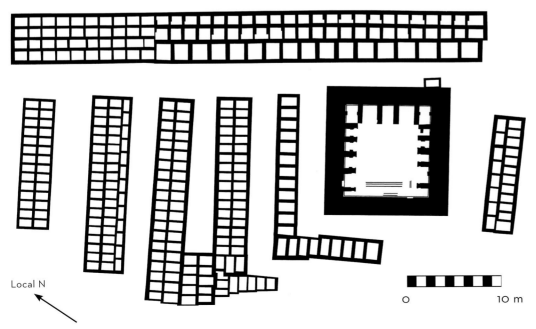

FIGURE C16. Plan of King Djer's tomb complex at Umm el-Qaab (Bestock 2009, fig. 13). The main burial chamber was surrounded by 318 subsidiary tombs. Of the hundreds of stelae published by Petrie from 1900 to 1901, seventy-three came from this tomb complex: sixty belonged to women, one to a "dwarf," and twelve were too fragmentary to identify. Catalog Nos. 116 and 117 were recovered from this complex, but their original place within it is unknown. The miniature ivory cylindrical vessel and two stone bowls (Catalog Nos. 63119–20) were recovered from subsidiary grave O2

Local N

0   10 m

there has long been speculation as to whether the individuals buried at Abydos were human sacrifices, or if they had been granted tombs near the king for use at the time of their natural deaths. The architecture of the tombs, with their shared walls, would make it difficult to roof tombs at different times, suggesting sacrifice. Evidence for sacrifice also comes from King Aha's funerary enclosure. There, a physical anthropologist has identified stains caused by strangulation on the teeth of the interred (Galvin 2005). However, in a more recent publication (Doughetry 2010), it is stated that "there is no conclusive evidence for human sacrifice here [Hierakonpolis] or at Abydos." Thus, the debate surrounding the circumstances of the subsidiary burials continues. However, what is clear is the prestige that came from being buried near the king, and the influence of royal authority at the dawn of the Dynastic period.   EVM

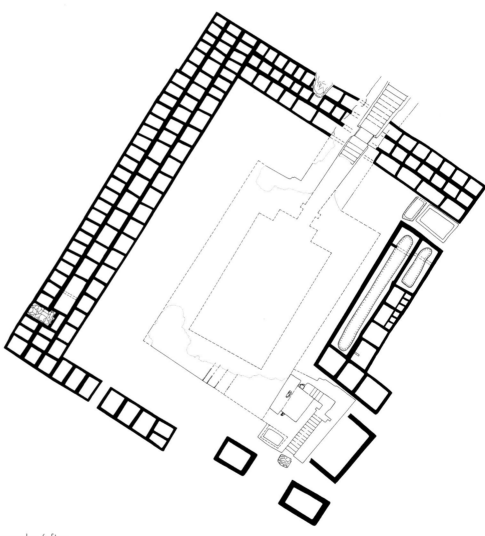

FIGURE C17. Plan of King Den's tomb complex (after Dreyer et al. 1993). It contained 142 subsidiary tombs. Of the hundreds of stelae published by Petrie from 1900 to 1901, thirty-nine came from this tomb complex. Sixteen belonged to women, nine to men, and fourteen were too fragmentary to identify. The reduction in subsidiary graves at this time corresponds to a change in the layout of the tomb complex — the subsidiary chambers being more evenly distributed around the sides of the complex (after Dreyer et al. 1993, fig. 13)

Local N

0   10 m

116. FUNERARY STELA

Limestone
Dynasty 1, reign of Djer, ca. 2950 BC
Abydos, Umm el-Qaab, tomb O, subsidiary burial of Djer
Gift of the Egypt Exploration Fund, 1902
H: 31.9; W: 14.7 cm
OIM E5863

116

This roughly hewn limestone round-top stela is eroded by sand and weather. The top half was carved with raised hieroglyphic signs and the lower half was left blank. This stela belonged to a female courtier of King Djer, as attested by the seated woman determinative 𓁐. Her name, which is written from right to left as 𓊃𓈖𓂝𓂋, has been read in several ways, of which the most convincing is *sšm.t kȝ* (*≠i*) "She Who Guides My Ka." Her titles are: 𓅃𓂀 *mȝ(ȝ.t) Hr* "She Who Beholds Horus"; 𓅃𓏤, *ḥᶜ(.t) (ḫnᶜ) Hr* "(Female) Servant of Horus"; and 𓂝𓃩, *ᶜ(.t) Stẖ* "She Who Lifts Up Seth." The responsibilities of individuals bearing these titles are not clear. What is certain, however, is that burial in the royal funerary complex was a sign of prestige.   EVM

PUBLISHED (SELECTED)

Helck 1987, p. 119; D. Jones 2000, pp. 349.1300, 353.1314, 421.1561; Klasens 1956, pp. 26, fig, 7.126, pp. 31-32, no. 126; Petrie 1901a, pp. 32-33, pl. 27.96; Sabbahy 1993, pp. 81-87, fig. 1B

253

117. FUNERARY STELA

Limestone
Dynasty 1, reign of Djer, ca. 2950 BC
Abydos, Umm el-Qaab, tomb O, subsidiary burial of Djer
Gift of the Egypt Exploration Fund, 1902
H: 38.9; W: 22.0 cm; T: 10.3
OIM E5865

117

This roughly hewn limestone stela belonged to a female courtier of King Djer whose name is , *Ḥtp(.t)* "She Who is Content." Many stelae in this complex belonged to women, documenting the high status of women in Early Dynastic society. No titles accompany her name. EVM

PUBLISHED (SELECTED)

Klasens 1956, p. 26, fig. 7.86, p. 28, no. 86; MacArthur 2010, p. 135; Petrie 1901a, pp. 32–33, pls. 26.86, 29B.86

118. FUNERARY STELA

Limestone
Dynasty 1, reign of Den, ca. 2950 BC
Abydos, Umm el-Qaab, tomb T, subsidiary burial of Den
Gift of the Egypt Exploration Fund, 1902
H: 29.6; W: 2.7 cm
OIM E5869

118

This stela belonged to a female courtier of King Den. Only her name, whose translation is difficult, is given. The difficulty stems from the outline style of the hieroglyphs that leads to confusion between signs. The *ka* arms 𓂓 can be easily identified, but the second sign could be either the *r* mouth 𓂋, or the *i̓r* eye 𓁹. Kaplony argued for the latter, proposing that the pupil was painted rather than carved. In that case, the name could be rendered *i̓r(.t)-kꜣ* "That Which My Ka Created." Kaplony alternatively suggested that the second sign could be the *r* mouth, which could be rendered *kꜣ(=i̓)-i̓r(=i̓)-* "My Companion is My Ka." EVM

PUBLISHED (SELECTED)

Kahl 1994, p. 443 n. 169; Kaplony 1963, pp. 191, 429–30; Klasens 1956, pp. 30–31; Petrie 1901a, pp. 32–33, pls. 27.136, 30A.136

TWO BOWLS FROM SUBSIDIARY BURIALS OF KING DJER

These vessels were found by Petrie's excavation team in one of the subsidiary burials positioned along the northern side of King Djer's burial chamber. These stone containers are among several thousand that were buried around these royal tombs, although most were found in fragments. The quantity and quality of such artifacts attest to the concentration of wealth and craft specialization around the First Dynasty royal court. The expertise of these royal craftsmen is clear from such vessels, with better interior smoothing and more highly polished exteriors than is generally seen in earlier types of stone working. According to Petrie's monograph, at least two other vessels, both cylindrical in form, were also found in subsidiary burial O2 (Petrie 1901a, pl. 53). AS

119. BOWL

Dolomite marble
Dynasty 1, ca. 2950 BC
Umm el-Qaab, subsidiary burial of
King Djer, tomb O2
Gift of the Egypt Exploration Fund,
1900–1901
H: 7.5; D: 13.2 cm
OIM E6044

PUBLISHED

Petrie 1901a, pl. 51c.250

119

120

120. JAR

Dolomite marble
Dynasty 1, ca. 2950 BC
Abydos, Umm el-Qaab, subsidiary
burial of King Djer, tomb O2
Gift of the Egypt Exploration Fund,
1900–1901
H: 4.4; D: 5.1 cm
OIM E6045

PUBLISHED

Petrie 1901a, pl. 51e.281

THE TOMB OF AN OFFICIAL AT ABYDOS

The Temenos of Osiris I had wished to excavate since I first saw it in 1887. It was undoubtedly one of the oldest centres of worship, and had a long history to be unraveled. — Petrie 1902, p. 1

In 1902, Petrie began excavating the ancient town of Abydos, in the low-lying center of the site where the main temple to the god Osiris once stood. That structure was built on top of an earlier shrine to the jackal god Khenty-imentiu. In antiquity, a town had sprung up and spread out along the temple. After the Old Kingdom, an enclosure wall was built, its foundations set into the rubbish of deserted houses. This enclosed space is known as the "Temenos of Osiris," and it was there, among the deserted houses and debris, that Petrie found a few large tombs, several smaller burials, and votive deposits (see "Petrie and the Discovery of Earliest Egypt" in this volume).

Of the burials, tomb M19 seemed to have been of particular interest to Petrie "This was the richest tomb of all ... exceptional in having much finer vases than the others." The tomb contained nearly one hundred vessels of stone (calcite, slate, diorite, and siltstone) and ceramic plates, bowls, jars, and cylinders (fig. C18).

The owner's name and administrative titles were not preserved, and so his relationship to the king and the state is unknown. As expected for such an early burial, the body interred in tomb M19 was not mummified. However, his tomb was carefully prepared, with stone vessels arranged at his head and against the northern wall, and ceramic vessels stacked against the eastern and southern walls. The tomb itself was relatively large in comparison to other tombs in the vicinity, and it seems to have been roofed. The splendor of such a tomb demonstrates the growth and wealth of the burgeoning Egyptian bureaucracy. EVM

FIGURE C18. Tomb M19

121   122   123   124   125

126   127   128   129

121. JAR

Calcite
Abydos, Temenos of Osiris,
tomb M19
Dynasty 1, reign of Merneith,
ca. 2950 BC
Gift of the Egypt Exploration Fund,
1901–1902
H: 17; D: 10.5 cm
OIM E7612

The Oriental Institute Museum
has at least twenty of the stone
vessels recovered from tomb M19.

PUBLISHED

Petrie 1902, pp. 16–21, pl. 46.36

122. JAR

Calcite
Abydos, Temenos of Osiris,
tomb M19
Dynasty 1, reign of Merneith,
ca. 2950 BC
Gift of the Egypt Exploration Fund,
1901–1902
H: 11.8; D: 11.9 cm
OIM E7623

PUBLISHED

Petrie 1902, pp. 16–21, pl. 47.6

123. JAR

Calcite
Abydos, Temenos of Osiris,
tomb M19
Dynasty 1, reign of Merneith,
ca. 2950 BC
Gift of the Egypt Exploration Fund,
1901–1902
H: 22.2; 7.4 cm
OIM E7618

PUBLISHED

Petrie 1902, pp. 16–21, pl. 46.7

124. BOWL

Calcite
Abydos, Temenos of Osiris,
tomb M19
Dynasty 1, reign of Merneith,
ca. 2950 BC
Gift of the Egypt Exploration Fund,
1901–1902
H: 11.1; D: 16.5 cm
OIM E7624

PUBLISHED

Petrie 1902, pp. 16–21, pl. 47.17

125. JAR

Calcite
Abydos, Temenos of Osiris,
tomb M19
Dynasty 1, reign of Merneith,
ca. 2950 BC
Gift of the Egypt Exploration Fund,
1901–1902
H: 7.5; D: 9 cm
OIM E7613

PUBLISHED

Petrie 1902, pp. 16–21, pl. 46.19

126. BOWL

Baked clay
Abydos, Temenos of Osiris,
tomb M19
Dynasty 1, reign of Merneith,
ca. 2950 BC
Gift of the Egypt Exploration Fund,
1901–1902
L: 17.3; W 12.0; H: 3.6 cm
OIM E7734

PUBLISHED

Petrie 1902, pp. 16–21, pl. 41.75

127. BOWL

Baked clay
Abydos, Temenos of Osiris, tomb
M19
Dynasty 1, reign of Merneith, ca.
2950 BC
Gift of the Egypt Exploration Fund,
1901–1902
H: 5.5; D: 10.6 cm
OIM E7743

PUBLISHED

Petrie 1902, pp. 16–21, pl. 41.83

128. BOWL

Calcite
Abydos, Temenos of Osiris, tomb
M19
Dynasty 1, reign of Merneith, ca.
2950 BC
Gift of the Egypt Exploration Fund,
1901–1902
H: 2.5; D: 9.2 cm
OIM E7611

PUBLISHED

Petrie 1902, pp. 16–21, pl. 47.8

129. BOWL

Slate
Abydos, Temenos of Osiris, tomb
M19
Dynasty 1, reign of Merneith, ca.
2950 BC
Gift of the Egypt Exploration Fund,
1901–1902
H: 3.6; D: 16.0 cm
OIM E7784

PUBLISHED

Petrie 1902, pp. 16–21, pl. 47.4

CONCORDANCE OF MUSEUM REGISTRATION NUMBERS

Registration Number	Catalog / Figure Number	Description
ASHMOLEAN MUSEUM OF ART AND ARCHAEOLOGY		
AN1892.1171	Cat. No. 80	The Battlefield Palette
AN1896–1908 E.517	Cat. No. 81	Statue of King Khasekhem
THE ORIENTAL INSTITUTE OF THE UNIVERSITY OF CHICAGO		
OIM C209	Figure 16.1	Narmer Palette (cast)
OIM E734	Cat. No. 39	Painted vessel
OIM E768	Cat. No. 34	Painted vessel
OIM E805	Cat. No. 61	Pebble stone
OIM E858	Cat. No. 13	Straight-spouted jar
OIM E905	Cat. No. 22, Figure 7.3	Bowl
OIM E935	Figure 7.7	Stone vessel
OIM E940	Cat. No. 28	Painted bowl
OIM E1708	Cat. No. 26	Polished Red-ware dish
OIM E1814	Cat. No. 25	Black-Topped jar with pot mark
OIM E1826	Cat. No. 23	Bottle
OIM E4725	Cat. No. 93	Disk-shaped mace-head
OIM E4732	Cat. No. 64	Scorpion figurine
OIM E4739	Cat. No. 94	Pear-shaped mace-head
OIM E5189	Cat. No. 31	Painted vessel
OIM E5230	Cat. No. 32	Painted funnel
OIM E5234	Cat. No. 33	Painted vessel
OIM E5241	Figure 10.2	Jar with wavy handles
OIM E5256	Cat. No. 6	Fish-shaped palette
OIM E5279	Cat. No. 51	Rectangular palette
OIM E5283	Cat. No. 47	Rhomboid palette
OIM E5330	Cat. No. 27	Rough-ware jar
OIM E5653	Cat. No. 75	Stylized tag
OIM E5811	Cat. No. 21, Figure 7.3	Double beaker
OIM E5816	Cat. No. 15, Figures 7.5 and 10.2	Vessel with wavy handles
OIM E5863	Cat. No. 116	Funerary stela
OIM E5865	Cat. No. 117	Funerary stela
OIM E5869	Cat. No. 118	Funerary stela
OIM E5899	Cat. No. 82	Fragment of inscribed storage vessel
OIM E5912	Cat. No. 4	Bracelet
OIM E5916	Figure 7.10	Ivory comb
OIM E5920	Figure 7.11	Bone spoon
OIM E5929	Cat. No. 86	Label with inked inscription
OIM E5930	Cat. No. 88	Rim of bowl with *serekh*
OIM E5933	Cat. No. 84	Inscribed jar fragment
OIM E5952	Cat. No. 109	Furniture leg
OIM E5954	Cat. No. 63	Cylindrical vessel
OIM E6002	Cat. No. 97	Arrowhead
OIM E6004	Cat. No. 100	Arrowhead
OIM E6007	Cat. No. 101	Arrowhead
OIM E6008	Cat. No. 98	Arrowhead
OIM E6009	Cat. No. 99	Arrowhead
OIM E6015	Cat. No. 95	Arrowhead
OIM E6044	Cat. No. 119	Bowl
OIM E6045	Cat. No. 120	Jar
OIM E6046	Cat. No. 102	Pear-shaped mace-head
OIM E6057	Cat. No. 113	Game piece
OIM E6058	Cat. No. 90	Fragment of a label
OIM E6096	Cat. No. 96	Arrowhead
OIM E6105	Cat. No. 83, Figure 2.13	Inscribed ivory
OIM E6146	Cat. No. 91	Label with image of King Den
OIM E6147	Cat. No. 104	Furniture inlay
OIM E6151	Cat. No. 54	Bi-truncated, regular blade tool
OIM E6168	Cat. No. 62	Bowl fragment with inscription
OIM E6184	Cat. No. 105	Furniture inlay
OIM E6185	Cat. No. 106	Furniture inlay
OIM E6186	Cat. No. 107	Furniture inlay
OIM E6192	Cat. No. 85	Tag
OIM E6213	Cat. No. 115	Fragment of a bracelet
OIM E6224	Cat. No. 110	Model chisel
OIM E6229	Cat. No. 111	Model harpoon
OIM E6240	Cat. No. 112	Ax head
OIM E6252	Cat. No. 87	Sealing
OIM E6320	Cat. No. 14	Model chisel
OIM E6439A–D	Cat. No. 103	Throwstick
OIM E6446	Cat. No. 92	Fragment of a crystal vessel
OIM E6651	Cat. No. 73	Model *nw/nemset* vessel
OIM E6718	Cat. No. 89	Sealing of King Narmer
OIM E6901	Cat. No. 108	Furniture leg
OIM E7354	Cat. No. 58	Sickle blade
OIM E7411	Cat. No. 59	Spiked flint tool
OIM E7535	Cat. No. 56	Sickle blade
OIM E7538	Cat. No. 55	Sickle blade
OIM E7558	Cat. No. 57	Sickle blade
OIM E7611	Cat. No. 128, Figure 7.9	Bowl (catalog only)
OIM E7612	Cat. No. 121, Figure 7.9	Jar (catalog only)
OIM E7613	Cat. No. 125, Figure 7.9	Jar (catalog only)

Registration Number	Catalog / Figure Number	Description	Registration Number	Catalog / Figure Number	Description
OIM E7618	Cat. No. 123, Figure 7.9	Jar (catalog only)	OIM E10862	Figures 7.7, C3	Stone vessel
OIM E7623	Cat. No. 122, Figure 7.9	Jar (catalog only)	OIM E10864	Figure 10.1	Stone vessel
OIM E7624	Cat. No. 124, Figure 7.9	Bowl (catalog only)	OIM E11054	Cat. No. 49	"Pelta-shaped" palette
			OIM E11063	Cat. No. 44	Bowl
OIM E7734	Cat. No. 126	Bowl (catalog only)	OIM E11085	Cat. No. 45	Jar
OIM E7738	Figure 10.2	Jar with wavy handles	OIM E11250	Cat. No. 78	Fish-tail knife
OIM E7743	Cat. No. 127	Bowl (catalog only)	OIM E11252	Cat. No. 77	Fish-tail knife
OIM E7774	Figure 10.6	Wine jar	OIM E11258	Cat. No. 8	Arrowhead
OIM E7784	Cat. No. 129	Bowl (catalog only)	OIM E11264	Cat. No. 7	Arrowhead
OIM E7895	Cat. No. 114	Lioness game piece	OIM E11265	Cat. No. 9	Arrowhead
OIM E7897	Cat. No. 67	Baboon	OIM E11463	Cat. No. 52	Falcon palette
OIM E7900	Cat. No. 72	Model hes jar	OIM E11469	Figure 8.5	Palette
OIM E7910	Cat. No. 74	Figurine of a youth	OIM E11470	Cat. No. 53	Composite animal palette
OIM E7911	Cat. No. 70	Votive plaque	OIM E11473	Cat. No. 48	Double-bird palette
OIM E7960	Cat. No. 69	Baboon	OIM E11912	Cat. No. 19	Cylindrical vessel
OIM E7961	Cat. No. 66	Female figurine	OIM E11917	Cat. No. 60	Blade
OIM E8208	Cat. No. 65	Frog	OIM E12170	Cat. No. 50	Elephant palette
OIM E8302	Cat. No. 68	Baboon	OIM E12322	Cat. No. 5	Decorated ostrich egg
OIM E8315	Cat. No. 71	Model hes jar	OIM E16950	Figure C15	Mehen game board
OIM E8907	Cat. No. 11	Hooked ornament or pin	OIM E18243	Cat. No. 29	Painted bowl with animal head
OIM E8922	Cat. No. 35, Figure C3	Painted vessel	OIM E18253	Cat. No. 24	Jar
OIM E8923	Cat. No. 1	Jar with hunting scene	OIM E21901	Figure 9.1	Ripple-burnished jar
OIM E9026	Cat. No. 20, Figure 7.3	Bowl	OIM E23662	Figure 9.11	Sealing
			OIM E23666	Figure 9.6	Gold bracelet
OIM E9345	Cat. No. 36	Painted vessel	OIM E23726	Figure 9.8	Palette
OIM E9366	Figure 7.10	Ivory comb	OIM E23727	Figure 9.6	Copper spearhead
OIM E10533	Cat. No. 79	Ripple-flaked knife	OIM E23758	Figure 9.2	Jug
OIM E10581	Cat. No. 30, FIgure 8.3	Painted vessel	OIM E24058	Figure 9.10	Archaic Horus Incense Burner
			OIM E24061	Figure 9.3	Faience jar
OIM E10592	Figure 11.2	Cylinder seal	OIM E24062	Figure 9.3	Faience jar
OIM E10609	Cat. No. 41, Figure 7.7	Jar with lug handles	OIM E24069	Cat. No. 10, Figure 9.7	Qustul Incense Burner
OIM E10610	Cat. No. 43	Jar	OIM E24119	Figure 9.13	Bowl
OIM E10688	Cat. No. 3	Carved tusk	OIM E24153	Figure 9.14	Bowl
OIM E10695	Cat. No. 76	Amulet in form of a man	OIM E24159	Figure 9.6	Mace-head
OIM E10758	Cat. No. 37	Painted vessel	OIM E24197	Figure 9.5	Vessel stand
OIM E10759	Cat. No. 38, Figure 8.3	Painted vessel	OIM E26072	Cat. No. 12	Jar with wavy handles
OIM E10762	Cat. No. 2, Figure 8.3	Painted vessel	OIM E26112	Cat. No. 17, Figures 7.5 and 10.2	Vessel with wavy handles
OIM E10782	Figure 8.3	Painted vessel	OIM E26239	Frontispiece	Painted vessel
OIM E10790	Cat. No. 42	Squat jar with lug handles	OIM E26240	Figure 8.3	Painted vessel
OIM E10795	Figure 7.7	Stone vessel	OIM E26815	Cat. No. 16, Figures 7.5 and 10.2	Vessel with wavy handles
OIM E10853	Cat. No. 40, Figure 10.1	Stone vessel	OIM E28207	Figure 10.5	Meidum bowl
OIM E10855	Figure 10.1	Stone vessel	OIM E29255	Cat. No. 18, Figures 7.5 and 10.2	Vessel with wavy handles
OIM E10856	Figure 7.7	Stone vessel			
OIM E10859	Cat. No. 46	Bird-shaped vessel	OIM E29871	Figure 4.4	Painted vessel

CHECKLIST OF THE EXHIBIT

Sequence Dating

OIM E5816	Vessel with wavy handles
OIM E26815	Vessel with wavy handles
OIM E26112	Vessel with wavy handles
OIM E29255	Vessel with wavy handles
OIM E11912	Cylindrical vessel

The Physical Setting

OIM E8923	Jar with hunting scene
OIM E10762	Painted vessel
OIM E10688	Carved tusk
OIM E12322	Decorated ostrich egg
OIM E5912	Bracelet
OIM E5256	Fish-shaped palette
OIM E11264	Arrowhead
OIM E11258	Arrowhead
OIM E11265	Arrowhead

Trade and Contact

OIM E24069	Qustul Incense Burner
OIM E26072	Jar with wavy handles
OIM E858	Straight-spouted jar
OIM E8907	Hooked ornament or pin
OIM E6320	Model chisel

Culture of the Predynastic Period

Pottery

OIM E905	Bowl
OIM E9026	Bowl
OIM E5811	Double beaker
OIM E1814	Black-Topped jar with pot mark
OIM E1708	Polished Red-ware dish
OIM E1826	Bottle
OIM E18253	Jar
OIM E5330	Rough-ware jar
OIM E18243	Painted bowl with animal head
OIM E940	Painted bowl
OIM E10581	Painted vessel

OIM E10758	Painted vessel
OIM E10759	Painted vessel
OIM E5189	Painted vessel
OIM E5230	Painted funnel
OIM E5234	Painted vessel
OIM E9345	Painted vessel
OIM E26239	Painted vessel
OIM E8922	Painted vessel
OIM E734	Painted vessel

Stonework

OIM E5283	Rhomboid palette
OIM E11473	Double-bird palette
OIM E11054	"Pelta-shaped" palette
OIM E12170	Elephant palette
OIM E11463	Falcon palette
OIM E5279	Rectangular palette
OIM E11470	Composite animal palette
OIM E10853	Stone vessel
OIM E10609	Jar with lug handles
OIM E768	Painted vessel
OIM E10859	Bird-shaped vessel
OIM E11063	Bowl
OIM E11085	Jar
OIM E10610	Jar
OIM E10790	Squat jar with lug handles

Religion

OIM E6168	Bowl fragment with inscription
OIM E5954	Cylindrical vessel
OIM E4732	Scorpion figurine
OIM E8208	Frog
OIM E7960	Baboon
OIM E7897	Baboon
OIM E8302	Baboon
OIM E7961	Female figurine
OIM E8315	Model *hes* jar
OIM E7900	Model *hes* jar
OIM E6651	Model *nw/nemset* vessel

OIM E7911	Votive plaque
OIM E7910	Figurine of a youth
OIM E10695	Amulet in form of a man
OIM E5653	Stylized tag
OIM E11252	Fish-tail knife
OIM E11250	Fish-tail knife
OIM E10533	Ripple-flaked knife

Writing

OIM E5899	Fragment of inscribed storage vessel
OIM E6192	Tag
OIM E6252	Sealing
OIM E5933	Inscribed jar fragment
OIM E5929	Label with inked inscription
OIM E6105	Inscribed ivory

Tools

OIM E6151	Bi-truncated regular blade tool
OIM E7354	Sickle blade
OIM E7538	Sickle blade
OIM E7535	Sickle blade
OIM E7558	Sickle blade
OIM E11917	Blade
OIM E805	Pebble stone
OIM E7411	Spiked flint tool

The Rise of the State

OIM C209	Narmer Palette (cast)
AN1892.1171	Battlefield Palette
AN1896–1908 E.517	Statue of King Khasekhem
OIM E6146	Label with image of King Den
OIM E5930	Rim of bowl with *serekh*

OIM E6718	Sealing of King Narmer
OIM E4725	Disk-shaped mace-head
OIM E4739	Pear-shaped mace-head
OIM E6058	Fragment of a label
OIM E6046	Pear-shaped mace-head
OIM E6002	Arrowhead
OIM E6004	Arrowhead
OIM E6007	Arrowhead
OIM E6008	Arrowhead
OIM E6009	Arrowhead
OIM E6015	Arrowhead
OIM E6096	Arrowhead
OIM E6439A–D	Throwstick
OIM E6446	Fragment of a crystal vessel
OIM E6147	Furniture inlay
OIM E6184	Furniture inlay
OIM E6185	Furniture inlay
OIM E6186	Furniture inlay
OIM E5952	Furniture leg
OIM E6901	Furniture leg
OIM E6213	Fragment of a bracelet
OIM E7895	Lioness game piece
OIM E6057	Game piece
OIM E6224	Model chisel
OIM E6240	Ax head
OIM E6229	Model harpoon
OIM E5863	Funerary stela
OIM E5865	Funerary stela
OIM E5869	Funerary stela
OIM E6045	Jar
OIM E6044	Bowl

BIBLIOGRAPHY

Adams, Barbara

1987   *The Fort Cemetery at Hierakonpolis*. London: Kegan Paul International.

1995   *Ancient Nekhen: Garstang in the City of Hierakonpolis*. Egyptian Studies Association 3. New Malden: SIA Publishing.

1999   "Early Temples at Hierakonpolis and Beyond." In *Centenary of Mediterranean Archaeology, 1897-1997* (International Symposium, Cracow, October 1999), pp. 15–28. Krakow: Jagiellonian University.

2000a   *Excavations in the Locality 6 Cemetery at Hierakonpolis, 1979-1985*. British Archaeological Reports, International Series 903. Oxford: Archeopress.

2000b   "Dish of Delight and Coleoptera." In *Studies on Ancient Egypt in Honour of H. S. Smith*, edited by Anthony Leahy and John Tait, pp. 1–9. London: Egypt Exploration Society.

In press   *Fancy Stone Vessels from the Early Dynastic Royal Tombs at Abydos*. Studien zur Archäologie und Geschichte Altägyptens. Heidelberg.

Adams, Barbara, and Krzysztof M. Ciałowicz

1997   *Protodynastic Egypt*. Princes Risborough: Shire.

Adams, Barbara, and Renée F. Friedman

1992   "Imports and Influences in the Predynastic and Protodynastic Settlement and Funerary Assemblages at Hierakonpolis." In *The Nile Delta in Transition: 4th-3rd Millennium B.C.* (Proceedings of the Seminar Held in Cairo, 21–24 October 1990, at the Netherlands Institute of Archaeology and Arabic Studies), edited by Edwin C. M. van den Brink, pp. 317–38. Tel Aviv: Edwin C. M. van den Brink.

Adams, Barbara, and Naomi Porat

1996   "Imported Pottery with Potmarks from Abydos." In *Aspects of Early Egypt*, edited by Jeffrey Spencer, pp. 98–107. London: British Museum Press.

Adams, William Y.

1985   "Doubts about the Lost Pharaohs." *Journal of Near Eastern Studies* 44: 185–92.

Alexanian, Nicole

1998   "Die Reliefdekoration des Chasechemui, aus dem sogenannten Fort in Hierakonpolis." In *Les critères de datation stylistiques à l'Ancien Empire*, edited by Nicolas Grimal, pp. 1–21. Cairo: Institut français d'archéologie orientale.

Algaze, Guillermo

1993   *The Uruk World System: The Dynamics of Expansion of Early Mesopotamian Civilization*. Chicago: University of Chicago Press.

2001a   "Initial Social Complexity in Southwestern Asia: The Mesopotamian Advantage." *Current Anthropology* 42/2: 199–233.

2001b   "The Prehistory of Imperialism: The Case of Uruk Period Mesopotamia." In *Uruk Mesopotamia and Its Neighbors: Cross-cultural Interactions in the Era of State Formation*, edited by Mitchell S. Rothman, pp. 27–83. Santa Fe: School of American Research Press.

2008   *Ancient Mesopotamia at the Dawn of Civilization: The Evolution of an Urban Landscape*. Chicago: University of Chicago Press.

Amer, Mustafa

1936   "The Excavations of the Egyptian University in the Prehistoric Site at Maadi, near Cairo: The First Two Seasons' Work (1930/31 and 1932)." *Journal of the Royal Anthropological Institute of Great Britain and Ireland* 66, pp. 65–69.

Amiran, Ruth

1969   *Ancient Pottery of the Holy Land*. Jerusalem: Masada.

1974   "An Egyptian Jar Fragment with the Name of Narmer from Arad." *Israel Exploration Journal* 24: 4–12.

Amiran, Ruth; O. Ilan; and C. Arnon

1983   "Excavations at Small Tel Malhata: Three Narmer Serekhs." *Israel Museum Journal* 2: 75–83.

Anđelković, Branislav

1995   *The Relations between Early Bronze Age I Canaanites and Upper Egyptians*. Centre for Archaeological Research 14. Belgrade: Faculty of Philosophy.

2002   "Southern Canaan as an Egyptian Protodynastic Colony." *Cahiers Caribéens d'Egyptologie* 3–4: 75–92.

2004   "The Upper Egyptian Commonwealth: A Crucial Phase of the State Formation Process." In *Egypt at Its Origins: Studies in Memory of Barbara Adams* (Proceedings of the International Conference Origin of the State: Predynastic and Early Dynastic Egypt, Krakow, 28 August–1 September 2002), edited by Stan Hendrickx, Renée F. Friedman, Krzysztof M. Ciałowicz, and Marek Chłodnicki, pp. 535–46. Orientalia Lovaniensia Analecta 138. Leuven: Peeters.

2006   "Models of State Formation in Predynastic Egypt." In *Archaeology of Early Northeastern Africa: In Memory of Lech Krzyżaniak*, edited by Karla Kroeper, Marek Chłodnicki, and Michał Kobusiewicz, pp. 593–609. Studies in African Archaeology 9. Poznan: Poznan Archaeological Museum.

2008   "Parameters of Statehood in Predynastic Egypt." In *Egypt at Its Origins* 2 (Proceedings of the International Conference Origin of the State, Predynastic and Early Dynastic Egypt, Toulouse, France, 5–8 September 2005), edited by Béatrix Midant-Reynes and Yann Tristant, pp. 1039–56. Orientalia Lovaniensia Analecta 172. Leuven: Peeters.

2009   "Hegemony for Beginners: Egyptian Activity in the Southern Levant during the Second Half of the Fourth Millennium B.C." Public lecture delivered September 11, 2009, at the Sterling Memorial Library Lecture Hall, Yale Egyptological Institute in Egypt and Department of Near Eastern Languages and Civilizations, Yale University.

In press   "Factors of State Formation in Protodynastic Egypt." In *Egypt at Its Origins* 3 (Proceedings of the Third International Colloquium Origin of the State, Predynastic and Early Dynastic Egypt, London, 27 July–1 August 2008), edited by Renée F. Friedman and P. N. Fiske. Orientalia Lovaniensia Analecta 205. Leuven: Peeters.

Forthcoming "The Molding Power of Ideology: Political Transformations of Predynastic Egypt."

Anderson, Benedict

1983   *Imagined Communities*. London: Verso.

Anderson, Wendy

1992   "Badarian Burials: Evidence of Social Inequality in Middle Egypt during the Early Predynastic Era." *Journal of the American Research Center in Egypt* 29: 51–66.

Arkell, Anthony J.

1953   *Shaheinab: An Account of the Excavation of a Neolithic Occupation Site Carried out for the Sudan Antiquities Service in 1945–50*. London: Oxford University Press.

Arnold, Dorothea, and Janine Bourriau

1993   *An Introduction to Ancient Egyptian Pottery*. Mainz: Philipp von Zabern.

Aston, Barbara

1994   *Ancient Egyptian Stone Vessels: Materials and Forms*. Studien zur Archäologie und Geschichte Altägyptens 5. Heidelberg: Heidelberger Orientverlag.

Aston, Barbara; James Harrell; and Ian Shaw

2000   "Stone." In *Ancient Egyptian Materials and Technology*, edited by Paul Nicholson and Ian Shaw, pp. 5–77. Cambridge: Cambridge University Press.

Asselberghs, Henri M.

1961   *Chaos en Beheersing: Documenten uit het aenolithisch Egypte*. Documenta et Monumenta Orientis Antiqui 8. Leiden: Brill.

Ayrton, Edward R., and William L. S. Loat

1911   *Pre-dynastic Cemetery at El-Mahasna*. Egypt Exploration Fund 31. London: Egypt Exploration Fund.

Baba, Masahiro

2008   "Pottery-making Tools: Worked Sherds from HK11C Square B4, Hierakonpolis." In *Egypt at Its Origins* 2 (Proceedings of the International Conference Origin of the State, Predynastic and Early Dynastic Egypt, Toulouse, France, 5–8 September 2005), edited by Béatrix Midant-Reynes and Yann Tristant, pp. 7–20. Orientalia Lovaniensia Analecta 172. Leuven: Peeters.

2009   "Pottery Production at Hierakonpolis during the Naqada II Period: Toward a Reconstruction of the Firing Technique." *British Museum Studies in Ancient Egypt and Sudan* 13: 1–23.

Baduel, Nathalie

2008   "Tegumentary Paint and Cosmetic Palettes in Predynastic Egypt: Impact of those Artefacts on the Birth of the Monarchy." In *Egypt at Its Origins* 2 (Proceedings of the International Conference Origin of the State, Predynastic and Early Dynastic Egypt, Toulouse, France, 5–8 September 2005), edited by Béatrix Midant-Reynes and Yann Tristant, pp. 1057–90. Leuven: Peeters.

Bagh, Tine

2004   "First Dynasty Jewellery and Amulets: Finds from the Royal Naqada Tomb: Proposed Reconstructions, Comparisons and Interpretations." In *Egypt at Its Origins* 2 (Proceedings of the International Conference Origin of the State, Predynastic and Early Dynastic Egypt, Toulouse, France, 5–8 September 2005), edited by Béatrix Midant-Reynes and Yann Tristant, pp. 591–605. Leuven: Peeters.

Baines, John

1994   "On the Status and Purposes of Ancient Egyptian Art." *Cambridge Archaeological Journal* 4: 67–94.

1995   "Origins of Egyptian Kingship." In *Ancient Egyptian Kingship*, edited by David O'Connor and David P. Silverman, pp. 95–156. Probleme der Ägyptologie 9. Leiden: Brill.

1999   "Defining Social Complexity in Early Egypt: Levels of Pattering in the Evidence." Paper presented at the World Archaeological Congress 4, January 10–14, 1999. Cape Town.

2004   "The Earliest Egyptian Writing: Development, Context, Purpose." In *The First Writing: Script Invention as History and Process*, edited by Stephen D. Houston, pp. 150–89. Cambridge: Cambridge University Press.

2007   *Visual and Written Culture in Ancient Egypt*. Oxford: Oxford University Press.

Baines, John, and Norman Yoffee

1998   "Order, Legitimacy and Wealth in Ancient Egypt and Mesopotamia." In *Archaic States*, edited by Gary M. Feinman and Joyce Marcus, pp. 199–260. Santa Fe: School of American Research Press.

Bar-Adon, Pessaḥ

1980   *The Cave of the Treasure: The Finds from the Caves in Naḥal Mishmar*. Jerusalem: Israel Exploration Society.

Bard, Kathryn

1987   "The Geography of Excavated Predynastic Sites and the Rise of Complex Society in Egypt." *Journal of the American Research Center in Egypt* 24: 81–93.

1989   "The Evolution of Social Complexity in Predynastic Egypt: An Analysis of the Naqada Cemeteries." *Journal of Mediterranean Archaeology* 2: 223–48.

1994   *From Farmers to Pharaohs: Mortuary Evidence for the Rise of Complex Society.* Sheffield: Sheffield Academic Press.

Bar-Yosef Mayer, D.

2002   "Egyptian-Canaanite Interaction during the Fourth and Third Millennia BCE: The Shell Connection." In *Egypt and the Levant: Interrelations from the 4th through the Early 3rd Millennium BCE,* edited by Edwin C. M. van den Brink and Thomas E. Levy, pp. 129–35. London: Leicester University Press.

Baumgartel, Elise J.

1947   *The Cultures of Prehistoric Egypt.* London: Oxford University Press.

1955   *The Cultures of Prehistoric Egypt* 1. 2nd revised edition. London: Oxford University Press.

1960   *The Cultures of Prehistoric Egypt* 2. London: Oxford University Press.

1965   "What Do We Know About the Excavations at Merimda?" *Journal of the American Oriental Society* 85: 502–11.

1970   *Petrie's Naqada Excavation: A Supplement.* London: Bernard Quaritch.

Beit-Arieh, Itzhaq, and Ram Gophna

1999   "The Egyptian Protodynastic (Late EB I) Site at Tel Ma'ahaz: A Reassessment." *Tel Aviv* 26/2: 191–207.

Ben-Tor, Amnon

1975   *Two Burial Caves of the Proto-Urban Period at Azor, 1971.* Qedem 1. Jerusalem: Hebrew University.

Bestock, Laurel

2008   "The Early Dynastic Funerary Enclosures of Abydos." *Archéo-Nil* 18: 42–59.

2009   *The Development of Royal Funerary Cult at Abydos: Two Funerary Enclosures from the Reign of Aha.* Menes, Studien zur Kultur und Sprache der ägyptischen Frühzeit und des Alten Reiches 6. Wiesbaden: Harrassowitz.

Błaszczyk, Katarzyna

2008   "The Royal Figurine(?) from Tell el-Farkha." In *Studies in Ancient Art and Civilization* 12: 57–61.

Bourke, Stephen J.

2002   "The Origins of Social Complexity in the Southern Levant: New Evidence from Teleilat Ghassul, Jordan." *Palestine Exploration Quarterly* 134: 2–27.

Braidwood, Robert J., and Linda S. Braidwood

1960   *Excavations in the Plain of Antioch,* Volume 1: *The Earier Assemblages A-J.* Oriental Institute Publications 61. Chicago: Univesity of Chicago Press.

Brandl, B.

1989   "Observations on the Early Bronze Age Strata of Tel Erani." *L'urbanisation de la Palestine à l'âge du Bronze ancien: Bilan et perspectives des recherches actuelles* (Actes du Colloque d'Emmaüs, 20–24 octobre 1986), edited by Pierre de Miroschedji, pp. 357–88. British Archaeological Reports, International Series 527. Oxford: British Archaeological Reports.

1992   "Evidence for Egyptian Colonization in the Southern Coastal Plain and Lowlands of Canaan during the EB I Period." In *The Nile Delta In Transition: 4th-3rd Millennium BC* (Proceedings of the Seminar Held in Cairo, October 21–24, 1990, at the Netherlands Institute of Archaeology and Arabic Studies), edited by Edwin C. M. van den Brink, pp. 441–77. Tel Aviv: Edwin C. M. van den Brink.

Braun, Eliot

1989   "The Problem of the Apsidal House: New Aspects of Early Bronze I Domestic Architecture in Israel, Jordan and Lebanon." *Palestine Exploration Quarterly* 121: 1–43.

2001   "Proto and Early Dynastic Egypt and Early Bronze I–II of the Southern Levant: Uneasy C 14 Correlations." *Radiocarbon* 43: 1202–18.

2002   "Chapter 11: Egypt's First Sojourn In Canaan." In *Egypt and the Levant: Interrelations from the 4th through the Early 3rd Millennium BCE,* edited by Edwin C. M. van den Brink and Thomas E. Levy, pp. 173–89. London: Leicester University Press.

2003   "South Levantine Encounters with Ancient Egypt around the Beginning of the Third Millennium." In *Ancient Perspectives on Egypt,* edited by Roger Matthews and Cornelia Römer, pp. 21–37. London: University College London Press, Institute of Archaeology.

2004   "Egypt and the Southern Levant: Shifting Patterns of Relationships during Dynasty 0." In *Egypt at Its Origins: Studies in Memory of Barbara Adams (Proceedings of the International Conference Origin of the State: Predynastic and Early Dynastic Egypt, Krakow, 28 August-1 September 2002),* edited by Stan Hendrickx, Renée F. Friedman, Krzysztof M. Ciałowicz, and Marek Chłodnicki, pp. 507–17. Leuven: Peeters.

2009   "South Levantine Early Bronze Age Chronological Correlations with Egypt in Light of the Narmer Serekhs from Tel Erani and Arad: New Interpretations." http://www.britishmuseum.org/research/onlIne_journals/bmsaes/issue_13/braun.aspx (accessed 9/7/10; in press: British Museum Studies In Ancient Egypt and Sudan).

Braun, Eliot, and Edwin C. M. van den Brink

1998   "Some Comments on the Late EB I Sequence of Canaan and the Relative Dating of Tomb U-j at Umm el Ga'ab and Graves 313 and 787 from Minshat Abu Omar with Imported Ware: Views from Egypt and Canaan." *Egypt and the Levant* 7: 71–94.

Brewer, Douglas, and Renée F. Friedman

1989   *Fish and Fishing in Ancient Egypt*. Warminster: Aris & Phillips.

Breyer, Francis Amadeus Karl

2002   "Die Schriftzeugnisse des prädynastichen Königsgrabes U-j in Umm el-Qaab: Versuch einer Neuinterpretation." *Journal of Egyptian Archaeology* 88: 53–65.

Brunton, Guy

1937   *Mostagedda and the Tasian Culture*. British Museum Expedition to Middle Egypt, First and Second Years, 1928, 1929. London: Bernard Quaritch.

Brunton, Guy, and Gertrude Caton-Thompson

1928   *The Badarian Civilisation and Predynastic Remains near Badari*. London: British School of Archaeology in Egypt and Bernard Qaritch.

Buchez, Nathalie

In press   "A Reconsideration of Predynastic Chronology: The Contribution of Adaïma." In *Egypt at Its Origins 3* (Proceedings of the Third International Colloquium Origin of the State, Predynastic and Early Dynastic Egypt, London, 27 July–1 August 2008), edited by Renée F. Friedman and P. N. Fiske. Orientalia Lovaniensia Analecta 205. Leuven: Peeters.

Buchez, Nathalie, and Béatrix Midant-Reynes

2007   "Le site prédynastique de Kom el-Khilgan (Delta oriental): Données nouvelles sur les processus d'unification culturelle au IVe millénaire." *Bulletin de l'Institut français d'archéologie orientale* 107: 43–70.

Bussmann, Richard

In press   "Local Traditions in Early Egyptian Temples." In *Egypt at Its Origins 3* (Proceedings of the Third International Colloquium Origin of the State, Predynastic and Early Dynastic Egypt, London, 27 July–1 August 2008), edited by Renée F. Friedman and P. N. Fiske. Orientalia Lovaniensia Analecta 205. Leuven: Peeters.

Buszek, A.

2008   "Dwarf Figurines from Tell el-Farkha." In *Studies in Ancient Art and Civilization* 12, edited by J. Śliwa, pp. 35–55. Krakow: Instytut Archeologii Uniwersytetu Jagiellońskiego.

Butzer, Karl W.

1976   *Early Hydraulic Civilization in Egypt: A Study in Cultural Ecology*. Chicago: University of Chicago Press.

1995   "Environmental Change in the Near East and Human Impact on the Land." In *Civilizations of the Ancient Near East*, edited by Jack M. Sasson, John

Baines, Gary Beckman, and Karen S. Rubinson, pp. 123–51. New York: Charles Scribner's Sons.

Campagno, Marcelo

2002   "On the Predynastic 'Proto-States' of Upper Egypt." *Göttinger Miszellen* 188: 49–60.

Capart, Jean

1905   *Primitive Art in Egypt*. London: H. Grevel.

Carneiro, Robert L.

In prep.   "The Circumscription Theory: A Clarification, Amplification, and Reformulation."

Carter, Howard

1933   *The Tomb of Tut•Ankh•Amen*, Volume 3. London: Cassell.

Case, Humphrey, and Joan Crowfoot Payne

1962   "Tomb 100: The Decorated Tomb at Hierakonpolis." *Journal of Egyptian Archaeology* 48: 5–18.

Chłodnicki, Marek, and Krzysztof M. Ciałowicz

2002   "Polish Excavations at Tell el-Farkha (Ghazala) in Nile Delta. Preliminary Report 1998–2001." *Archeologia* 53: 63–118.

2003   "Tell el-Farkha (Ghazala) 1998–2002." *Archéo-Nil* 13: 47–54.

2004   "Polish Excavations at Tell el-Farkha (Ghazala) in the Nile Delta. Preliminary Report 2002–2003." *Archeologia* 55: 47–74.

2007   "Golden Figures from Tell el-Farkha." *Studies in Ancient Art and Civilization* 10: pp. 7–21.

2008   "Tell el-Farkha (Ghazala) Season 2006." *Polish Archaeology in the Mediterranean* 18: 127–53.

Chłodnicki, Marek; R. Fattovich; and S. Salvatori

1991   "Italian Excavations in the Nile Delta: Fresh Data and New Hypotheses on the 4th Millennium Cultural Development of Egyptian Prehistory." *Rivista di Archeologia* 15: 5–33.

Ciałowicz, Krzysztof M.

1986   "Predynastic Mace-Heads: Principles and Criteria of the Typological Classification." *Recherches Archéologiques de 1984*: 100–04.

1992   "Problèmes de l'interprétation du relief prédynastique tardif: Motif du palmier et des girafes." *Studies in Ancient Art and Civilization* 4: 7–18.

1998   "The Earliest Evidence for Egypt's Expansion into Nubia?" *Gdansk Archaeological Museum African Reports* 1: 17–22.

2001   *La naissance d'un royaume: L'Égypte dès la période prédynastique à la fin de la I*ère *dynastie*. Krakow: Księgarnia Akademicka.

2005   "Les Cultures de Basse-Égypte." *Dossiers d'archéologie* 307: 30–37.

2007a   "Tell el-Farkha." In *Seventy Years of Polish Archaeology in Egypt*, edited by Ewa Laskowska-Kusztal, pp. 67–78. Warsaw: Polish Centre of Mediterranean Archaeology, University of Warsaw.

2007b   *Ivory and Gold in the Delta: Excavations at Tell el-Farkha*. Krakow: Institute of Archaeology, Jagiellonian University.

2008   "The Nature of the Relation between Lower and Upper Egypt in the Protodynastic Period: A View from Tell el-Farkha" In *Egypt at Its Origins 2 (Proceedings of the International Conference Origin of the State, Predynastic and Early Dynastic Egypt, Toulouse, France, 5–8 September 2005)*, edited by Béatrix Midant-Reynes and Yann Tristant, pp. 501–13. Orientalia Lovaniensia Analecta 172. Leuven: Peeters.

2009   "The Early Dynastic Administrative-cultic Centre at Tell el-Farkha." *British Museum Studies in Ancient Egypt and Sudan* 13: 83–123.

Cichowski, Krzysztof

2008   "The Brewery Complex from Tell el-Farkha: Archaeological Aspects of the Discovery." In *Egypt at Its Origins 2 (Proceedings of the International Conference Origin of the State, Predynastic and Early Dynastic Egypt, Toulouse, France, 5–8 September 2005)*, edited by Béatrix Midant-Reynes and Yann Tristant, pp. 33–40. Leuven: Peeters.

Collon, Dominique

1988   *First Impressions: Cylinder Seals in the Ancient Near East*. London: British Museum Press.

Commenge, Catherine, and David Alon

2002   "Chapter 8. Competitive Involution and Expanded Horizons: Exploring the Nature of Interaction between Northern Negev and Lower Egypt (c. 4500–3600 BCE)." In *Egypt and the Levant: Interrelations from the 4th through the Early 3rd Millennium BCE*, edited by Edwin C. M. van den Brink and Thomas E. Levy, pp. 139–53. London: Leicester University Press.

Commenge-Pellerin, Catherine

1990   *La poterie de Safadi (Beersheva) au IVe millénaire avant l'ère chrétienne*. Paris: Association Paléorient.

Coote, Jeremy, and Anthony Shelton

1992   *Anthropology, Art, and Aesthetics*. Oxford: Clarendon Press.

Costin, Cathy L.

1991   "Craft Specialization: Issues in Defining, Documenting, and Exploring the Organization of Production." In *Archaeological Method and Theory*, edited by Michael Schiffer, pp. 1–56. Tucson: University of Arizona Press.

Cottrell, Fred

1955   *Energy and Society: The Relation Between Energy, Social Change, and Economic Development*. New York: McGraw-Hill.

Crubézy, Eric; Thierry Janin; and Béatrix Midant-Reynes

2002   *Adaïma*, Volume 2: *La nécropole prédynastique*. Fouilles de l'Institut français d'archéologie orientale 47. Cairo: Institut français d'archéologie orientale.

Curvers, Hans H., and Glenn M. Schwartz

2007   "Urban Origins, Collapse, and Regeneration in the Jabbul Plain." *Les Annales Archéologiques Arabes Syriennes* 45–46 (2002/2003): 75–84.

Darnell, Deborah

2002   "Gravel of the Desert and Broken Pots in the Road." In *Egypt and Nubia, Gifts of the Desert*, edited by Renée F. Friedman, pp. 156–77. London: British Museum Press.

Darnell, John C.

2002   *Theban Desert Road Survey in the Egyptian Western Desert*, Volume 1: *Gebel Tjauti Rock Inscriptions 1–45 and Wadi el-Ḥôl Rock Inscriptions 1–45*. Oriental Institute Publications 119. Chicago: The Oriental Institute.

Davies, W. Vivian, and Renée F. Friedman

1998   *Egypt*. London: British Museum Press.

Davis, Whitney

1983   "Artists and Patrons in Predynastic and Early Dynastic Egypt." *Studien zur Altägyptischen Kultur* 10: 119–40.

1992   *Masking the Blow: The Scene of Representation in Late Prehistoric Egyptian Art*. Berkeley: University of California Press.

Debono, Fernand, and Bodil Mortensen

1988   *The Predynastic Cemetery at Heliopolis: Season March–September 1950*. Deutsches Archäologisches Institut, Abteilung Kairo, Archäologische Veröffentlichungen 63. Mainz am Rhein: Philipp von Zabern.

1990   *El Omari: A Neolithic Settlement and Other Sites in the Vicinity of Wadi Hof, Helwan*. Deutsches Archäologisches Institut, Abteilung Kairo, Archäologische Veröffentlichungen 82. Mainz am Rhein: Philipp von Zabern.

De Putter, Thierry; Stijn Bielen; Paul De Paepe; Stan Hendrickx; and Valerie Schelstraete

2000   "Les mille et un vases de pierre des premières dynasties à Bruxelles. " *Pierres égyptiennes ... Chefs d'œuvre pour l'éternité*, edited by Christina Karlshausen and Thierry De Putter, pp. 49–62. Mons: Faculté Polytechnique de Mons.

DeVries, Carl E.

1976   "The Oriental Institute Decorated Censer from Nubia." In *Studies in Honor of George R. Hughes*, edited by Janet H. Johnson and Edward F. Wente, pp. 55–74. Studies in Ancient Oriental Civilization 39. Chicago: The Oriental Institute.

Dollfus, Geneviève, and Zeidan Kafafi

1986   "Preliminary Results of the First Season of the Joint Jordano-French Project at Abu Hamid." *Annual of the Department of Antiquities of Jordan* 30: 353–79.

Dougherty, Sean

2010   "Death in Fragments: Piecing Together the Skeletons of HK6." *Nekhen News* 22: 6–7.

Dreyer, Günter

1986   Elephantine 8. *Der Tempel des Satet: Die Funde der Frühzeit und des Alten Reiches.* Deutsches Archäologisches Institut, Abteilung Kairo, Archäologische Veröffentlichungen 39. Mainz: Philipp von Zabern.

1990   "Umm el-Qaab: Nachuntersuchungen im frühzeitlichen Königsfriedhof, 3./4. Vorbericht." *Mitteilungen des Deutschen Archäologischen Instituts, Abteilung Kairo* 46: 53–90.

1993   "Horus Krokodil, ein Gegenkönig der Dynastie 0." In *Followers of Horus*, edited by Renée F. Friedman and Barabara Adams, pp. 259–63. Oxford: Oxbow.

1998   Umm el-Qaab 1. *Das prädynastische Königsgrab U-j und seine frühen Schriftzeugnisse.* Deutsches Archäologisches Institut, Abteilung Kairo, Archäologische Veröffentlichungen 86. Mainz am Rhein: Philipp von Zabern.

2000   "Egypt's Earliest Historical Event." *Egyptian Archaeology* 16: 6–7.

Dreyer, Günter; A. Effland; U. Effland; E.-M. Engel; R. Hartmann; Ulrich Hartung; C. Lacher; Vera Müller; and A. Pokorny

2006   "Umm el-Qaab: Nachuntersuchungen im frühzeitlichen Königsfriedhof, 16./17./18. Vorbericht." *Mitteilungen des Deutschen Archäologischen Instituts, Abteilung Kairo* 62: 67–130.

Dreyer, Günter; E.-M. Engel; Ulrich Hartung; Thomas Hikade; E. Christiana Köhler; Frauke Pumpenmeir; Angela von den Driesch; and J. Peters

1996   "Umm el-Qaab: Nachuntersuchungen im frühzeitlichen Königsfriedhof, 7./8. Vorbericht. *Mitteilungen des Deutschen Archäologischen Instituts, Abteilung Kairo* 52: 11–81.

Dreyer, Günter; R. Hartmann; Ulrich Hartung; Thomas Hikade; H. Köpp; C. Lacher; Vera Müller; A. Nerlich; and A. Zink

2003   "Umm el-Qaab: Nachuntersuchungen im frühzeitlichen Königsfriedhof, 13./14./15. Vorbericht." *Mitteilungen des Deutschen Archäologischen Instituts, Abteilung Kairo* 59: 67–138.

Dreyer, Günter; Ulrich Hartung; and Frauke Pumpenmeier

1993   "Umm el-Qaab. Nachuntersuchungen im frühzeitlichen Königsfriedhof, 5./6. Vorbericht." *Mitteilungen des Deutschen Archäologischen Instituts, Abteilung Kairo* 49: 48–62.

Dreyer, Günter; Urlich Hartung; Thomas Hikade; E. Christiana Köhler; Vera Müller; and Frauke Pumpenmeier

1998   "Umm el-Qaab. Nachuntersuchungen im frühzeitlichen Königsfriedhof, 9./10. Vorbericht." *Mitteilungen des Deutschen Archäologischen Instituts, Abteilung Kairo* 54: 77–167.

Drioton, Étienne, and Jacques Vandier

1975   *L'Égypte: Des origines à la conquête d'Alexandre.* Paris: Presses Universitaires de France.

Drower, Margaret S.

1985   *Flinders Petrie: A Life in Archaeology.* London: Victor Gollancz.

Earle, Timothy K.

1997   *How Chiefs Come to Power: The Political Economy in Prehistory.* Stanford: Stanford University Press.

Earle, Timothy K., and Jonathon E. Ericson

1977   *Exchange Systems in Prehistory.* New York: Academic Press.

Eisenberg, Emanuel, and Raphael Greenberg

2006   "Chapter 8. Area EY: The Eisenberg-Yogev Excavations, 1981–1982, 1985–1986." In *Bet Yerah: The Early Bronze Age Mound*, Volume 1: *Excavation Reports, 1933-1986*, edited by Raphael Greenberg, Emanuel Eisenberg, Sarit Paz, and Yitzhak Paz, pp. 339–468. Israel Antiquities Authorities Reports 30. Jerusalem: Israel Antiquities Authorities.

Eiwanger, Josef

1984   Merimde-Benisalâme 1. *Die Funde der Urschicht.* Deutsches Archäologisches Institut, Abteilung Kairo, Archäologische Veröffentlichungen 47. Mainz: Philipp von Zabern.

1988   Merimde-Benisalâme 2. *Die Funde der mittleren Merimde-Kultur.* Deutsches Archäologisches Institut, Abteilung Kairo, Archäologische Veröffentlichungen 51. Mainz: Philipp von Zabern.

1992   Merimde-Benisalâme 3. *Die Funde der jüngeren Merimde-Kultur.* Deutsches Archäologisches Institut, Abteilung Kairo, Archäologische Veröffentlichungen 59. Mainz: Philipp von Zabern.

2007   "Benisalâme." In *Begegnung mit der Vergangenheit: 100 Jahre in Ägypten*, edited by Günter Dreyer and Daniel Polz, pp. 69–76. Mainz: Philipp von Zabern.

Eldar, I., and Y. Baumgarten

1993   "Neveh Noy." In *The New Encyclopedia of Archaeological Excavations In the Holy Land 1-4*, edited by Ephraim Stern, pp. 163–65. Jerusalem: Israel Exploration Society.

Emery, Walter B.

1961   *Archaic Egypt.* Baltimore: Penguin Books.

Endesfelder, Erika

1991 "Die Formierung der altägyptischen Klassengesell-schaft: Probleme und Beobachtungen." In *Probleme der frühen Gesellschaftsentwicklung im Alten Ägyp-ten*, edited by Erika Endesfelder, pp. 5–62. Berlin: Humboldt-Universität zu Berlin.

Engelmayer, Reinhold

1965 *Die Felsgravierungen im Distrikt Sayala-Nubien.* Berichte des Österreichischen Nationalkomitees der UNESCO-Aktion für die Rettung der Nubi-schen Altertümer 2; Österreichische Akademie der Wissenschaften, Philosophisch-Historische Klasse, Denkschriften 90. Vienna: Hermann Böhlaus Nachf.

Fagan, Brian M.

1987 *New Treasures of the Past: Fresh Finds that Deepen Our Understanding of the Archaeology of Man.* New York: Barron's.

Fahmy, Ahmed

1999 "Plant Macro Remains from HK43: An Interim Re-port." *Journal of the American Research Center in Egypt* 36: 14–18.

2000 "What They Ate: Plant Remains from HK43." *Nekhen News* 12: 19.

Fairservis, Walter A., Jr.

1986 *The Hierakonpolis Project Season January to May 1981: Excavation of the Archaic Remains East of the Niched Gate.* Occasional Papers in Anthropology 3. Pough-keepsie: Vassar College.

Faltings, Dina A.

1998a "Canaanites at Buto in the Early Fourth Millennium BC." *Egyptian Archaeology* 13: 29–32.

1998b *Die Keramik der Lebensmittelproduktion im Alten Reich.* Studien zur Archäologie und Geschichte Altägyp-tens 14. Heidelberg: Heidelberger Orientverlag.

1998c "Ergebnisse der neuen Ausgrabungen in Buto: Chronologie und Fernbeziehungen der Buto-Maadi-Kultur neu überdacht." In *Stationen: Beiträge zur Kul-turgeschichte Ägyptens — Rainer Stadelmann gewidmet*, edited by Heike Guksch and Daniel Polz, pp. 39–45. Mainz: Philipp von Zabern.

1998d "Recent Excavations in Tell el-Fara'în/Buto: New Finds and their Chronological Implications." In *Proceedings of the Seventh International Congress of Egyptologists, Cambridge, 3–9 September 1995*, edited by Christopher Eyre, pp. 365–75. Orientalia Lovanien-sia Analecta 82. Leuven: Peeters.

2002 "The Chronological Frame and Social Structure of Buto in the Fourth Millennium BCE." In *Egypt and the Levant: Interrelations from the 4th through the Early 3rd Millennium BCE*, edited by Edwin C. M. van den Brink and Thomas E. Levy, pp. 165–70. London: Leicester University Press.

Faltings, Dina A.; P. Ballet; F. Förste; P. French; C. Ihde; H. Sahlmann; J. Thomalsky; C. Thumshirn; and A. Wodzinska.

2000 "Zweiter Vorbericht über die Arbeiten in Buto von 1996 bis 1999." *Mitteilungen des Deutschen Archäologi-schen Instituts, Abteilung Kairo* 56: 131–79.

Faltings, Dina A., and E. Christiana Köhler

1996 "Vorbericht über die Ausgrabungen des DAI in Tell el-Fara'în/Buto 1993 bis 1995." *Mitteilungen des Deutschen Archäologischen Instituts, Abteilung Kairo* 52: 88–114.

Finkelstein, Israel; David Ussishkin; and Jennifer Peersmann

2006 "Chapter 3. Area J." In Megiddo 4: *The 1998-2000 Sea-sons*, edited by Israel Finkelstein, David Ussishkin, and Baruch Halpern, pp. 29–53. Monograph Series 24. Tel Aviv: Institute of Archaeology.

Finkenstaedt, Elizabeth

1980 "Regional Painting Style in Prehistoric Egypt." *Zeit-schrift für ägyptische Sprache und Altertumskunde* 107: 116–20.

Firth, Cecil M.

1912 *The Archaeological Survey of Nubia, Report for 1908-1909.* Cairo: Government Press.

1915 *The Archaeological Survey of Nubia, Report for 1909-1910.* Cairo: Government Press.

1927 *The Archaeological Survey of Nubia, Report for 1910-1911.* Cairo: Government Press.

Fischer, Henry G.

1962 "The Cult and the Nome of the Goddess Bat." *Journal of the American Research Center in Egypt* 1: 7–24.

Frangipane, Marcella

2001 "Centralization Processes in Greater Mesopotamia: Uruk 'Expansion' as the Climax of Systemic Interac-tions among Areas of the Greater Mesopotamian Region." In *Uruk Mesopotamia and Its Neighbors: Cross-cultural Interactions in the Era of State Formation*, edited by Mitchell S. Rothman, pp. 307–47. Santa Fe: School of American Research Press.

Frankfort, Henri

1930 "The Cemeteries of Abydos: Work of the Season 1925–26, II: Description of Tombs." *Journal of Egyp-tian Archaeology* 16/3–4: 213–19.

1948 *Kingship and the Gods. A Study of Ancient Near Eastern Religion as the Integration of Society and Nature.* Chi-cago: University of Chicago Press.

Fried, Morton H.

1960 "On the Evolution of Social Stratification and the State." In *Culture in History*, edited by Stanley Dia-mond, pp. 713–31. New York: Columbia University Press.

Friedman, Renée F.

1994 Predynastic Settlement Ceramics of Upper Egypt: A Comparative Study of the Ceramics of Hemamieh, Nagada and Hierakonpolis. Ph.D. dissertation, University of California, Berkeley.

1999 "Badari Grave Goup 569." In *Studies in Egyptian Antiquities: A Tribute to T. G. H. James*, edited by W. Vivian Davies, pp. 1–11. British Museum Occasional Papers 123. London: British Museum Press.

2004a "Elephants at Hierakonpolis." In *Egypt at Its Origins: Studies in Memory of Barbara Adams* (Proceedings of the International Conference Origin of the State: Predynastic and Early Dynastic Egypt, Krakow, 28 August–1 September 2002), edited by Stan Hendrickx, Renée F. Friedman, Krzysztof M. Ciałowicz, and Marek Chłodnicki, pp. 131–68. Orientalia Lovaniensia Analecta 138. Leuven: Peeters.

2004b "He's Got a Knife! Burial 412 at HK 43." *Nekhen News* 16: 8–9.

2006 "New Tombs and New Thoughts at HK6." *Nekhen News* 18: 11–12.

2008a "The Cemeteries of Hierakonpolis." *Archéo-Nil* 18: 8–29.

2008b "Excavating Egypt's Early Kings: Recent Discoveries in the Elite Cemetery at Hierakonpolis." In *Egypt at Its Origins* 2 (Proceedings of the International Conference Origin of the State, Predynastic and Early Dynastic Egypt" Toulouse, France, 5–8 September 2005), edited by Béatrix Midant-Reynes and Yann Tristant, pp. 1157–94. Orientalia Lovaniensia Analecta 172. Leuven: Peeters.

2009 "Hierakonpolis Locality HK29A: The Predynastic Ceremonial Center Revisited." *Journal of the American Research Center in Egypt* 45: 79–103.

2010 "The Early Royal Cemetery at Hierakonpolis: An Overview." In *Recent Discoveries and Latest Researches in Egyptology* (Proceedings of the First Neapolitan Congress of Egyptology. Naples, June 18–20, 2008), edited by Francesco Raffaele, Massimiliano Nuzzolo, and Ilaria Incordino, pp. 67–86. Wiesbaden: Harrassowitz.

Friedman, Renée F., and Joseph Hobbs

2002 "A 'Tasian' Tomb in Egypt's Eastern Desert." In *Egypt and Nubia: Gifts of the Desert*, edited by Renée F. Friedman, pp. 178–91. London: British Museum Press.

Friedman, Renée F.; Wim Van Neer; and Veerle Linseele

In press "The Elite Predynastic Cemetery at Hierakonpolis: 2009–2010 Update." In *Egypt at Its Origins* 3 (Proceedings of the Third International Colloquium Origin of the State, Predynastic and Early Dynastic Egypt, London, 27 July–1 August 2008), edited by Renée F. Friedman and P. N. Fiske. Orientalia Lovaniensia Analecta 205. Leuven: Peeters.

Galvin, John

2005 "Abydos: Life and Death at the Dawn of Egyptian Civilzation." *National Geographic* 207/4: 120.

Gamer-Wallert, Ingrid

1970 *Fische und Fishchkulte im Alten Ägypten*. Ägyptologische Abhandlungen 21. Wiesbaden: Harrassowitz.

Gardiner, Alan H.

1957 *Egyptian Grammar: Being an Introduction to the Study of Hieroglyphs*. 3rd edition. Oxford: Griffith Institute.

Garstang, John

1903 *Maḥâsna and Bêt Khallâf*. Egyptian Research Account 7. London: Egyptian Research Account.

Gatto, Maria Carmela

2000 "The Most Ancient Evidence of the A-Group Culture in Lower Nubia." In *Recent Research into the Stone Age of Northeastern Africa*, edited by Lech Krzyżaniak, Karla Kroeper, and Michał Kobusiewicz, pp. 105–17. Studies in African Archaeology 7. Poznan: Poznan Archaeological Museum.

2002 "Ceramic Traditions and Cultural Territories: The Nubian Group in Prehistory." *Sudan and Nubia* 6: 9–19.

2006 "The A-Group, a Reassessment." *Archéo-Nil* 16: 61–76.

2006/07 "'Je voidrai te montrer un truc.' A Short Note on a Possible A-Group-related Cemetery at the Sixth Cataract of the Nile (Sudan)." *Cahier de recherches de l'Institut de papyrologie et d'égyptologie de Lille* 17: 115–19.

2009 "Egypt and Nubia in the 5th–4th Millennia BCE: A View from the First Cataract and Its Surroundings." *British Museum Studies in Ancient Egypt and Sudan* 13: 125–45.

Gatto, Maria Carmela, and Serena Giuliani

2006/07 "Nubians in Upper Egypt: Results of the Survey in the Aswan-Kom Ombo Region (2005–2006)." *Cahier de recherches de l'Institut de papyrologie et d'égyptologie de Lille* 26: 121–30.

Gazit, Dan, and Ram Gophna

1993 "Appendi." In "An Unfortified Late Bronze Age Site at Gerar: Survey Finds," by Dan Gazit and Ram Gophna, p. 152. *'Atiqot* 22: 152, 15*–19*. [Hebrew with English summary]

Geller, Jeremy R.

1992 "From Prehistory to History: Beer in Egypt." In *The Followers of Horus: Studies Dedicated to Michael Allen Hoffman, 1944-1990*, edited by Renée F. Friedman and Barbara Adams, pp. 19–26. Oxford: Oxbow.

Gilead, Isaac

1992 "New Archaeo-metallurgical Evidence for the Beginnings of Metallurgy in the Southern Levant: Excavations at Tell Abu Matar Beersheba (Israel)

1990–1991." *Institute for Archaeo-Metallurgic Studies* 18: 11–14.

Glubok, Shirley

1962   *The Art of Ancient Egypt.* New York: Athenaeum.

Goebs, Katja

2008   *Crowns in Egyptian Funerary Literature: Royalty, Rebirth and Destruction.* Oxford: Griffith Institute.

Golani, Amir

2004   "Salvage Excavations at the Early Bronze Age Site of Afridar, Ashqelon—Area E." *'Atiqot* 45: 9–62.

Gopher, Avi, and Tsvika Tsuk

1996   "The Chalcolithic Assemblage." In *The Nahal Qanah Cave: Earliest Gold In the Southern Levant*, edited by Avi Gopher, pp. 91–139. Monograph Series 12. Tel Aviv: Institute of Archaeology, University of Tel Aviv.

Gophna, Ram

1972   "Egyptian First Dynasty Pottery from Tel Halif Terrace." *Museum Haaretz Bulletin* 14: 47–56.

1978   "'En Besor: An Egyptian First Dynasty Staging Post in the Northern Negev." *Expedition* 20: 5–7.

1990   "The Egyptian Pottery of 'En Besor." *Tel Aviv* 17: 144–62.

1993   "A Faience Statuette from 'En Besor." *Tel Aviv* 20: 29–32.

Gophna, Ram, and Edwin C. M. van den Brink

2002   "Chapter 18. Core-Periphery Interaction between Pristine Egyptian Nagada IIIb State, Late Early Bronze Age I Canaan, and Terminal A-Group Lower Nubia: More Data." In *Egypt and the Levant: Interrelations from the 4th through the Early 3rd Millennium BCE*, edited by Edwin C. M. van den Brink and Thomas E. Levy, pp. 280–85. London: Leicester University Press.

Goren, Yuval, and P. Fabian

2002   *Kissufim Road: A Chalcolithic Mortuary Site.* Israel Antiquities Authority Reports 16. Jerusalem: Israel Antiquities Authority.

Gorzalczany, Amir, and Ya'aqov Baumgarten

2005   "Ḥorbat Petora (North)." *Hadashot Arkheologiyot* 117. http://www.hadashot-esi.org.il/report_detail_eng.asp?id=241&mag_id=110 (accessed 9/7/2010)

Graff, Gwenola

2009   *Les peintures sur vases de Nagada I-Nagada II: Nouvelle approche sémiologique de l'iconographie prédynastique.* Egyptian Prehistory Monographs 6. Leuven: Leuven University Press.

Graff, Gwenola; Merel Eyckerman; and Stan Hendrickx

In press   "Architectural Elements on Decorated Pottery and Ritual Presenting of Desert Animals." In *Egypt at Its Origins* 3 (Proceedings of the Third International Colloquium Origin of the State, Predynastic and Early Dynastic Egypt, London, 27 July–1 August 2008), edited by Renée F. Friedman and P. N. Fiske. Orientalia Lovaniensia Analecta 205. Leuven: Peeters.

Green, Christine

1987   *Temple Furniture from the Sacred Animal Necropolis at North Saqqara 1964–1976.* Fifty-third Excavation Memoir. London: Egypt Exploration Society.

Greenberg, Raphael, and Emanuel Eisenberg

2002   "Egypt, Bet Yerah and Early Canaanite Urbanization." In *Egypt and the Levant: Interrelations from the 4th through the Early 3rd Millennium BCE*, edited by Edwin C. M. van den Brink and Thomas E. Levy, pp. 213–22. London: Leicester University Press.

Greenberg, Raphael; David Wengrow; and Sarit Paz

2010   "Cosmetic Connections: An Egyptian Relief Carving from Early Bronze Age Tel Bet Yerah (Israel)." *Antiquity* 84/324. http://antiquity.ac.uk/projgall/greenberg324/ (accessed 9/7/2010).

Griffith, Francis Ll.

1896   *Beni Hasan* 3. Archaeological Survey of Egypt 5. London: Egypt Exploration Fund.

Habachi, Labib, and Werner Kaiser

1985   "Ein Friedhof der Maadikultur bei es-Saff." *Mitteilungen des Deutschen Archäologischen Instituts, Abteilung Kairo* 41: 43–46

Hall, Emma S.

1986   *The Pharaoh Smites His Enemies: A Comparative Study.* Munich: Deutscher Kunstverlag.

Hansen, Donald P.

1965   "The Relative Chronology of Mesopotamia, Part II: The Pottery Sequence at Nippur from the Middle Uruk to the End of the Old Babylonian Period (3400–1600 B.C.)." In *Chronologies in Old World Archaeology*, edited by Robert W. Ehrich, pp. 201–13. Chicago: University of Chicago Press.

Hartmann, Rita

In press   "The Chronology of Naqada I Tombs in the Predynastic Cemetery U at Abydos." In *Egypt at Its Origins* 3 (Proceedings of the Third International Colloquium Origin of the State, Predynastic and Early Dynastic Egypt, London, 27 July–1 August 2008), edited by Renée F. Friedman and P. N. Fiske. Orientalia Lovaniensia Analecta 205. Leuven: Peeters.

Hartung, Ulrich

1993   "III. Importkeramik aus Grab U-j. Umm el-Qaab: Nachuntersuchungen im frühzeitlichen Königsfriedhof, 5./6. Vorbericht." *Mitteilungen des Deutschen Archäologischen Instituts, Abteilung Kairo* 49: 49–55.

1998   "Zur Entwicklung des Handels und zum Beginn wirtschaftlicher Administration im prädynastischen Ägypten." *Studien zur Altägyptischen Kultur* 26: 35–50.

2001   Umm el-Qaab 2. *Importkeramik aus dem Friedhof U in Abydos (Umm el-Qaab) und die Beziehungen Ägyptens zu Vorderasien im 4. Jahrtausend v. Chr.* Deutsches Archäologisches Institut, Abteilung Kairo, Archäologische Veröffentlichungen 92. Mainz am Rhein: Philipp von Zabern.

2003a   "Predynastic Subterranean Dwellers in Maadi, Cairo." *Egyptian Archaeology* 22: 7–9.

2003b   "Maadi, fouille de sauvetage aux confins du Caire." *Archéo-Nil* 13: 29–36.

2003c   "Bouto, fouille d'habitat dans le Delta du Nil." *Archéo-Nil* 13: 73–76.

2004   "Rescue Excavations in the Predynastic Settlement of Maadi." In *Egypt at Its Origins: Studies in Memory of Barbara Adams* (Proceedings of the International Conference Origin of the State: Predynastic and Early Dynastic Egypt, Krakow, 28 August–1 September 2002), edited by Stan Hendrickx, Renée F. Friedman, Krzysztof M. Ciałowicz, and Marek Chłodnicki, pp. 337–56. Orientalia Lovaniensia Analecta 138. Leuven: Peeters.

2006   "Bemerkungen zur Architektur und Chronologie der unterirdischen und halbunterirdischen Bauten in der prädynastischen Siedlung von Maadi." In *Timelines: Studies in Honour of Manfred Bietak*, edited by Ernst Czerny, I. Hein, H. Hunger, D. Melman, A. Schwab, pp. 35–44. Orientalia Lovaniensia Analecta 149/2. Leuven: Peeters.

2007a   "Maadi. Predynastic Settlement on the Outskirts of Cairo." In *Meeting the Past: 100 Years in Egypt: German Archaeological Institute Cairo 1907–2007*, edited by Ute Rummel, pp. 96–109. Cairo: Institutum Archaeologicum Germanicum.

2007b   "Buto. Settlement and Sacred Site in the Northwestern Nile Delta." In *Meeting the Past: 100 Years in Egypt: German Archaeological Institute Cairo 1907–2007*, edited by Ute Rummel, pp. 110–30. Cairo: Institutum Archaeologicum Germanicum.

2007c   "Der Fortgang der Untersuchungen am Tell von Buto: Hin "Berg" an Informationen wartet auf Entschlüsselung." In *Begegnung mit der Vergangenheit: 100 Jahre in Ägypten*, edited by Günter Dreyer and Daniel Polz, pp. 60–68. Mainz: Philipp von Zabern.

2007d   "Puzzlearbeit zwischen Neubauten: Neue archäologische Untersuchungen in Maadi." In *Begegnung mit der Vergangenheit: 100 Jahre in Ägypten*, edited by Günter Dreyer and Daniel Polz, pp. 126–29. Mainz: Philipp von Zabern.

2008   "Recent investigations at Tell el-Fara'în/Buto." In *Egypt at Its Origins* 2 (Proceedings of the International Conference Origin of the State, Predynastic and Early Dynastic Egypt, Toulouse, France, 5–8 September 2005), edited by Béatrix Midant-Reynes and Yann Tristant, pp. 1155–219. Orientalia Lovaniensia Analecta 172. Leuven: Peeters.

2010   "Hippopotamus Hunters and Bureaucrats: Elite Burials at Cemetery U at Abydos." In *Recent Discoveries and Latest Researches in Egyptology* (Proceedings of the First Neapolitan Congress of Egyptology, Naples, June 18–20, 2008), edited by Francesco Raffaele, Massimiliano Nuzzolo, and Ilaria Incordino, pp. 107–20. Wiesbaden: Harrassowitz.

Hartung, Ulrich; Larry J. Exner; Friedel Feindt; Donald L. Glusker; Yuval Goren; Rolf Kohring; Patrick E. McGovern; Axel Pape; Naomi Porat; and Thomas Schlüter

2001   "Importkeramik aus dem Friedhof U in Abydos." In *Umm el-Qaab 2. Importkeramik aus dem Friedhof U in Abydos (Umm el-Qaab) und die Beziehungen Ägyptens zu Vorderasien im 4. Jahrtausend v. Chr.*, edited by Ulrich Hartung, pp. 5–70. Deutsches Archäologisches Institut, Abteilung Kairo, Archäologische Veröffentlichungen 92. Mainz: Philipp von Zabern.

Hartung, Ulrich; Mohammed Abd el-Gelil; Angela von den Driesch; Gamal Fares; Rita Hartmann; Thomas Hikade; and Christian Ihde

2003a   "Vorbericht über neue Untersuchungen in der prädynastischen Siedlung von Maadi." *Mitteilungen des Deutschen Archäologischen Instituts, Abteilung Kairo* 59: 149–98.

Hartung, Ulrich; Pascale Ballet; Frédéric Béguin; Janine Bourriau; Peter French; Tomasz Herbich; Peter Kopp; Guy Lecuyot; and Anne Schmitt

2003b   "Tell el-Fara'în – Buto 8. Vorbericht." *Mitteilungen des Deutschen Archäologischen Instituts, Abteilung Kairo* 59: 199–267.

Hartung, Ulrich; Pascale Ballet; Frédéric Béguin; Janine Bourriau; Delphine Dixneuf; Angela von den Driesch; Peter French; Rita Hartmann; Tomasz Herbich; Chiori Kitagawa; Peter Kopp; Guy Lecuyot; Marie-Dominique Nenna; Anne Schmitt; Gonca Şenol; and Ahmet Şenol

2007   "Tell el-Fara'în — Buto 9. Vorbericht." *Mitteilungen des Deutschen Archäologischen Instituts, Abteilung Kairo* 63: 69–165.

Hassan, Fekri A.

1993   "Town and Village in Ancient Egypt: Ecology, Society and Urbanization." In *The Archaeology of Africa: Food, Metals and Towns*, edited by Thurstan Shaw, Paul Sinclair, Bassey Andah, and Alex Okpoko, pp. 551–69. London and New York: Routledge.

Hassan, Fekri A.; Alejandro Jiménez Serrano; and Geoffrey J. Tassie

2006   "The Sequence and Chronology of the Protodynastic and Dynasty I Rulers." In *Archaeology of Northeastern Africa: In Memory of Lech Krzyżaniak*, edited by Karla Kroeper, Marek Chłodnicki, and Michał Kobusiewicz, pp. 687–713. Studies in African Archaeology 9. Poznan: Poznan Archaeological Museum.

Hawass, Zahi; Fekri A. Hassan; and Achilles Gautier

1988   "Chronology, Sediments, and Subsistence at Merimda Beni Salama." *Journal of Egyptian Archaeology* 74: 31–38.

Helck, Wolfgang

1987   *Untersuchungen zur Thinitenzeit.* Ägyptologische Abhandlungen 45. Wiesbaden: Harrassowitz.

Hellström, Pontus, and Hans Langballe

1970   *The Rock Drawings*, Volume 1: *The Scandinavian Joint Expedition to Sudanese Nubia.* Copenhagen, Oslo, and Stockholm: Scandinavian University Books.

Hendrickx, Stan

1989   De grafvelden der Naqada-cultuur in Zuid-Egypte, met bijzondere aandacht voor het Naqada III grafveld te Elkab. Interne chronologie en sociale differentiatie. PhD dissertation, Katholieke Universiteit, Leuven.

1994   Elkab 5: *The Naqada III Cemetery.* Brussels: Musées Royaux d'Art et d'Histoire.

1995   *Analytical Bibliography of the Prehistory and the Early Dynastic Period of Egypt and Northern Sudan.* Egyptian Prehistory Monographs 1. Leuven: Leuven University Press.

1996a   "The Relative Chronology of the Naqada Culture, Problems and Possibilities." In *Aspects of Early Egypt*, edited by Jeffrey Spencer, pp. 36–69. London: British Museum Press.

1996b   "Two Protodynastic Objects in Brussels and the Origin of the Bilobate Cult-Sign of Neith." *Journal of Egyptian Archaeology* 82: 23–42.

2002   "Bovines in Egyptian Predynastic and Early Dynastic Iconography." In *Droughts, Food and Culture: Ecological Change and Food Security in Africa's Later Prehistory*, edited by Fekri A. Hassan, pp. 275–318. New York: Kluwer Academic/Plenum Publishers.

2006a   "Predynastic–Early Dynastic Chronology." In *Ancient Egyptian Chronology*. edited by Erik Hornung, Rolf Krauss, and David A. Warburton, pp. 55–93, 487–88. Handbook of Oriental Studies, Section One, The Near and Middle East 83. Leiden: Brill.

2006b   "The Dog, the *Lycaon pictus* and Order over Chaos in Predynastic Egypt." In *Archaeology of Early Northeastern Africa: In Memory of Lech Krzyżaniak*, edited by Karla Kroeper, Marek Chłodnicki, and Michał Kobusiewicz, pp. 723–49. Studies in African Archaeology 9. Poznan: Poznan Archaeological Museum.

2008   "Rough Ware as an Element of Symbolism and Craft Specialisation at Hierakonpolis' Elite Cemetery HK6." In *Egypt at Its Origins* 2 (Proceedings of the International Conference Origin of the State, Predynastic and Early Dynastic Egypt, Toulouse, France, 5–8 September 2005), edited by Béatrix Midant-Reynes and Yann Tristant, pp. 61–85. Orientalia Lovaniensia Analecta 172. Leuven: Peeters.

In press   "L'iconographie de la chasse dans le contexte social prédynastique." *Archéo-Nil* 20.

Hendrickx, Stan, and Laurent Bavay

2002   "The Relative Chronological Position of Egyptian Predynastic and Early Dynastic Tombs with Objects Imported from the Near East and the Nature of Interregional Contacts." In *Egypt and the Levant: Interrelations from the 4th through the Early 3rd Millennium BCE*, edited by Edwin C. M. van den Brink and Thomas E. Levy, pp. 58–80. London: Leicester University Press.

Hendrickx, Stan; Stijn Bielen; and Paul De Paepe

2001   "Excavating in the Museum: The Stone Vessel Fragments from the Royal Tombs at Umm el-Qaab in the Egyptian Collection of the Royal Museums for Art and History at Brussels." *Mitteilungen des Deutschen Archäologischen Instituts, Abteilung Kairo* 57: 73–108.

Hendrickx, Stan, and Merel Eyckerman

2010   "Continuity and Change in the Visual Representations of Predynastic Egypt." In *Recent Discoveries and Latest Researches in Egyptology (Proceedings of the First Neapolitan Congress of Egyptology, Naples, June 18–20, 2008)*, edited by Francesco Raffaele, Massimiliano Nuzzolo, and Ilaria Incordino, pp. 121–44. Wiesbaden: Harrassowitz.

In press   "Tusks and Tags: Between the Hippopotamus and the Naqada Plant." In *Egypt at Its Origins* 3 (Proceedings of the Third International Colloquium Origin of the State, Predynastic and Early Dynastic Egypt, London, 27 July–1 August 2008), edited by Renée F. Friedman and P. N. Fiske. Orientalia Lovaniensia Analecta 205. Leuven: Peeters.

Hendrickx, Stan; Dina Faltings; Lies Op de Beeck; Dietrich Raue; and Chris Michiels

2002   "Milk, Beer and Bread Technology during the Early Dynastic Period." *Mitteilungen des Deutschen Archäologischen Instituts, Abteilung Kairo* 58: 277–304.

Hendrickx, Stan, and Renée F. Friedman

2003   "Gebel Tjauti Rock Inscription 1 and the Relationship between Abydos and Hierakonpolis during the Early Naqada III Period." *Göttinger Miszellen* 196: 95–109.

Hendrickx, Stan; Renée F. Friedman; and Merel Eyckerman

2010   "Early Falcons." In *Vorspann oder formative Phase? Ägypten und der Vordere Orient 3500–2700 v. Chr., Leipzig, 07.09–08.09.2007*, edited by Ludwig Morenz and Robert Kuhn. Wiesbaden: Harrassowitz.

Hendrickx, Stan; Renée F. Friedman; and Fabienne Loyens

2000   "Experimental Archaeology Concerning Black-Topped Pottery from Ancient Egypt and the Sudan." *Cahiers de la céramique égyptienne* 6: 171–87.

Hendrickx, Stan; Dirk Huyge; and Barbara Adams

1997/98   "Le scorpion en silex du Musée Royal de Mariemont et les silex figuratifs de l'Égypte pré- et protodynastique." *Les Cahiers de Mariemont* 28–29: 6–33.

Hendrickx, Stan; Heiko Riemer; Frank Förster; and John C. Darnell

2009 "Late Predynastic/Early Dynastic Rock Art Scenes of Barbary Sheep Hunting from Egypt's Western Desert: From Capturing Wild Animals to the Women of the 'Acacia House.'" In *Desert Animals in the Eastern Sahara: Status, Economic Significance and Cultural Reflection in Antiquity* (Proceedings of an interdisciplinary ACACIA workshop held at the University of Cologne, December 14–15, 2007), edited by Heiko Riemer, Frank Förster, Michael Herb, and Nadja Pöllath, pp. 189–244. Colloquium Africanum 4. Cologne: Heinrich-Barth Institut.

Hendrickx, Stan, and C. Van Winkel

1993 "Fragments de récipients décorés en pierre provenant de la nécropole royale des premières dynasties à Abydos (Haute-Égypte)." *Bulletin des Musées Royaux d'Art et d'Histoire* 64: 5–36.

Hikade, Thomas

2003 "Getting the Ritual Right — Fishtail Knives in Predynastic Egypt." In *Egypt — Temple of the Whole World: Studies in Honour of Jan Assmann*, edited by Sibylle Meyer, pp. 137–51. Leiden: Brill.

2004a "Some Thoughts on Chalcolithic and Early Bronze Age Flint Scrapers in Egypt." *Mitteilungen des Deutschen Archäologischen Instituts, Abteilung Kairo* 60: 57–68.

2004b "Prestige and Skill — Fishtail Knives in Predynastic Egypt." *Nekhen News* 16: 9–10.

2010 "Stone Tool Production." In *UCLA Encyclopedia of Egyptology*, edited by Willeke Wendrich, pp. 6–9. http://digital2.library.ucla.edu/viewItem.do?ark=21198/zz0025h6kk.

Hikade, Thomas; Gillian Pyke; and D'Arne O'Neill

2008 "Excavations at Hierakonpolis HK29B and HK25: The Campaigns of 2005/2006." *Mitteilungen des Deutschen Archäologischen Instituts, Abteilung Kairo* 64: 153–88.

Hoffman, Michael A.

1982 *The Predynastic of Hierakonpolis: An Interim Report.* Egyptian Studies Association 1. Giza and Macomb: Alden Press.

1991 *Egypt before the Pharaohs.* Revised and updated. Austin: University of Texas.

Hoffman, Michael A.; Hany A. Hamroush; and Ralph O. Allen

1986 "A Model of Urban Development for the Hierakonpolis Region from Predynastic through Old Kingdom Times." *Journal of the American Research Center in Egypt* 23: 175–88.

Holmes, Diane L.

1989 *The Predynastic Lithic Industries of Upper Egypt: A Comparative Study of the Lithic Traditions of Badari, Nagada, and Hierakonpolis.* British Archaeological Reports, International Series 469. Oxford: British Archaeological Reports.

1992a "Chipped Stone-working Craftsmen, Hierakonpolis and the Rise of Civilization in Egypt." In *The Followers of Horus: Studies Dedicated to Michael Allen Hoffman, 1944-1990*, edited by Renée F. Friedman and Barbara Adams, pp. 37–44. Oxford: Oxbow.

1992b "The Evidence and Nature of Contacts between Upper and Lower Egypt during the Predynastic: A View from Upper Egypt." In *The Nile Delta in Transition: 4th-3rd Millennium BC* (Proceedings of the Seminar Held in Cairo, 21–24 October 1990, at the Netherlands Institute of Archaeology and Arabic Studies), edited by Edwin C. M. van den Brink, pp. 301–16. Tel Aviv: Edwin C. M. van den Brink.

Honegger, Mathieu

2004a "The Pre-Kerma Settlement: New Elements Throw Light on the Rise of the First Nubian Kingdom." In *Nubian Studies 1998* (Proceedings of the Ninth International Conference of the International Society of Nubian Studies, August 21–26, 1998), edited by Timothy Kendall, pp. 22–23. Boston: Museum of Fine Arts.

2004b "The Pre-Kerma Period." In *Sudan Ancient Treasures: An Exhibition of Recent Discoveries from the Sudan National Museum*, edited by Derek Welsby and Julie Anderson, pp. 61–63. London: British Museum Press.

2004c "The Pre-Kerma Settlement at Kerma." In *Sudan Ancient Treasures: An Exhibition of Recent Discoveries from the Sudan National Museum*, edited by Derek Welsby and Julie Anderson, pp. 64–69. London: British Museum Press.

Houston, Stephen D., editor

2004 *The First Writing. Script Invention as History and Process.* Cambridge: Cambridge University Press.

Huyge, Dirk

2004 "A Double-powerful Device for Regeneration: The Abu Zaidan Knife Handle Reconsidered." In *Egypt at Its Origins: Studies in Memory of Barbara Adams* (Proceedings of the International Conference Origin of the State: Predynastic and Early Dynastic Egypt, Krakow, 28 August–1 September 2002), edited by Stan Hendrickx, Renée F. Friedman, Krzysztof M. Ciałowicz, and Marek Chłodnicki, pp. 823–36. Orientalia Lovaniensia Analecta 138. Leuven: Peeters.

Jaeschke, Helena

2004 "The Stone Statue Fragments from HK6." In *Egypt at Its Origins: Studies in Memory of Barbara Adams* (Proceedings of the International Conference Origin of the State: Predynastic and Early Dynastic Egypt, Krakow, 28 August–1 September 2002), edited by Stan Hendrickx, Renée F. Friedman, Krzysztof M. Ciałowicz, and Marek Chłodnicki, pp. 46–65. Orientalia Lovaniensia Analecta 138. Leuven: Peeters.

Jeffreys, David G., and Anna Tavares

1994   "The Landscape of Early Dynastic Memphis." *Mitteilungen des Deutschen Archäologischen Instituts, Abteilung Kairo* 50: 143–73.

Jiménez Serrano, Alejandro

2002   *Royal Festivals in the Late Predynastic Period and the First Dynasty.* British Archaeological Reports, International Series 1976. Oxford: Archaeopress.

Johnson, Allen W., and Timothy K. Earle

1987   *The Evolution of Human Societies: From Foraging Group to Agrarian State.* Stanford: Stanford University Press.

Jones, Dilwyn

2000   *An Index of Ancient Egyptian Titles, Epithets and Phrases of the Old Kingdom.* 2 volumes. British Archaeological Reports, International Series 866. Oxford: Archaeopress.

Jones, Jana

2008   "Pre- and Early Dynastic Textiles: Technology, Specialisation and Administration during the Process of State Formation." In *Egypt at Its Origins* 2 (Proceedings of the International Conference Origin of the State, PreDynastic and Early Dynastic Egypt, Toulouse, France, 5–8 September 2005), edited by Béatrix Midant-Reynes and Yann Tristant, pp. 99–132. Orientalia Lovaniensia Analecta 172. Leuven: Peeters.

Jucha, Mariusz A.

2005   *The Pottery of the Predynastic Settlement (Phases 2 to 5).* Tell el-Farkha 2. Poznan: Poznan Archaeological Museum.

2008   "Wavy-Handled and Cylindrical Jars in the Nile Delta: A View from Tell el-Farkha." *Studies in Ancient Art and Civilization* 12: 63–74.

In press   "The Development of Pottery Production during the Early Dynastic Period and the Beginning of the Old Kingdom: A View from Tell el-Farkha." In *Egypt at Its Origins* 3 (Proceedings of the Third International Colloquium Origin of the State, Predynastic and Early Dynastic Egypt, London, 27 July 1–August 2008), edited by Renée F. Friedman and P. N. Fiske. Orientalia Lovaniensia Analecta 205. Leuven: Peeters.

Junker, Hermann

1929   "Vorläufiger Bericht über die Grabung der Akademie der Wissenschaften in Wien auf der neolithischen Siedlung von Merimde-Benisalâme (Westdelta) vom 1. bis 30. März 1929." *Anzeiger der Akademie der Wissenschaften in Wien* 16–18: 156–250.

1930a   "Vorläufiger Bericht über die zweite Grabung der Akademie der Wissenschaften in Wien auf der vorgeschichtlichen Siedlung Merimde-Benisalâme vom 7. Februar bis 8. April 1930." *Anzeiger der Akademie der Wissenschaften in Wien* 5–13: 21–83.

1930b   "Bericht über die vom Deutschen Institut für Ägyptische Altertumskunde nach dem Ostdelta-Rand unternommene Erkundgsfahrt." *Mitteilungen des Deutschen Archäologischen Instituts, Abteilung Kairo* 1: 3–37.

1932   "Vorbericht über die von der Akademie der Wissenschaften in Wien in Verbindung mit dem Egyptiska Museet in Stockholm unternommenen Grabungen auf der neolithischen Siedlung von Merimde-Benisalâme vom 6. November 1931 bis 20. Jänner 1932." *Anzeiger der Akademie der Wissenschaften in Wien* 1–4: 36–97.

1933   "Vorläufige Bericht über die Grabungen auf der neolithischen Siedlung von Merimde-Benisalâme." *Anzeiger der Akademie der Wissenschaften in Wien* 16–17: 54–97.

1934   "Vorbericht über die fünfte von der Akademie der Wissenschaften in Wien und dem Egyptiska Museet in Stockholm unternommene Grabung auf der neolithischen Siedlung Merimde-Benisalâme vom 13. Februar bis 26. März 1934." *Anzeiger der Akademie der Wissenschaften in Wien* 10: 118–32.

1940   "Vorbericht über die siebente Grabung der Akademie der Wissenschaften in Wien auf der vorgeschichtlichen Siedlung Merimde-Benisalâme vom 25. Januar bis 4. April 1939." *Ägyptologische Studien* 1–4: 3–25.

1955   "Die Feinde auf dem Sockel der Chasechem-Statuen und die Darstellung von geopferten Tieren." In *Ägyptologische Studien: Hermann Grapow zum 70. Geburtstag gewidmet*, edited by Otto Firchow, pp. 162–75. Deutsche Akademie der Wissenschaften, Institut für Orientforschung, Veröffentlichung 29. Berlin: Akademie-Verlag.

Kahl, Jochem

1994   *Das System der ägyptischen Hieroglyphenschrift in der Dynastie 0–3.* Göttinger Orientforschungen IV. Reihe, Ägypten 29. Wiesbaden: Harrassowitz.

2001   "Hieroglyphic Writing during the Fourth Millennium BC: An Analysis of Systems." *Archéo-Nil* 11: 103–25.

2003   "Die frühen Schriftzeugnisse aus dem Grab U-j in Umm el-Qaab." *Chronique d'Égypte* 78: 112–35.

2004   Frühägyptisches Wörterbuch. Dritte Lieferung, ḥ–ḫ. Wiesbaden: Harrassowitz.

Kaiser, Werner

1957   "Zur inneren Chronologie der Naqadakultur." *Archaeologia Geographica* 6: 69–77.

1961   "Bericht über eine archäologisch-geologische Felduntersuchung in Ober- und Mittelägypten." *Mitteilungen des Deutschen Archäologischen Instituts, Abteilung Kairo* 17: 1–53.

1983   "Zu den ⸗ der älteren Bilddarstellungen und der Bedeutung von *rpw.t*." *Mitteilungen des Deutschen Archäologischen Instituts, Abteilung Kairo* 39: 261–96.

Kaiser, Werner, and Günter Dreyer

1982   "Umm el-Qaab. Nachuntersuchungen im frühzeitlichen Königsfriedhof, 2. Vorbericht." *Mitteilungen des Deutschen Archäologischen Instituts, Abteilung Kairo* 38: 211–69.

Kaiser, Werner, and Andrea Zaugg

1988   "Zum Fundplatz der Maadikultur bei Tura." *Mitteilungen des Deutschen Archäologischen Instituts, Abteilung Kairo* 44: 121–24.

Kansa, E.; Stan Henrickx; Thomas E. Levy; and Edwin C. M. van den Brink

2002   "Nahal Tillah Reed Decorated Pottery: Aspects of Early Bronze Age IB Ceramic Production and Egyptian Counterparts." In *In Quest of Ancient Settlements and Landscapes: Archaeological Studies in Honour of Ram Gophna*, edited by Edwin C. M. van den Brink and Eli Yannai, pp. 193–218. Tel Aviv: Tel Aviv University, Ramot Publishing.

Kantor, Helene J.

1948   "A Predynastic Ostrich Egg with Incised Decorations." *Journal of Near Eastern Studies* 7: 46–51.

1974   "Ägypen." In *Frühe Stufen der Kunst*, edited by Machteld J. Mellink and Jan Filip, pp. 227–56. Propyläen Kunstgeschicht 13. Berlin: Propyläen Verlag.

1992   "The Relative Chronology of Egypt and Its Foreign Correlations before the First Intermediate Period." In *Chronologies In Old World Archaeology*, edited by Robert W. Ehrich, pp. 3–21. 3rd edition. Chicago: University of Chicago Press.

Kaplony, Peter

1958   "Zu den beiden Harpunenzeichen der Narmerpalette." *Zeitschrift für ägyptische Sprache und Altertumskunde* 83: 76–78.

1963   *Die Inschriften der ägyptischen Frühzeit.* 3 volumes. Wiesbaden: Harrassowitz.

2002   "The Bet Yerah Jar Inscription and the Annals of King Dewen-Dewen as 'King Narmer Redivivus.'" In *Egypt and the Levant: Interrelations from the 4th through the Early 3rd Millennium BCE*, edited by Edwin C. M. van den Brink and Thomas E. Levy, pp. 450–64. London: Leicester University Press.

Kelterborn, Peter

1984   "Towards Replicating Egyptian Predynastic Flint Knives." *Journal of Archaeological Science* 11/6: 433–53.

Kemp, Barry J.

1968   "Merimda and the Theory of House Burials in Prehistoric Egypt." *Cahiers d'Égyptologie* 85: 22–33.

1977   "The Early Development of Towns in Egypt." *Antiquity* 51: 185–200.

1989   *Ancient Egypt: Anatomy of a Civilization.* London: Routledge.

2000   "The Colossi from the Early Shrine at Coptos in Egypt." *Cambridge Archaeological Journal* 10/2: 211–42.

2006   *Ancient Egypt. Anatomy of a Civilization.* 2nd revised edition. London: Routledge.

Kempinski, Aharon, and Isaac Gilead

1991   "New Excavations at Tel Erani: A Preliminary Report of the 1985–1988 Seasons." *Tel Aviv* 18: 164–91.

Kendall, Timothy

2007   "Mehen, the Ancient Egyptian Game of the Serpent." In *Ancient Board Games in Perspective: Papers from the 1990 British Museum Colloquium, with Additional Contributions*, edited by Irving L. Finkel, pp. 33–45. London: British Museum Press.

Khalaily, Hamudi

2004   "An Early Bronze Age Site at Ashqelon, Afridar — Area F." *'Atiqot* 45: 121–59.

el-Khouli, Ali

1978   *Egyptian Stone Vessels: Predynastic Period to Dynasty III: Typology and Analysis.* 3 volumes. Mainz am Rhein: Philipp von Zabern.

Klasens, Adolf

1956   "Een grafsteen uit de eerste dynastie." *Oudheidkundige Mededelingen uit het Rijksmuseum van Oudheden te Leiden* 37: 12–34.

Klemm, Rosemarie, and D. D. Klemm

1998   "Evolution of Methods for Prospection, Mining and Processing of Gold in Egypt." In *Proceedings of the First International Conference on Ancient Egyptian Mining and Metallurgy and Conservation of Metallic Artifacts, Cairo, Egypt, 10-12 April 1995*, edited by F. A. Esmael, pp. 341–54. Cairo: Ministry of Culture, Supreme Council of Antiquities.

Kobusiewicz, Michał; Jacek Kabaciński; Romuald Schild; Joel D. Irish; and Fred Wendorf

2004   "Discovery of the First Neolithic Cemetery in Egypt's Western Desert." *Antiquity* 78: 566–78.

Köhler, E. Christiana

1998   Tell el-Fara'în – Buto 3. *Die Keramik von der späten Naqada-Kultur bis zum frühen Alten Reich (Schlichten III bis VI).* Mainz am Rhein: Philipp von Zabern.

1999   "Re-assessment of a Cylinder Seal from Helwan." *Göttinger Miszellen* 168: 49–56.

2002   "History or Ideology? New Reflections on the Narmer Palette and the Nature of Foreign Relations in Predynastic Egypt." In *Egypt and the Levant: Interrelations from the 4th through the Early 3rd Millennium BCE*, edited by Edwin C. M. van den Brink and Thomas E. Levy, pp. 499–513. London: Leicester University Press.

2004   "On the Origins of Memphis — The New Excavations in the Early Dynastic Necropolis at Helwan."

In *Egypt at Its Origins: Studies in Memory of Barbara Adams* (Proceedings of the International Conference Origin of the State: Predynastic and Early Dynastic Egypt, Krakow, 28 August–1 September 2002), edited by Stan Hendrickx, Renée F. Friedman, Krzysztof M. Ciałowicz, and Marek Chłodnicki, pp. 295–315. Orientalia Lovaniensia Analecta 138. Leuven: Peeters.

2005   "The Interaction between and the Roles of Upper and Lower Egypt in the Formation of the Egyptian State: Another Review." In *Conférence internationale: L'Égypte pré- et protodynastique. Les origines de l'état, Toulouse, France, 5-8 sept. 2005, Livret des Résumés*, edited by Béatrix Midant-Reynes and Yann Tristant, pp. 58–60. Toulouse. http://origines2.free.fr/annexes/resumes.pdf

2008a   "Formation of the Ancient Egyptian State." http://warandgame.wordpress.com/2008/08/05/formation-of-the-ancient-egyptian-state/

2008b   "The Interaction between and the Roles of Upper and Lower Egypt in the Formation of the Egyptian State: Another Review." In *Egypt at Its Origins* 2 (Proceedings of the International Conference Origin of the State, Predynastic and Early Dynastic Egypt, Toulouse, France, 5–8 September 2005), edited by Béatrix Midant-Reynes and Yann Tristant, pp. 515–43. Orientalia Lovaniensia Analecta 172. Leuven: Peeters.

2010   "Theories of State Formation." In *Egyptian Archaeology*, edited by Willeke Wendrich, pp. 36–54. Chichester: Wiley-Blackwell.

Krzyżaniak, Lech

1993   "New Data on the Late Prehistoric Settlement at Minshat Abu Omar (Eastern Nile Delta)." In *Environmental Change and Human Culture in the Nile Basin and Northern Africa until the Second Millennium BC* (Proceedings of the International Symposium, 5–10 September, 1988), edited by dans Lech Krzyżaniak, Michał Kobusiewicz, and John Alexander, pp. 321–25. Poznan: Poznan Archaeological Museum.

Kubiak-Martens, Lucy, and Jerzy J. Langer

2008   "Predynastic Beer Brewing as Suggested by Botanical and Physicochemical Evidence from Tell el-Farkha, Eastern Delta." In *Egypt at Its Origins* 2 (Proceedings of the International Conference Origin of the State, Predynastic and Early Dynastic Egypt, Toulouse, France, 5–8 September 2005), edited by Béatrix Midant-Reynes and Yann Tristant, pp. 427–41. Orientalia Lovaniensia Analecta 172. Leuven: Peeters.

Lange, Mathias

2006   *Wadi Shaw - Wadi Sahal. Studien zur holozänen Besiedlung der Laqiya-Region (Nordsudan)*. Africa Praehistorica 19. Cologne: Heinrich-Barth Institut.

Lansing, Ambrose

1935   "The Museum's Excavations at Hierakonpolis: The Egyptian Expedition 1934–1935." *Bulletin of the Metropolitan Museum of Arts* 30: 37–45.

Levy, Thomas E.

1986   "The Chalcolithic Period." *Biblical Archaeologist* 49: 82–108.

1987   Shiqmim 1. *Studies Concerning Chalcolithic Societies in the Northern Negev Desert, Israel (1982-1984)*. British Archaeological Reports, International Series 356. Oxford: British Archaeological Reports.

Levy, Thomas E.; Edwin C. M. van den Brink; Yuval Goren; and David Alon

1995   "New Light on King Narmer and the Protodynastic Egyptian Presence in Canaan." *Biblical Archaeologist* 58: 26–35.

Levy, Thomas E.; David Alon; Yorke Rowan; Edwin C. M. van den Brink; Caroline Grigson; Augustin Holl; Patricia Smith; Paul Goldberg; Alan J. Witten; Eric Kansa; John Moreno; Yuval Yekutieli; Naomi Porat; Jonathan Golden; Leslie Dawson; and Morag Kersel

1997   "Egyptian-Canaanite Interaction at Nahal Tillah, Israel (ca. 4500–3000 B.C.E.): An Interim Report on the 1994–1995 Excavations." *Bulletin of American Schools of Oriental Research* 307: 1–51.

Linseele, Veerle, and Wim Van Neer

2009   "Exploitation of Desert and Other Wild Game in Ancient Egypt: The Archaeological Evidence from the Nile Valley." In *Desert Animals in the Eastern Sahara: Status, Economic Significance and Cultural Reflection in Antiquity* (Proceedings of an interdisciplinary ACACIA workshop held at the University of Cologne December 14–15, 2007), edited by Heiko Riemer, Frank Förster, Michael Herb, and Nadja Pöllath, pp. 47–78. Colloquium Africanum 4. Cologne: Heinrich-Barth Institut.

Linseele, Veerle; Wim Van Neer; and Renée F. Friedman

2009   "Special Animals from a Special Place? The Fauna from HK29A at Predynastic Hierakonpolis." *Journal of the American Research Center in Egypt* 45: 105–36.

Linseele, Veerle; Wim Van Neer; and Stan Hendrickx

2007   "Evidence for Early Cat Taming in Egypt." *Journal of Archaeological Science* 34/12: 1081–90.

Logan, Thomas J.

1990   "The Origins of the *Jmy-wt* Fetish." *Journal of the American Research Center in Egypt* 27: 61–69.

Lovell, Jaimie

2008   "Horticulture, Status and Long-Range Trade in Chalcolithic Southern Levant: Early Connections with Egypt." In *Egypt at Its Origins* 2 (Proceedings of the International Conference Origin of the State, Predynastic and Early Dynastic Egypt, Toulouse, France, 5–8 September 2005), edited by Béatrix

Midant-Reynes and Yann Tristant, pp. 741–62. Orientalia Lovaniensia Analecta 172. Leuven: Peeters.

Lucas, Alfred

1932   "Black and Black-topped Pottery." *Annales du Service des Antiquités de l'Égypte* 32: 93–96.

MacArthur, Elise

2010   "The Conception and Development of the Egyptian Writing System." In *Visible Language: Inventions of Writing in the Ancient Middle East and Beyond*, edited by Christopher Woods, pp. 115–36. Oriental Institute Museum Publications 32. Chicago: The Oriental Institute.

Macdonald, Eann

1932   *Prehistoric Fara in Beth-Pelet* 2. British School of Archaeology in Egypt and Egyptian Research Account 52. London: British School of Archaeology in Egypt.

Mączyńska, Agnieszka

2003   "Lower Egyptian Culture from the Central Tell at Tell el-Farkha." In *Cultural Markers in the Later Prehistory of Northeastern Africa and Recent Research* (Proceedings of the International Symposium, 29 August–2 September 2000, Poznan), edited by Lech Krzyżaniak, Karla Kroeper, and Michał Kobusiewicz, pp. 213–25. Poznan: Poznan Archaeological Museum.

2004   "Pottery Tradition at Tell el-Farkha." In *Egypt at Its Origins: Studies in Memory of Barbara Adams* (Proceedings of the International Conference Origin of the State: Predynastic and Early Dynastic Egypt, Krakow, 28 August–1 September 2002), edited by Stan Hendrickx, Renée F. Friedman, Krzysztof M. Ciałowicz, and Marek Chłodnicki, pp. 421–41. Orientalia Lovaniensia Analecta 138. Leuven: Peeters.

2006   "Egyptian-Southern Levantine Interaction in the 4th and 3rd Millennium B.C. — A View from Tell el-Farkha." In *Archaeology of Northeastern Africa: In Memory of Lech Krzyżaniak*, edited by Karla Kroeper, Marek Chłodnicki, and Michał Kobusiewicz, pp. 945–57. Studies In African Archaeology 9. Poznan: Poznan Archaeological Museum.

2008   "Some Remarks on Egyptian-Southern Levantine Interrelations in the First Half of the 4th Millennium BC." In *Egypt at Its Origins* 2 (Proceedings of the International Conference Origin of the State, Predynastic and Early Dynastic Egypt, Toulouse, France, 5–8 September 2005), edited by Béatrix Midant-Reynes and Yann Tristant, pp. 763–81. Orientalia Lovaniensia Analecta 172. Leuven: Peeters.

Mallory-Greenough, Leanne M.

2002   "The Geographical, Spatial, and Temporal Distribution of Predynastic and First Dynasty Basalt Vessels." *Journal of Egyptian Archaeology* 88: 67–94.

Mallory-Greenough, Leanne M.; John D. Greenough; and J. Victor Owen

1999   "The Stone Source of Predynastic Basalt Vessels: Mineralogical Evidence for Quarries in Northern Egypt." *Journal of Archaeological Science* 26: 1261–72.

Marfoe, Leon

1982   *A Guide to the Oriental Institute Museum*. Chicago: University of Chicago Press.

Marinova, Elena, and Wim Van Neer

2009   "An Elephant's Last Meal." *Nekhen News* 21: 10–11.

Mazar, Amihai, and Pierre de Miroschedji

1996   "Hartuv, an Aspect of the Early Bronze I Culture of Southern Israel." *Bulletin of American Schools of Oriental Research* 302: 1–40.

McGovern, Patrick E.

2001   "The Origins of the Tomb U-j Syro-Palestinian Type Jars as Determined by Neutron Activation Analysis." In Umm el-Qaab 2. *Importkeramik aus dem Friedhof U in Abydos (Umm el-Qaab) und die Beziehungen Ägyptens zu Vorderasien im 4. Jahrtausend v. Chr.*, edited by Ulrich Hartung, pp. 407–16. Deutsches Archäologisches Institut, Abteilung Kairo, Archäologische Veröffentlichungen 92. Mainz: Philipp von Zabern.

McGovern, Patrick E.; Ulrich Hartung; Virginia R. Badler; Donald L. Glusker; Lawrence J. Exner

1997   "The Beginnings of Winemaking and Viniculture in the Ancient Near East and Egypt." *Expedition* 39: 3–21.

McNamara, Liam

2008   "The Revetted Mound at Hierakonpolis and Early Kingship: A Re-interpretation." In *Egypt at Its Origins* 2 (Proceedings of the International Conference Origin of the State, Predynastic and Early Dynastic Egypt, Toulouse, France, 5–8 September 2005), edited by Béatrix Midant-Reynes and Yann Tristant, pp. 901–36. Orientalia Lovaniensia Analecta 172. Leuven: Peeters.

Menghin, Oswald, and Mustafa Amer

1932   *The Excavations of the Egyptian University in the Neolithic Site at Maadi: First Preliminary Report (Season 1930-1931)*. Cairo: Misr-Sokkar Press.

1936   *The Excavations of the Egyptian University in the Neolithic Site at Maadi: Second Preliminary Report (Season 1932)*. Cairo: Government Press.

Merpert, N. Y., and O. G. Bolshakov

1964   "Раннединастическое поселение Хор-Дауд." In Древняя Нубиа, edited by B. B. Piotrovsky pp. 83–177. Moscow: Издателство "Наука." ["Early Dynastic Settlement of Hor-Da'ud." In *Ancient Nubia*, edited by B. B. Piotrovsky pp. 83–177. Moscow: Nauka]

Midant-Reynes, Béatrix

1987   "Contribution à l'étude de la société prédynastique: Le cas du couteau 'ripple-flake.'" *Studien zur Altägyptischen Kultur* 14: 185–224.

2000   *The Prehistory of Egypt from the First Egyptians to the First Pharaohs.* Translated by Ian Shaw. Oxford: Blackwell.

2003   *Aux origines de l'Égypte: Du néolithique à l'émergence de l'état.* Paris: Fayard.

Midant-Reynes, Béatrix; Hugues Boisson; Nathalie Buchez; Éric Crubézy; Stan Hendrickx; and Frédéric Jallet

1997   "Le site prédynastique d'Adaïma: Rapport de la huitième campagne de fouille." *Bulletin de l'Institut français d'archéologie orientale* 97: 201–19.

Midant-Reynes, Béatrix, and Nathalie Buchez

In prep.   *Kôm el-Khilgan: Une nécropole prédynastique et un habitat Hyksôs dans le Delta oriental du Nil.* Cairo.

Midant-Reynes, Béatrix; François Briois; Nathalie Buchez; Morgan De Dapper; Sylvie Duchesne; Bruno Fabry; Christiane Hochstrasser-Petit; Luc Staniaszek; and Yann Tristant

2003   "Kôm el-Khilgan: Un nouveau site dans le Delta." *Archéo-Nil* 13: 55–64.

2004   "Kom el-Khilgan: A New Site of the Predynastic Period in Lower Egypt; The 2002 Campaign." In *Egypt at Its Origins: Studies in Memory of Barbara Adams* (Proceedings of the International Conference Origin of the State: Predynastic and Early Dynastic Egypt, Krakow, 28 August–1 September 2002), edited by Stan Hendrickx, Renée F. Friedman, Krzysztof M. Ciałowicz, and Marek Chłodnicki, pp. 465–86. Orientalia Lovaniensia Analecta 138. Leuven: Peeters.

Midant-Reynes, Béatrix; G. Bréand; François Briois; Nathalie Buchez; N. Delhopital; R. el-Hajaoui; A. Emery-Barbier; S. Guérin; F. Guyot; Christiane Hochstrasser-Petit; J. Lesur; S. Marchand; M. Minotti; F. Mourot; I. Regulski; L. Torchy; and Yann Tristant

In prep.   *Tell el-Iswid (Sud), 2007-2010.* Fouilles de l'Institut français d'archéologie orientale. Cairo.

Mienis, H. K.

2007   "Shells." In "Tel Malot (East): Final Report," by Edwin C. M. van den Brink. *Hadashot Arkheologiyot* 119. http://www.hadashot-esi.org.il/report_detail_eng.asp?id=478&mag_id=112&print=nopic (accessed 7/29/2010)

Milevski, Ianir

2010   *Early Bronze Age Goods Exchange in the Southern Levant: A Marxist Perspective.* London: Equinox.

de Miroschedji, Pierre

1998   "Les égyptiens au Sinaï du nord et en Palestine au Bronze ancien." In *Le Sinaï durant l'antiquité et le moyen âge: 4000 ans d'histoire pour un désert* (Actes du colloque Sinaï qui s'est tenu à l'UNESCO du 19 au 21 septembre 1997), edited by Dominique Valbelle and Charles Bonnet, pp. 20–32. Paris: Errance.

2000   "La Palestine, Gaza et l'Égypte au Bronze ancien, chapitre III, les sites archéologiques." In *Gaza Méditerranéenne: Histoire et archéologie en Palestine*, by Jean-Baptiste Humbert, pp. 27–30. Paris: Errance.

2001   "Gaza et l'Égypte de l'époque prédynastique à l'Ancien Empire: Premiers résultats des fouilles de Tell es-Sakan." *Bulletin del la Société Française d'Égyptologie* 152: 28–52.

de Miroschedji, Pierre, and Moain Sadek

2008   "Sakan, Tell es-." In *The New Encyclopedia of Archaeological Excavations in the Holy Land 5, Supplementary Volume*, edited by Ephraim Stern, pp. 2027–29. Jerusalem and Washington, DC: Israel Exploration Society and Biblical Archaeology Society.

Möller, Georg, and Alexander Scharff

1969   *Die archäologischen Ergebnisse des vorgeschichtlichen Gräberfeldes von Abusir El-Meleq.* Wissenschaftliche Veröffentlichung der Deutschen Orient-Gesellschaft 49. Osnabrück: Otto Zeller.

Moorey, P. Roger S.

1987   "On Tracking Cultural Transfers in Prehistory: The Case of Egypt and Lower Mesopotamia in the Fourth Millennium BC." In *Centre and Periphery in the Ancient World*, edited by Michael Rowlands, Mogens T. Larsen, and Kristian Kristiansen, pp. 36–46. Cambridge: Cambridge University Press.

Mortensen, Bodil

1985   "Four Jars from the Maadi Culture Found in Giza." *Mitteilungen des Deutschen Archäologischen Instituts, Abteilung Kairo* 41: 145–47.

1991   "Change in the Settlement Pattern and Population in the Beginning of the Historical Period." *Ägypten und Levante* 2: 11–37.

Morenz, Ludwig D.

2004   *Bild-Buchstaben und symbolische Zeichen: Die Herausbildung der Schrift in der hohen Kultur Altägyptens.* Fribourg: Academic Press; Göttingen: Vandenhoeck & Ruprecht.

Muir, Arthur H., Jr.

2009   "Eggsplosion!" *Nekhen News* 21: 18–19.

Muir, Arthur H., Jr., and Renée F. Friedman

In press   "Analysis of Predynastic Ostrich Eggshells from Hierakonpolis and Beyond." In *Egypt at Its Origins* 3 (Proceedings of the Third International Colloquium Origin of the State, Predynastic and Early Dynastic Egypt, London, 27 July 1–August 2008), edited by Renée F. Friedman and P. N. Fiske. Orientalia Lovaniensia Analecta 205. Leuven: Peeters.

Müller, Hans Wolfgang

1959 "Ein neues Fragment einer reliefgeschmückten Schminkpalette aus Abydos." *Zeitschrift für ägyptische Sprache und Altertumskunde* 84: 68–70.

Müller, Vera

2008 "Nilpferdjagd und geköpfte Feinde: Zu zwei Ikonen des Feindvernichtungsrituals." In *Zeichen aus dem Sand: Streiflichter aus Ägyptens Geschichte zu Ehren von Günter Dreyer*, edited by Eva-Maria Engel, Vera Müller, and Ulrich Hartung, pp. 477–93. Menes 5. Wiesbaden: Harrassowitz.

Müller-Wollermann, Renata

2003 "Zoologische Gärten als Mittel der Herrschaftslegitimation im Alten Ägypten." *Die Welt des Orients* 33: 31–43.

Murnane, William J.

1987 "Appendix C. The Gebel Sheikh Suleiman Monument: Epigraphic Remarks." In "The Metropolitan Museum Knife Handle and Aspects of Pharaonic Imagery before Narmer," by Bruce B. Williams and Thomas J. Logan, pp. 282–84. *Journal of Near Eastern Studies* 46: 245–85.

Needler, Winifred

1967 "A Rock-drawing on Gebel Sheikh Suliman (near Wadi Halfa) Showing a Scorpion and Human Figures." *Journal of the American Research Center in Egypt* 6: 87–91.

1984 *Predynastic and Archaic Egypt in the Brooklyn Museum.* Wilbour Monographs 9. Brooklyn: The Brooklyn Museum.

Newberry, Percy E.

1893 *Beni Hasan* 1. Archaeological Survey of Egypt 1. London: Egypt Exploration Fund

Nissen, Hans J.; Peter Damerow; and Robert K. Englund

1993 *Archaic Bookkeeping: Early Writing and Techniques of Economic Administration in the Ancient Near East.* Chicago: University of Chicago Press.

Nordström, Hans-Åke

1972 *Neolithic and A-Group Sites.* The Scandinavian Joint Expedition to Sudanese Nubia 3. Copenhagen, Oslo, and Stockholm: Scandinavian University Books.

2004 "The Nubian A-Group: Perceiving a Social Landscape." In *Nubian Studies 1998* (Proceedings of the Ninth Conference of the International Society of Nubian Studies, August 21–26, 1998, Boston), edited by Timothy Kendall, pp. 134–44. Boston: Department of African-American Studies, Northeastern University.

O'Connor, David

1992 "Status of Early Egyptian Temples: An Alternative Theory." In *The Followers of Horus: Studies Dedicated to Michael Allen Hoffman, 1944-1990,* edited by Barbara

Adams and Renée F. Freedman, pp. 83–98. Oxford: Oxbow Books.

1993 *Ancient Nubia: Egypt's Rival in Africa.* Philadelphia: The University of Museum, University of Pennsylvania.

2002 "Context, Function and Program: Understanding Ceremonial Slate Palettes." *Journal of the American Research Center in Egypt* 39: 5–25.

2004 "Narmer's Enigmatic Palette." *Archaeology Odyssey* 7/5: 6–23, 52–53.

2009 *Abydos: Egypt's First Pharaohs and the Cult of Osiris.* London: Thames & Hudson.

Op de Beeck, Lies

2004 "Possibilities and Restrictions for the Use of Maidum-bowls as Chronological Indicators." *Cahiers de la céramique égyptienne* 7: 239–80.

Oren, Eliezer D.

1989 "Early Bronze Age Settlement in Northern Sinai: A Model for Egypto-Canaanite Interconnections." In *L'urbanisation de la Palestine à l'âge du Bronze ancien: Bilan et perspectives des recherches actuelles* (Actes du Colloque d'Emmaüs, 20–24 octobre 1986), edited by Pierre de Miroschedji, pp. 389–405. British Archaeological Reports, International Series 527. Oxford: British Archaeological Reports.

Oren, Eliezer D., and Yuval Yekutieli

1992 "Taur Ikhbeineh: Earliest Evidence for Egyptian Interconnections." In *The Nile Delta in Transition: 4th-3rd Millennium BC* (Proceedings of the Seminar Held in Cairo, 21–24, October, 1990, at the Netherlands Institute of Archaeology and Arabic Studies), edited by Edwin C. M. van den Brink, pp. 361–84. Tel Aviv: Edwin C. M. van den Brink.

Patch, Diana

1995 "A 'Lower Egyptian Costume': Its Origins, Development and Meaning." *Journal of the American Research Center in Egypt* 32: 93–116.

Payne, Joan Crowfoot

1987 "Appendix to 'Naqada Excavations Supplement.'" *Journal of Egyptian Archaeology* 73: 181–89.

Peet, T. Eric

1914 *The Cemeteries of Abydos, Part 2: 1911-1912.* Egypt Exploration Fund 34. London: Egypt Exploration Fund.

Peet, T. Eric, and William L. S. Loat

1913 *The Cemeteries of Abydos, Part 3: 1912-1913.* Egypt Exploration Fund 35. London: Egypt Exploration Fund.

Perrot, Jean

1955 "The Excavations at Tell Abu Matar, near Beersheba." *Israel Exploration Journal* 5: 17–40.

1959   "Statuettes en ivoire et autres objets en ivoire et en os provenant des gisements préhistoriques de la région de Béershéba." *Syria* 36: 8–19.

1984   "Structures d'habitat, mode de vie et environnement: Les villages des pasteurs de Beershéva, dans le Sud d'Israël, au IVᵉ millénaire avant l'ère chrétienne." *Paléorient* 10: 75-96.

Perrot, Jean, and Daniel Ladiray

1980   *Tombes à ossuaires de la région côtière palestinienne au ive millénaire avant l'ère chrétienne.* Mémoires et travaux du Centre de Recherches Préhistoriques Français de Jérusalem 1. Paris: Association Paléorient.

Perry, Patricia

In press   "Sources of Power in Predynastic Hierakonpolis: Legacies for Egyptian Kingship." In *Egypt at Its Origins* 3 (Proceedings of the Third International Colloquium Origin of the State, Predynastic and Early Dynastic Egypt, London, 27 July–1 August 2008), edited by Renée F. Friedman and P. N. Fiske. Orientalia Lovaniensia Analecta 205. Leuven: Peeters.

Petrie, William M. Flinders

1892   *Ten Years' Digging in Egypt.* London: Religious Tract Society.

1894   *A History of Egypt.* 1st edition. London: Methuen.

1896   *Koptos.* London: Bernard Quaritch.

1899   "Sequences in Prehistoric Remains." *Journal of the Anthropological Institute of Great Britain and Ireland* 29: 295–301.

1900   *The Royal Tombs of the First Dynasty,* Part 1. London: Egypt Exploration Fund.

1901a   *The Royal Tombs of the Earliest Dynasties,* Part 2. London: Egypt Exploration Fund.

1901b   *Diospolis Parva: The Cemeteries of Abadiyeh and Hu 1898-9.* London: Egypt Exploration Fund.

1902   *Abydos,* Part 1. Egypt Exploration Fund 22. London: Egypt Exploration Fund.

1903   *Abydos,* Part 2. Egypt Exploration Fund 24. London: Egypt Exploration Fund.

1907   *Gizeh and Rifeh.* London: British School of Archaeology in Egypt.

1914   *Tarkhan 2.* London: British School of Archaeology in Egypt.

1917   *Tools and Weapons.* British School of Archaeology in Egypt and Egyptian Research Account 30. London: British School of Archaeology in Egypt. Reprint, Aris & Phillips, 1974.

1920a   *Prehistoric Egypt Illustrated by over 1,000 Objects in University College, London.* British School of Archaeology in Egypt and Egyptian Research Account 31. London: British School of Archaeology in Egypt.

1920b   *Prehistoric Egypt: Corpus of Prehistoric Pottery and Palettes.* London: British School of Archaeology in Egypt.

1921   *Corpus of Prehistoric Pottery and Palettes.* British School of Archaeology in Egypt and Egypt. Research Account 32. London: British School of Archaeology in Egypt.

1925   *Tombs of the Courtiers and Oxyrhynkhos.* London: British School of Archaeology in Egypt.

1931   *Seventy Years in Archaeology.* London: Sampson Low & Marston.

1939   *The Making of Egypt.* London: Sheldon Press.

1953   *Ceremonial Slate Palettes and Corpus of Proto-Dynastic Pottery.* British School of Egyptian Archaeology 66. London: British School of Archaeology in Egypt.

Petrie, William M. Flinders, and James E. Quibell

1896   *Naqada and Ballas, 1895.* British School of Archaeology in Egypt 1. London: Bernard Quaritch.

Petrie, William M. Flinders; Gerald A. Wainwright; and Ernest Mackay

1912   *The Labyrinth Gerzeh and Mazghuneh.* London: School of Archaeology in Egypt, University College.

Piquette, Kathryn E.

2004   "Representing the Human Body on Late Predynastic and Early Dynastic Labels." In *Egypt at Its Origins: Studies in Memory of Barbara Adams* (Proceedings of the International Conference Origin of the State: Predynastic and Early Dynastic Egypt, Krakow, 28 August–1 September 2002), edited by Stan Hendrickx, Renée F. Friedman, Krzysztof M. Ciałowicz, and Marek Chłodnicki, pp. 923–47. Orientalia Lovaniensia Analecta 138. Leuven: Peeters.

Porat, Naomi

1997   "Petrography and Composition of the Pottery." In Tell el-Fara'în – Buto 1. *Ergebnisse zum frühen Kontext Kampagnen der Jahre 1983-1989,* edited by Thomas von der Way, pp. 223–31. Deutsches Archäologisches Institut, Abteilung Kairo, Archäologische Veröffentlichungen 83. Mainz: Philipp von Zabern.

Porat, Naomi, and Yuval Goren

2001   "Petrography of the Naqada IIIa Canaanite Pottery from Tomb U-j in Abydos." In *Umm el-Qaab 2. Abydos (Umm el-Qaab) und die Beziehungen Ägyptens zu Vorderasien im 4. Jahrtausend v. Chr.,* edited by Ulrich Hartung, pp. 466–81. Deutsches Archäologisches Institut, Abteilung Kairo, Archäologische Veröffentlichungen 92. Mainz: Philipp von Zabern.

2002   "Petrography of the Naqada IIIa Canaanite Pottery from Tomb U-j in Abydos." In *Egypt and the Levant: Interrelations from the 4th through the early 3rd Millennium BC,* edited by Edwin C. M. van den Brink and Thomas E. Levy, pp. 252–70. London: Leicester University Press.

Postgate, Nicholas; Tao Wang; and Toby A. H. Wilkinson

1995   "The Evidence for Early Writing: Utilitarian or Ceremonial?" *Antiquity* 69: 459–80.

Quibell, James E.

1898   "Slate Palette from Hierakonpolis." *Zeitschrift für ägyptische Sprache und Altertumskunde* 36: 81–84.

1900   *Hierakonpolis* 1. Egypt Research Account 4. London: Bernard Quaritch.

1904–05   *Catalogue général: Archaic Objects.* Cairo: Institut français d'archéologie orientale.

Quibell, James E., and Frederick W. Green

1902   *Hierakonpolis* 2. Egypt Research Account 5. London: Bernard Quaritch.

Quirke, Stephen

2010a   "Petrie at Abydos in 1900: Margaret Murray's Album." *Egyptian Archaeology* 36: 6–7.

2010b   *Hidden Hands: Egyptian Workforces in Petrie Excavation Archives, 1880–1924.* London: Duckworth.

Randall-MacIver, David, and Arthur C. Mace

1902   *El Amrah and Abydos, 1899–1901.* Memoir of the Egyptian Exploration Society 23. London: Egypt Exploration Fund.

Reeves, Nicholas

1990   *The Complete Tutankhamun.* London: Thames & Hudson.

Redford, Donald B.

1986   *Pharaonic King-lists, Annals, and Day-books: A Contribution to the Study of the Egyptian Sense of History.* Mississauga: Benben.

Reinold, Jacques

2000   *Archéologie au Soudan: Les civilisations de Nubie.* Paris: Errance

2007   *La nécropole néolithique d'el-Kadada au Soudan Central: Les cimetières A et B.* Fouilles de la Section Français des Antiquités du Soudan 1. Paris: Éditions Recherche sur les civilisations.

Reisner, George A.

1910   *The Archaeological Survey of Nubia, Report for 1907–1908,* Bulletin 1: *Archaeological Report.* Cairo: National Printing Department.

Renfrew, Colin, and John Cherry

1986   *Peer Polity Interaction and Socio-political Change.* Cambridge: Cambridge University Press.

Riemer, Heiko, and Rudolph Kuper

2000   "'Clayton Rings': Enigmatic Ancient Pottery in the Eastern Sahara." *Sahara* 12: 91–100.

Rizkana, Ibrahim, and Jürgen Seeher

1987   Maadi 1. *The Pottery of the Predynastic Settlement: Excavations at the Predynastic Site of Maadi and Its Cemeteries conducted by Mustafa Amer and Ibrahim Rizkana on behalf of the Department of Geography, Faculty of Arts of Cairo University 1930–1953.* Deutsches Archäologisches Institut, Abteilung Kairo, Archäologische

Veröffentlichungen 64. Mainz am Rhein: Philipp von Zabern.

1988   Maadi 2. *The Lithic Industries of the Predynastic Settlement.* Deutsches Archäologisches Institut, Abteilung Kairo, Archäologische Veröffentlichungen 65. Mainz am Rhein: Philipp von Zabern.

1989   Maadi 3. *The Non-lithic Small Finds and the Structural Remains of the Predynastic Settlement.* Deutsches Archäologisches Institut, Abteilung Kairo, Archäologische Veröffentlichungen 80. Mainz am Rhein: Philipp von Zabern.

1990   Maadi 4. *The Predynastic Cemeteries of Maadi and Wadi Digla.* Deutsches Archäologisches Institut, Abteilung Kairo, Archäologische Veröffentlichungen 81. Mainz am Rhein: Philipp von Zabern.

Rosellini, Hippolito

1977   *Monumenti dell'Egitto e della Nubia,* Vol. 2: *Monumenti civili.* Geneva: Éditions de belles-lettres. (reproduction of the 1834 original)

Roth, Ann Macy

1992   "The *psš-kf* and the 'Opening of the Mouth' Ceremony." *Journal of Egyptian Archaeology* 78: 113–47.

Rowan, Yorke M.

2006   "Chapter 11. The Chipped Stone Assemblage at Gilat." In *Archaeology, Anthropology and Cult: The Sanctuary at Gilat, Israel,* edited by Thomas E. Levy, pp. 507–74. London: Equinox.

Rowan, Yorke M.; Thomas E. Levy; David Alon; and Yuval Goren

2006   "Chapter 12. Gilat's Ground Stone Assemblage: Stone Fenestrated Stands, Bowls, Palettes and Related Artifacts." In *Archaeology, Anthropology and Cult: The Sanctuary at Gilat, Israel,* edited by Thomas E. Levy, pp. 575–684. London: Equinox.

Sabbahy, Lisa K.

1993   "Evidence for the Titulary of the Queen from Dynasty One." *Göttinger Miszellen* 135: 81–87.

el-Sanussi Ashraf, and M. Jones

1997   "A Site of the Maadi Culture near the Giza Pyramids." *Mitteilungen des Deutschen Archäologischen Instituts, Abteilung Kairo* 53: 241–53.

el-Sayed, Ramadan

1975   *Documents relatifs à Saïs et ses divinités.* Bibliothèque d'études 69. Cairo: Institut français d'archéologie orientale.

Scamuzzi, Ernesto

1965   *Egyptian Art in the Egyptian Museum of Turin.* New York: Harry N. Abrams.

Scharff, Alexander

1928   "Some Prehistoric Vases in the British Museum and Remarks on Egyptian Prehistory." *Journal of Egyptian Archaeology* 14: 261–76.

Schulman, Alan R.

1976 "Egyptian Seal Impressions from 'En Besor." 'Atiqot (English series) 11: 16–26.

1991/92 "Narmer and the Unification: A Revisionist View." Bulletin of the Egyptological Seminar 11: 79–94.

Seele, Keith

1974 "Excavations Between Abu Simbel and the Sudan Border: A Preliminary Report." Journal of Near Eastern Studies 33: 1–43.

Service, Elman R.

1962 Primitive Social Organization: An Evolutionary Perspective. New York: Random House.

Sharvit, J.; E. Galili; B. Rosen; and Edwin C. M. van den Brink

2002 "Predynastic Maritime Traffic along the Carmel Coast of Israel: A Submerged Find from North Atlit Bay." In In Quest of Ancient Settlements and Landscapes: Archaeological Studies in Honour of Ram Gophna, edited by Edwin C. M. van den Brink and Eli Yannai, pp. 159–66. Tel Aviv: Tel Aviv University, Ramot Publishing.

Smith, Harry S.

1966 "The Nubian B-Group." Kush 14: 69–124.

1994 "The Princes of Seyala in Lower Nubia." In Hommages à Jean Leclant, Volume 2: Nubie, Soudan, Éthiopie, edited by Catherine Berger, Gisèle Clerc, and Nicolas Grimal, pp. 362–76. Bibliothèque d'étude 106/2. Cairo: Institut français de l'archéologie orientale.

Smith, Harry S., and Lisa L. Giddy

1985 "Nubia and Dakhla Oasis in the Late Third Millennium BC: The Present Balance of Textual and Archaeological Evidence." In Mélanges offert à Jean Vercoutter, edited by Francis Geus and Florence Thill, pp. 317–30. Paris: Éditions Recherche sur les civilizations.

Smith, William Stevenson

1949 A History of Egyptian Sculpture and Painting in the Old Kingdom. 2nd edition. Boston: Museum of Fine Arts.

Sobas, Magdalena

2009 "Tell el-Farkha 2006–2008: Ceramics from Cult Room No. 211." Studies in Ancient Art and Civilization 13: 25–42.

Spencer, A. Jeffrey

1980 Catalogue of Egyptian Antiquities in the British Museum, Volume 5: Early Dynastic Objects. London: British Museum.

1993 Early Egypt: The Rise of Civilisation in the Nile Valley. London: British Museum Press.

Stevenson, Alice

2009a "Palette." In UCLA Encyclopedia of Egyptology, edited by Willike Wendrich. Los Angeles: http://escholarship.org/uc/item/7dh0x2n0

2009b The Predynastic Egyptian Cemetery of el-Gerzeh: Social Identities and Mortuary Practices. Orientalia Lovaniensia Analecta 186. Leuven: Peeters.

In press "Egypt and Mesopotamia." In The Sumerian World, edited by H. Crawford. London: Routledge.

Stocks, Denys A.

2003 Experiments in Egyptian Archaeology: Stoneworking Technology in Ancient Egypt. London: Routledge.

Storemyr, Per

2009 "A Prehistoric Geometric Rock Art Landscape by the First Nile Cataract." Archéo-Nil 19: 121–50.

Takamiya, Izumi H.

2004 "Development of Specialisation in the Nile Valley during the 4th Millennium BC." In Egypt at Its Origins: Studies in Memory of Barbara Adams (Proceedings of the International Conference Origin of the State: Predynastic and Early Dynastic Egypt, Krakow, 28 August–1 September 2002), edited by Stan Hendrickx, Renée F. Friedman, Krzysztof M. Ciałowicz, and Marek Chłodnicki, pp. 1027–39. Orientalia Lovaniensia Analecta 138. Leuven: Peeters.

2008 "Firing Installations and Specialization: A View from Recent Excavations at Hierakonpolis Locality 11C." In Egypt at Its Origins 2 (Proceedings of the International Conference Origin of the State, Predynastic and Early Dynastic Egypt, Toulouse, France, 5–8 September 2005), edited by Béatrix Midant-Reynes and Yann Tristant, pp. 187–202. Orientalia Lovaniensia Analecta 172. Leuven: Peeters.

Teeter, Emily

2003 Ancient Egypt: Treasures from the Collection of the Oriental Institute. Oriental Institute Museum Publications 23. Chicago: The Oriental Institute.

Trigger, Bruce G.

1985 "The Rise of Egyptian Civilization." In Ancient Egypt: A Social History, edited by Bruce G. Trigger, Barry J. Kemp, David O'Connor, and Alan B. Lloyd, pp. 1–70. Cambridge: Cambridge University Press.

2003 Understanding Early Civilizations. A Comparative Study. Cambridge: Cambridge University Press.

Tristant, Yann

2004 L'habitat prédynastique de la Vallée du Nil: Vivre sur les rives du Nil aux Ve et IVe millénaires. British Archaeological Reports, International Series 1287. Oxford: Hedges.

In press L'occupation humaine dans le delta du Nil (Égypte) aux 5e et 4e millénaires: Approche géo-archéologique à partir de la région de Samara (delta oriental).

Tristant, Yann; Morgan De Dapper; and Béatrix Midant-Reynes

2007   "Recherches géo-archéologiques sur le site pré- et protodynastique de Kôm el-Khilgan (Delta du Nil). Résultats préliminaires des campagnes de prospection 2002–2004." In *Proceedings of the Ninth International Congress of Egyptologists, Grenoble, 6–12 septembre 2004*, edited by Jean-Claude Goyon and Christine Cardin, pp. 1841–50. Orientalia Lovaniensia Analecta 150. Leuven: Peeters.

2008   "Human Occupation of the Nile Delta during Pre- and Early Dynastic Times: A View from Kom el-Khilgan." In *Egypt at Its Origins* 2 (Proceedings of the International Conference Origin of the State, Predynastic and Early Dynastic Egypt, Toulouse, France, 5–8 September 2005), edited by Béatrix Midant-Reynes and Yann Tristant, pp. 463–82. Orientalia Lovaniensia Analecta 172. Leuven: Peeters.

Tutundžić, Sava P.

1989   "Relations between Late Predynastic Egypt and Palestine: Some Elements and Phenomena." In *L'urbanisation de la Palestine à l'âge du Bronze ancien: Bilan et perspectives des recherches actuelles* (Actes du Colloque d'Emmaüs, 20–24 octobre 1986), edited by Pierre de Miroschedji, pp. 423–32. British Archaeological Reports, International Series 527. Oxford: British Archaeological Reports.

1993   "A Consideration of Differences between the Pottery Showing Palestinian Characteristics in the Maadian and Gerzean Cultures." *Journal of Egyptian Archaeology* 79: 33–55.

Ucko, Peter J.

1968   *Anthropomorphic Figurines of Predynastic Egypt and Neolithic Crete with Comparative Material from the Prehistoric Near East and Mainland Greece*. Royal Anthropological Institute of Great Britian and Ireland, Occasional Paper 24. London: Andrew Szmidla.

Ussishkin, David

1980   "The Ghassulian Shrine at En-gedi." *Tel Aviv* 7: 1–44.

van den Brink, Edwin C. M.

1989   "A Transitional Late Predynastic: Early Dynastic Settlement Site in the Northeastern Nile Delta, Egypt." *Mitteilungen des Deutschen Archäologischen Instituts, Abteilung Kairo* 45: 55–108.

1996   "The Incised Serekh Signs of Dynasties 0–1, Part 1: Complete Vessels." In *Aspects of Early Egypt*, edited by Jeffrey Spencer, pp. 140–58. London: British Museum Press.

1998   "Late Protodynastic–Early First Dynasty Egyptian Finds in Late Early Bronze Age I Canaan: An Update." In *Proceedings of the Seventh International Congress of Egyptologists, Cambridge, 3–9 September 1995*, edited by Christopher Eyre, pp. 215–25. Orientalia Lovaniensia Analecta 82. Leuven: Peeters.

van den Brink, Edwin C. M., and Eliot Braun

2002   "Wine Jars with Serekhs from Early Bronze Lod: Appellation Vallée du Nil Contrôlée, but for Whom?" In *In Quest of Ancient Settlements and Landscapes: Archaeological Studies in Honor of Ram Gophna*, edited by Edwin C. M. van den Brink and Eli Yannai, pp. 167–92. Ramot: Tel Aviv.

2006   "South Levantine Influences on Egyptian Stone and Pottery Production: Some Rare Examples." In *Archaeology of Northeastern Africa: In Memory of Lech Krzyżaniak*, edited by Karla Kroeper, Marek Chłodnicki, and Michał Kobusiewicz, pp. 817–25. Studies in African Archaeology 9. Poznan: Poznan Archaeological Museum.

2008   "Appraising South Levantine-Egyptian Interaction: Recent Discoveries from Israel and Egypt." In *Egypt at Its Origins* 2 (Proceedings of the International Conference Origin of the State, Predynastic and Early Dynastic Egypt, Toulouse, France, 5–8 September 2005), edited by Béatrix Midant-Reynes and Yann Tristant, pp. 643–88. Orientalia Lovaniensia Analecta 172. Leuven: Peeters.

van den Brink, Edwin C. M., and Ram Gophna

2004   "Protodynastic Storage Jars from the Area of Sheikh Zuweid, Northern Sinai: Another Entrêpot along the Way(s)-of-Horus?" In *Egypt at Its Origins: Studies in Memory of Barbara Adams* (Proceedings of the International Conference Origin of the State: Predynastic and Early Dynastic Egypt, Krakow, 28 August–1 September 2002), edited by Stan Hendrickx, Renée F. Friedman, Krzysztof M. Ciałowicz, and Marek Chłodnicki, pp. 487–506. Orientalia Lovaniensia Analecta 138. Leuven: Peeters.

van den Brink, Edwin C. M.; Ram Gophna; and Asher Ovadiah

2007   "Burial Cave 2 in the Azor-Holon Cemetery: An Early Bonze Age I Tomb with Egyptian Finds." *Egypt and the Levant* 17: 59–71.

van den Brink, Edwin C. M., and Tzach Kanias

2010   "Modi'in, H. Hadat: Preliminary Report." *Hadashot Arkheologiyot: Excavations and Surveys in Israel* 122. http://www.hadashot-esi.org.il/report_detail_eng.asp?id=1435&mag_id=117 (accessed 7/22/2010).

Vandier, Jacques

1952   *Manuel d'archéologie égyptienne*, Volume 1: *Les époques de formation*, Part 1: *La préhistoire*. Paris: A. & J. Picard.

van Haarlem, William M.

2001   "Tell Ibrahim Awad." *Egyptian Archaeology* 18: 33–36.

2002   "The Ivory Objects from Tell Ibrahim Awd." *Egyptian Archaeology* 20: 16–17.

Van Neer, Wim; Veerle Linseele; and Renée F. Friedman

2004   "Animal Burials and Food Offerings at the Elite Cemetery HK6 in Hierakonpolis." In *Egypt at Its Origins: Studies in Memory of Barbara Adams* (Proceedings of the International Conference Origin of the State: Predynastic and Early Dynastic Egypt, Krakow, 28 August–1 September 2002), edited by Stan Hendrickx, Renée F. Friedman, Krzysztof M. Ciałowicz, and Marek Chłodnicki, pp. 67–130. Orientalia Lovaniensia Analecta 138. Leuven: Peeters.

In press   "More Animal Burials from the Predynastic Elite Cemetery of Hierakonpolis (Upper Egypt): The 2008 Season." In *Proceedings of the Ninth Meeting of the International Council for Archaeozoology Working Group "Archaeozoology of Southwest Asia and Adjacent Areas."* Oxford: Oxbow.

van Walsem, R.

1978   "The *Psš-kf.* An Investigation of an Ancient Egyptian Funerary Instrument." *Oudheidkundige Mededelingen uit het Rijksmuseum van Oudheden te Leiden* 58: 193–249.

Vaudou, Émilie

2008   "Les sépultures subsidiaires des grandes tombes de la 1re dynastie égyptienne." *Archéo-Nil* 18: 148–65.

te Velde, H.

1988   "Some Remarks on the Mysterious Language of the Baboons." In *Funerary Symbols and Religion: Essays Dedicated to Professor M. S. G. Heerma van Voss on the occasion of his retirement from the Chair of the History of Ancient Religions at the University of Amsterdam,* edited by Jacques H. Kamstra, H. Milde, and K. Wagtendonk, pp. 129–36. Kampen: J. H. Kok.

von Bissing, Friedrich W.

1913   *Tongefässe 1: Bis zum Beginn des Alten Reiches.* Catalogue général des antiquités égyptiennes du Musée du Caire 66. Vienna: A. Holzhausen.

von der Way, Thomas

1993   *Untersuchungen zur Spätvor- und Frühgeschichte Unterägyptens.* Studien zur Archäologie und Geschichte Altägyptens 8. Heidelberg: Heidelberger Orientverlag.

1997   Tell el-Fara'în – Buto 1. *Ergebnisse zum frühen Kontext Kampagnen der Jahre 1983-1989.* Deutsches Archäologisches Institut, Abteilung Kairo, Archäologische Veröffentlichungen 83. Mainz: Philipp von Zabern.

2007   "Auf der Suche nach dem alten Buto – der "Stecknadel im Heuhaufen." In *Begegnung mit der Vergangenheit: 100 Jahre in Ägypten,* edited by Günter Dreyer and Daniel Polz, pp. 55–59. Mainz: Philipp von Zabern.

Watrin, L.

2002   "Tributes and the Rise of a Predatory Power: Unraveling the Intrigue of EB I Palestinian Jars Found by Amélineau at Abydos." In *Egypt and the Levant: Interrelations from the 4th through the Early 3rd Millennium BCE,* edited by Edwin C. M. van den Brink and Thomas E. Levy, pp. 450–63. London: Leicester University Press.

Weill, Raymond

1961   Recherches sur la Ire dynastie et les temps prépharaoniques. 2 volumes. Bibliothèque d'étude 38. Cairo: Institut français d'archéologie orientale.

Wendrich, Willeke

2010   "Egyptian Archaeology." In *Egyptian Archaeology,* edited by Willeke Wendrich, pp. 1–14. Chichester: Wiley-Blackwell.

Wengrow, David

2006   *The Archaeology of Early Egypt: Social Transformations in North-East Africa, 10,000 to 2650 BC.* Cambridge: Cambridge University Press.

Whitehouse, Helen

2009   *Ancient Egypt and Nubia in the Ashmolean Museum.* Oxford: Ashmolean Museum.

Wilkinson, Toby A. H.

1985   "The Horus Name and the Form and Significance of the Serekh in the Royal Egyptian Titulary." *Journal for the Society of the Study of Egyptian Antiquities* 15/3: 98–104.

1996   *State Formation in Egypt: Chronology and Society.* British Archaeological Reports, International Series 651. Cambridge Monographs in African Archaeology 40. Oxford: Tempus Reparatum.

1999   *Early Dynastic Egypt.* London and New York: Routledge

2000a   "Political Unification: Towards a Reconstruction." *Mitteilungen des Deutschen Archäologischen Instituts, Abteilung Kairo* 56: 377–95.

2000b   *Royal Annals of Ancient Egypt: The Palermo Stone and Its Associated Fragments.* London: Kegan Paul International.

2001   *Early Dynastic Egypt.* 2nd edition. London and New York: Routledge.

2003   *Genesis of the Pharaohs: Dramatic New Discoveries that Rewrite the Origins of Ancient Egypt.* London: Thames & Hudson.

Williams, Bruce B.

1980   "The Lost Pharaohs of Nubia." *Archaeology* 33/5: 14–21.

1986   *Excavations Between Abu Simbel and the Sudan Frontier, Part 1: The A-Group Royal Cemetery at Qustul: Cemetery L.* Oriental Institute Nubian Expedition 3. Chicago: The Oriental Institute.

1987   "Forebears of Menes in Nubia, Myth or Reality." *Journal of Near Eastern Studies* 46: 15–26.

1988   *Decorated Pottery and the Art of Naqada III: A Documentary Essay.* Münchner ägyptologische Studien 45. Munich: Deutscher Kunstverlag.

1989   *Excavations Between Abu Simbel and the Sudan Frontier, Parts 2, 3, and 4: Neolithic, A-Group, and Post-A-Group Remains from Cemeteries W, V, S, Q, T, and a Cave East of*

Cemetery K. Oriental Institute Nubian Expedition 4. Chicago: The Oriental Institute.

1990   *Excavations Between Abu Simbel and the Sudan Frontier, Part 7: Twenty-fifth Dynasty and Napatan Remains at Qustul: Cemeteries W and V.* Oriental Institute Nubian Expedition 7. Chicago: The Oriental Institute.

2006   "A-Group Society in the Context of Northeastern Africa." In *Archaeology of Early Northeastern Africa in Memory of Lech Krzyżaniak*, edited by Karla Kroeper, Marek Chłodnicki, and Michał Kobusiewicz, pp. 177–94. Studies in African Archaeology 9. Poznan: Poznan Archaeological Museum.

Williams, Bruce B., and Thomas J. Logan

1987   "The Metropolitan Museum Knife Handle and Aspects of Pharaonic Imagery before Narmer." *Journal of Near Eastern Studies* 46: 245–86.

Wilson, Karen, and Joan Barghusen

1989   *The Oriental Institute Museum: Highlights from the Collection.* Chicago: The Oriental Institute.

Wilson, Penelope

2006   "Prehistoric Settlement in the Western Delta: A Regional and Local View from Sais (Sâ el-Hagar)." *Journal of Egyptian Archaeology* 92: 76–126.

Wilson, Penelope, and Gregory Gilbert

2003   "The Prehistoric Period at Saïs (Sâ el-Hagar)." *Archéo-Nil* 13: 65–72.

Yadin, Yigael

1963   *The Art of Warfare in Biblical Lands*, Volume 1. New York: McGraw-Hill.

Yannai, Eli

2002   "Imported Finds from the 'Ein Assawir Tombs (Israel) and Their Significance in Understanding the Chronological Synchronization between Israel, Egypt and Eastern Anatolia." In *Egypt and the Levant: Interrelations from the 4th through the Early 3rd Millennium BCE*, edited by Edwin C. M. van den Brink and Thomas E. Levy, pp. 334–45. London: Leicester University Press.

Yeivin, S.

1960   "Early Contacts Between Canaan and Egypt." *Israel Exploration Journal* 10: 193–203.

Yekutieli, Yuval

1998   The Early Bronze I of North Sinai: Social, Economic and Spatial Aspects. PhD dissertation, Tel Aviv University.

2004   "The Desert, the Sown and the Egyptian Colony." *Egypt and the Levant* 14: 1–9.

2006   "The Ceramics of Tel 'Erani, Layer C." *Journal of the Serbian Archaeological Society* 22: 225–42.

Yoffee, Norman

2002   "The Evolution of Simplicity: Review of *Seeing Like a State*, by J. C. Scott." *Current Anthropology* 42: 767–69.

2005   *Myths of the Archaic State: Evolution of the Earliest Cities, States and Civilizations.* Cambridge: Cambridge University Press.

Yurco, Frank

1995   "Narmer: First King of Upper and Lower Egypt, A Reconsideration of His Palette and Macehead." *Journal of the Society for the Study of Egyptian Antiquities* 25: 85–95.